Recently Acceded Members of the World Trade Organization

Kenji Takamiya

Recently Acceded Members of the World Trade Organization

Membership, the Doha Development Agenda, and Dispute Settlement

palgrave
macmillan

Kenji Takamiya
Manila, Philippines

ISBN 978-981-13-9158-3 ISBN 978-981-13-9159-0 (eBook)
https://doi.org/10.1007/978-981-13-9159-0

This Palgrave Macmillan imprint is published by the registered company Springer Nature Singapore Pte Ltd.
The registered company address is: 152 Beach Road, #21-01/04 Gateway East, Singapore 189721, Singapore

Preface

Developing and transition economies that acceded to the multilateral trading system since the establishment of the World Trade Organization (WTO) in 1995 had made extensive market access commitments in the course of membership negotiations. After joining the multilateral trading system, however, these recently acceded members (RAMs) generally expressed reservations against further market opening in the Doha Round launched in 2001, also known as the Doha Development Agenda (DDA). At the same time, a number of RAMs have been aggressively using the dispute settlement mechanism (DSM) at the WTO, partly to address issues related to their terms of accession. Using the economy theories of trade agreements and negotiations as a guide for intellectual inquiries, this book assesses motivations accounting for the RAM's evolving behaviors in the multilateral trading system.

The volume was substantially written when I was at the University of Cambridge in 2012–2015. I would like to express my sincere gratitude to Professor Amrita Narlikar, presently President of the GIGA German Institute of Global and Area Studies. I could not compete the research without her constant encouragement, in addition to valuable technical advice while she was still in Cambridge and thereafter. I am also grateful to Dr. Pieter van Houten, Dr. Kun-Chin Lin, and Professor Richard Rex, all from the University of Cambridge. I would also like to acknowledge funding provided by the Cambridge Political Economy Society Trust and the Joint Japan/World Bank Graduate Scholarship Programme, among others.

The research entailed overseas travels to five countries (Ecuador, Georgia, People's Republic of China, Switzerland, and Viet Nam), and I am grateful to officials of the government agencies and business associations, as well as colleagues of international organizations and academia for welcoming me for necessary interviews. While their valuable contributions are kept anonymous in the text of the book, all of them very pleasantly spent their precious time to talk with me, despite their busy schedules. Special thanks also go to Jacob Dreyer, Commissioning Editor and Anushangi Weerakoon, Editorial Assistant of Palgrave Macmillan.

The views expressed and the conclusions reached are those of mine in my personal capacity, and these do not reflect views of my employer and scholarship sponsors, their policies and activities, or any national political questions.

Manila, Philippines Kenji Takamiya

Contents

Abbreviations

ACP	African, Caribbean and Pacific
ADB	Asian Development Bank
AFTA	ASEAN Free Trade Area
Amcham	American Chamber of Commerce
ASEAN	Association of Southeast Asian Nations
ATC	Agreement on Textiles and Clothing
AVEs	ad valorem equivalents
BAG	Business Association of Georgia
BATNA	best alternative to a negotiated agreement
BBC	British Broadcasting Corporation
BFA	Framework Agreement on Bananas
BOP	balance of payments
BTA	bilateral trade agreement
CCTV	China Central Television
CEPT	Common Effective Preferential Tariff
CET	Common External Tariff
CFA	Catfish Farmers of America
CIEM	Central Institute for Economic Management
CIS	Commonwealth of Independent States
CU	customs union
DDA	Doha Development Agenda
DOC	Department of Commerce
DSB	Dispute Settlement Body
DSM	dispute settlement mechanism
DSU	Dispute Settlement Understanding
EAP	East Asia and the Pacific

EC	European Communities
ECA	Europe and Central Asia
ECU	European Currency Unit
EEC	European Economic Community
EU	European Union
FDI	foreign direct investment
FIEs	foreign-invested enterprises
FTA	free trade area/agreement
FYROM	Former Yugoslav Republic of Macedonia
GAO	General Accounting Office
GATS	General Agreement on Trade in Services
GATT	General Agreement on Tariffs and Trade
GCC	Gulf Cooperation Council
GDP	gross domestic product
GMS	Greater Mekong Subregion
GSP	generalized system of preferences
IBRD	International Bank for Reconstruction and Development
IDA	International Development Association
IEO	Independent Evaluation Office
IFC	International Finance Corporation
IFI(s)	international financial institution(s)
IMF	International Monetary Fund
IT	individual treatment
ITA	Information Technology Agreement
LDCs	least-developed countries
MET	market economy treatment
MFA	Multifibre Arrangement
MFN	most-favored nation
MNCs	multi-national corporations
MOFCOM	Ministry of Commerce
MOFTEC	Ministry of Foreign Trade and Economic Cooperation
MOU(s)	memorandum/a of understanding
NAMA	non-agricultural market access
NCIEC	National Committee for International Economic Cooperation
NME(s)	non-market economy/ies
OECD	Organisation for Economic Co-operation and Development
OTEXA	Office of Textiles and Apparel
PBL	policy-based lending
PCA	Partnership and Cooperation Agreement
PNBV	National Plan for Good Living
PNTR	permanent normal trade relations
PRC	People's Republic of China

PTAs	preferential trade agreements
RAM(s)	recently acceded member(s)
RMB	Renminbi
ROW	rest of the world
RTAs	regional trade agreements
SCM	Subsidies and Countervailing Measures
SOEs	state-owned enterprises
SVEs	small, vulnerable economies
TBT	technical barriers to trade
TiSA	Trade in Services Agreement
TNC	Trade Negotiations Committee
TPP	Trans-Pacific Partnership
TPRM	trade policy review mechanism
TPS	transitional product-specific safeguard
TRAINS	trade analysis information system
TRIMs	Trade-Related Investment Measures
TRIPS	Trade-Related Aspects of Intellectual Property Rights
UN	United Nations
UNCTAD	United Nations Conference on Trade and Development
US/U.S.	United States
USDOC	United States Department of Commerce
USTR	United States Trade Representative
VASEP	Viet Nam Association of Seafood Exporters and Producers
VCCI	Viet Nam Chamber of Commerce and Industry
VER(s)	voluntary exports restraint(s)
VITAS	Viet Nam Textile and Apparel Association
VRAM(s)	very recently acceded member(s)
WTO	World Trade Organization

List of Tables

Chapter 4

Chapter 5

Chapter 6

Chapter 7

CHAPTER 1

Background and Theoretical Framework

1 Background

Countries that acceded to the World Trade Organization (WTO) since its establishment in 1995 generally made substantial commitments as part of the membership negotiations, often beyond what were previously required for the incumbent members at the equivalent stage of development. Article XII of the Marrakesh Agreement Establishing the World Trade Organization (WTO Agreement), which came into effect in 1995 and provides rules on accession to the multilateral trading system, reads that an applicant may accede "*on terms to be agreed between it and the WTO*" (WTO, 1995a, p. 15), without further elaboration of what these terms are. The absence of pre-defined conditions for membership left determination of terms of accession to tough negotiations between each applicant and incumbent members. While the earlier General Agreement on Tariffs and Trade (GATT) 1947—a predecessor of the present WTO—also had a similar provision on accession (Article XXXIII),[1] it allowed newly independent territories (former colonies of the incumbent GATT contracting parties) to exercise a privilege of semi-automatic accession without making substantial membership commitments

[1]Basra (2012) provided an observation that the legal provision of accession under the WTO Agreement maintains a similarity with that of GATT, while asymmetry in bargaining positions between acceding countries and strong incumbents such as the United States (US) has been increasingly visible at the WTO accession negotiations.

K. Takamiya, *Recently Acceded Members of the World Trade Organization*, https://doi.org/10.1007/978-981-13-9159-0_1

(Article XXVI: 5(c)). The differential treatment created a substantial gap in the depth and scope of trade policy commitments made between many developing countries that acceded under the old GATT system (and became founding members of the WTO) and the more recently acceded members (RAMs) that joined the WTO after 1995.[2]

The RAMs' commitments made in their terms of accession, in excess of what were required for incumbent developing members, took two forms: deeper and wider market access commitments and so-called WTO-plus and WTO-minus obligations. Under terms of accession, the RAMs bound their tariffs at an average rate of 10.75% for industrial products—or non-agricultural market access (NAMA) in the WTO jargon—and 17.07% for agricultural products, substantially lower than the level committed by other developing countries (28.9% for NAMA and 60.95% for agriculture). Their binding coverage amounted to 100% of tariff lines. While the RAMs made these extensive market access commitments, all they received from incumbent members in return was essentially a consolidation of existing market access on the permanent most-favored nation (MFN) basis (GATT Article I),[3] mostly without

[2]Unless specified otherwise, "RAMs" referred to in this book comprise members that acceded to the multilateral trading system based on the Article XII of the WTO Agreement after 1995 and were parties to the Doha Round as of December 2008 (when its negotiations on the draft modalities papers were concluded), excluding the European Union (EU) member states and least-developed countries (LDCs). These RAMs include: Albania, Armenia, Cape Verde, People's Republic of China, Croatia, Ecuador, Former Yugoslav Republic of Macedonia, Georgia, Jordan, Kyrgyz Republic, Moldova, Mongolia, Oman, Panama, Saudi Arabia, Chinese Taipei, Tonga, Viet Nam, and Ukraine (WTO, 2008a). The EU adopts a common external trade policy and has a collective membership of its own at the WTO. LDCs are not expected to make new commitments for further liberalization during the Doha Round and are not part of the RAMs group. Croatia subsequently withdrew from the RAMs group upon its EU accession in 2013. The other new members that joined the WTO after conclusion of the draft December 2008 modalities are outside of the scope of this research. Presently, the RAMs as of 2008 and these more recently acceded members are collectively called "Article XII Members." See the WTO Web site: http://www.wto.org/english/tratop_e/dda_e/negotiating_groups_e.htm.

[3]The non-discrimination principle, comprising MFN and national treatment, is one of the key pillars of the multilateral trading system. GATT Article I on MFN stipulates that the WTO members shall not discriminate certain trading partners against others, and like products should be treated equally with respect to border measures. Article III on national treatment requires non-discrimination of foreign and home like products behind the border.

reciprocal and incremental tariff cuts. At the same time, some of the RAMs had to accept the so-called WTO-plus (obligation beyond the existing multilateral rules) and WTO-minus (exceptions to the current multilateral rules, including those applicable on the side of the incumbent members[4]) in their terms of accession.[5] While all WTO members, old and new, had accepted the single undertaking of the WTO Agreement (including most of its annexes on multilateral trade agreements, dispute settlement understanding, and the trade policy review mechanism[6]) in principle, WTO-plus and minus provisions were designated aside from this general requirement[7] and were imposed uniquely upon the RAMs through their accession processes. In particular, some of the WTO-minus provisions mostly took the form of time-bound allowance for the incumbent members to exercise targeted discrimination against a number of RAMs continuously from the pre-accession period. Thus, while the RAMs joined the multilateral trading system that supposedly functions on the basis of the non-discrimination principle, some forms of discrimination targeted to them remained in the post-accession period.

Typically, WTO accession is depicted as a process of developing and transition countries' integration to a globalizing market economy through multilateral trade liberalization (see Lanoszka, 2001). In a statement entitled "26 years of accession experience and best practices" in 2012, Pascal Lamy, then WTO's Director-General, remarked:

[4]As further reviewed in this book, some WTO-minus provisions take the form of time-bound allowance for the incumbent WTO members to continue discriminatory trade policy measures against the new entrants. Another typical case of WTO-minus provisions accords the transition period for the new members to implement the multilateral rules after accession.

[5]"WTO-plus" and "WTO-minus" are not legally defined terms. In an attempt to distinguish various provisions in RAM's protocol of accession, Charnovitz (2008, p. 869) proposes the following taxonomy: "*WTO-plus and WTO-minus obligations should be understood as obligations that are either greater than or less than what is required by general WTO law.*" Some authors and practitioners do not make distinction between plus and minuses, and call them all "WTO-plus," on the ground that both are stipulated in the form of additional commitments made by the RAMs in their terms of accession.

[6]The WTO trade policy review mechanism comprises regular surveillance of each member's trade policy for enhancing transparency (Annex 3, WTO Agreement).

[7]Technically speaking, protocols of accession of the RAMs (including WTO-plus and minuses) have become integral parts of the WTO Agreement upon their membership, but these depart from the original Uruguay Round package.

> WTO accessions are key elements in strengthening trade multilateralism. It is the WTO trade pathway to domestic reforms, competitiveness and growth. It is a uniquely WTO approach to development... For acceding governments, benefit of WTO membership is obvious. It provides new opportunities for trade, attracts investments and sustains economic growth.[8]

Ironically, however, some elements of these earlier terms of accession appear to have backfired in the post-membership phase. In the course of market access negotiations of the Doha Round launched in 2001, also known as the Doha Development Agenda (DDA),[9] a coalition[10] among the 19 RAMs took a position that, given the substantive commitments they had already made at the time of accession negotiations, only a moderate (or no) liberalization on their part should be required for both NAMA and agriculture. As a coalition, the RAMs collectively submitted the negotiating proposals on market access following this hardened line, which read as follows:

> (I)n the process of accession the RAMs assumed extensive level of commitments in all WTO areas, distinguishing thereby the group from the rest of the membership. In this regard, RAMs consider that the aim of this development round should not be to deepen already existing discrepancies between developing members, or to disadvantage those that have done their share in contributing extensively to the world trading system. Instead, members should pursue an approach that takes into account different realities which exist among their schedules and envisages more balanced outcome. (WTO, 2007a, p. 1; 2007b, p. 1)

There is probably little doubt that a majority of the post-1995 RAMs effectively used terms of WTO accession for consolidating their efforts of

[8]Opening remark at the Beijing 2012 Round Table for Least-Developed Countries (LDCs) on Best Practices in the WTO Accession Process organized in Beijing, China, on 29 May–1 June 2012, found in the WTO Web site: http://www.wto.org/english/news_e/sppl_e/sppl231_e.htm.

[9]The WTO explains that the Doha Round "*is also known semi-officially as the **Doha Development Agenda** as a fundamental objective is to improve the trading prospects of developing countries*" in its Web site. In line with the WTO practice, the book also adopts both terms and uses them interchangeably. See the WTO Web site page on the Doha Round: https://www.wto.org/english/tratop_e/dda_e/dda_e.htm.

[10]See Narlikar (2003, 2012) on the role of coalition at negotiations in the multilateral trading system.

integration to the global economy, as reflected in the market access commitments at the time of membership. However, at least on the surface, they are now pointing to the same accession commitments as a source of difficulty to their continuous engagement in multilateral trade liberalization at the post-membership stage. Observing China's[11] performance in the Doha Round, for instance, Lim and Wang (2010) comment that the country's negotiating position has been hardened for this reason. However, this change of policy orientation, before and after accession, is somewhat puzzling. If the RAMs pursued international economic integration through accession on the premise that it would serve their own economic benefits, there should be no obvious reason to discontinue the liberalization efforts at the Doha Round in the post-accession period.

In contrast to their defensive positions at the DDA market access negotiations, a number of RAMs have been proactively utilizing WTO's dispute settlement mechanism in relation to their terms of accession, as have actually been observed for China and Viet Nam. The accession protocol for these two East Asian transition countries designated them as "non-market economies" (NMEs).[12] The NME status allows WTO members to refer to costs of the third surrogate country in calculation of dumping margins (as prices in transition economies are allegedly distorted), leaving the RAMs in a vulnerable position in anti-dumping investigations. Likewise, the special transitional product-specific safeguard (TPS) provision inserted in China's terms of accession[13] significantly relaxed the usual multilateral disciplines on eligibility for safeguard actions by its trading partners (Messerlin, 2004).[14] These measures were part of targeted discrimination that the incumbent WTO members had

[11] It is WTO's common practice to refer to People's Republic of China just as China (as presented in its Web site: http://www.wto.org/english/thewto_e/whatis_e/tif_e/org6_e.htm). Where the text of this book adopts this term, it is solely for the purpose of reflecting WTO's practice, without any political connotation.

[12] See Snyder (2001) on the origins of the NME idea, particularly in the European context.

[13] The TPS provision eases the WTO members' resort to targeted safeguard against China. See Chapter 4 on this China-specific WTO-minus provision and the relevant dispute settlement case.

[14] Legal scholars criticize the WTO-plus and WTO-minus provisions on the ground that they undermine the rule of law by creating "two-tier" membership (Polouektov, 2002) and fragmenting the unity of WTO law (Charnovitz, 2008; Qin, 2003). Among economists, Martin (2010) presents a negative view on WTO-minus provisions, as having created a precedent of discriminatory trade restriction at departure from the MFN principle.

imposed on the non-members prior to their accession, and were retained as WTO-minus provisions continuously in the post-accession period.

Ecuador is another RAM that has actively been using the WTO dispute settlement mechanism, partly in relation to its banana exports to the European Union (EU). European countries had long provided preferences to imports from its former colonies in African, Caribbean, and Pacific (ACP) regions, and, as a result, banana exports from other regions—Latin America in particular—had practically been discriminated. Thus, the EU's discrimination was a source of concern for Ecuador as a major banana producing country, before and even for some time after its accession to the WTO. In contrast, many other new WTO members have not been involved in such disputes at all.

2 Research Question and Relevance

2.1 Research Question

A puzzle is that, whereas most of the RAMs were engaged in non-discriminatory trade liberalization through the multilateral trading system in the pre-membership phase, many of them disengaged from further market opening at the WTO in the post-membership phase, with notable exceptions for involvement in dispute settlement cases by some. Against this background, the proposed research poses a question on how these developments are taking place—in particular, what accounts for the RAMs' pre- and post-accession policy orientations toward and within the multilateral trading system.

Specifically, this book sheds light on two distinctive areas of merchandize trade policies,[15] namely (i) non-discriminatory market access liberalization, including through accession and the DDA negotiations on NAMA and agriculture and (ii) countering discrimination through dispute settlement and other multilateral schemes of trade liberalization. Essentially, whereas market access negotiations are aimed at reduction of MFN bound tariffs across a wide range of products (and have economy-wide implications), targeted discrimination typically takes the form of partial (and hence specific) departures from the

[15] The RAMs' negotiating claims vis-à-vis terms of accession are strongest and most relevant in the areas of trade in goods, where they form a coalition for the Doha Round. For this reason, trade in services and intellectual property rights are not direct coverage of this research.

MFN treatment. Thus, these are usually treated as separate issues. At the same time, both commonly relate to trade liberalization,[16] and comprehensive coverage of the two is important in analyzing the RAMs' broad trade policy orientations. It is worth clarifying that the research focuses on trade policy orientation from the side of the RAMs, and it does not provide a comprehensive account of policy-making on the side of their trading partners. This would be an important agenda for future research.

2.2 *Specific Areas of Research*

Further details on the two specific areas of analysis (market accession negotiations and countering discrimination) are presented below, together with elaboration of the overall research relevance, from both policy and academic points of view.

2.2.1 Market Access Negotiations

The analysis of the market access liberalization primarily examines the RAMs' policy objectives on NAMA and agriculture in the accession process and the DDA negotiations. On the latter, the research primarily assesses the process toward the conclusion of the so-called July 2008 package, which marked the last major milestone before subsequent deadlock of the entire Doha Round and culminated into its so-called draft "modalities" papers by December 2008.[17] While the RAMs were collectively seeking differential treatment in the Doha Round, details of their negotiating claims and results varied across different subgroups within the coalition, so were outcomes partly reflected in its draft December 2008 modalities papers.[18] A close look reveals that the new WTO members designated as

[16] Market access negotiations for the membership relate to trade liberalization by acceding countries, while the dispute settlement is envisaged to help lift certain (WTO-inconsistent) protectionist measures by the defendant. The DDA market access negotiations are aimed at mutual trade liberalization among the members.

[17] Draft December 2008 modalities papers of the DDA negotiations adopted a Swiss formula for NAMA and a tiered formula for agriculture as prime yardsticks for tariff cuts among participating members. Most of the RAMs, but not all, were excluded from the proposed obligations. See WTO (2008a, 2008b).

[18] In 2008, the DDA negotiations on NAMA and agriculture almost reached a grand consensus among WTO members, except that the US and India could not agree on the exact terms of the special safeguard for farm products by developing countries.

the RAMs comprised the following subgroups of economies with distinctive characters and trade policy positions[19]:

- **Low-income economies in transition, including Albania, Armenia, Georgia,[20] Kyrgyz Republic, Mongolia, and Moldova**. With an exception of Mongolia, low-income economies in transition come from Central Asia and Eastern Europe. They formed a sub-coalition of their own within a larger RAMs group and were most vocally arguing for the differential treatment at the Doha Round. The low-income economies in transition had bound their tariffs at the low single-digit level in their terms of accession, exhibiting the most liberal trade policy orientation among the RAMs subgroups, but were refusing to make further concessions during the DDA market access negotiations. Their defensive negotiating position was mostly accommodated by the WTO members.
- **"Formula" countries, including Croatia, China, Oman, and Chinese Taipei**. Unlike most of the other RAMs, these four economies ended up with negotiating their own tariff cuts at the Doha Round. The draft DDA modalities[21] stipulate prospective trade liberalization by these RAMs based on the designated formula, albeit with the longer implementation period (by 3 years, for NAMA) and at a moderate rate (for agriculture) specifically allowed for them.[22] Thus, while still seeking differential treatment as RAMs, these formula countries appeared to be accepting the virtue of market opening

[19] Presented country subgrouping primarily reflects RAM's self-designation in their negotiating proposals (WTO, 2007a, 2007b) and treatments under draft December 2008 modalities papers (WTO, 2008a, 2008b). However, the composition was not always fixed in the course of the DDA negotiations, and the official documentation on negotiation is not precisely clear in its articulation. So, the typology here reflects a certain degree of flexible discretion by the author.

[20] At a later stage of the Doha Round, Georgia withdrew from the sub-coalition among low-income economies in transition, particularly for NAMA negotiations. The case study on Georgia in Chapter 3 sheds some light also on other low-income economies in transition, to assess whether there was any unique background applicable only to Georgia but not to others.

[21] See further elaboration of the draft December 2008 modalities of the Doha Round in Chapter 2.

[22] Because of the membership to the Gulf Cooperation Council, Oman was further exempted from reduction of bound tariff below 5% after applying modalities.

through the Doha Round, on top of what they had previously accepted for accession. The depth of market access commitments made in their terms of accession varies.

- **"Very" recently acceded members (VRAMs), including Cape Verde, Former Yugoslav Republic of Macedonia, Saudi Arabia, Tonga, Viet Nam, and Ukraine**: The VRAMs were exempted from making any further concessions during the Doha Round, on the grounds that they just recently started implementing terms of accession in parallel. The depth of their accession commitments varies, but stays mostly at the average tariff level higher than those of the low-income economies in transition. While the VRAMs did not accept the formula-based tariff cuts, they were relatively less vocal or even silent in claiming the RAMs' cause of differential treatment in the Doha Round.
- **"Small, vulnerable economies" (SVEs), including Ecuador, Jordan, and Panama** from the RAMs. The "SVE" designation cuts across all WTO members with a small share in the world trade, not specific to the RAMs. The SVEs that were concurrently RAMs retained the average tariff rate at the two-digit level bound in their terms of accession, much higher than those of most of the other RAMs. For the Doha Round, the SVEs had been granted a differential treatment of somewhat moderate tariff cuts (for both NAMA and agriculture) with a grace period of three years (for NAMA).

Observations of positions at the market access negotiations of the WTO alone do not provide a full picture of the RAMs' trade policy orientation. To retain a broader picture of the RAMs' recent trade liberalization in scope, the research also reviews the policy stance outside of the multilateral trading system. Interestingly, on the one hand, a majority of the RAMs (most of the low-income economies in transition, the SVEs, and the VRAMs) appear to have been undertaking autonomous trade liberalization even beyond their accession commitments on the voluntary basis, despite their disengagement from formula-based tariff cuts at the Doha Round. On the other hand, the RAMs whose autonomous liberalization somewhat stalled were those that negotiated formula-based tariff cuts relatively proactively in the Doha Round ("formula" countries).[23] Good or bad, regional trade agreements also emerged as trade policy

[23] See Chapter 2 for further details.

instruments.[24] This appears to suggest that these RAMs were simply picking their own avenue of post-accession trade policy reform, but were not necessarily discontinuing liberalization itself at the cost of foregoing gains from trade through market opening.[25]

2.2.2 Countering Long-Standing Discrimination

Another element of the research sheds light on how the RAMs have been reacting to targeted discrimination that dates back to the pre-accession period. Having previously been outside of the multilateral trading system, some of the RAMs had to suffer from a number of targeted discriminatory measures from the incumbent members of the WTO. These include not only the NME designation for anti-dumping disputes and TPS-like undisciplined safeguard measures, but also lack of the unconditional MFN status and possible exclusion from the quota removal under the WTO Agreement on Textiles and Clothing,[26] among others. While some of these costs of previous non-membership have been removed through or soon after the RAMs' WTO accession, a number of targeted discriminatory measures remained for some countries. This research looks into the RAMs' long-standing endeavors to counter the targeted discrimination through and after WTO accession.

Under the DDA mandate, the WTO members were negotiating refinement of a number of existing multilateral rules, including those on some

[24] This book primarily addresses MFN-based trade liberalization, both within the WTO and through each country's domestic reforms. Assessment of regional trade agreements is less comprehensive and focuses primarily upon those that formed an important context for MFN-based liberalization. This is partly because there are existing research works that address the issue of multilateralism versus regionalism, but also because, unlike the case of non-discriminatory market-opening, preferential tariff-cuts may not necessarily bring about welfare gains, due to trade diversion among other reasons. Thus, MFN-based liberalization and preferential liberalization are not directly comparable. In fact, customs unions, one form of the regional trade agreements, may even require their members to raise tariff rates, as recently observed for a number of RAMs that joined the Eurasian Economic Union (EAEU). According to the Word Bank (2005), regional trade agreements accounted for only a very small share (10%) of tariff liberalization among developing countries in 1983–2003. See Bhagwati (2008) on critical accounts of preferential trade agreements.

[25] See Bhagwati (2002a) on the case for free trade.

[26] The Agreement on Textile and Clothing required elimination of relevant quotas among WTO members by 2005, but it was not applicable for exports from the non-member countries. Thus, the non-members were to be discriminated.

forms of trade remedies.[27] For certain RAMs still in the process of transition to market economies, the negotiations provided an avenue to redress the discriminatory treatment inscribed in the terms of accession, in parallel with individual dispute settlement proceeding among parties concerned. Among the RAMs, China in particular accorded a high priority to making progress in the rules negotiations on anti-dumping (Messerlin, 2004), while the talk itself appeared to be stagnating. This research assesses development of RAMs' negotiating positions in the Doha Round, particularly in response to the NME provision inscribed in the terms of accession.

Analysis is also conducted on how the RAMs were coping with trade remedies by their trading partners through the WTO dispute settlement system, mostly focusing on cases substantially completed by early years of their membership, up to 31 December 2012.[28] While NME and TPS provisions included in the terms of accession of China and Viet Nam were explicitly discriminatory and protectionist in nature, the WTO membership also provided access to the dispute settlement mechanism for the RAMs to cope with them. In fact, these two East Asian RAMs in transition have proactively been utilizing this new avenue to counter protectionist measures by their trading partners. Trade remedy cases related to RAMs' terms of accession on long-standing discrimination in early years after membership include:

- United States—Anti-dumping and Countervailing Duties (China)
- European Community—Fasteners (China)
- United States—Tyres (China)
- United States—Shrimp (Viet Nam)
- European Union—Footwear (China).

However, these two East Asian transition economies were not the only RAMs that have been coping with the long-standing discrimination through dispute settlement with major trading partners. Beyond the area

[27] In the WTO context, "trade remedies" are contingent protections exercised by importing countries, including safeguard, anti-dumping, and countervailing duties.

[28] To focus on recourse to WTO dispute settlement in early years of their membership, this book mainly covers trade remedy cases whose original panel or Appellate Body report (when appealed) was circulated by 31 December 2012. For the United States–Fasteners (China) case, the compliance panel was composed after circulation of the Appellate Body report on 15 July 2011, and the panel and Appellate Body reports in the compliance proceedings were circulated on 7 August 2015 and 18 January 2016, respectively. See WTO (2011, 2016a, 2016b).

of trade remedies, one prominent case was Ecuador's involvement in the EC—Bananas III dispute that lasted until 8 November 2012.

Despite the obvious disadvantage, the RAMs appear to have fared well in most of the cases, except for one safeguard dispute. This research looks into the RAMs' positions taken in these cases. It also reviews previous efforts to remove the targeted discrimination first through the accession process, as well as similar cases of pre-accession bilateral disputes.[29]

2.3 Relevance of the Research

The post-1995 accession process clearly created a new category of WTO members—the RAMs, on top of the conventional grouping of developed and developing countries.[30] A total of 36 members that joined the WTO through the post-1995 accession process already account for over one-fifth of the entire membership (that counted 164 as of 29 July 2016). Furthermore, the new members include large trading nations of systemic importance to the global economy, such as China.[31] For these reasons, the RAMs' post-accession policy orientation increasingly carries weight in the multilateral trading system. Thus, a close look at their positions and behavior entails practical policy relevance. Particularly on China, the present trade disputes with the United States reflect the latter's frustration and perception that the momentum to proceed with transition to a market economy observed at the time of the WTO accession negotiations has been lost, if not reversed, once the country joined the club in 2001. To understand the origin of today's disputes, it is extremely important to know what exactly China's motivation for the WTO accession and post-accession agendas was.

[29]This research looks into the RAMs' pre- and post-accession engagement in the multilateral trading system in relation to their membership. For this reason, most of the other disputes on issues not directly related to the WTO membership and terms of accession are not covered. Also, observations of dispute settlements on targeted discrimination inevitably touch upon both complainants (the RAMs) and respondents (the United States and the EU) but, in line with the overall objective of the research, the primary focus of analysis is the former.

[30]Tyagi (2012) observes this discriminated status of the RAM as "a second-class citizen."

[31]The Russian Federation joined the WTO quite recently on 22 August 2012, and it was still outside of the formal RAMs negotiating group in the process toward concluding the July 2008 package of the Doha Round and the draft December 2008 modalities papers. For this reason, its trade policy has not been assessed in detail in this research. See Tarr (2007) and World Bank (1999) on issues related to Russia's WTO accession.

Intellectually, the research is an attempt to contribute to the understanding of political economy of the multilateral trading system, especially its theoretical rationale. Surprisingly, among academic circles, there is no solid consensus on what exactly is the purpose of the multilateral trading system. To be precise, there is probably no disagreement in saying that one of its institutional aspirations is non-discriminatory trade liberalization (or "*substantial reduction of tariffs and other barriers to trade and to the elimination of discriminatory treatment in international trade relations*"), as stated in the preamble of the WTO Agreement (WTO, 1995a, p. 6). However, a real question is why there has to be an international regime to pursue this objective. A country gains from trade through its own autonomous trade liberalization (and is free to take this advantage with or without the presence of the multilateral institution). Then, what is the value added of the WTO (or GATT before it) in supporting market opening by its current and prospective members?[32] This has been a long-standing question among scholars of the multilateral trading system. For instance, Regan (2006) wrote:

> What are trade agreements for? Despite all the academic discussion of trade agreements, we have no generally accepted account of what they are supposed to do. Broadly speaking, trade agreements promote global economic efficiency by restraining certain sorts of national behaviour. But what sorts, specifically? (Regan, 2006, pp. 951–952)

In fact, as further elaborated in the third section (on argument, theories, and hypotheses) of this chapter, a number of theories have been developed by scholars in an attempt to answer this question, but most of them have not necessarily been followed up by empirical research in the form of detailed qualitative case studies. In particular, no previous studies systematically revealed the objective of engagement in the WTO actually conceived by policy-makers and negotiators on the basis of primary materials, such as policy statements, memoirs, and interviews. The most straightforward approach to confirm the role of the multilateral trading system is to find out what motivated the countries to participate in its various liberalization schemes. Through careful studies of the record of the RAMs' actual engagement in the WTO, this research reveals the functions of the multilateral trading system as perceived directly by its stakeholders.

[32] Implicitly, this question places a presumption that states use and design the international institutions to further their goals (Koremenos, Lipson, & Snidal, 2004).

3 Argument, Theories, and Hypotheses

3.1 Main Argument

As observed, the form and extent of the RAMs' engagement in pre- and post-membership multilateral trade liberalization vary. As an overall proposition, the research places an assumption that countries envisage different roles for various schemes of multilateral trade liberalization (accession, the Doha Round, and dispute settlement) at the WTO. Individual RAMs should have certain economic objectives to be achieved through specific functions of the multilateral trading system, and they would remain engaged in the multilateral liberalization process only where these schemes efficiently serve their desired goals. Otherwise, they would refrain from utilizing the multilateral process and act more autonomously. In this argument, what counts is RAMs' trade policy objectives envisaged to be achieved through each function of the multilateral trading system. As a conceptual framework, the research draws upon a number of economic theories to identify what these possible agendas could be, and which scheme of multilateral trade liberalization is best suited to accommodate them, for subsequent confirmation through case studies. The theories also provide some predictions on what types of economies would possess what kind of objectives.

3.2 Conceptual Framework for Analyzing Multilateral Trade Liberalization[33]

3.2.1 General Thrust of Trade Theories

The conventional trade theory of international economics tells that, essentially, welfare gains from trade can be derived from autonomous trade liberalization, at least for small economies (Bhagwati, 2002b; Krugman, 1997). By simply opening the domestic market to the rest of

[33] This section is organized primarily around theories introduced by economists, but it also refers to the same or similar concepts of rationales for international trade agreements and negotiations conceived by lawyers and political scientists. Typically, while theories presented in the formal writing by economists tend to be modeled more rigorously (and often mathematically), works by others (including informal writing by economists) allow for more relaxed interpretation of the unique trade policy objectives. Where a particular economic theory is referred to in this paper, it is meant to be encompassing not only the former but also the latter perspectives, from holistic points of views.

the world unilaterally, the country can achieve more efficient resource allocation, production, and consumption, and this can be accomplished with or without membership to the multilateral trading system. The very fact that the RAMs went through considerable length to join the WTO, however, implies that there were more specific reasons for them to have joined the club. A number of economic theories (on commitment, juggernaut, terms of trade externality, and domino) provide some insights into these objectives[34] and inference on how they may possibly affect the RAMs' trade policy positions at the WTO. Following the theories and inferences, the research will place working hypotheses on the relationship between RAMs' economic characteristics on the one hand and their engagement in the multilateral trading system on the other hand. Broadly speaking, the theories on international trade agreements could be categorized into two groups: those pertaining to market access liberalization in general and the other on recovery of the more specific cost of the outsider status, outlined as follows together with their resulting hypotheses.

3.2.2 Market Access Liberalization for Merchandize Trade

3.2.2.1 Case for Unilateral Policy Commitment

The "commitment" theory emphasizes the role of the trade agreement as an anchor to support domestically driven trade liberalization (Maggi & Rodriguez-Clare, 1998; Staiger & Tabellini, 1987).[35] As stated above, a country gains from trade by unilateral liberalization. However, this economy-wide gain primarily takes the form of surplus for the consumers (who enjoy cheaper imports) that outweighs loss for the

[34] Robert Baldwin (2012b), Hoekman and Kostecki (2009), and the WTO (2007c) summarize some of key economic theories of the multilateral trading system.

[35] In this paper, the commitment theory is presented as a broad notion that the role of the WTO is to help the government tie its own hands to implement and sustain domestic reforms. Among the commitment theorists, Staiger and Tabellini (1987) specifically address importance of credibility over policy's time-consistency among domestic businesses, whereas Maggi and Rodriguez-Clare (1998) emphasize the role of multilateral trade agreements to foreclose pressures from vested interests. The latter view is shared by some legal scholars including McGinnis and Movsesian (2000), Petersmann (1986), and Regan (2006). Gerhart (2003) specifically calls it the "inward-looking and economic" constitutional vision of the WTO (to distinguish it from another "external, participatory" constitutional vision of the WTO, that addresses trade policies of other member countries, rather than one's own).

import-competing industries (who may lose out from exposure to international competition). Whereas the former group is scattered, the latter is better organized to lobby for protection, thereby potentially posing difficulty for the government undertaking unilateral trade liberalization (Petersmann, 1986). In some cases, domestic businesses may not even start necessary restructuring simply at the ignorance of the government's policy announcement on prospective liberalization. In such instances, the market-opening commitment through the multilateral trade agreement may serve as a credible anchor for the government to enforce policy implementation and prevent its reverse in the future. The trade agreement will lock in the government's reform initiatives, and once locked in, commitments made would be enforceable through the dispute settlement system, further enhancing the government's position and credibility among the domestic constituencies.[36] Thus, the commitment theory assumes that the government concludes international trade agreements to "tie its own hands" in support of domestic reforms, as eloquently illustrated in the WTO's own publication:

> Under WTO rules, once a commitment has been made to liberalize a sector of trade, it is difficult to reverse. The rules also discourage a range of unwise policies. For businesses, that means greater certainty and clarity about trading conditions. For governments it can often mean good discipline... Quite often, governments use the WTO as a welcome external constraint on their policies: "we can't do this because it would violate the WTO agreements". (WTO, 2009, p. 14)

One important feature of the commitment theory is its primary focus on a single country's own unilateral trade liberalization, and reciprocal tariff cuts by trading partners are not necessarily assumed.[37]

[36] It also signals government's commitment to improve business environment externally to foreign investors. For instance, the prospect for Viet Nam's WTO accession in 2007 brought about increase in foreign direct investment (FDI) (Hanh, 2011), as elaborated in Chapter 5. See Sam and Thu (2005) on the country's financial sector reform in preparation for WTO accession.

[37] In fact, Maggi and Rodriguez-Clare (2007) extend the commitment theory model to encompass terms of trade externality in a single framework. However, their work clearly distinguishes the role of accession to a trade agreement to enhance credibility through unilateral commitments on the one hand and that of reciprocal negotiations to contain terms of trade externality on the other hand.

The government ties its own hands to catalyze or consolidate its domestic reforms, and trade liberalization by trading partners is not expected to play any role. As stated above, this is broadly how the market access commitments of the WTO accession process work. In the membership negotiations, the acceding governments make unilateral tariff binding commitments, while incumbent members of the WTO are not expected to make additional commitments (beyond extending the existing tariff rates on the MFN basis). In the commitment theory, the only motivation for a country's engagement in the multilateral trading system is the will of its own government to proceed with domestic reforms.

A majority of the RAMs are economies in transition, and it is very plausible that they might have used terms of WTO accession as a straightforward commitment device for unilateral trade liberalization as part of their own market-oriented reform.[38] However, the other RAMs that were not undertaking reforms would make little use of market access commitments for accession. In line with the commitment theory, the first hypothesis of this research focuses on this domestic reform objective of market access commitments through WTO accession:

- *Reforming economies (especially, those in transition to a market economy) would make extensive market access commitments for WTO accession, while others would make little use of them (Hypothesis 1).*

3.2.2.2 Case for Trade Reciprocity

Unlike the commitment theory of unilateral liberalization, the two strands of theories on the multilateral trading system emphasize the role of reciprocity. Among them, ***the "juggernaut" theory*** on mobilization of exports business interests (Baldwin, 1994, 2006, 2012a) presumes a mercantilist orientation in multilateral trade negotiations[39] or, what Krugman (1991) called "***GATT-think***," comprising three basic principles as follows:

[38] See tariff data and further details on accession commitments presented in Chapter 2.

[39] The juggernaut theory also draws upon the insights of the "protection for sale" model (Grossman & Helpman, 1994), more explicitly featuring the role of campaign contributions and party finance in representative democracy. However, the model addresses protectionism and trade policy in general, rather than multilateral trade liberalization alone, and could not explain a country's preference for the latter. (See the Sect. 3.3 of this chapter.) Milner (1988, 1997) also presents a similar view that trade policy is formulated through interactions among domestic actors, including business entities.

1. Exports are good.
2. Imports are bad.
3. Other things equal, an equal increase in imports and exports is good. (Krugman, 1991, p. 15)

In line with its third principle on reciprocity ("*Other things equal, an equal increase in imports and exports is good.*"), trade negotiators acting out of GATT-think would offer market access only when the counterparts from other WTO members would reciprocate them. Conversely, opening of the foreign markets would also be conditioned upon liberalization of home markets, and this reciprocity constraint should induce domestic export industries to lobby for such liberalization against resistance from import-competing industries (Goldstein, 1998).[40] With the support from export businesses, the government could achieve more extensive trade liberalization than possible by its autonomous action alone.[41] Once the process of reciprocal liberalization kicks in, the export industries grow as their business opportunities expand and so do their political influence, while import-competing industries shrink. In turn, this will automatically fulfill the political conditions toward further market opening.

Under this juggernaut model, the driving force for multilateral trading liberalization is export business interests, as reflected in the first principle of GATT-think. ("Exports are good.") Accordingly, export-oriented economies should opt for more proactive engagement in the multilateral liberalization process. In contrast, import-oriented economies that lack this impetus would stay out of reciprocal liberalization and may just claim the second principle of GATT-think ("Imports are bad"). In the absence of sufficient export interests, there is no reason

[40]One open question is to what extent mobilization of export interests through reciprocity is actually an outcome purposefully desired by the reform-minded policy-makers seeking liberalization, rather than an unintended result of domestic politics. Baldwin himself just indicates that trade policy is endogenous, determined through an interaction between the economy and its political system (Baldwin, 1994, 2006). In fact, negotiating governments themselves may be eager to seek export markets on behalf of their domestic industries. Ethier (2004) presents a political externalities model whereby the government claims credits for negotiating foreign market access liberalization to increase exports to the trading partners.

[41]Krugman (1991) indicates that GATT-think is conceptually wrong (as it departs from the conventional trade theory prescribing unilateral liberalization) yet mostly turns out to produce good results (of reciprocal liberalization, through the political process of engaging export interests) in practice.

to stay engaged in the complex multilateral negotiations, and instead, they would straightforwardly pursue liberalization autonomously outside of the multilateral trading system.[42] An important proposition of this theory is reciprocity, which is a key feature of the multilateral trade rounds including the DDA,[43] but not necessarily of the WTO accession negotiations where acceding governments make unilateral tariff binding commitments. These considerations of GATT-think and the juggernaut theory lead to the following hypothesis on the DDA market access negotiations.

- *Only export-oriented economies would stay proactively engaged in the post-accession market access negotiations of the Doha Round, while others would pursue autonomous liberalization (Hypothesis 2-a).*

Another strand of the rationale for reciprocity, ***the theory on "terms of trade externality,"*** assumes that large countries use the multilateral trading system to escape from Prisoner's Dilemma (Bagwell & Staiger, 1999, 2002).[44] If the economy is sufficiently large to be able to affect the world price through its trade policy, it would be reluctant to cut tariffs alone as it may worsen its terms of trade. To the contrary, the country would be induced to raise tariffs to improve its terms of trade (as per the theory of optimal tariffs), and this move may trigger its trading partners to do the same. However, retaliations and a possibly resulting tariff war would leave all countries worse off, in a situation where terms of trade might not improve (as all try to raise tariffs) while economic efficiency would also be sacrificed (due to higher protection). The reciprocity built into the multilateral trade negotiations would remove such Prisoner's Dilemma by ensuring that one's tariff cuts would be replicated

[42] This is partly because, whereas an increase of imports would facilitate any form of trade liberalization, unilateral and reciprocal alike, only an increase of exports would stimulate reciprocal liberalization. As a result, only economies enhancing their export orientation over and above the import orientation would opt for reciprocal liberalization, and others would choose a simpler autonomous route. The juggernaut theory literature does not explicitly make this point.

[43] Legal foundations of reciprocity and its derivatives are reviewed in Chapter 2.

[44] The economic theory of terms of trade externality shares an insight of neo-liberal institutionalism of international politics that emphasizes the role of multilateral institutions to promote international cooperation among individual states and derive the globally optimal solution (WTO, 2007c).

by others, thereby maintaining terms of trade unchanged among trading partners. This theory's underlying presumption, that each country cares about terms of trade in the first place, may probably sound rather unrealistic, and its practical relevance is often questioned (Ethier, 2007; Hoekman & Kostecki, 2009; Regan, 2006).[45] At the same time, it gives an insight that, at least on theoretical grounds, reciprocity and the size of the economy may matter.

Like the case of juggernaut theory, reciprocity plays a central role, which is a unique feature of the market access negotiations of the Doha Round but not typically in those of accession. However, the primary motivation of the government is to self-discipline its own temptation to manipulate terms of trade, and only economies large enough to be able to affect international prices through its tariff setting would need such a discipline. Small economies could not affect terms of trade in the first place and hence would not have this motivation to stay engaged in the reciprocal trade negotiations. Their only source of welfare gains is efficiency, rather than terms of trade, and that can be pursued through autonomous liberalization without engagement in the multilateral negotiations through the Doha Round. From this observation, the hypothesis that could be inferred would be:

- *Only large economies would stay proactively engaged in the market access negotiations of the Doha Round, while others would pursue autonomous liberalization (Hypothesis 2-b).*

Overall, what could be inferred from these theories is an insight that envisaged roles for market access negotiations for unilateral liberalization under the WTO accession and those for reciprocal liberalization under the Doha Round could be completely different. While the former directly catalyzes the acceding country's domestic reforms by serving as a commitment device and appeal to the needs of reforming economies across the board, the latter has more specific functions (mobilization of export business interests and containment of terms of trade manipulation) that cater to the needs of only a small set of countries characterized by the increasing export orientation and large size. Thus, these theories

[45] For this reason, between the two theories explaining the role of reciprocity in trade negotiations, juggernaut would probably have a higher level of real policy relevance than terms of trade externality.

should provide one possible explanation on why a majority of RAMs were effectively engaged in the WTO accession process by making extensive market access commitments, but many of them ceased to do so in the DDA market access negotiations.[46] On the one hand, many RAMs were transition economies undertaking reforms, and the WTO accession served as a mechanism to catalyze unilateral liberalization. On the other hand, only a handful of RAMs were export oriented or large, and others had no pressing reason to stay engaged in the reciprocal negotiations of the Doha Round. However, even RAMs that were relatively proactive at the DDA did not try to play a prominent leading role to move the entire round forward, and there is a need for closer examination of the extent of these theories' relevance in real-life trade policy-making.

3.2.3 Recovering Cost of Prior Non-membership

The "domino" theory focuses on the cost of staying out of the rule-based international regime as a driver for expansion of its membership (Baldwin, 1994, 1995, 2006, 2012a). While the conclusion of a trade agreement and the resulting deepening of integration create trade among its members, they also bring about trade diversion away from non-members. As per the domino theory, the latter triggers non-members to join the agreement to recover the lost export markets, or to cope with the adverse impacts that arise from the trade policy of other countries (Gerhart, 2003).[47] An underlying proposition is that countries join trade agreements from a defensive motivation (Gruber, 2001),[48] not necessarily out of the intent to willingly open their own market. In fact, the original domino theory was derived as a conceptual framework explaining expansion of regional trade agreements (RTAs),[49] but it may also

[46]The WTO's own publication comments on the commitment theory as follows: "*(I)t may explain why a country joins the GATT/WTO, but not why it would need reciprocal negotiations to reduce its tariffs. Once a Member, a country could unilaterally commit to reduce its tariff*" (WTO, 2007c, p. 91).

[47]Gerhart (2003) called this the "external, participatory" constitutional visions of the WTO.

[48]The domino theory originally conceptualized by Economist Richard Baldwin (including his use of the North American Free Trade Agreement as one of the illustrative cases) was later replicated by Political Scientist Lloyd Gruber.

[49]At departure from the MFN principle, GATT Article XXIV allows formation of customs unions and free trade areas under certain conditions. This exceptional clause on RTAs assumes reciprocity.

be applicable to the WTO accession (Lissovolik & Lissovolik, 2004[50]). While many incumbent members of the WTO typically tended to accord the MFN treatment even to non-members on a voluntary basis, there were certain discriminatory measures targeted at certain economies. In the course of WTO accession, the RAMs might have sought unconditional consolidation of the existing MFN access to export markets[51] and mostly managed to secure permanent MFN status by accession. However, some of the discrimination remained, partly as WTO-minus provisions in terms of accession. The domino theory gives an insight that the removal of such costs of previous non-membership[52] could be the RAMs' motivation for engagement in the multilateral trading system, leading to another hypothesis:

- *Countries that face the discriminatory costs of prior non-membership would stay engaged in the relevant multilateral liberalization schemes, while others would refrain from such activities (Hypothesis 3).*

Targeted discrimination could be redressed through various WTO schemes. Among them, the RAMs' first line of defense in this endeavor would be accession negotiations. However, where terms of accession

[50] In this work, authors estimated possible positive impacts of accession by Russia.

[51] A majority of the RAMs are economies in transition from the former communist bloc and, as previously excluded from the multilateral trading system, these NMEs were not granted a permanent normal trade relations (PNTR) status by the US—the world's largest economy—under its domestic law (Section 402 of 1974 Trade Act commonly known as the Jackson–Vanik amendment). Such a discriminatory treatment would become illegal under the MFN principle of the multilateral trading system and, for these transition economies, accession to the WTO was an avenue to redress this problem and secure permanent access to the key export market. See Rhodes and Jackson (1999) on the US domestic laws related to WTO accession. To be precise, Article XIII of the WTO Agreement still allows an exception whereby the incumbent members opt out from WTO relations with new members but, in practice, all the RAMs have been accorded the PNTR status by the time of accession or mostly within a few years after that. See Cooper (2012).

[52] One may argue that, strictly speaking, given that some of these discriminatory treatments were maintained even after the RAMs' WTO membership (at least for a certain period of time), they alone were not necessarily the cost of the outsider status. However, the non-members could not resort to the WTO dispute settlement mechanism to counter targeted trade restrictions by the incumbent members in the pre-accession period. Thus, the discrimination and the lack of access to the dispute settlement mechanism combined were clearly the cost of the outsider status.

could not fully resolve the problem (as a result of accession negotiations or due to the nature of discrimination), the RAMs would resort to other schemes of multilateral trade liberalization, such as the dispute settlement mechanism or the DDA negotiations in the post-accession period. In particular, the dispute settlement mechanism could serve as a powerful instrument for the WTO members to claim their legal right through the multilateral litigation. Dispute settlement cannot overrule the existing multilateral trade agreements and the RAMs' terms of accession, but it can serve as an instrument to deter abuse of these rules by older WTO members.[53] Thus, access to the dispute settlement itself could be one important purpose of the WTO accession for the RAMs that had long suffered from targeted discrimination.

3.3 Supplementary Explanation and Other Theories

One potentially important issue that is not explicitly addressed in depth in the theories outlined above is the complexity of institutional processes under different schemes of multilateral trade liberalization. Above all, the Doha Round is an attempt to liberalize trade policy of all WTO members through negotiations among them, whereas the WTO accession and dispute settlement essentially focus on one country's policy and require negotiations and litigation involving a smaller number of direct stakeholders. Thus, the Doha Round is much more complex than other forms of multilateral trade liberalization. As partly eluded to in the formulation of the hypotheses, a consideration of these different levels of complexities may partly reveal the possible explanation on why, for instance, most of the RAMs were proactively engaged in the accession process but not in the Doha Round. In particular, when the objective of engagement in the multilateral trading system is to catalyze the domestic reforms (as assumed in Hypothesis 1), the country would bind its market access commitments through the relatively simpler accession process, but would hesitate to go through the complex process of the Doha Round. Instead, it would opt for autonomous trade liberalization (that does not require any international negotiations and agreements) to achieve its objective

[53] This is not to say that countering discrimination that dates back to the pre-accession period is the only objective for recourse to dispute settlement at the WTO. Obviously, the dispute settlement mechanism can address all other issues related to the covered agreements.

more efficiently in the post-accession period. The only exceptional cases would be when the country has other motivations (such as mobilizing export business interests, containing terms of trade externality, or redressing remaining discrimination, as assumed in the other hypotheses) whose merit deserves efforts of proactive engagement in the complex multilateral negotiation process. While the issue of institutional complexity would not be a central theme of existing trade theories and this research, it could well supplement theories adopted in the thesis in explaining the RAMs' behaviors and would be revisited in the final chapter.[54]

At the same time, it should be noted that theories presented herewith are only those that explain government's possible motivation and the rationale for engagement in the multilateral trading system, and are not meant to be an exhaustive listing of all concepts related to the formulation of trade policy at large. These include, for instance, the influential "protection for sale" model (Grossman & Helpman, 1994) illustrating how domestic business constituencies affect the government's policy-making trough election contributions, and various economic models presenting distributive impacts of international trade (such as the Stolper–Samuelson theorem[55]). These theories do not assume the presence of any multilateral institutions and are not meant to explain the motivation and rationale for countries' resort to international trade agreements, negotiations, and litigation. The latter is the central theme of this thesis, and the base theories have been selected out of this consideration.

4 Methodology and Case Selection

4.1 Research Methodology

The research adopts the case study method as the main tool of enquiry. It primarily draws upon the "method of difference" (Odell, 2001) of comparing cases that possess different independent variables (causes)

[54]The institutional aspects of multilateral trade liberalization are briefly touched upon in Chapter 7. It compares not only various trade liberalization schemes under the WTO auspices but also policy-based lending by international financial institutions (IFIs). Where relevant, IFIs' contribution to trade liberalization is also referred to in other chapters, to present a holistic picture of the role of all multilateral institutions involved.

[55]Stolper and Samuelson (1941). Rogowski (2004) extends the Stolper–Samuelson theorem for analysis of coalition formation for rent-seeking within the domestic economy.

and dependent variables (effects), so as to confirm possible causalities spelled out in each hypothesis.[56] After presenting an overview of WTO's accession process and post-accession trade policy performances of the 19 RAMs, including their collective behavior as a negotiating coalition, the research undertakes the preliminary cross-country examination of each hypothesis based on the policy and economic data available for all the RAMs. In line with the overall argument and hypotheses, the independent variables are the RAMs' unique economic characteristics, including the reform orientation for Hypothesis 1, export orientation for Hypothesis 2-a, the size of the economy for Hypothesis 2-b, and discrimination faced since the pre-accession period for Hypothesis 3. The dependent variables are the RAMs' actual engagement in (and disengagement from) various schemes of multilateral trade liberalization at the WTO, including accession, the Doha Round, and dispute settlement. Macroeconomic and policy data (such as balance-of-payments statistics and applied and bound tariff rates) was consulted for identification of the RAMs' economic characteristics and, where relevant, the state of actual engagement in the WTO activities.

However, the research goes beyond simple observations of the cross-country data alone, and the preliminary observation is followed by more specific case studies of a small number of selected economies, as well as comparison of the findings to evaluate the hypotheses in further detail. The advantage of such a small number case study is that it allows careful review of each country's trade policy positions taken in the process of actual policy-making, negotiations, and litigation, beyond what could be observed through the large number empirical studies. Even when certain independent variables are found to be correlated with the dependent variables on the basis of data alone, it does not necessarily establish that the former caused the latter in a way predicted by the theory.[57] For instance, Hypothesis 1 presumes correlation between the

[56] Ideally, for strictly rigorous confirmation of correlation between independent and dependent variables, all other variables should be controlled. As Odell (2001) notes, however, it is extremely difficult to find two (or more) cases that are completely identical except for independent and dependent variables in the real world. The research overcomes this challenge by relying on qualitative observation of the policy-making and negotiation process, beyond mere comparison of variables in the form of data alone, so as to find what actually accounted for decisions by policy-makers and negotiators in each case study.

[57] In other words, correlation does not guarantee causality.

RAMs' reform orientation and the depth of WTO accession commitments. However, such a review of policy data alone does not prove that the domestic reform was actually the country's motivation for accession as assumed in the commitment theory. This can be verified only through more direct inquiries on the RAMs' policy objectives, which require more qualitative assessments of the positions taken and arguments made in the membership process.

This qualitative assessment was conducted through a careful review of the original WTO documents (remarks at the ministerial conferences; memorandums of foreign trade regime; protocols of accession, including working party reports; minutes, negotiating proposals, and chair's reports of the DDA negotiations on NAMA, agriculture, and rules; reports and minutes of trade policy reviews; and panel and Appellate Body reports, as well as minutes of the Dispute Settlement Body), reports by other international organizations (particularly, international financial institutions active in the area of trade policy), domestic policy and research documents, personal memories, letters, and commentaries by negotiators, policy-makers, and other stakeholders, media coverage, and so on. Given that the launch of the accession process for a number of RAMs dates back to the time of pre-1995 GATT system (before establishment of the WTO), the research also entailed extensive archival search of documents of the day. It presents numerous citations of texts from these primary documents.

Documentary information was supplemented by face-to-face interviews with senior trade policy officials, business representatives, and international organizations in capitals of the RAMs selected for case studies, and in Geneva, Switzerland (where the WTO is located). Overall, 57 interviews were conducted through eight trips to Beijing, China (19–30 October, 2013), Geneva, Switzerland (1–31 July, 15–19 September, and 28 September–5 October in 2012, and 24 September–4 October, 2014), Hanoi, Viet Nam (13–19 October, 2013), Quito, Ecuador (21 November–3 December, 2013), and Tbilisi, Georgia (10–16 November, 2013). At a minimum, policy-makers of trade ministries, representatives of the major nationwide business associations, and the staff of international financial institutions were interviewed in the capital of each case study country (while, depending on the country, hearing was conducted also with other stakeholders, such as those from other ministries, academia, and the sectoral business association). In Geneva, interviews were held mainly with trade negotiators based in the WTO permanent missions of the most RAMs (including the case study countries) and the staff members of the concerned divisions at the WTO secretariat. These interviews provided insights into the RAMs' policy objectives and background, beyond what were stated in the official documents.

4.2 *Selected Case Countries*

Among the RAMs, Georgia, People's Republic of China, Viet Nam, and Ecuador have been chosen as cases.[58] All of them share a common background of joining the WTO through the Article XII accession process since 1995.[59] Their independent variables (characteristics of the economy) vary, making them suitable candidates to evaluate the hypotheses.[60] Georgia is a small transition economy with a chronic current account deficit, and the country did not suffer from targeted discrimination by incumbent members before and after the WTO accession.[61] China is also a transition economy undertaking domestic reforms. At the same time, it is a large country with a high degree of export orientation (the world's second largest economy and the largest exporter with huge current account surplus). Whereas China obtained the permanent MFN status from the United States after the WTO membership, it remained qualified by the

[58] Among low-income economies in transition, Albania and Macedonia are in the process of EU accession. Mongolia could be another interesting case (Tsogtbaatar, 2005), but is not listed due to unlikely availability of reliable pre-accession tariff data.

[59] As the RAMs, these countries also share a common feature of being non-LDC emerging market economies and non-EU member states with autonomous trade policy-making.

[60] In principle, each hypothesis can be examined by only two case countries that differ in one independent variable assumed under each hypothesis. However, a conclusion drawn for each hypothesis becomes more reliable by also including cases that share the same orientation in the independent variable specifically assumed for each hypothesis but differ in those assumed for other hypotheses. For instance, if all economies that shared the characteristics of undertaking reforms but differed in their export orientation undertook extensive market access commitments (while non-reforming economies did not), such a result enhances validity of Hypothesis 1 by its confirmation that the reform orientation, not export orientation, was the common feature among them, hence the determinant of the depth of market access commitments for accession. This is a merit of including more than two cases for each hypothesis.

[61] Georgia was accorded the PNTR status by the United States only in the year of its WTO accession (2000), but there is no evidence indicating that the country's exports had been adversely affected by discrimination. Also, there was no explicit discriminatory WTO-minus provision in Georgia's terms of accession.

discriminatory provisions included in the terms of accession, such as those on NME, TPS, and textile safeguard. As an East Asian transition economy with an outward-oriented growth strategy, Viet Nam has similar characteristics as those of China, but it ran short of China in terms of the economy size (medium) and export orientation (previously, the current account had been in deficit, which sharply increased immediately after WTO accession[62]). Viet Nam received the permanent MFN status through the WTO accession but was designated as NME, albeit not for TPS as was the case for China. Unlike these transition economies, Ecuador ceased to pursue active domestic reforms before the launch of the WTO membership process. The country is relatively small. Its current account had been in deficit, but it turned to surplus during the Doha Round.[63] Ecuador suffered from discrimination under the EU's banana import regime before and long after its WTO membership.

In relation to Hypothesis 1, these case countries include three transition economies undertaking domestic reforms (China, Georgia, and Viet Nam) and the non-reformer (Ecuador). With regard to Hypothesis 2-a, the cases include an export-oriented economy (China), an import-oriented economy (Georgia), and those that experienced a change of the external position in the course of the Doha Round (Viet Nam and Ecuador). For examination of Hypothesis 2-b, a large economy (China) and smaller ones (others) are covered. As to Hypothesis 3, whereas three of them (China, Viet Nam, and Ecuador) continuously suffered from targeted discrimination since the pre-WTO accession period, such a cost of previous non-member status was not a major concern for the other (Georgia). One methodological challenge is that the RAMs that have consistently been export oriented tended to be large at the same time, and this coincidence raises the difficulty in determining which one of these economic characteristics was more relevant purely on the basis of data alone. The case study approach overcomes this problem by introducing more qualitative observations of the government's policy objective for the country concerned (China).

[62] In more recent years since 2011, Viet Nam's current account turned into a surplus, recording 4.9% of gross domestic product (GDP) in 2014, while it returned to a deficit at 0.1% of GDP in 2015 (IMF, 2018a).

[63] In 2000, Ecuador introduced dollarization as its monetary policy and does not have its own currency. Chapter 6 examines the implication of this unique macroeconomic policy arrangement. In more recent years since 2009, after the deadlock of the Doha Round in 2008, Ecuador's current account tuned into deficit again, except in 2016 when a surplus at 1.4% of GDP was recorded. See IMF (2018b).

These four cases also differ in their dependent variables (the state of engagement in multilateral liberalization schemes at the WTO), as summarized below on each of them:

- **Georgia**. The country had made very liberal market access commitments for accession, at the bound rate of 7.4% on average, but had been very vocal in seeking differentiated treatment in the early phase of the DDA negotiations, disengaging itself from the multilateral process. After WTO accession, Georgia instead undertook substantial autonomous liberalization, particularly for industrial goods. It has not been involved in any disputes at the WTO.
- **People's Republic of China**. The country made an accession commitment of bound tariff rates at around 10% on average, and it has also been actively engaged in the DDA negotiations on market access and rules, as well as a number of WTO-minus trade remedy disputes against the United States and the EU. China was one of the few RAMs that envisaged to pursue further market opening based on the DDA formulas. However, its autonomous liberalization almost completely stalled after WTO accession.
- **Viet Nam**. The country's average bound tariff rate was 11.5%, slightly higher than China's. Compared with the other RAMs, it was much less vocal in the DDA negotiations. The country has been undertaking some autonomous tariff cuts after WTO accession. Viet Nam resorted to the dispute settlement mechanism at WTO against the United States on the trade remedy measures claimed to be related to the WTO-minus provision.
- **Ecuador**. The country's average bound tariff rate was 21.7%, highest (together with Panama) among all the RAMs. Ecuador had been advocating ambitious liberalization of agricultural trade through the DDA negotiations, but there has been little move towards autonomous market opening, both before and after WTO accession. Ecuador filed a dispute settlement case against the EU on the latter's banana import regime.

As outlined above, case countries made different levels of market access commitments in the course of accession, in relation to Hypothesis 1. They also represent all four sub-groupings of the RAMs in the DDA market access negotiations (China as a formula country; Georgia as a low-income economy in transition; Viet Nam as a VRAM; and Ecuador as an SVE), in relation to Hypotheses 2-a and 2-b, and include those that filed disputes at the WTO (China, Viet Nam, and Ecuador[64]) and a non-disputant (Georgia) in relation to Hypothesis 3. The case studies allow comparison across these countries with regard to their different behaviors at the multilateral trading system.[65]

5 Literature Survey[66]

There is an immense number of literature on WTO membership, including works providing general accounts of the RAMs' activities conducted prior to accession (Braga & Cattaneo, 2009a, 2009b; Hoekman & Roy, 2000; Langhammer & Lücke, 1999; Michalopoulos, 2002; Milthorp, 2009; Smith, 1996; WTO, 2010a, 2010b). Most of cross-country empirical works point to a trend of increasingly demanding terms and process of securing WTO membership (Evenett & Braga, 2005, 2006; Grynbeg, Dugal, & Razzaque, 2006; Jones, 2009; Lacey, 2007). The data confirms that the bar has become significantly higher for the newly acceding countries, mostly irrespective of their levels of development,[67] and the time required to complete the accession process has increased for each additional membership. Other research has found that many acceding economies still bind the tariff

[64]Interestingly, Viet Nam had NME anti-dumping disputes with the United States on similar products before (on catfish) (Davis, 2006) and after (shrimp) WTO accession. The examination of the pre-accession case would allow identification of the country's initial expectation for the WTO membership in relation to trade remedy disputes. See Chapter 5.

[65]Four hypotheses on market access negotiations for accession (Hypothesis 1), those under the Doha Round (Hypotheses 2-a and 2-b), and redressing discrimination (Hypothesis 3) are evaluated for each of the four RAMs. So, all in all, they represent a total of sixteen sub-cases.

[66]For brevity and selectivity, this section does not list the entire literature on WTO accession. In particular, those related to regionalism (Ferrantino, 2010; Huang, 2009; Pomfret, 2010; Tumbarello, 2005, 2007a) are not covered.

[67]Pelc (2011) provided a cross-country empirical evidence showing that de jure depth of tariff liberalization (gap between a pre-accession MFN rate and a post-accession bound rate) was negatively correlated with import market size of the accession countries, except in the case of LDCs. VanGrasstek (2001) presented a historical perspective that the trend of increasing demands on accession countries was a reflection of a changing focus of multilateral trade negotiations among developed countries, from tariffs alone to behind-the-border measures.

rates at the level higher than their applied rates for market access liberalization of trade in goods (Bacchetta & Drabek, 2002; Drabek & Bacchetta, 2004; Martin, 2010).

There are also ample studies on the economic impact of WTO membership, at both cross-country and country levels. In a widely cited empirical study on 175 countries over a 50-year period, for instance, Rose (2004a) found that there was little evidence that GATT/WTO membership had a substantial positive effect on the expansion of trade.[68] To the contrary, Subramanian and Wei (2007) provided counter-evidence that the WTO had strong positive impacts, albeit unevenly across members,[69] and Tomz, Goldstein, and Rivers (2007) showed that, once non-formal members (colonies, or de facto or provisional members) were counted as participants to the multilateral trading system, the conclusion by Rose would be reversed. A majority of country-specific quantitative estimates and qualitative analysis of welfare impacts related to China's accession (Anderson, Huang, & Ianchovichina, 2004a, 2004b; Bhattasali, Li, & Martin, 2004; Drabek & Woo, 2010; Francois & Spinanger, 2004; Ianchovichina & Martin, 2001, 2004; Martin, 2003; Mattoo, 2003, 2004), whereas other countries and regions also caught some researchers' attention (Anderson, 1999; Koukhartchouk & Maurel, 2003; Michalopoulos, 1998; Tumbarello, 2007b).

However, the empirical research on the new WTO member's post-membership policy orientation (beyond implementation of accession commitments) is relatively scarce. One notable exception on trade in goods is a study by Rose (2004b). Through cross-country regression of a comprehensive set of trade policy data (comprising 68 tariffs and non-tariff measures), for 168 countries in the period from 1950 to 1998, it found that almost no measure of trade liberalization was significantly correlated to GATT/WTO accession. One important limitation of this

[68]Rose (2005) also compared contributions of three different multilateral and plurilateral institutions to increase of trade. He concluded that Organisation for Economic Co-operation and Development membership had a consistently large positive effect, while impacts of the GATT/WTO and the International Monetary Fund have been weaker. Rose (2010) further presented an overview of the debates on relevance of GATT/WTO so far, with his latest view on the subject.

[69]This point was picked up by a counter response by Rose (2007). Allee and Scalera (2012), Felbermayr and Kohler (2010), and Tang and Wei (2009) also presented findings with similar orientations.

work, however, is its time span of up to the late 1990s. Back then, most of today's RAMs were still non-members and are treated as such. Thus, specificity of the RAMs as new members with unique terms of accession is not reflected. In services, Eschenbach and Hoekman (2006) found that WTO accession commitments did not bring about a positive impact on the quality of policy of European and transition economies. The latter study is mainly intended to address the implementation of accession commitments and does not cover the RAMs' policy positions in the Doha Round and dispute settlement.

Single-country researches featuring post-accession policy are mostly on China.[70] For instance, Lawrence (2008), Lim and Wang (2010), Mallon and Whalley (2004), Sally (2011), and Whalley (2006) took stock of China's trade policy performance after accession, on multilateral, regional, bilateral, and unilateral fronts, and Green (2004) looked into the country's bilateral negotiations on the market economy status, particularly with the EU. From a legal point of view, Tyagi (2012) reviewed dispute settlement cases related to the RAMs' protocols of accession, mainly on China. However, at the moment, there is no qualitative case study literature covering China's post-accession performance at the WTO from comparative perspectives with the other RAMs'.

There are a number of empirical studies conducted with an attempt to verify the economic theories on trade agreements and negotiations. In support of the commitment theory, Staiger and Tabellini (1999) presented the statistical evidence showing that, during the Tokyo Round, the United States triggered exceptions from the formula-based tariff cuts less readily in sectors characterized by the high level of protection (while the reverse was true in its resort to the escape clause). Fugazza and Robert-Nicoud (2010) claimed validity of the juggernaut theory based on their finding that the United States granted the immediate duty-free access status to its RTA partners particularly in sectors where the country had made the deepest Uruguay Round commitments (to make an argument that the Uruguay Round triggered subsequent trade liberation, albeit preferentially). Bagwell and Staiger (2011) found correlation between the tariff cuts negotiated by the RAMs and the ratios of their

[70]Pietras (1998) reviewed experiences of earlier WTO membership by a number of Eastern European economies in transition (Poland, Czech Republic, Romania, and Hungary), with some reference to their post-accession trade policy response. These EU member states are not designated as RAMs.

import volumes to the word price and took it as empirical verification of the terms of trade externality theory. Another work by Broda, Limão, and Weinstein (2006) found that non-WTO members and the United States set the high tariffs in sectors where they had market power, and took it as proof of relevance of terms of trade consideration. Based on the statistical data for 145 countries in 1995–2005, Egger and Larch (2008) observed that formation of RTAs created incentives for the outsiders to join the existing RTAs or to form new RTAs, and Sapir (2001) presented a similar finding on European integration in 1960–1992, both allegedly in line with the domino theory.

Critical limitation of these existing empirical studies is their exclusive reliance on indirect economic and policy statistics. These works were aimed at establishing a statistical correlation between variables selected by the authors, who then interpreted such correlation as the evidence of theory relevance. However, none of them directly asked whether policy-makers or trade negotiators "actually" conceived the motivations envisaged in the theories in their past engagement in the multilateral trading system. Considering that there is not yet a consensus on the role of the WTO in trade liberalization in the academic circle, the absence of such a study is a crucial omission in the scholarship. The book fills this gap through careful reviews of statements by and interviews with the stakeholders involved in actual policy-making and negotiations. Although the research uses available economic and policy data to support the argument, it substantially draws also upon the qualitative information, so as to reveal each country's objective for engagement in the multilateral trading system in a more direct manner.

6 Structure of the Book

The book is structured around introduction and overview to cover the entire RAMs and four specific case studies on the selected countries. This first chapter on background provides the research question, main arguments, theoretical frameworks, and hypotheses. The second chapter on overview presents general features of negotiations and terms of WTO accession, the RAMs' collective claims at the Doha Round as a negotiating coalition, and their overall performance in accession-related dispute settlements. At the same time, it provides a preliminary examination of the hypotheses on the basis of cross-country statistical data available for the 19 RAMs. These are followed by four chapters of country case studies, whereby hypotheses are examined in further detail against the RAMs' performance in both market access liberalization and countering discrimination. Each case study traces the relevant country context, evolution of the country's trade policy, and positions for negotiations and litigation with regard to market access liberalization and trade remedies.[71] The book is wrapped up with the concluding chapter, which summarizes and compares the findings from the case studies. In essence, the research reveals that, while the theories applicable primarily to WTO accession and dispute settlement (commitment and domino) worked just as envisaged, relevance of those for reciprocal DDA market access negotiations (juggernaut and terms of trade eternality) is, at best, verified only with qualifications. The conclusion also provides some suggestions for future research, as well as relevant policy recommendations.

7 Conclusion

This research is probably the first serious attempt to examine the RAMs' trade policy positions and performance from a comparative cross-country perspective, cutting across both pre- and post-accession periods. While the main focus of the research relates to the accession of the RAMs and their post-accession trade policy orientation, in a member-driven institution like the WTO, positions of individual members ultimately help shape the collective orientation of the entire regime. As WTO membership expands, the RAMs' positions will have increasingly important stakes in formulating the future of the multilateral trading system. In this sense, albeit indirectly, the research is also an attempt to shed some light on the changing face of the global governance on international trade.

References

Allee, T. L., & Scalera, J. E. (2012). The divergent effects of joining international organizations: Trade gains and the rigors of WTO accession. *International Organization, 66*(2), 243–276.

Anderson, K. (1999). *Vietnam's transforming economy and WTO accession.* Singapore: Institute of Southeast Asian Studies.

[71] In this exercise, the international and domestic factors are reviewed along with the relevant hypotheses, with an assumption that the two are interconnected (Goldstein, 1998, 2012; Milner, 1997; Putnam, 1988).

Anderson, K., Huang, J., & Ianchovichina, E. (2004a). Will China's WTO accession worsen farm household incomes? *China Economic Review, 15*, 443–456.

Anderson, K., Huang, J., & Ianchovichina, E. (2004b). The impact of WTO accession on Chinese agriculture and rural poverty. In D. Bhattasali, S. Li, & W. Martin (Eds.), *China and the WTO: Accession, policy reform, and poverty reduction strategies* (pp. 101–116). Washington, DC: World Bank.

Bacchetta, M., & Drabek, Z. (2002). *Effects of WTO accession on policy-making in sovereign states: preliminary lessons from the recent experience of transition countries* (Development and Economic Research Division Staff Working Paper DERD-2002-02). Retrieved from World Trade Organization website: http://www.wto.org/english/res_e/reser_e/derd200202_e.htm.

Bagwell, K., & Staiger, R. W. (1999). An economic theory of GATT. *American Economic Review, 89*(1), 215–248.

Bagwell, K., & Staiger, R. W. (2002). *The economics of the world trading system*. Cambridge: MIT Press.

Bagwell, K., & Staiger, R. W. (2011). What do trade negotiators negotiate about? Empirical evidence from the World Trade Organization. *American Economic Review, 101*(4), 1238–1273.

Baldwin, R. E. (1994). *Toward an integrated Europe*. London: Centre for Economic Policy Research.

Baldwin, R. E. (1995). A domino theory of regionalism. In R. Baldwin, P. Haaparanta, & J. Kiander (Eds.), *Expanding membership of the European Union* (pp. 25–48). Cambridge: Cambridge University Press.

Baldwin, R. E. (2006). Multilateralising regionalism: Spaghetti bowls as building blocs on the path to global free trade. *The World Economy, 29*(11), 1451–1518.

Baldwin, R. E. (2012a). Preferential trading arrangements. In A. Narlikar, M. Daunton, & R. M. Stern (Eds.), *The Oxford handbook on the World Trade Organization* (pp. 632–654). Oxford: Oxford University Press.

Baldwin, R. E. (2012b). The case for a multilateral trade organization. In A. Narlikar, M. Daunton, & R. M. Stern (Eds.), *The Oxford handbook on the World Trade Organization* (pp. 29–39). Oxford: Oxford University Press.

Basra, H. (2012). Increased legalization or politicization? A comparison of accession under the GATT and WTO. *Journal of World Trade, 46*(4), 937–960.

Bhagwati, J. (2002a). *Free trade today*. Princeton: Princeton University Press.

Bhagwati, J. (2002b). Introduction: The unilateral freeing of trade versus reciprocity. In J. Bhagwati (Ed.), *Going alone: The case for relaxed reciprocity in freeing trade* (pp. 1–30). Cambridge: MIT Press.

Bhagwati, J. (2008). *Termites in the trading system: How preferential arrangements undermine free trade*. Oxford: Oxford University Press.

Bhattasali, D., Li, S., & Martin, W. (2004). Impacts and policy implications of WTO accession for China. In D. Bhattasali, S. Li, & W. Martin (Eds.), *China and the WTO: Accession, policy reform, and poverty reduction strategies* (pp. 1–17). Washington, DC: World Bank.

Braga, C. A. P., & Cattaneo, O. (2009a). Introduction. In C. A. P. Braga & O. Cattaneo (Eds.), *The WTO and accession countries* (Vol. 1, pp. xi–xlvii). Cheltenham: Edward Elgar.

Braga, C. A. P., & Cattaneo, O. (2009b). *Everything you always wanted to know about WTO accession (But were afraid to ask)* (Policy Research Working Paper, WPS5156). Retrieved from World Bank website: http://www-wds.worldbank.org/external/default/WDSContentServer/WDSP/IB/2009/11/05/000158349_20091105161912/Rendered/PDF/WPS5116.pdf.

Broda, C., Limão, N., & Weinstein, D. (2006). *Optimal tariffs: The evidence* (Working Paper No. 12033). Retrieved from National Bureau of Economic Research website: http://www.nber.org/papers/w12033.

Charnovitz, S. (2008). Mapping the law of WTO accession. In M. E. Janow, V. Donaldson, & A. Yanovich (Eds.), *The WTO: Governance, dispute settlement, and developing countries* (pp. 855–920). Huntington: Juris.

Cooper, W. H. (2012). *The Jackson-Vanik amendment and candidate countries for WTO accession: Issues for congress*. Washington, DC: Congressional Research Service.

Davis, C. L. (2006). Do WTO rules create a level playing field? Lessons from the experience of Peru and Vietnam. In J. S. Odell (Ed.), *Negotiating trade: Developing countries in the WTO and NAFTA* (pp. 219–256). Cambridge: Cambridge University Press.

Drabek, Z., & Bacchetta, M. (2004). Tracing the effects of WTO accession on policy-making in sovereign states: Preliminary lessons from the recent experience of transition countries. *World Economy, 27*(7), 1083–1125.

Drabek, Z., & Woo, W. T. (2010). Who should join the WTO and why? A cost-benefit analysis of WTO membership. In Z. Drabek (Ed.), *Is the World Trade Organization attractive enough for emerging economies? Critical essays on the multilateral trading system* (pp. 249–294). Basingstoke: Palgrave Macmillan.

Egger, P., & Larch, M. (2008). Interdependent preferential trade agreement memberships: An empirical analysis. *Journal of International Economics, 76*, 384–399.

Eschenbach, F., & Hoekman, B. (2006). Services policies in transition economies: On the EU and WTO as commitment mechanism. *World Trade Review, 5*(3), 415–443.

Ethier, W. J. (2004). Political externalities, nondiscrimination, and a multilateral world. *Review of International Economics, 12*(3), 303–320.

Ethier, W. J. (2007). The theory of trade policy and trade agreements: A critique. *European Journal of Political Economy, 23*, 605–623.

Evenett, S. J., & Braga, C. A. P. (2005). WTO accession: Lessons from experience (Trade Note 22, June 6). Retrieved from World Bank website: http://www-wds.worldbank.org/external/default/WDSContentServer/WDSP/IB/2005/07/28/000160016_20050728140916/Rendered/PDF/331270TradeNote22.pdf.

Evenett, S. J., & Braga, C. A. P. (2006). WTO accession: Moving the goalposts? In R. Newfarmer (Ed.), *Trade, Doha, and development: A window into the issues* (pp. 231–243). Washington, DC: World Bank.

Felbermayr, G., & Kohler, W. (2010). Does WTO membership make a difference at the extensive margin of world trade? In Z. Drabek (Ed.), *Is the World Trade Organization attractive enough for emerging economies? Critical essays on the multilateral trading system* (pp. 217–248). Basingstoke: Palgrave Macmillan.

Ferrantino, M. J. (2010). Policy anchors: Do free trade agreements and WTO accessions serve as vehicles for developing-country policy reform? In Z. Drabek (Ed.), *Is the World Trade Organization attractive enough for emerging economies? Critical essays on the multilateral trading system* (pp. 91–138). Basingstoke: Palgrave Macmillan.

Francois, J. F., & Spinanger, D. (2004). WTO accession and the structure of China's motor vehicle sector. In D. Bhattasali, S. Li, & W. Martin (Eds.), *China and the WTO: Accession, policy reform, and poverty reduction strategies* (pp. 191–210). Washington, DC: World Bank.

Fugazza, M., & Robert-Nicoud, F. (2010). *The 'emulator effect' of the Uruguay round on US regionalism* (CEP Discussion Paper No. 973). Retrieved from Centre for Economic Performance website: http://cep.lse.ac.uk/pubs/download/dp0973.pdf.

Gerhart, P. M. (2003). The two constitutional visions of the world trade organization. *University of Pennsylvania Journal of International Economic Law, 24*(1), 1–75.

Goldstein, J. (1998). International institutions and domestic politics: GATT, WTO, and the liberalization of international trade. In A. O. Kruger (Ed.), *The WTO as an international organization* (pp. 133–152). Chicago: University of Chicago Press.

Goldstein, J. (2012). Trade liberalization and domestic politics. In A. Narlikar, M. Daunton, & R. M. Stern (Eds.), *The Oxford handbook on the World Trade Organization* (pp. 64–82). Oxford: Oxford University Press.

Green, S. (2004). *China's quest for market economy status* (Chatham House Briefing Note). Retrieved from Royal Institute of International Affairs website: https://www.chathamhouse.org/sites/files/chathamhouse/public/Research/Asia/bnmay04.pdf.

Grossman, G. M., & Helpman, E. (1994). Protection for sale. *The American Economic Review, 84*(4), 833–850.

Gruber, L. (2001). Power politics and the free trade bandwagon. *Comparative Political Studies, 34*(7), 703–741.

Grynbeg, R., Dugal, M., & Razzaque, M. A. (2006). *An evaluation of the terms of accession to the World Trade Organization: A comparative assessment of services and goods sector commitments by WTO members and acceding countries.* London: Commonwealth Secretariat.

Hanh, P. T. H. (2011). Does WTO accession matter for the dynamics of foreign direct investment and trade? Vietnam's experience. *Economics of Transition, 19*(2), 255–285.

Hoekman, B. M., & Kostecki, M. M. (2009). *The political economy of the world trading system: The WTO and beyond* (2nd ed.). Oxford: Oxford University Press.

Hoekman, B., & Roy, J. (2000). Benefiting from WTO accession and membership. In B. Hoekman & J. Zarrouk (Eds.), *Catching up with the competition: Trade opportunities and challenges for Arab countries* (pp. 307–324). Ann Arbor: University of Michigan Press.

Huang, C. (2009). Bilateralism and multilateralism: Taiwan's trade liberalization trajectory. *The Hague Journal of Diplomacy, 4*, 37–59.

Ianchovichina, E., & Martin, W. (2001, December). Trade liberalization in China's accession to WTO. *Journal of Economic Integration, 16*(4), 421–445.

Ianchovichina, E., & Martin, W. (2004). Economic impacts of China's accession to the WTO. In D. Bhattasali, S. Li, & W. Martin (Eds.), *China and the WTO: Accession, policy reform, and poverty reduction strategies* (pp. 211–236). Washington, DC: World Bank.

International Monetary Fund. (2018a). *Viet Nam: 2018 article IV consultation* (IMF Country Report No. 18/215). Washington, DC: Author.

International Monetary Fund. (2018b). *World economic outlook (October): Challenges to steady growth.* Washington, DC: Author.

Jones, K. (2009). The political economy of WTO accession: The unfinished business of universal membership. *World Trade Review, 8*(2), 279–314.

Koremenos, B., Lipson, C., & Snidal, D. (2004). The rational design of international institutions. In B. Koremenos, C. Lipson, & D. Snidal (Eds.), *The rational design of international institutions* (pp. 1–39). Cambridge: Cambridge University Press.

Koukhartchouk, O., & Maurel, M. (2003). *Accession to the WTO and EU enlargement: What potential from trade increase?*. London: Centre for Economic Policy Research.

Krugman, P. (1991, November/December). The move toward free trade zones. *Economic Review—Federal Reserve Bank of Kansas City, 76*(6), 5–25.

Krugman, P. (1997). What should trade negotiators negotiate about? *Journal of Economic Literature, 35*(1), 113–120.

Lacey, S. (2007). The view from the other side of the table: WTO accession from the perspective of WTO members. In J. Streatfeild & S. Lacey (Eds.), *New Reflections on International Trade* (pp. 75–98). London: Cameron May.

Langhammer, R. J., & Lücke, M. (1999). WTO accession issues. *World Economy, 22*(6), 837–873.

Lanoszka, A. (2001). The World Trade Organization accession process: Negotiating participation in a globalizing economy. *Journal of World Trade, 35*(4), 575–602.

Lawrence, R. Z. (2008). China and the multilateral trading system. In B. Eichengreen, Y. C. Park, & C. Wyplosz (Eds.), *China, Asia, and the new world economy* (pp. 145–167). Oxford: Oxford University Press.

Lim, C. L., & Wang, J. Y. (2010). China and the Doha development agenda. *Journal of World Trade, 44*(6), 1309–1331.

Lissovolik, B., & Lissovolik, Y. (2004). *Russia and the WTO: The "gravity" of outsider status* (Working Paper No. WP/04/159). Retrieved from the International Monetary Fund website: http://www.imf.org/external/pubs/ft/wp/2004/wp04159.pdf.

Maggi, G., & Rodríguez-Clare, A. (1998). The value of trade agreements in the presence of political pressures. *Journal of Political Economy, 106*(3), 574–601.

Maggi, G., & Rodríguez-Clare, A. (2007). A political-economy theory of trade agreements. *American Economic Review, 97*(4), 1374–1406.

Mallon, G., & Whalley, J. (2004). *China's post accession WTO stance* (Working Paper No. 10649). Retrieved from National Bureau of Economic Research website: http://www.nber.org/papers/w10649.

Martin, W. (2003). Implication of reform and WTO accession for China's agricultural policies. In S. D. Rozelle & D. A. Summer (Eds.), *Agriculture trade and policy in China: Issues, analysis and implications* (pp. 1–27). Aldershot: Ashgate.

Martin, W. (2010). Development implications of WTO accession procedures. In Z. Drabek (Ed.), *Is the World Trade Organization attractive enough for emerging economies? Critical essays on the multilateral trading system* (pp. 13–36). Basingstoke: Palgrave Macmillan.

Mattoo, A. (2003). China's accession to the WTO: The services dimension. *Journal of International Economic Law, 6*(2), 299–339.

Mattoo, A. (2004). The services dimension of China's accession to the WTO. In D. Bhattasali, S. Li, & W. Martin (Eds.), *China and the WTO: Accession, policy reform, and poverty reduction strategies* (pp. 117–139). Washington, DC: World Bank.

McGinnis, J. O., & Movsesian, M. L. (2000). The world trade constitution. *Harvard Law Review, 114*(2), 511–605.

Messerlin, P. A. (2004). China in the WTO: Antidumping and safeguards. In D. Bhattasali, S. Li, & W. Martin (Eds.), *China and the WTO: Accession, policy reform, and poverty reduction strategies* (pp. 29–47). Washington, DC: World Bank.

Michalopoulos, C. (1998). *WTO accession for countries in transition* (Policy Research Working Paper No. 1934). Retrieved from World Bank website: http://www-wds.worldbank.org/external/default/WDSContentServer/WDSP/IB/1998/06/01/000009265_3980702115733/Rendered/PDF/multi0page.pdf.

Michalopoulos, C. (2002). WTO accession. In B. M. Hoekman, A. Mattoo, & P. English (Eds.), *Development, trade, and the WTO: A handbook* (pp. 61–70). Washington, DC: World Bank.

Milner, H. V. (1997). *Interests, institutions and information: Domestic politics and international relations*. Princeton: Princeton University Press.

Milner, H. V. (1988). *Resisting protectionism: Global industries and the politics of international trade*. Princeton: Princeton University Press.

Milthorp, P. (2009). WTO accessions: The story so far. *The Hague Journal of Diplomacy, 4*, 103–112.

Narlikar, A. (2003). *International trade and developing countries: Bargaining coalitions in the GATT & WTO*. London: Routledge.

Narlikar, A. (2012). Collective agency, systemic consequences: Bargaining coalitions in the WTO. In A. Narlikar, M. Daunton, & R. M. Stern (Eds.), *The Oxford handbook on the World Trade Organization* (pp. 184–209). Oxford: Oxford University Press.

Odell, J. S. (2001). Case study methods in international political economy. *International Studies Perspectives, 2*(2), 161–176.

Pelc, K. J. (2011). Why do some countries get better WTO accession terms than others? *International Organization, 65*(4), 639–672.

Petersmann, E.-U. (1986). Trade policy as a constitutional problem: On the 'domestic policy functions' of international trade rules. *Aussenwirtschaft, 41*, 405–439.

Pietras, J. (1998). The role of the WTO for economies in transition. In A. O. Kruger (Ed.), *The WTO as an international organization* (pp. 353–362). Chicago: University of Chicago Press.

Polouektov, A. (2002). Non-market economy issues in the WTO anti-dumping law and accession negotiations: Revival of a two-tier membership? *Journal of World Trade, 36*(1), 1–37.

Pomfret, R. (2010). Regional trading arrangements and WTO membership: Substitutes or complements? In Z. Drabek (Ed.), *Is the World Trade Organization attractive enough for emerging economies? Critical essays on the multilateral trading system* (pp. 176–195). Basingstoke: Palgrave Macmillan.

Putnam, R. D. (1988). Diplomacy and domestic politics: The logic of two-level games. *International Organization, 42*(3), 427–460.

Qin, J. Y. (2003). "WTO-plus" obligations and their implications for the World Trade Organization legal system: An appraisal of China accession protocol. *Journal of World Trade, 37*(3), 483–552.

Regan, D. H. (2006). What are trade agreements for? Two conflicting stories told by economists, with a lesson for lawyers. *Journal of International Economic Law, 9*(4), 951–988.

Rhodes, S. A., & Jackson, J. H. (1999). United States law and China's WTO accession process. *Journal of International Economic Law, 2*(3), 497–510.

Rogowski, R. (2004). Commerce and coalitions: How trade affects domestic political alignments. In J. A. Frieden & D. A. Lake (Eds.), *International political economy: Perspectives on global power and wealth* (4th ed., pp. 318–326). London: Routledge. (Original work published 2000).

Rose, A. K. (2004a, March). Do we really know that the WTO increase trade? *American Economic Review, 94*(1), 98–114.

Rose, A. K. (2004b). Do WTO members have more liberal trade policy? *Journal of International Economics, 63,* 209–235.

Rose, A. K. (2005). Which international institutions promote international trade? *Review of International Economics, 13*(4), 682–698.

Rose, A. K. (2007). Do we really know that the WTO increases trade? Reply. *American Economic Review, 97*(5), 2019–2025.

Rose, A. K. (2010). The effect of membership in the GATT/WTO on trade: Where do we stand? In Z. Drabek (Ed.), *Is the World Trade Organization attractive enough for emerging economies? Critical essays on the multilateral trading system* (pp. 195–216). Basingstoke: Palgrave Macmillan.

Sally, R. (2011). *Chinese trade policy after (almost) ten years in the WTO: A post-crisis stocktake* (ECIPE Occasional Paper No. 2/2011). Brussels: European Centre for International Political Economy.

Sam, P. V., & Thu, V. T. (2005). Preparation by Viet Nam's banking sector for WTO accession. In P. Gallagher, P. Low, & A. Stoler (Eds.), *Managing the challenges of WTO participation: 45 case studies* (pp. 621–633). Cambridge: Cambridge University Press.

Sapir, A. (2001). Domino effects in Western European regional trade, 1960–1992. *European Journal of Political Economy, 17,* 377–388.

Smith, M. G. (1996). Accession to the WTO: Key strategic issues. In J. J. Scott (Ed.), *The world trading system: Challenges ahead* (pp. 167–181). Washington, DC: Institute for International Economics.

Snyder, F. (2001). The origins of the 'nonmarket economy': Ideas, pluralism and power in EC anti-dumping law about China. *European Law Journal, 7*(4), 369–424.

Staiger, R. W., & Tabellini, G. (1987). Discretionary trade policy and excessive protection. *American Economic Review, 77*(5), 823–837.

Staiger, R. W., & Tabellini, G. (1999). Do GATT rules help governments make domestic commitments? *Economics and Politics, 11*(2), 109–144.

Stolper, W., & Samuelson, P. (1941). Protection and real wages. *Review of Economic Studies, 9*(1), 58–73.

Subramanian, A., & Wei, S. (2007, May). The WTO promotes trade, strongly but unevenly. *Journal of International Economics*, 72(1), 151–175.

Tang, M., & Wei, S. (2009). The value of making commitments externally: Evidence from WTO accessions. *Journal of International Economics, 78,* 216–229.

Tarr, D. (2007). *Russian WTO accession: What has been accomplished, what can be expected* (Policy Research Working Paper No. 4428). Retrieved from World Bank website: http://www-wds.worldbank.org/external/default/WDSContentServer/WDSP/IB/2007/12/04/000158349_20071204105142/Rendered/PDF/wps4428.pdf.

Tomz, M., Goldstein, J. L., & Rivers, D. (2007). Do we really know that WTO increases trade? Comment. *American Economic Review, 97*(5), 2005–2018.

Tsogtbaatar, D. (2005). Mongolia's WTO accession: Expectations and realities of WTO membership. In P. Gallagher, P. Low, & A. L. Stoler (Eds.), *Managing the challenges of WTO participation: 45 case studies* (pp. 409–419). Cambridge: Cambridge University Press.

Tumbarello, P. (2005). *Regional trade integration and WTO accession: Which is the right sequencing? An application to the CIS* (Working Paper No. WP/05/94). Retrieved from International Monetary Fund website: http://www.imf.org/external/pubs/ft/wp/2005/wp0594.pdf.

Tumbarello, P. (2007a). *Are regional trade agreements in Asia stumbling or building blocks? Implications for the Mekong-3 countries* (Working Paper No. WP/07/53). Retrieved from International Monetary Fund website: http://www.imf.org/external/pubs/ft/wp/2007/wp0753.pdf.

Tumbarello, P. (2007b). Vietnam's WTO accession: Opportunities and challenges. In International Monetary Fund, *Viet Nam: Selected issues* (IMF Country Report No. 07/385). Washington, DC: International Monetary Fund.

Tyagi, M. (2012). Flesh on a legal fiction: Early practice in the WTO accession protocols. *Journal of International Economic Law, 15*(2), 391–441.

VanGrasstek, C. (2001). Why demands on acceding countries increase over time: A three-dimensional analysis of multilateral trade diplomacy. In United Nations Conference on Trade and Development, *WTO Accession and Development Policies* (UNCTAD/DITC/TNCD/11) (pp. 78–95). Retrieved from United Nations Conference on Trade and Development website: http://unctad.org/en/Docs/ditctncd11_en.pdf.

Whalley, J. (2006). China in the world trading system. *CESifo Economic Studies, 52*(2/206), 215–245.

World Bank. (1999). *Russian trade policy reform for WTO accession* (World Bank Discussion Paper No. 401). Washington, DC: Author.

World Bank. (2005). *Global economic prospects 2005: Trade, regionalism, and development.* Washington, DC: Author.

World Trade Organization. (1995). *The results of the Uruguay round of multilateral trade negotiations: Legal texts.* Geneva: Author. (Original work published by the GATT Secretariat 1994).

World Trade Organization. (2000a). *European Communities—Regime for the importation, sale and distribution of bananas: Request by the European Communities for arbitration under article 22.6 of the DSU—Decision by the arbitrators* (WT/DS27/ARB/ECU). Geneva: Author.

World Trade Organization. (2000b). *European Communities—Regime for the importation, sale and distribution of bananas: Recourse to article 22.7 of the DSU by Ecuador* (WT/DS27/54). Geneva: Author.

World Trade Organization. (2000c). *Dispute settlement body: 30 November 2000* (WT/DSB/M/91). Geneva: Author.

World Trade Organization. (2007a). *Negotiating group on market access: Market access for non-agricultural products—Negotiating proposals by recently acceded members (RAMs)* (TN/MA/W/83). Geneva: Author.

World Trade Organization. (2007b). *Committee on agriculture special session: Negotiating proposals by recently acceded members (RAMs)* (TN/AG/GEN/24). Geneva: Author.

World Trade Organization. (2007c). *World trade report 2007—Six decades of multilateral trade cooperation: What have we learned?* Geneva: Author.

World Trade Organization. (2008a). *Negotiating group on market access: Fourth revision of draft modalities for non-agricultural market access* (TN/MA/W/103/Rev.3). Geneva: Author.

World Trade Organization. (2008b). *Committee on agriculture, special session: Revised draft modalities for agriculture* (TN/AG/W/4/Rev.4). Geneva: Author.

World Trade Organization. (2009). *10 benefits of the WTO trading system.* Geneva: Author.

World Trade Organization. (2010a). *Technical note on the accession process: Note by the secretariat—Revision* (WT/ACC/10/Rev/4). Geneva: Author.

World Trade Organization. (2010b). *Technical note on the accession process: State of play and information on current accessions, note by the secretariat—Revision* (WT/ACC/11/Rev.9). Geneva: Author.

World Trade Organization. (2011). *European Communities—Definitive anti-dumping measures on certain iron or steel fasteners from China: Report of the appellate body* (WT/DS397/AB/R). Geneva: Author.

World Trade Organization. (2016a). *European Communities—Definitive anti-dumping measures on certain iron or steel fasteners from China—Recourse to article 21.5 of the DSU by China: Report of the appellate body* (WT/DS397/AB/RW). Geneva: Author.

World Trade Organization. (2016b). *European Communities—Definitive anti-dumping measures on certain iron or steel fasteners from China—Recourse to article 21.5 of the DSU by China: Report of the appellate body*—Addendum (WT/DS397/AB/RW/Add.1). Geneva: Author.

CHAPTER 2

The RAMs' Accession and Post-membership Activities: An Overview

1 Introduction

Further to the first chapter that introduced the theoretical framework for analyzing the RAMs' policy performances, this chapter first presents an overview of the WTO accession process and post-membership activities in the multilateral trading system. Thereafter, the RAMs' trade policy positions are empirically analyzed in light of the hypotheses inferred from theoretical framework, comprising the commitment theory that underlines the role of trade agreements to enhance unilateral domestic reforms; GATT-think, juggernaut and terms of trade externality theories that accords the prime role of the multilateral trading system to its reciprocity principle; and the domino theory that points to the cost of the outsider status as a motivation to join the trade agreement (albeit its origin to explain the proliferation of regional trade agreements). The hypotheses comprise: *Reforming economies (especially, those in transition to a market economy) would make extensive market access commitments for WTO accession, while others would make little use of them (Hypothesis 1); Only export-oriented economies would stay proactively engaged in the post-accession market access negotiations of the Doha Round, while others would pursue autonomous liberalization (Hypothesis 2-a); Only large economies would stay proactively engaged in the market access negotiations of the Doha Round, while others would pursue autonomous liberalization (Hypothesis 2-b); and Countries that face the discriminatory cost of prior non-membership would stay engaged in the relevant multilateral*

K. Takamiya, *Recently Acceded Members of the World Trade Organization*, https://doi.org/10.1007/978-981-13-9159-0_2

liberalization schemes, while others would refrain from such activities (Hypothesis 3). The analysis in this chapter offers preliminary cross-country observations primarily on the basis of macroeconomic and policy statistics available for all 19 RAMs covered by this research, which are to be followed by more specific case studies on four selected economies in the subsequent chapters.

Section 2 presents a factual summary of the WTO membership process, and the third section tracks the RAMs' post-accession policy performances within the multilateral trading system, at the Doha Round negotiations and in dispute settlement cases. The fourth section attempts to provide a preliminary explanation of the RAMs' behaviors based on the macroeconomic and policy data in relation to the hypotheses, and the fifth section provides concluding remarks.

2 WTO Accession at a Glance

2.1 Practice of the WTO Membership Process[1]

The codified procedural rule on WTO accession is rather simple. Article XII on accession of the Marrakesh Agreement Establishing the World Trade Organization (the WTO Agreement), which came into effect when the organization was established in 1995, just reads:

> Any State or separate customs territory possessing full autonomy in the conduct of its external commercial relations and of the other matters provided for in this Agreement and the Multilateral Trade Agreements may accede to this Agreement, on terms to be agreed between it and the WTO. Such accession shall apply to this Agreement and the Multilateral Trade Agreements annexed thereto.... Decisions on accession shall be taken by the Ministerial Conference. The Ministerial Conference shall approve the agreement on the terms of accession by a two-thirds majority of the Members of the WTO. (WTO, 1995a, p. 15)

Over time, the customary practice of the accession process evolved, as spelled out in a note "Accession to the World Trade Organization:

[1] This sub-section draws on the Technical Note on the Accession Process prepared by the WTO secretariat (WTO, 2010). See a handbook on accession released as a WTO publication for more comprehensive information on the accession process (Williams, 2008).

Procedures for Negotiations under Article XII" (WTO, 1995b, 2014), prepared by the secretariat in 1995 (and updated in 2014) in consultation with the interested members.

The accession process starts with submission of the application for membership to the Director-General by the prospective member. Upon verification by the Director-General, the request is transmitted to the WTO's General Council, which in turn establishes the Working Party among the interested incumbent members. The terms of reference of this Working Party are to examine the application and to submit to the General Council (or the Ministerial Conference) recommendations which usually include a draft Protocol of Accession. In the early phase of the accession process, the applicant submits the Memorandum of the Foreign Trade Regime, as well as related information including copies of legislation (laws and regulations) in place, forward-looking legislative action plans, and data on applied duty rates, agricultural domestic support and export subsidies, and services. Submission of the memorandum is followed by an exchange of written questions and replies between the applicant and the Working Party, before the first meeting of the latter is convened for the examination of the applicant's trade regime. Once these fact-finding works are sufficiently advanced, the Working Party negotiates the terms of accession with the applicant. These negotiations are mainly about compliance with general WTO rules on trade in goods, services, and intellectual property rights. Commitments made by the applicant are reflected into the Working Group Report (or, exceptionally, the Protocol of Accession itself), to be cross-referenced in the draft Protocol of Accession. While the membership of the Working Party is open to the entire WTO membership and its negotiations are often described as being "multilateral" (WTO, 2010), in practice, only interested members[2] join the Working Party, and negotiations are actually conducted on the plurilateral basis.[3]

The plurilateral negotiations are only part of the broader accession process. In parallel, bilateral negotiations are conducted individually

[2]Among WTO members, Australia, Canada, the EU, Japan, and the United States participated in all past Working Parties (Williams, 2008).

[3]In the WTO, "multilateral" means "involving all members," whereas "plurilateral" means "involving some members" only. See glossary in the WTO Web site: http://www.wto.org/english/thewto_e/glossary_e/glossary_e.htm.

with the incumbent WTO members concerned.[4] It is in these bilateral negotiations where market access commitments for trade in goods and services are negotiated. Outcomes of individual bilateral negotiations are ultimately consolidated by the secretariat into draft Goods and Services Schedules, which are to be annexed to the Protocol of Accession for extension to all WTO members on the MFN basis. In other words, results of the bilateral negotiations are multilateralized through the accession process. It should be noted that these bilateral negotiations conducted as part of the accession process are distinct from other bilateral trade agreements aimed at establishing trade relations between the incumbent and applicant countries (that often precede WTO accession but may not necessarily be multilateralized in a formal manner). The completed Working Group Report, including the draft Protocol of Accession, is forwarded to the General Council (or the Ministerial Conference), which adopts the Report by consensus.[5] The acceding government becomes a WTO member 30 days after notifying its acceptance (domestic ratification) of the Protocol. The length to complete the whole accession process varies, as presented in Table 1 that summarizes the records of all the RAMs covered by this research. The longest among these 19 RAMs was over 15 years for China. A flow chart summarizing procedural steps for WTO accession is presented in Appendix.

2.2 *Open-Ended Rule on Terms of Accession*

Whereas well-established procedures exist for the WTO membership process, there is no pre-defined prescription on the content of terms of accession, in terms of its substance. The only rule that relates to the terms of accession of the applicant government is that these are "to be agreed between it and the WTO" as stated in Article XII of the Marrakesh Agreement. The agreement does not place any limit on the extent of these terms, and in that sense, possibility is open-ended and the incumbent members could seek any concessions. In fact, this

[4] The contents of individual bilateral negotiations are confidential.

[5] Article IV of the WTO Agreement stipulates that the General Council conducts the functions of the Ministerial Conference in intervals of the latter's meetings. Article IX of the WTO Agreement says that, for decision-making, consensus takes precedence over voting.

Table 1 WTO accession process and timetable

WTO members	*Application*	*Working party established*	*Memorandum*	*Draft working party report*	*Report adopted by council*	*Membership*	*Total time*
Albania	Nov-92	Dec-92	Jan-95	Jul-99	Jul-00	Sep-00	7 years 10 months
Armenia	Nov-93	Dec-93	Apr-95	Mar-97	Dec-02	Feb-03	9 years 3 months
Cape Verde	Nov-99	Jul-00	Jul-03	Jun-05	Dec-07	Jul-08	8 years 8 months
China	Jul-86	Mar-87	Feb-87	Dec-94	Nov-01	Dec-01	15 years 5 months
Chinese Taipei	Jan-92	Sep-92	Oct-92	Mar-98	Nov-01	Jan-02	10 years
Croatia	Sep-93	Oct-93	Jun-94	Aug-98	Jul-00	Nov-00	7 years 2 months
Ecuador	Sep-92	Oct-92	May-92	Oct-94	Jul-95	Jan-96	3 years 4 months
FYROM	Dec-94	Dec-94	Apr-94	May-02	Oct-02	Apr-03	8 years 3 months
Georgia	Jul-96	Jul-96	Jul-97	Feb-99	Oct-99	Jun-00	4 years 1 month
Jordan	Jan-94	Jan-94	Oct-94	Apr-99	Dec-99	Apr-00	6 years 4 months
Kyrgyz Republic	Feb-96	Apr-96	Aug-96	Apr-98	Oct-98	Dec-98	2 years 10 months
Moldova	Nov-93	Dec-93	Dec-96	Jul-99	May-01	Jul-01	7 years 4 months
Mongolia	Jul-91	Oct-91	Jan-92	Dec-94	Jul-96	Jan-97	5 years 6 months
Oman	Apr-96	Jun-96	Jun-96	Mar-99	Oct-00	Nov-00	4 years 7 months
Panama	Aug-91	Oct-91	Jun-93	May-96	Oct-96	Sep-97	5 years 1 month
Saudi Arabia	Jun-93	Jul-93	Jul-94	Oct-05	Nov-05	Dec-05	12 years 6 months
Tonga	Jun-95	Nov-95	May-98	Mar-03	Dec-05	Jul-07	12 years 1 month
Ukraine	Nov-93	Dec-93	Jul-94	Mar-04	Feb-08	May-08	14 years 6 months
Viet Nam	Jan-95	Jan-95	Sep-96	Nov-04	Nov-06	Jan-07	12 years

Note FYROM = Former Yugoslav Republic of Macedonia
Source WTO (2010)

particular provision on accession in the present WTO is quite similar to its predecessor in GATT 1947, stipulated as Article XXXIII.[6] However, the pre-1995 rule on accession to the multilateral trading system had a number of qualifications. Firstly, Article XXVI: 5 (c) of GATT 1947 allowed semi-automatic accession for former colonies of the contracting parties, just with sponsorship by the latter:

> If any of the customs territories, in respect of which a contracting party has accepted this Agreement, possesses or acquires full autonomy in the conduct of its external commercial relations and of the other matters provided for in this Agreement, such territory shall, upon sponsorship through a declaration by the responsible contracting party establishing the above-mentioned fact, be deemed to be a contracting party. (WTO, 1995a, p. 526)

Secondly, developing countries were exempted from the reciprocal trade liberalization at the previous rounds of multilateral trade negotiation under the old GATT system. Article XXXVI: 8 in Part IV on trade and development of GATT 1947 says:

> The developed contracting parties do not expect reciprocity for commitments made by them in trade negotiations to reduce or remove tariffs and other barriers to the trade of less-developed contracting parties. (WTO, 1995a, p. 534)

The 1979 Enabling Clause (or "Decision on Differential and More Favourable Treatment, Reciprocity, and Fuller Participation of Developing Countries") restated and institutionalized this non-reciprocity principle.[7] The non-reciprocity practically excluded developing countries from substantive negotiations at trade rounds and had been practiced until the Uruguay Round (the last multilateral trade negotiations under the old GATT system). As a result, generally, most of developing countries achieved only little trade liberalization through tariff binding at trade negotiations under the pre-1995 multilateral trading system (and resorted

[6]WTO (1995a, p. 467).

[7]Whereas Part IV of GATT has been interpreted as a statement of non-binding aspirations (or best efforts undertakings), the Enabling Clause defined and codified key legal rights and obligations of the developing countries (Keck & Low, 2004).

mostly to autonomous market-opening or other forms of unilateral liberalization under the auspices of international financial institutions [IFIs], such as the International Monetary Fund [IMF] and the World Bank[8]). Finally, these GATT contracting parties became members of the WTO without making further market accession commitments at the time of its establishment in 1995. Article XI on original membership of the WTO Agreement provides automatic membership of the countries that participated in the Uruguay Round:

> The contracting parties to GATT 1947 as of the date of entry into force of this Agreement, and the European Communities, which accept this Agreement and the Multilateral Trade Agreements and for which Schedules of Concessions and Commitments are annexed to GATT 1994 and for which Schedules of Specific Commitments are annexed to GATS shall become original Members of the WTO. (WTO, 1995a, p. 14)

Thus, generally less substantive market access commitments of developing countries as of 1994 under the old GATT system were simply carried over to the new WTO in 1995. As a result, these developing member countries joined the WTO only with modest commitments of the day.

Interestingly, the open-ended nature of negotiating terms of accession to the multilateral trading system makes a sharp contrast with that of the global monetary system.[9] Article II on membership of Articles of Agreement of the IMF says;

> The original members of the Fund shall be those of the countries represented at the United Nations Monetary and Financial Conference whose governments accept membership before December 31, 1945... Membership shall be open to other countries at such times and in

[8]Of 21 percentage points cuts in average weighted tariffs of all developing countries between 1983 and 2003, unilateral reforms (including autonomous reforms and other forms of unilateral liberalization under IFIs' adjustment lending and WTO accession) accounted for about two-thirds of liberalization, while the Uruguay Round and regional trade agreements accounted for about 25 and 10%, respectively. See World Bank (2005).

[9]Membership to the IMF is a prerequisite of the membership to the International Bank for Reconstruction and Development (IBRD), known as the World Bank. Membership to the IBRD in turn is a prerequisite for membership to its subsidiaries under the World Bank Group, such as the International Development Association (IDA) and the International Finance Corporation (IFC).

Table 2 Average bound tariff rates of the WTO members (%)

	NAMA	*Agriculture*
Developed countries	6.1	12.5
RAMs	10.75	17.07
Para 6	24.7	–
Developing countries	28.9	60.95
SVEs	40.2	67.6
LDCs	43.0	75.8

Note LDCs = least-developed countries; NAMA = non-agricultural market access; RAMs = recently-acceded members; SVEs = small, vulnerable economies
Source WTO (2007a, 2007b)

> accordance with such terms as may be prescribed by the Board of Governors. These terms, including the terms for subscriptions, shall be based on principles consistent with those applied to other countries that are already members. (IMF, 2011a, p. 3).

Unlike the case of the WTO (that practically differentiates incumbent members that were party to the Final Act of the Uruguay Round under the old GATT system and the newcomers that joined the WTO after 1995), terms of membership to the IMF are qualified by the consistent principle of equality (between founding members that were parties to the Bretton Woods Conference and subsequent applicants for the IMF membership).[10]

With this unique open-ended nature, terms of WTO accession for the RAMs were not restrained by the precedents of incumbent members. As Table 2 shows, the post-1995 RAMs generally achieved a much greater degree of market access commitments in terms of average bound tariff rates, compared with the incumbent developing member countries of the WTO.[11] The RAMs' bound tariff rates for NAMA and agriculture

[10]This does not mean that IFIs, such as the IMF and the World Bank, completely refrain from advocating trade liberalization by member countries. However, their trade-related conditionality is set as part of their policy-based lending operations after membership, rather than up front as terms of accession. On IFIs' trade-related operations, see the IMF (2005a, 2005b), the Independent Evaluation Office (IEO) of the IMF (2009), the World Bank (2011), and the World Bank Independent Evaluation Group (2006).

[11]The data presented in Table 2 was submitted by the RAMs during the Doha Round negotiations in 2007. See WTO (2007a, 2007b).

average at the rate of 10.75 and 17.07%, respectively, substantially lower than those of developing countries at large (28.9 and 60.95%). Apart from these relatively low average levels of bound tariff rates, the RAMs' binding coverage amounts to nearly 100% of tariff lines. The bound tariff data appears to indicate the post-1995 RAMs' relatively more successful record of utilizing the multilateral trading system in favor of their own trade liberalization. However, at least on average, their bound rates are still higher than those of developed countries (6.1% for NAMA and 12.5% for agriculture), and there appears to be some room for further improvement.[12]

Apparently, the economic benefits of RAMs' market access commitments have been firmly demonstrated. The conventional trade theory tells that, the more a country opens its market to the rest of the world, the more welfare gains accrue to it, simply as a result of its own liberalization. Tariff cuts bring in imports from trading partners that produce certain products relatively more efficiently. That in turn allows the liberalizing country to shift domestic resources to the sector where it has comparative advantage for more efficient production and exports. Tariff bindings provide certainty to private exporters and importers, and further facilitate the flow of international trade. In fact, the trade creation effects of market-opening have been verified by existing empirical studies. In the period of 1995–2011, the RAMs' trade in goods and services, respectively, recorded the growth rates of 15 and 12%, much higher than those of global records (9 and 8%). For this entire period, the value of the RAMs' merchandize trade increased by 650% approximately, at a pace more than a double of that of the entire world (250%). Their share of the world trade also more than doubled from 7 to 15% (WTO, 2012).[13] Subramanian and Wei (2007) found that new WTO member countries that acceded after conclusion of the Uruguay Round

[12] Also, as revealed in this chapter, many RAMs bound tariffs within their applied level, and some observers question the extent of value added by the WTO (Hoekman & Kostecki, 2009; Martin, 2010). At the same time, it is well recognized that even tariff binding above the applied rate has some benefits of enhancing certainty of market access (Francois & Martin, 2002).

[13] Osakwe (2011) also notes that, in the period of 1995–2009, the value of merchandize trade by the RAMs grew at an average annual rate of 13%, at the pace much faster than the growth of global merchandize trade at 7%. In 1995–2008, the overall trade value of all the RAMs increased by around 500%, compared with expansion of the world trade at about 200%. The RAMs' share of world trade increased from 6 to 12% in 1995–2009.

captured more trade gains than old developing member countries. Allee and Scalera (2012) also statistically revealed a strong link between accession commitments and future trade volumes. The more stringent post-1995 accession process seems to have worked favorably for the RAMs, at least on these economic grounds.[14]

2.3 *Mostly One-Sided Negotiations for Applicant's Commitments*

Apart from the open-ended nature of the content of terms of WTO accession, another important feature of membership negotiations is its one-sidedness. Simply put, the prime focus of the market access negotiations is liberalization on the side of the applicant country, mostly without reciprocal market-opening by incumbent members. This is not explicitly stated formally in the WTO Agreement, but has emerged as a prevailing practice of accession. Marc Bacchetta and Zdenek Drabek of the WTO secretariat noted this "unwritten rule":

> It should also be noted that countries are joining the WTO under what may be called status quo for the incumbent countries. The acceding countries cannot negotiate any change in the incumbent countries' commitments of market access nor can they negotiate any change in the rules of the WTO Agreements. The acceding country is joining the WTO under the existing commitments of the Members. As any new member of a "club" has to abide by the rules of the club he/she wants to join, countries acceding into the WTO must accept the terms and conditions of the WTO as they stand. This is an unwritten but fully respected "rule" of accession. (Bacchetta & Drabek, 2002, p. 6)

Under Article I of GATT 1994 (and similar provisions throughout the WTO Agreement), WTO members are required to extend the most-favored nation (MFN) treatment to all members across the board and this formal requirement is applicable only among membership. However, many developed countries typically—but not entirely—had already accorded the MFN treatment equally to WTO members and

[14] As these studies show, the RAMs' market access commitments through accession have probably been a source of gains from these economic points of view. However, in the Doha Round, these were also treated negatively as excessive concessions given by the RAMs, more from the mercantilist perspective. The RAMs' latter point of views is covered in this chapter's third section on the Doha Round.

non-members alike (or even preferences to developing countries), and incumbent members are not asked to provide additional preferential market access to the applicant country through the accession process. For these reasons, a conventional view is that the accession only secures certainty of MFN access to the incumbent members that already exists, but does not create additional markets for new members (Braga & Cattaneo, 2009a, 2009b; Drabek & Bacchetta, 2004; Drabek & Woo, 2010).

In fact, one could take a view that even assurance of the existing MFN access alone could have a practical value by giving predictability of business opportunities to exporters. This was arguably the case for transition economies whose MFN access to the United States—the world's largest market—had been subjected to annual review, hence uncertain. Under Title IV of the US Trade Act of 1974, non-market economies were denied the normal trade relations with the United States unless they fulfilled freedom-of-emigration conditions stipulated in Sector 402, or were only granted a presidential waiver that is subject to congressional disapproval. The provision, known as the Jackson–Vanik Amendment, initially served as trade restrictions against the communist regime under the Cold War, but has remained in force even after its end. Such a denial of the normal trade relations would be a violation of the MFN principle once these transition economies become WTO members. Article XIII of the WTO Agreement still allows members to "opt out" from WTO relations with certain trading partners but, in practice, most of the RAMs in transition have been granted the permanent normal trade relations (PNTR) status by the United States within a few years of WTO accession.[15]

However, the actual trade impacts of PNTR are rather questionable and not so obvious across the RAMs in transition. Table 3 shows the volume of exports from such RAMs to the United States, in the year when PNTR became effective and three years before and after that. It appears that PNTR has not affected exports of transition economies, except in East Asia (China, Mongolia, and Viet Nam).

Actually, observation of the absolute volume alone may even exaggerate PNTR's trade creation effects, as it may be reflecting increase of overall trade also with the rest of the world (that may be attributable to other factors). Alternatively, Table 4 presents the US share of RAM's exports.

[15]For the Jackson Vanik Amendment and PNTR, see reports prepared for the US Congress by the Congressional Research Service (Cooper, 2012; Pregelj, 2005a, 2005b).

Table 3 Transition economies—exports to the United States (millions of US dollars)

WTO members (PNTR effectiveness)	*Year −3*	*Year −2*	*Year −1*	*Year 0*	*Year +1*	*Year +2*	*Year +3*
Albania (2000)	2.07	3.44	1.29	2.33	2.01	5.42	2.27
Armenia (2005)	28.91	57.19	97.10	109.51	65.82	75.89	52.84
China (2002)	42,003.00	52,162.00	54,395.00	70,064.00	92,633.00	125,155.00	163,348.00
Georgia (2000)	4.22	13.91	16.27	6.42	31.64	17.09	15.36
Kyrgyz Republic (2000)	18.19	7.60	11.30	2.90	7.08	36.06	6.52
Moldova (2012)	12.46	22.01	15.73	–	–	–	–
Mongolia (1999)	17.79	25.40	29.40	46.32	130.24	144.52	165.72
Ukraine (2006)	719.00	1507.00	956.00	1202.00	1058.00	1949.00	251.00
Viet Nam (2006)	3940.00	5025.00	5924.00	7845.00	10,105.00	11,869.00	11,356.00

Note PNTR = permanent normal trade relations
Source IMF (2003, 2010, 2012)

Table 4 Transition economies—exports share of the United States (%)

WTO members (PNTR effectiveness)	*Year −3*	*Year −2*	*Year −1*	*Year 0*	*Year +1*	*Year +2*	*Year +3*
Albania (2000)	1.46	1.67	0.47	0.90	0.66	1.64	0.51
Armenia (2005)	8.34	8.34	13.43	11.24	6.68	6.59	5.00
China (2002)	21.55	20.93	20.40	21.51	21.15	21.11	21.41
Georgia (2000)	1.83	4.20	4.51	1.95	5.58	2.96	3.30
Kyrgyz Republic (2000)	2.98	1.49	2.49	0.58	1.49	7.43	1.12
Moldova (2012)	0.97	1.43	0.77	–	–	–	–
Mongolia (1999)	4.19	5.63	8.52	12.93	24.31	27.72	31.63
Ukraine (2006)	2.96	4.62	2.81	3.15	2.15	2.91	0.63
Viet Nam (2006)	19.56	18.97	18.26	19.70	20.81	18.93	19.89

Note PNTR = permanent normal trade relations
Source IMF (2003, 2010, 2012)

Even in East Asia, the share of exports to the United States has been quite stable before and after PNTR effectiveness, except for Mongolia. Effects of de facto reciprocity seem limited here.

However, for RAMs that have also been targets of more explicit protectionism by incumbent WTO members, accession was still an important avenue to redress this imbalance. For instance, prior to WTO accession, China and Viet Nam had been concerned about possible exclusion from export opportunities that would arise from gradual phasing-out of quotas under the Uruguay Round Agreement on Textiles and Closing. For these particular RAMs, WTO accession provided an avenue to claim the natural right of MFN access to their trading partners. This is where accession negotiations were expected to bring about liberalization at the side of incumbent members, at departure from the rest of the membership process whose focus is reforms exclusively at the side of applicants. However, the transition to a less discriminatory regime was not necessarily instant and immediate. The terms of accession for China had a special provision to allow the incumbent members to trigger targeted safeguard actions against its textile and clothing exports and the United States unilaterally introduced a similar mechanism also against Viet Nam.[16] China's terms of accession also entailed reservations by some other incumbent members over immediate removals of restrictive measures on the selected products.

[16] Both were in place only for a short period of time after their respective WTO membership. See Chapter 4 on People's Republic of China and Chapter 5 on Viet Nam.

Incidentally, these two East Asian RAMs in transition have been the target of trade remedies by the United States and the EU and their terms of WTO accession provided other special WTO-minus provisions to ease imposition of import restrictions, in much longer time spans. Firstly, both RAMs are continuously treated as NMEs in anti-dumping investigations for 15 years (in the case of China) and 12 years (in the case of Viet Nam), so as to allow their trading partners to use the price and cost of the third surrogate country in calculation of dumping margins. The NME treatment for anti-dumping has its root in the Cold War, whereby countries from the West attempted to restrict imports from the East in their bilateral trade relations (Snyder, 2001). The treatment of this matter in the multilateral rule is rather light and is stated only in the 1995 Interpretative Note to Paragraph 1 of GATT Article VI on anti-dumping. Para 2 of this Ad Article VI reads:

> It is recognized that, in the case of imports from a country which has a complete or substantially complete monopoly of its trade and where all domestic prices are fixed by the State, special difficulties may exist in determining price comparability…, and in such cases importing contracting parties may find it necessary to take into account the possibility that a strict comparison with domestic prices in such a country may not always be appropriate. (WTO, 1995a, pp. 545–546)

The Interpretative Note, initially inserted at the proposal by Czechoslovakia at the annual GATT Review Session for 1954–1955, just points to the technical difficulty to find comparable prices in transition economies. However, domestic legislations and practices in the United States and the EU went further to adopt the price of the surrogate third county. Such a discretion marks a substantive departure from the principle of using domestic price and cost as a normal value for determination of dumping margins (stipulated in GATT Article VI and the Uruguay Round agreement on its implementation, known as the Agreement on Anti-Dumping). However, through the WTO accession process, a part of these discriminatory practices was codified into terms of accession of these two RAMs. Secondly, China's terms of accession also allow WTO members' recourse to a Transitional Product-Specific Safeguard (TPS) mechanism, which is severely less disciplined than the normal safeguard under GATT Article XIX and the Agreement on Safeguard. Like the NME designation, the TPS provision poses challenges to China to seize the full benefits of supposedly non-discriminatory market access under the multilateral trading system.

Another type of discrimination for the previous non-members arose as a result of preferences accorded to other economies. This was particularly true for Ecuador as the world's largest banana exporter. The 1989 Fourth Lomé Convention signed between the EU and its 70 former colonies from African, Caribbean and Pacific (ACP) regions accorded preferential market access to the latter for products including bananas (WTO, 1997). In effect, the preference for ACP countries was discrimination to their Latin American competitors, including Ecuador, and GATT contracting parties even accorded an MFN waiver to the EU to justify the Lomé Convention in 1996 (so-called Lomé waiver) (GATT, 1994). Unlike many other Latin American countries, Ecuador was not a WTO member back then and could not join the multilateral negotiations or dispute settlement to resolve this problem to its satisfaction. This matter was not addressed explicitly in Ecuador's terms of accession, however, and the discrimination remained even after the country's WTO membership.[17]

To sum up, WTO accession is primarily a process aimed at unilateral trade liberalization on the side of applicants, while some liberalization also occurred through removal of discrimination from the side of the incumbents, particularly in the area of textile and clothing.[18] Some RAMs have continuously been subjected to a number of specific discriminatory measures by their trading partners, which represent a departure from the MFN principle of the multilateral trading system.

3 The RAMs' Post-accession Performance

3.1 Reciprocity in the Doha Development Agenda

Unlike the case of mostly one-sided negotiations for accession to the multilateral trading system (where the RAMs made unilateral market

[17]As the Fourth Lomé Convention was subsequently replaced by the 2000 Cotonou Agreement, the WTO accorded another waiver at the Doha Ministerial Conference in 2001 (so-called Doha waiver) (WTO, 2001e).

[18]In truth, for the East Asian RAMs, the perceived value of quota liberalization in textile and clothing was not trivial, and this issue is addressed in Chapters 4 on People's Republic of China and Chapter 5 on Viet Nam.

access commitments), in principle, multilateral trade rounds under the GATT/WTO auspices (such as the Doha Round) are deemed to be conducted on a more reciprocal basis. Under this reciprocity principle, WTO members sitting at both sides of the negotiating table are meant to exchange market access commitments on the "mutually advantageous basis," as stated in GATT Article XXVIII bis: 1 on tariff negotiations:

> The contracting parties recognize that customs duties often constitute serious obstacles to trade; thus negotiations on a reciprocal and mutually advantageous basis, directed to the substantial reduction of the general level of tariffs and other charges on imports and exports and in particular to the reduction of such high tariffs as discourage the importation even of minimum quantities, and conducted with due regard to the objectives of this Agreement and the varying needs of individual contracting parties, are of great importance to the expansion of international trade. The CONTRACTING PARTIES may therefore sponsor such negotiations from time to time. (WTO, 1995a, p. 529)

While this principle of reciprocity for trade rounds has traditionally been carved out by another principle of non-reciprocity as a special and differential treatment for developing countries (in Part IV of GATT and the 1979 Enabling Clause), the Doha Ministerial Declaration appears to have at least partially extended the reciprocity to developing countries, with a somewhat relaxed language of "less than full reciprocity." Its paragraph 16 on NAMA reads:

> We agree to negotiations which shall aim, by modalities to be agreed, to reduce or as appropriate eliminate tariffs, including the reduction or elimination of tariff peaks, high tariffs, and tariff escalation, as well as non-tariff barriers..... The negotiations shall take fully into account the special needs and interests of developing and least developed country participants, including through less than full reciprocity in reduction commitments, in accordance with the relevant provisions of Article XXVIII bis of GATT 1994 and the provisions cited in..... (WTO, 2001a, pp. 3–4)

Still, to what extent "less than full reciprocity" differs from non-reciprocity of free-riding is a matter of debate and interpretation. In practice, however, there appears to be some expectation in the Doha Round that emerging market economies participate in the negotiations in a substantive manner, and they appear to be acting accordingly. The former Direct-General Pascal Lamy noted:

> The emergence of some developing countries as key players and as real contributors to global dialogue on trade and economics is a fundamental feature of this new geo-political reality. These emerging powers — China, India, Brazil, Mexico, Indonesia, Malaysia, South Africa — and many others — Thailand, Chile, Turkey — are no longer policy takers.[19]

In any event, even non-reciprocity or less than full reciprocity is meant to relieve market access commitments required from developing countries (including the RAMs), rather than those from developed countries (including many founding members of the WTO).[20] Given that developed countries are not covered by this special and differential treatment through the Doha Round, the RAMs should be able to seek reciprocal market access commitments at least from these wealthier WTO members, if they so wish. Such prospect of reciprocity is one important difference between market access negotiations for accession and those under the Doha Round.[21]

3.2 Emergence of the RAMs Group at Market Access Negotiations

Generally, the RAMs have been taking defensive positions during the DDA market access negotiations, on both NAMA and agriculture. The RAMs' defensive positions are a reflection of extensive market access commitments made earlier at the time of their accession, that was first recognized officially for the Doha Round in the 2001 Ministerial Declaration. Its paragraph 9 reads:

[19] Richard Snape Lecture by Director-General Pascal Lamy on 26 November 2012 in Melbourne, Australia. See the WTO Web site: http://www.wto.org/english/news_e/sppl_e/sppl258_e.htm.

[20] It is noteworthy that the Enabling Clause just states '*(t)he developed countries do not expect reciprocity..., i.e., the developed countries do not expect the developing countries, in the course of trade negotiations, to make contributions...*', but it does not preclude the possibility that developing countries seek reciprocity from developed countries or among themselves. See the legal text in the WTO Web site: https://www.wto.org/english/docs_e/legal_e/enabling1979_e.htm.

[21] In this sense, even less than full reciprocal market access negotiations of the Doha Round could paradoxically be more reciprocal than those of the accession negotiations, whereby the RAMs mostly made unilateral tariff binding commitments.

> We note with particular satisfaction that this Conference has completed the WTO accession procedures for China and Chinese Taipei. We also welcome the accession as new Members, since our last Session, of Albania, Croatia, Georgia, Jordan, Lithuania, Moldova and Oman, and note the extensive market-access commitments already made by these countries on accession. These accessions will greatly strengthen the multilateral trading system, as will those of the 28 countries now negotiating their accession. (WTO, 2001a, p. 2)

In the reciprocal setting, countries that previously made more commitments than others would be reluctant to offer further concession at the present time, unless there are reasons to use reciprocity offensively for their mercantilist advantage. Thus, there have been increasingly stronger calls by the RAMs for greater flexibility through the Doha Round, but with different degrees among individual economies. Across the RAMs, those most vocal were transition economies from Eastern Europe, Caucasus, and Central Asia, including Albania, Armenia, Croatia, Georgia, Kyrgyz Republic, and Moldova, often in the form of submitting joint communications among some of them. All in all, they turned in 8 negotiating proposals (excluding a corrigendum and a revision) in the period of 2001–2007 (WTO, 2001d, 2003a, 2005a, 2005b, 2005c, 2005d, 2006a, 2006b, 2007c, 2008c). They often pointed to domestic adjustment difficulties that arose from the preceding trade liberalization.

> However, the strength of our economies and the competitiveness of our industries in other countries' markets still seem to be in some discrepancy to our tariff profiles. The liberalization process has undoubtedly shown its rewarding side, but has nonetheless significantly exposed domestic industries that were undergoing the difficult process of transformation and transition to tough international competition. At the same time one could not neglect the current disparities in the level of tariff protection among WTO Members… From the position of recently acceded Members that have already made significant market access liberalization commitments, it is difficult to envisage a situation where we would be again asked to make further significant commitments in such a short period of time and from incomparably low level of tariffs comparing to the majority of other Members. (WTO, 2003a, p. 1)

Among them, four low-income economies in transition (Armenia, Georgia, Kyrgyz Republic, and Moldova) also formed a coalition of their own and sought the same treatment as those for LDCs and other vulnerable developing countries. As a very recently acceded member (VRAM), Saudi Arabia filed a communication that no further market access commitment should be expected from the country (WTO, 2006c). Two Latin American small, vulnerable economies (SVEs) of Ecuador and Panama submitted a joint communication and sought recognition as RAMs (WTO, 2006d), despite their relatively high bound tariff rates. Jordan, another SVE from Middle East, filed two negotiating proposals seeking more equal treatment of the RAMs and further agricultural liberalization by other developing countries (WTO, 2001b, 2001c). Oman indicated that RAMs' commitments during the Doha Round should be voluntary and autonomous (WTO, 2002a). While China kept some cautious attitude for the RAMs (WTO, 2003b), the country also proposed the formula-based tariff cuts for NAMA among both developed and developing countries, including the RAMs (WTO, 2002b, 2003c). Thus, China's position toward multilateral liberalization has been more positive than most of the other RAMs from the outset,[22] while its level of engagement was far short of what developed countries had expected.[23]

In the course of the Doha Round, the RAMs' overall concerns have been increasingly recognized and addressed in the Work Program adopted in 2004, known as the July package or "Framework" agreement. Its paragraph 47 reads:

> The particular concerns of recently acceded Members will be effectively addressed through specific flexibility provisions. (WTO, 2004a, p. A-7).

Still, at the stage of the Hong Kong Ministerial Conference, there was only awareness of the RAMs' unique standing, but no concrete course of actions was laid out. Paragraph 58 and Annex A on agriculture of the Hong Kong Ministerial Declaration reads:

[22] See Chapter 4 on People's Republic of China.

[23] Comments on China by representatives from the United States and the EU at the 2013 WTO Public Forum session on "Looking beyond MC9: How to deal with reciprocity and flexibility in moving forward on the Doha Development Agenda?". See the WTO Web site: http://www.wto.org/english/forums_e/public_forum13_e/programme_e.htm.

> We recognize the special situation of recently-acceded Members who have undertaken extensive market access commitments at the time of accession. This situation will be taken into account in the negotiations... Concrete proposals have been made and discussed, but no specific flexibility provisions have commanded consensus. (WTO, 2004b, p. 11 and p. A-7)

To consolidate the position more firmly toward the conclusion of the July 2008 Package, the RAMs that had previously been acting individually or in small groups formed a larger RAMs group, and 15 of them filed a joint negotiating proposal on NAMA in 2007. This communication was initially drafted by Chinese Taipei, designated as the RAMs coordinator on behalf of the group. Its paragraph 4 says:

> RAMs would nevertheless like to reiterate that the future modalities must meet the mandate as set out in the Framework agreement, namely that "Recently Acceded Members shall have recourse to special provisions for tariff reductions". (WTO, 2007a, p. 2)

This joint negotiating proposal recognized different positions and contexts of smaller groups within the RAMs namely, the low-income economies in transition, the VRAMs, the SVEs and "the rest" (the formula countries), as stated in its paragraphs 5–6:

> RAMs group encompasses many different members that acceded to WTO at different stages under different conditions, while some of the accession processes ended very recently. To that end small low income countries in transition, such as Armenia, Moldova and Kyrgyz Republic have made the proposal to be exempted from further tariff reductions within the current round of negotiations. This proposal has received support by all members. Similarly, in view of their very recent accession processes and respective commitments that they just started to implement Saudi Arabia, Former Yugoslav Republic of Macedonia and Viet Nam requested that they too be exempted from undertaking any further commitments or concessions within the current round. The rest of RAMs considers that the appropriate level of flexibilities that should be awarded to them should be "developing plus" ... Furthermore, members of the group which meet the criteria for SVEs shall have recourse to such treatment. (WTO, 2007a, p. 2)

To summarize, it was proposed that the low-income economies in transition and the VRAMs be exempted from any further market access commitments, and SVEs be treated as such. On the other hand, it was suggested that the rest of the RAMs accept liberalization commitments albeit with some special flexibilities. The proposed flexibilities included, among others, an implementation period that was 5-year longer than that for other developing countries, a 5-year grace period, and a coefficient that was 1.5 times higher than that for other developing countries. As was apparently seen in China's negotiating proposal, these formula countries have been expressing a relatively more positive attitude toward trade liberalization through the Doha Round. The RAMs also submitted a joint negotiating proposal separately for agriculture, including similar differentiation among them (WTO, 2007b).

Ultimately, positions of the RAMs were broadly accommodated in the July 2008 packages for NAMA and agriculture, which were the height of the entire Doha Round negotiations before the prolonged period of deadlock thereafter. While negotiations at that time did not reach final conclusion of the round, due to disagreement between the United States and India (sided by China) on special safeguard for agriculture by developing countries, there was a broad consensus on the content of the package across WTO membership. The outcome of the package fed into the text of draft modalities that were subsequently finalized by the chairs of NAMA and agriculture negotiations by December 2008. Paragraphs 18–20 on the RAMs of the draft NAMA modalities read:

> The RAMs shall apply the modality provided for in either paragraphs 5, 6 and 7 or paragraph 13, as applicable... In addition, the RAMs applying the formula shall be granted an extended implementation period of 3 equal rate reductions to that provided in paragraph 6(f) to implement their Doha commitments. The first reduction shall be implemented on 1 January of the year following the entry into force of the DDA results. Each successive reduction shall be made effective on 1 January of each of the following years.... Albania, Armenia, Cape Verde, Former Yugoslav Republic of Macedonia, Kyrgyz Republic, Moldova, Mongolia, Saudi Arabia, Tonga, Viet Nam and Ukraine shall not be required to undertake tariff reductions beyond their accession commitments. (WTO, 2008a, p. 9)

Paragraphs 5, 6 and 7 refer to the Swiss formula and some flexibilities applicable to developing countries. Under the simple Swiss formula, required tariff cuts were generally deeper on higher tariffs, while a higher coefficient envisaged for developing countries mitigated the reductions.

Oman accepted the formula, but was exempted from reducing bound tariffs below 5%. Paragraph 13 is on a flexibility provided for SVEs with a share of less than 0.1% of world trade in industrial goods. The SVEs were exempted from formula-based tariff cuts and required to cut tariffs at the level differentiated by their respective binding coverage. An additional three-year grace period was accorded to the SVEs that were also the RAMs. The low-income economies in transition and the VRAMs were completely exempted from tariff cuts requirements. It should be noted that Georgia, which had initially acted as a low-income economy in transition and could have been eligible for exemption, was no longer listed as such in the draft NAMA modalities, as the country probably chose to be covered by the formula on a voluntary basis.[24]

The rest of the RAMs were to cut tariffs in accordance with the formula as applicable to developing countries, albeit in a slightly longer transition period of 3 years. The implication of the formula adoption by these RAMs should not be underestimated. Unlike most developing countries that maintained the overhang between their bound tariff rates and applied tariff rates, some of these RAMs (notably, China and Chinese Taipei) had little water above their accession commitments. As a result, implementation of the formula would immediately cut into their applied tariffs. For this reason, despite the cautious posture presented as the RAMs, they would end up with liberalizing more than other emerging market economies with protectionist orientations. Although the modalities were formally prepared as chairs' papers, the RAMs broadly accepted these, and they were aware of this potential outcome of formula implementation.

For agriculture, draft December 2008 modalities were based on the tiered formula. As in the case of the Swiss formula for NAMA, there would be more cuts for higher bound tariffs, while the levels of tariffs were categorized by tiers. Again, developing countries have more exceptions. As for NAMA, the agriculture modality broadly reflected the RAMs' positions, with differentiated treatments across them. Firstly, the VRAMs and the low-income economies in transitions were exempted from any tariff cuts. Paragraph 67 of the draft modalities says:

[24] See Chapter 3 on Georgia. The country was one of the vocal advocates of differential treatments for transition economies in the early phase of the Doha Round and was also waived from market access commitments on agriculture later in the July 2008 package. However, its status in the late stage of the NAMA negotiations was rather ambiguous in the text of the draft December 2008 modalities paper.

> Saudi Arabia, the Former Yugoslav Republic of Macedonia, Viet Nam, Tonga and Ukraine, as very recently-acceded Members and small low-income RAMs with economies in transition[12], shall not be required to undertake reductions in final bound tariffs. (WTO, 2008b, p. 15)

Unlike the case of NAMA, the footnote 12 to this paragraph lists Georgia as one of the low-income economies in transition, together with Albania, Armenia, Georgia, Kyrgyz Republic, Moldova, and Mongolia. Secondly, the SVEs were entitled to undertake only moderate cuts. Paragraph 65 reads:

> Those small, vulnerable economies, including those among them which are ceiling binding and homogenously low binding countries... shall be entitled to moderate the cuts... by a further 10 ad valorem percentage points in each band. (WTO, 2008b, p. 15)

The rest of the RAMs were given a grace period of up to 1 year and the implementation period longer by up to 2 years. This adds 3 extra years for these RAMs to complete the Doha Round commitments, as in the case of NAMA. In addition, for agriculture, tariff-cutting obligations for these RAMs were further moderated as stated in paragraph 66:

> RAMs shall be entitled to moderate the cuts they would otherwise have been required to make under the tiered formula for developing country Members... by up to 8 ad valorem percentage points. All RAMs shall be entitled to exempt their final bound tariffs at or below 10 per cent from reductions in bound tariffs. (WTO, 2008b, p. 15)

Thus, unlike the case of NAMA whereby flexibility accorded to these RAMs accepting the formula was fairly limited, they were given a high degree of exemptions in agriculture. Actually, this was a common phenomenon seen for developing countries as a whole in the Doha Round agriculture negotiations. The use of the tiered formula was an exception for agriculture rather than the norm, and the special and differential treatment in agriculture for developing countries was the contentious point for the entire Doha Round at this stage.

As summarized in Table 5, within the RAMs group, those who would do the most cuts are those that accepted the formula with minimum qualifications for both NAMA and agriculture, including China, Chinese

Table 5 Potential tariff cuts by the RAMs under the December 2008 modalities

WTO members	*NAMA*	*Agriculture (market access)*
Albania	No reduction	No reduction as a low-income economy in transition
Armenia	No reduction	No reduction as a low-income economy in transition
Cape Verde	No reduction	Formula with smaller cuts (or no cuts on low tariffs). Extra grace and implementation periods
China	Formula with an extended implementation period	Formula with smaller cuts (or no cuts on low tariffs). Extra grace and implementation periods
Chinese Taipei	Formula with an extended implementation period	Formula with smaller cuts (or no cuts on low tariffs). Extra grace and implementation periods
Croatia	Formula with an extended implementation period	Formula with smaller cuts (or no cuts on low tariffs). Extra grace and implementation periods
Ecuador	SVE with an addition grace period as RAM	SVE (smaller reductions)
FYROM	No reduction	No reduction as VRAM
Georgia	Voluntary acceptance of the formula	No reduction as a low-income economy in transition
Jordan	SVE with an addition grace period as RAM	SVE (smaller reductions)
Kyrgyz Republic	No reduction	No reduction as a low-income economy in transition
Moldova	No reduction	No reduction as a low-income economy in transition
Mongolia	No reduction	No reduction as a low-income economy in transition
Oman	Formula with the extended implementation period and GCC allowance (no reduction below 5%)	Formula with smaller cuts (or no cuts on low tariffs). Extra grace and implementation periods
Panama	SVE with an addition grace period as RAM	SVE (smaller reductions)
Saudi Arabia	No reduction	No reduction as VRAM
Tonga	No reduction	No reduction as VRAM
Ukraine	No reduction	No reduction as VRAM
Viet Nam	No reduction	No reduction as VRAM

Note FYROM = Former Yugoslav Republic of Macedonia; GCC = Gulf Cooperation Council; RAM = recently acceded members; SVE = small, vulnerable economies; VRAM = very recently acceded member
Source WTO (2008a, 2008b); WTO Web site: http://www.wto.org

Taipei, and Croatia. They are followed by Oman with a small departure from NAMA formula and Georgia that voluntarily accepted the formula for NAMA but not for agriculture. The next in line are the SVEs including Ecuador, Jordan, and Panama, which were accorded special treatments of modified tariff cuts. The rest of the low-income economies in transition and the VRAMs (Albania, Armenia, Cape Verde,[25] Former Yugoslav Republic of Macedonia, Kyrgyz Republic, Moldova, Mongolia, Saudi Arabia, Tonga, Viet Nam, and Ukraine) did not make any prospective tariff-cutting commitments under the Doha Round.

At the Ministerial Conference in Geneva in 2009 and 2011, the RAMs further made joint statements echoing their special needs stated in the Hong Kong Ministerial Declaration (WTO, 2009, 2011). At the same time, the RAMs also called for other members to replicate their accession commitments as ambitious contributions to the Doha Round. Paragraph 2 of their 2011 communication reads:

> We emphasize that all of the RAMs during their accessions have made extensive commitments to the WTO believing such commitments are essential for a truly multilateral trading system, and to further promote global trade. The RAMs commitments to trade liberalization should encourage other Members to make due and ambitious contributions to the DDA negotiations. (WTO, 2011, p. 1)

In a sense that the RAMs were calling for further liberalization among WTO members during the Doha Round, this statement went beyond their defensive posture presented in their earlier joint communications. At least some of the RAMs within the groups seemed to be eager to pursue ambitious outcomes at the Doha Round.

3.3 *Redressing WTO-Minus Trade Remedies and Other Discrimination*

Apart from the market access negotiations, two East Asian RAMs in transition have been coping with their WTO-minus provisions on trade remedies inserted in their terms of accession in other multilateral avenues.

[25] To be precise, Cape Verde appears to be fully exempted from the formula-based tariff cuts as a VRAM only for NAMA, but not in agriculture. The modalities text does not provide any background on this point.

One venue to address this matter was the rules negotiations of the Doha Round. Paragraph 28 of the Doha Ministerial Declaration designated enhancement of existing disciplines on some forms of trade remedies as part of the work program of the round:

> In the light of experience and of the increasing application of these instruments by members, we agree to negotiations aimed at clarifying and improving disciplines under the Agreements on Implementation of Article VI of the GATT 1994 and on Subsidies and Countervailing Measures, while preserving the basic concepts, principles and effectiveness of these Agreements and their instruments and objectives, and taking into account the needs of developing and least-developed participants. In the initial phase of the negotiations, participants will indicate the provisions, including disciplines on trade distorting practices, that they seek to clarify and improve in the subsequent phase. (WTO, 2001a, p. 6)

Enhancement of trade remedy rules was one of the key priorities particularly for China. In the Doha Round negotiations on rules, the country sought revoking the NME provision of Ad Article VI. Its 2003 negotiating proposal reads:

> As we are all aware, one of the basic principles of this Organization is free trade which requires Members to establish market economic system. Therefore, no economy could ever accede to the WTO with a complete or substantially complete monopoly of its trade and with all domestic prices fixed by the State. Such clauses was [sic] established several decades ago when market economy was not prevailing. After 50 years of development, the circumstances for invoking such a clause do not exist anymore. And it is abused by some Members to provide unjustified protection to their domestic industries. Therefore, the "non market economy" clause contradicts with the real situation of WTO Members and should be revoked. (WTO, 2003d, pp. 3–4)

However, the question on whether the Doha Round was the right avenue to address this problem was somewhat debatable, and hence, China's ground for negotiating this matter at the rules negotiations was somewhat fragile. In the first place, it would have been questionable that rules negotiations at the Doha Round had a mandate of addressing Ad VI on top of the main Agreement on Anti-Dumping. Also, the Doha Round was not meant to be a venue to, in effect, renegotiate the RAMs' terms of accession themselves. Another important constraint was that, while the work program of the Doha Round inscribed in the 2001

Ministerial Declaration covered rules on anti-dumping and countervailing duties, it did not include negotiations on safeguard measures.

As a more practical solution, these two RAMs resorted to dispute settlement to cope with discriminatory trade remedies within the existing rules, outside of the Doha Round. Table 6 lists such dispute settlement cases on trade remedies filed by the RAMs as complainants in early years of their WTO membership. Out of these six selected cases, five of them were filed by China and one by Viet Nam. The respondent has always been the EU or the United States. Excluding one case on United States—Countervailing Measures, four cases (EU—Footwear; United States—Shrimp; EC—Fasteners; United States—Anti-Dumping and Countervailing Duties) related to broadly defined NME issues for anti-dumping and the one on TPS (United States—Tyres). For anti-dumping cases, China and Viet Nam adopted skillful legal tactics of focusing their arguments away from the narrowly defined price comparison issue (where they had acute disadvantage due to the WTO-minus provision) and instead criticized the trading partner's abuse of the NME designation (in excess of what was allowed under the terms of accession). However, in the TPS case, all arguments made by China were

Table 6 Trade remedy cases related to terms of accession involving RAM as a complainant

Short titles (respondent—[complainant])	*Cited provisions of accession protocol*	*Consultation request*	*Panel report*	*Appellate body report*
US—Countervailing Measures (China)	Article 15	25-May-12	14-Jul-14	18-Dec-2014
EU—Footwear (China)	Article 15	04-Feb-10	28-Oct-11	Not appealed
US—Shrimp (Viet Nam)	Part I, paragraph 1.2	01-Feb-10	11-Jul-11	Not appealed
US—Tyres (China)	Article 16.1, 16.3, 16.4, 16.6	14-Sep-09	13-Dec-10	05-Sep-11
EC—Fasteners (China)	Article 15	31-Jul-09	03-Dec-10	15-Jul-11
US—Anti-Dumping and Countervailing Duties (China)	Article 15	19-Sep-08	22-Oct-10	11-Mar-11

Note For the EC—Fasteners (China) case, the compliance proceedings started in 2013. The US—Shrimp case (Viet Nam) was followed by the US—Shrimp II case since 2012
Source WTO Web site: http://www.wto.org

straightforwardly rejected and, ultimately, no violations of relaxed disciplines under the terms of accession on the side of the United States were found by the panel and the Appellate Body. In the history of the WTO, this was the first time that a complainant completely lost the safeguard case, and probably a rare incident where a free trader argument lost against a protectionist one. In this sense, the incident demonstrated the devastating effect of discriminatory clause inserted in terms of accession.

Other than these dispute settlement cases on WTO-minus trade remedies initiated by transition economies, Ecuador also filed a dispute against the EU on the banana import regimes immediately after its WTO accession in 1996. The ACP preferences predate Ecuador's WTO accession, and it took 20 years for the dispute to be finally resolved through a series of litigations, arbitrations, and negotiations among the EU, the United States, and Latin American banana exporting countries.[26] At the same time, Ecuador called for ambitious agricultural liberalization at the Doha Round negotiations, especially in the area of tropical products including bananas, exhibiting some sign of proactive engagement compared with many other RAMs.[27]

4 Preliminary Examination of the RAMs' Policy Positions

4.1 *Accession as a Commitment Device to Support Domestic Reforms*

Casual observations of the RAMs' policy behaviors presented show that, overall, these new WTO members made much deeper market access commitments than the incumbent developing member countries, but most of them generally disengaged themselves from the DDA market access negotiations. Against this background, this research makes a proposition that this change in the RAMs' position is a reflection of the different functions envisaged for these two forms of market access negotiations. In particular, Hypothesis 1 assumes that, given its nature of unilateral commitments, the envisaged role of market access negotiations for accession is to support domestic reforms (as per the commitment theory). Accordingly,

[26] A news release "Banana Disputes: Historic signing ends 20 years of EU-Latin American banana disputes," found in the WTO Web site: http://www.wto.org/english/news_e/news12_e/disp_08nov12_e.htm.

[27] See Chapter 6 on Ecuador.

reforming economies should make best use of this envisaged function of the multilateral trading system, while others would not. In fact, the available cross-country tariff data presented in Table 7 appears to support this hypothesis. Most of the RAMs that made tariff binding commitments (presented as the "final bound" rates in the table) at the single-digit level are transition economies in Eastern Europe, Caucasus, and Central Asia (Albania, Armenia, Croatia, Macedonia, Georgia, Kyrgyz Republic, Moldova, and Ukraine). Other transition economies in East Asia (China, Mongolia, and Viet Nam) made commitments at rates slightly higher, but within a low two-digit level, while a number of non-transition economies like Chinese Taipei and Saudi Arabia also bound tariffs at relatively low levels. On the other hand, the average bound tariff rates of the two SVEs from Latin America (Ecuador and Panama) exceeded 20% and stand out as outliers among all the RAMs. This is probably because structural adjustments in Latin American economies were launched mainly as short-term responses to the debt crisis in the 1980s, and their reform momentum faded away by the time of WTO membership.[28]

Table 7 also presents the RAMs' average applied tariff rates at around the time of accession ("initial applied" or pre-accession rates, where possible) and the average applied tariff rates in 2008. Incremental tariff cuts for the WTO accession (from the initial rates to the final bound rates) are shown as "multilateral cuts" in the table. The data on pre-accession applied tariffs is not systematically available for all the RAMs, but there appears to be a tendency that most of the transition economies had low tariff rates even before the ultimate WTO membership, partly as a result of reforms undertaken in parallel with the accession process. Some of them bound tariffs to consolidate (or "lock in") the preceding trade liberalization at around these relatively low pre-accession rates. Other transition economies with slightly higher initial applied rates used the accession commitments to catalyze further tariff cuts.[29] Among

[28]The key multilateral instrument at the time of Latin American debt crisis in the 1980s was IFIs' policy-based lending, rather than GATT accession.

[29]Marc Bacchetta and Zdenek Drabek of the WTO secretariat noted these two different approaches of accession commitments, as follows: "*(O)ver the last decade most transition countries have made an exceptionally profound effort to liberalize their trade and investment regimes. Accession to the WTO has played an important albeit not exclusive role in this process of liberalization. The accession has been seen as critical for some countries such as China. In other countries, the autonomous measures taken by these countries have been more important in terms of the degree of liberalization*" (Bacchetta & Drabek, 2002, p. 35).

Table 7 Tariff liberalization of recently acceded members

WTO members (accession year)	*Initial applied*		*Final bound*	*Applied*	*Multilateral*	*Unilateral*	*Voluntary*
	%	*Year*	%	*2008 (%)*	*Cuts (%)*	*Cuts (%)*	*Cuts (%)*
Albania (2000)	10.6	2000	7.0	5.2	3.6	5.4	1.8
Armenia (2003)	8.6	2003	8.5	2.8	0.1	5.8	5.7
Cape Verde (2008)	10.4	2007	15.8	10.4	−5.4	0.0	5.4
China (2001)	15.9	2001	10.0	9.9	5.9	6.0	0.2
Chinese Taipei (2002)	7.8	2001	6.4	5.5	1.4	2.3	0.9
Croatia (2000)	6.4	2001	6.3	4.6	0.1	1.9	1.8
Ecuador (1996)	11.9	1996	21.7	11.3	−9.8	0.6	10.4
FYROM (2003)	8.3	2002	7.2	7.4	1.1	0.9	−0.2
Georgia (2000)	10.5	2001	7.4	1.0	3.1	9.5	6.4
Jordan (2000)	14.8	2000	16.3	10.8	−1.5	4.0	5.5
Kyrgyz Republic (1998)	4.8	2000	7.5	4.6	−2.7	0.2	2.9
Moldova (2001)	6.7	2007	7.0	4.4	−0.3	2.3	2.6
Mongolia (1997)	0.0	1999	17.5	5.0	−17.5	−5.0	12.5
Oman (2000)	5.7	2001	13.7	5.4	−8.0	0.2	8.3
Panama (1997)	32.3	1997	22.8	7.2	9.5	25.1	15.6
Saudi Arabia (2005)	5.7	2004	11.4	5.1	−5.7	0.6	6.3
Tonga (2007)	11.7	2009	17.6	11.7	−5.9	0.0	5.9
Ukraine (2008)	4.9	2007	5.8	4.8	−1.0	0.0	1.0
Viet Nam (2007)	16.8	2006	11.5	10.8	5.3	6.0	0.7

Note FYROM = Former Yugoslav Republic of Macedonia. Multilateral cuts are the differences between the initial applied rates and the final bound rates. Unilateral cuts are differences between the initial applied rates and the applied rates in 2008. Voluntary cuts are differences between unilateral cuts and multilateral cuts, which equal the differences between the final bound rates and the applied rates in 2008. Where substantial inconsistency was found on the 2008 applied tariff data for Armenia across WTO statistical databases, data more in line with the trend presented in the formal trade policy review has been adopted. Applied tariff data for Tonga in 2008 is not available, and the table presents the rate for 2009

Source WTO Trade Profiles and WTO Tariff Analysis Online in the WTO Web site: http://www.wto.org

non-transition economies, Chinese Taipei also appears to have utilized the WTO accession to cut its applied tariffs, albeit by a narrow margin. What is common particularly among transition economies was precedent of domestic reforms, and the WTO accession seems to have served the purpose of supporting the RAMs' unilateral trade liberalization, as stated in one of the WTO accession annual reports by the Director-General:

> WTO Membership has provided credibility to government reform policies and transmitted positive pro-market signals to businesses and investors around the world... WTO accession negotiations have served both as a catalyst for domestic reforms and as an instrument for locking-in these reforms. (WTO, 2012, p. 12)

In fact, the limited tariff data alone may not necessarily reveal RAMs' domestic reform orientation. One skeptical view would be that through membership negotiations, acceding governments were just forced to accept liberal market access commitments by incumbent members, reluctantly rather than willingly. One approach to examine the extent of domestic origin of the reforms is to assess whether these are limited only to the areas covered by WTO accession negotiations. If the RAMs undertook reforms exclusively in the areas of direct relevance to the multilateral trading system, the argument that they liberalized trade just as externally pressured by the incumbent WTO members (without any reform ownership from within the country) may possibly prevail. However, available data suggests otherwise. The World Bank's annual Doing Business reports ranks ease of the business environment across its member countries based on broad criteria of structural reforms (beyond the WTO-related areas).[30] Interestingly, as Table 8 shows, among its 185 economies across the globe, a majority of the RAMs (Albania, Armenia, China, Chinese Taipei, Croatia, Macedonia, Georgia, Kyrgyz Republic, Saudi Arabia, and Ukraine) ranked within top 50 performers that most advanced business friendly reforms.

[30]These include: starting a businesses, dealing with construction permits, getting electricity, registering property, getting credit, protecting investors, paying taxes, trading across borders, enforcing contracts, and resolving insolvency. Among them, trading across borders mainly address trade facilitation, rather than trade liberalization. Trade facilitation has emerged as one of the key issues of negotiations towards the Bali Ministerial Conference in 2012, but was not yet comprehensively covered by the multilateral trading system at the time of accession by most of the RAMs. See the World Bank Group's Doing Business Web site: http://www.doingbusiness.org/.

Table 8 Business environment and investment climate of recently acceded members

WTO members (accession year)	*Doing business ranking*							*Top 50 reformers*	*Applied tariffs*	
	2006	*2007*	*2008*	*2009*	*2010*	*2011*	*2012*	*2005–2012*	*%*	*Year*
Albania (2000)	120	136	86	82	82	82	85	50	5.0	2011
Armenia (2003)	34	39	44	43	48	55	32	19	2.8	2008
Cape Verde (2008)	125	132	143	146	132	119	122	–	10.2	2011
China (2001)	93	83	83	89	79	91	91	12	9.6	2011
Chinese Taipei (2002)	47	50	61	46	33	25	16	46	6.1	2011
Croatia (2000)	124	97	106	103	84	80	84	14	4.9	2011
Ecuador (1996)	123	128	136	138	130	130	139	–	10.1	2011
FYROM (2003)	92	75	71	32	38	22	23	5	7.0	2011
Georgia (2000)	37	18	15	11	12	16	9	1	1.5	2011
Jordan (2000)	78	80	101	100	111	96	106	–	10.0	2010
Kyrgyz Republic (1998)	90	94	68	41	44	70	70	10	4.6	2011
Moldova (2001)	103	92	103	94	90	81	83	–	4.6	2011
Mongolia (1997)	45	52	58	60	73	86	76	–	5.0	2011
Oman (2000)	55	49	57	65	57	49	47	–	5.6	2009
Panama (1997)	81	65	81	77	72	61	61	–	6.9	2011
Saudi Arabia (2005)	38	23	16	13	11	12	22	26	4.9	2011
Tonga (2007)	51	47	43	52	71	58	62	–	11.7	2011
Ukraine (2008)	128	139	145	142	145	152	137	20	4.5	2011
Viet Nam (2007)	104	91	92	93	78	98	99	–	9.8	2010

Note FYROM = Former Yugoslav Republic of Macedonia
Source World Bank & IFC (2006, 2007, 2008, 2009, 2010, 2012, 2013); WTO Trade Profiles in the WTO Web site: http://www.wto.org

These include RAMs in transitions, such as Albania, Armenia, China, Croatia, Georgia (ranked the first among all countries), Macedonia, Kyrgyz Republic, and Ukraine, and others that also made extensive tariff bindings commitments for WTO accession, such as Chinese Taipei and Saudi Arabia. The fact that these RAMs made substantial progress in the wide-ranging areas (including those not related to the WTO) suggests the domestic origin of their reforms.

On the other hand, two Latin American SVEs that retained relatively higher bound tariffs for the WTO accession were not ranked within top fifty. One critical constraint of this data is its limited period coverage (2005–2012), not necessarily concurrent with most RAMs' WTO accession dates. Still, there appears to be some indication that, at least from the medium-term perspective, RAMs that undertook extensive accession commitments pursued domestic reforms also by themselves.

As far as the RAMs are concerned, there appears to be a mutually enhancing influence between the country's domestic reform orientation and utilization of the WTO accession commitments. There is little doubt that, for WTO accession, acceding governments were under pressure to accommodate requests from older members of the multilateral trading system, but that does not seem to be the sole reason for their extensive market access commitments. Rather, reformers probably used these external pressures in their favor to justify liberalization at home. Chiedu Osakwe, former director of the WTO's accession division, has been long observing the RAMs' successful record of utilizing the accession process in support of their domestic reforms and concurs with this view[31]:

> In spite of the complexities and rigors of the WTO accession process, representatives of RAMs have acknowledged the high value of the accession process, as a necessary instrument for their domestic policy reform, specifically for economy-boosting trade liberalization... The accession process and results not only provide support for this argument, namely that multilateral rules help governments lock-in domestic reforms, but also demonstrate that the process and results were critical in generating momentum for trade liberalization in developing RAMs and economies in transition. (Osakwe, 2011, pp. 421–428)

[31] Based on 13 years of experience as a Counsellor in the WTO's Accession Division, Peter Milthorp also shared valuable insights on the membership process. See Milthorp (2009).

Observations of RAMs' performance on the basis of available cross-country statistics generally support Hypothesis 1. A majority of the RAMs were reforming economies, including those in transition to the market economy, and they made extensive market access commitments for WTO accession. Their reforms had domestic origins, and the WTO accession had a function of supporting unilateral liberalization. In contrast, a small number of RAMs were not active reformers by the time of their WTO accession, and their market access commitments were relatively limited.

4.2 *Export Orientation, Size of Economies, and Reciprocity*

Hypotheses 2-a and 2-b assume that the key functions of the Doha Round relate to its reciprocity principle, and only export-oriented (as per the juggernaut theory) or large economies (as per the terms of trade externality theory) would stay engaged in its market access negotiations. Available macroeconomic data on export orientation and market sizes supports this interpretation on the role of reciprocity at the Doha Round.

As to export orientation, among the 18 RAMs (excluding Croatia whose trade policy was probably guided by the prospect of joining the EU and adopting its common external trade policy, as it actually did later in 2013), China and Chinese Taipei were two members that accepted the formula-based tariff cuts with minimum qualifications. As presented in Table 9, both of them had been recording persistent current account surplus toward 2008, exhibiting the strong export orientation since the time of their WTO accessions (and even earlier). Presence of substantive export businesses in the domestic economy should induce the government to seek market access through the reciprocal trade liberalization process. The statement made by the Chinese Taipei delegation (at the Trade Negotiations Committee [TNC] in 2008) below is a clear testimony of such pursuit of the export interests through NAMA negotiations of the Doha Round:

> Now let me speak on behalf of my delegation… on NAMA, my delegation would reiterate that we need a real market access in this Round. We could

Table 9 Current account balance of the recently acceded members (% of GDP)

WTO members (membership)	*Around Accession*			*Toward 2008 modality*		
	Year −1	*Accession*	*Year +1*	*2006*	*2007*	*2008*
Albania (2000)	−3.9	−4.4	−3.2	−5.6	−10.4	−15.1
Armenia (2003)	−6.6	−6.8	−0.5	−1.8	−6.4	−11.8
Cape Verde (2008)	−14.7	−15.6	−15.2	−5.4	−14.7	−15.6
China (2001)	1.9	1.5	2.8	8.6	10.1	9.1
Chinese Taipei (2002)	6.5	9.1	10.2	7.0	8.9	6.9
Croatia (2000)	−7.0	−2.5	−3.7	−6.6	−7.2	−8.8
Ecuador (1996)	−4.1	−0.7	−3.0	4.4	3.6	2.5
FYROM (2003)	−8.5	−4.0	−8.2	−0.9	−7.0	−12.8
Georgia (2000)	−7.8	−4.4	−6.5	−15.1	−19.7	−22.6
Jordan (2000)	5.0	0.7	–	−11.5	−16.8	−9.3
Kyrgyz Republic (1998)	−8.3	−22.9	−15.7	−3.1	−0.2	−8.1
Moldova (2001)	−9.0	−4.9	−6.0	−11.4	−15.3	−16.3
Mongolia (1997)	−2.1	9.0	−5.8	6.5	6.3	−12.9
Oman (2000)	−3.1	16.1	9.9	15.4	5.9	8.3
Panama (1997)	−2.1	−5.0	−9.3	−3.1	−7.2	−11.9
Saudi Arabia (2005)	20.8	28.5	27.8	27.8	24.3	27.8
Tonga (2007)	−8.1	−8.6	−11.7	−8.1	−8.6	−11.7
Ukraine (2008)	−3.7	−7.1	−1.5	−1.5	−3.7	−7.1
Viet Nam (2007)	−0.3	−9.8	−11.9	−0.3	−9.8	−11.9

Note FYROM = Former Yugoslav Republic of Macedonia
Source IMF (2000, 2004, 2011b)

reach this objective, not only from the reasonable and balanced formula, but also from the success of sectorals. We would urge every Member to do its contribution.[32]

Chinese Taipei not only advocated formula-based tariff cuts but also sectoral initiatives (that require liberalization for specific sectors beyond general requirement by the formula). At an early stage of the Doha Round, China also proposed a formula-based tariff cuts among all WTO members (WTO, 2002b).

Interestingly, in contrast to their proactive engagement in the Doha Round, these two RAMs almost ceased to pursue autonomous trade liberalization after joining the multilateral trading system. Table 7 presents the incremental liberalization of applied tariffs each RAM had undertaken by 2008 beyond the WTO accession commitments (presented as "voluntary cuts"). While many RAMs continuously pursued autonomous liberalization outside of the multilateral trading system,[33] China and Chinese Taipei made little progress in trade liberalization beyond their final accession bound rates. As Table 8 on Doing Business ranking showed, the two RAMs had been among the top performers of advancing domestic reforms in other areas of structural reforms but, as far as MFN-based trade liberalization is concerned, they seem to be withholding autonomous actions and instead chose to pursue the multilateral path at the WTO.

Oman also recorded current account surplus in the years toward 2008, and so did Ecuador, as their external positions improved. Prospective commitments by these countries in the 2008 modalities were more moderate (as a Gulf Cooperation Council [GCC] country and SVE, respectively) than those for China and Chinese Taipei, but were more substantive compared with no obligations sought by most of the low-income economies in transition and the VRAMs. As a surplus country, Saudi Arabia's exemption from the formula appears to be an outlier case. Allegedly, its position was a reflection of the fact that the country had just joined the WTO in 2005 and was still implementing accession commitments, as stated in its negotiating proposal submitted in 2006:

[32] Statement on behalf of the Recently Acceded Members by the Separate Customs Territory of Taiwan, Penghu, Kinmen, and Matsu at the Informal TNC Meeting Monday 21 July 2008, retrieved from the WTO Web site: https://www.wto.org/.

[33] However, it should be noted that, for some members, substantial voluntarily cuts mainly reflect the shallow WTO accession commitments, rather than unilateral liberalization they pursued after their membership (presented as "unilateral cuts" in Table 7).

> In view of these considerations, especially the proximity in time of accession – only six months – it would not be fair or appropriate to require further reductions. This position will also be presented to the negotiating groups on Agriculture and Services, since the Kingdom made substantial concessions in these areas as well. The Kingdom also wishes to clarify that this position is without prejudice to the positions of other Members which acceded to the WTO prior to the Kingdom of Saudi Arabia. (WTO, 2006c, p. 2)

At the same time, Saudi Arabia is a major exporter of oil, which is a commodity not negotiated in the WTO, and thus its external position was probably not quite relevant to the negotiating stance at the Doha Round.[34]

Meanwhile, most of the RAMs that had been recording persistent current account deficit disengaged themselves from the market access negotiations of the Doha Round, and instead pursued post-accession trade liberalization autonomously outside of the multilateral trading system (see, for instance, records of Armenia, Georgia, and Kyrgyz Republic in Tables 7, 8, and 9[35]). These economies were also completely exempted from the formula-based tariff cuts in the draft December 2008 modalities papers, except for Georgia. Just like other low-income economies in transition, Georgia initially posed explicit reservation against further tariff cuts through the Doha Round, but the country seems to have become less vocal in claiming the RAMs' cause for flexibility later on. The share of its current account deficit (that recorded 22.6% of gross domestic product [GDP] in 2008) was biggest among all the RAMs, but the country ultimately withdrew from the low-income economies in transition coalition for NAMA and became more accommodating, albeit not for agriculture.

Aside from export interests, another economic rationale for participating in the reciprocal negotiations is containment of terms of trade externality among large economies. Table 10 shows volumes and world shares of the RAMs' imports, as an indication of the size of their economies.

[34]This interpretation could be selectively applicable to some other oil exporting countries, too. See Chapter 6 on Ecuador.

[35]As a more recent development after the deadlock of the Doha Round in 2008, Armenia and the Kyrgyz Republic joined EAEU in 2015 and adopted its higher common external tariff rates. See WTO (2018a).

Table 10 Market sizes of the recently acceded members

WTO members (membership)	*Imports in accession year*		*Imports in 2008*	
	Volume (US$ billions)	*World share (%)*	*Volume (US$ billions)*	*World share (%)*
Albania (2000)	1.1	0.02	5.3	0.03
Armenia (2003)	1.3	0.02	4.4	0.03
Cape Verde (2008)	0.8	0.00	0.8	0.00
China (2001)	243.6	3.83	1131.6	6.99
Chinese Taipei (2002)	112.8	1.71	240.7	1.49
Croatia (2000)	7.9	0.12	30.7	0.19
Ecuador (1996)	4.3	0.08	18.7	0.12
FYROM (2003)	2.3	0.03	6.8	0.04
Georgia (2000)	0.7	0.01	6.1	0.04
Jordan (2000)	4.6	0.07	16.8	0.10
Kyrgyz Republic (1998)	0.8	0.01	4.1	0.03
Moldova (2001)	0.9	0.01	4.1	0.03
Mongolia (1997)	0.5	0.01	3.6	0.02
Oman (2000)	5.0	0.08	23.1	0.14
Panama (1997)	3.0	0.05	9.1	0.06
Saudi Arabia (2005)	59.5	0.56	115.1	0.71
Tonga (2007)	0.1	0.00	0.2	0.00
Ukraine (2008)	85.5	0.53	85.5	0.53
Viet Nam (2007)	60.9	0.43	79.3	0.49

Note FYROM = Former Yugoslav Republic of Macedonia
Source IMF (2000, 2004, 2011b)

Here, too, the data seemingly verifies the hypothesis that larger economies would stay engaged in the reciprocal market access negotiations of the Doha Round. China and Chinese Taipei that accepted formula-based reciprocal tariff cuts are both relatively large economies that account for more than 1% of global imports, unlike the other RAMs. In particular, the size of the Chinese market had been growing rapidly, to reach nearly 7% by 2008, and quite significant. On the other hand, Chinese Taipei's global market share remained about 1.5%, and it is questionable if the economy of such size can still affect global price levels. In fact, no RAM made formal statements that referred to containment of terms of trade externality as a reason for their participation in the multilateral trading system. As Krugman (1991, p. 16) puts it, '*the optimal tariff argument... generally plays no part at all in real-world trade discussion.*' If reciprocity attracted a number of RAMs for their relatively active participation in the Doha Round negotiations, that was probably because of their export interests, rather than terms of trade externality. Here again, Georgia's case as a small economy requires further examination.

Findings from macroeconomic and policy data support the assumption that the envisaged function of the reciprocal market access negotiations of the Doha Round is different from those for unilateral commitments under WTO accession. As per Hypothesis 2-a, broadly speaking, only export-oriented economies engaged themselves proactively in the DDA market access negotiations, while other reforming economies pursued trade liberalization autonomously outside of the multilateral trading system. By implication, what takes precedence for the DDA market access negotiations was export orientation, rather than the government's willingness to reform as was the case for accession. There was also some evidence showing that, in line with Hypothesis 2-b, larger economies were more active in the Doha Round than smaller ones. However, given the absence of any remark on optimal tariffs by negotiators and policy-makers, the practical relevance of the terms of trade externality could be rather questionable.

4.3 Recovering the Cost of the Outsider Status

Hypothesis 3 presumes that some RAMs joined the multilateral trading system to redress discrimination encountered due to previous WTO non-membership (as per the domino theory). The RAMs would stay engaged in the relevant multilateral liberalization scheme as far as these costs of the outsider status exist, but those free from such constraints would not have to address these problems at the WTO in the first place. As explained in the second section of this chapter, incumbent WTO members typically accord the MFN treatment of broad-based market access (at least on the conditional basis) even to non-members, and the remaining discriminatory measures, if any, tend to take the form of more specific protections. For this reason, it would be misleading to gauge the level of the discrimination solely on the basis of average tariff data. Still, higher tariff data could partly be a weak reflection of these targeted discriminatory measures against the RAMs.

Table 11 compares the average rate of tariffs each RAM had faced against its exports in the pre-accession period (presented as "pre-accession country average" for a three-year period) and that for the entire world for the same period (presented as "pre-accession world

Table 11 Tariff barriers against the RAMs with international comparison (%)

WTO members (accession year)	*Pre-accession*	*Pre-accession*	*Post-accession*	*Dispute*
	Country average	*World average*	*Country average*	*Complaints*
Albania (2000)	6.69	8.72	5.72	0
Armenia (2003)	9.36	8.91	6.89	0
Cape Verde (2008)	4.67	7.59	9.97	0
China (2001)	11.94	8.60	11.47	12
Chinese Taipei (2002)	10.93	8.93	9.19	4
Croatia (2000)	7.71	8.72	7.04	0
Ecuador (1996)	10.75	8.77	10.34	3
FYROM (2003)	7.54	8.91	5.17	0
Georgia (2000)	6.02	8.72	7.84	0
Jordan (2000)	7.56	8.72	9.45	0
Kyrgyz Republic (1998)	10.97	9.12	8.79	0
Moldova (2001)	9.27	8.60	10.03	1
Mongolia (1997)	9.37	9.06	10.65	0
Oman (2000)	9.90	8.72	10.48	0
Panama (1997)	14.40	9.06	12.33	7
Saudi Arabia (2005)	10.47	7.80	7.57	0
Tonga (2007)	2.78	6.52	10.34	0
Ukraine (2008)	7.64	7.59	9.56	3
Viet Nam (2007)	8.50	6.52	9.96	2

Note Data is a three-year average of pre- and post-WTO accession periods for each RAM, except where data is available only for a shorter period. Regional averages cover developing countries of the region concerned, except for high-income non-OECD countries. OECD=Organisation for Economic Co-operation and Development
Source World Trade Indicators of the World Bank Web site: http://www.worldbank.org/; WTO Web site: http://www.wto.org/english/tratop_e/dispu_e/dispu_by_country_e.htm

average" for a three-year period). Surprisingly, some RAMs (Albania, Cape Verde, Croatia, Macedonia, Georgia, Jordan, and Tonga) faced ever lower tariffs than those for the rest of the world before their WTO accession. As far as the average tariff rate is concerned, these RAMs practically received preferences, rather than discrimination, prior to WTO accession.[36] However, the other RAMs faced higher tariffs in the pre-accession period. The table also shows the average tariff rate that the

[36]One possible reason for this seemingly paradoxical situation could be that the incumbent WTO members accorded more favorable market access to these RAMs prior to their membership, based on a refutable presumption that preferences accorded to the non-members were not required to be extended to the WTO members on the MFN basis.

RAMs faced in the post-accession period (presented as "post-accession country average," for a three-year period), as well as their record in their participation in the WTO dispute settlement mechanism as a complainant (presented as "dispute complaints"). Surprisingly, the trade barriers against some of the previously discriminated RAMs did not necessarily decline systematically in the post-accession period, and there appear to be some loose tendency that part of those RAMs that still faced the remaining restrictions (China, Chinese Taipei, Ecuador, Moldova, Panama, Ukraine, and Viet Nam) resorted to dispute settlement at the WTO as a complainant, while others did not.

The average tariff data does not necessarily reflect all forms of discrimination that the RAMs have faced since the pre-accession period, and dispute settlement is not the sole instrument to cope with such disadvantages. Also, dispute settlement can address other forms of trade barriers, not just discrimination against new members. In this sense, Table 11 is nothing more than a very generic illustration that discriminated economies tended to take certain actions at the WTO. Nonetheless, the limited available data seems to support Hypothesis 3, at least partially. Firmly reaching this conclusion would require more qualitative examination through case studies.

5 Conclusion

Preliminary observations on the basis of available cross-country statistics broadly support hypotheses inferred by economic theories on the roles of trade agreements and negotiations. While reforming economies generally tended to utilize market access commitments for WTO accession to catalyze and consolidate their unilateral trade liberalization (while others did not, as per Hypothesis 1), only a handful of export-oriented or relatively large economies remained proactively engaged in the market access negotiations later in the Doha Round (while others disengaged themselves from the multilateral process in favor of autonomous liberalization, as per Hypotheses 2-a and 2-b). These observations are in line with the assumption that the envisaged functions for market access negotiations under the WTO accession process and those for the Doha Round are different. While the role of unilateral accession commitments is to support the acceding government's own domestic reforms, only economies that can take potential advantages of reciprocity would stay engaged in the Doha Round. Likewise, there was a general tendency that the RAMs suffering from the discrimination more actively utilized the WTO dispute settlement (while other did not, as per Hypothesis 3).

However, these cross-country statistics may not necessarily reveal the whole picture. In particular, observations of the macroeconomic and policy data alone cannot prove that policy-makers and negotiators actually conceived the motivations for engagement in the multilateral trading system just as envisaged in the relevant economic theories (as elaborated in Chapter 1). Also, the analysis based on the data alone may not fully account for the nuanced behaviors of the individual RAMs. For instance, while it is true that export-oriented economies such as China have relatively been much more active than the other RAMs in the Doha Round, their level of pro-activeness was far from reaching the level of driving the entire round toward successful conclusion, implying that there must have been factors suppressing the country's will to use the multilateral liberalization process more effectively. Even if the macroeconomic data could explain why Georgia, as a small import-oriented economy, tried to disengage itself from the early phase of the DDA market access negotiations, it still leaves a puzzle on why the country became more accommodating later on. Above all, the analysis on the specific costs of the previous non-membership would require careful reviews of individual discriminatory measures (beyond the average level of tariff barriers), such as the NME designations for China and Viet Nam and the ACP preference against Ecuador. Analysis of these issues would have to be more context-specific and requires qualitative information. The next four chapters on Georgia, China, Viet Nam, and Ecuador present such analysis through country case studies.

References

Allee, T. L., & Scalera, J. E. (2012). The divergent effects of joining international organizations: Trade gains and the rigors of WTO accession. *International Organization, 66*(2), 243–276.

Bacchetta, M., & Drabek, Z. (2002). *Effects of WTO accession on policy-making in sovereign states: preliminary lessons from the recent experience of transition countries* (Development and Economic Research Division Staff Working Paper DERD-2002-02). Retrieved from World Trade Organization website: http://www.wto.org/english/res_e/reser_e/derd200202_e.htm.

Braga, C. A. P., & Cattaneo, O. (2009a). Introduction. In C. A. P. Braga & O. Cattaneo (Eds.), *The WTO and accession countries* (Vol. 1, pp. xi–xlvii). Cheltenham: Edward Elgar.

Braga, C. A. P., & Cattaneo, O. (2009b). *Everything you always wanted to know about WTO accession (But were afraid to ask)* (Policy Research Working Paper, WPS5156). Retrieved from World Bank website: http://www-wds.worldbank.org/external/default/WDSContentServer/WDSP/IB/2009/11/05/000158349_20091105161912/Rendered/PDF/WPS5116.pdf.

Cooper, W. H. (2012). *The Jackson-Vanik amendment and candidate countries for WTO accession: Issues for congress*. Washington, DC: Congressional Research Service.

Drabek, Z., & Bacchetta, M. (2004). Tracing the effects of WTO accession on policy-making in sovereign states: Preliminary lessons from the recent experience of transition countries. *World Economy, 27*(7), 1083–1125.

Drabek, Z., & Woo, W. T. (2010). Who should join the WTO and why? A Cost-benefit analysis of WTO membership. In Z. Drabek (Ed.), *Is the World Trade Organization attractive enough for emerging economies? Critical essays on the multilateral trading system* (pp. 249–294). Basingstoke: Palgrave Macmillan.

Francois, F. F., & Martin, W. (2002). Binding tariffs: Why do it? In B. Hoekman, A. Mattoo, & P. English (Eds.), *Development, trade, and the WTO: A handbook* (pp. 538–547). Washington, DC: World Bank.

General Agreement on Tariffs and Trade. (1994). *The fourth ACP-EEC convention of Lomé: Decision of 9 December 1994* (L/7604). Geneva: Author.

Hoekman, B. M., & Kostecki, M. M. (2009). *The political economy of the world trading system: The WTO and beyond* (2nd ed.). Oxford: Oxford University Press.

International Monetary Fund. (2000). *Ecuador: Selected issues and statistical annex* (IMF Staff Country Report No. 00/125). Washington, DC: Author.

International Monetary Fund. (2003). *Direction of trade statistics yearbook 2003*. Washington, DC: Author.

International Monetary Fund. (2004). *World economic outlook (September): The global demographic transition*. Washington, DC: Author.

International Monetary Fund. (2005a). *Review of fund work on trade*. Washington, DC: Author.

International Monetary Fund. (2005b). *Trade conditionality under fund-supported programs, 1990–2004 (background paper to the review of fund work on trade)*. Washington, DC: Author.

International Monetary Fund. (2009). *International financial statistics year book 2009*. Washington, DC: Author.

International Monetary Fund. (2011a). *Articles of the agreement of the International Monetary Fund (1944)*. Washington, DC: Author.

International Monetary Fund. (2011b). *World economic outlook (September): Slowing growth, rising risks*. Washington, DC: Author.

International Monetary Fund. (2012). *Direction of trade statistics yearbook 2012*. Washington, DC: Author.

Keck, A., & Low, P. (2004). *Special and differential treatment in the WTO: Why, when and how?* (Economic Research and Statistics Division Working Paper ERSD-2004-03). Retrieved from World Trade Organization website: http://www.wto.org/english/res_e/reser_e/ersd200403_e.htm.

Krugman, P. (1991, November/December). The move toward free trade zones. *Economic Review—Federal Reserve Bank of Kansas City, 76*(6), 5–25.

Martin, W. (2010). Development implications of WTO accession procedures. In Z. Drabek (Ed.), *Is the World Trade Organization attractive enough for emerging economies? Critical essays on the multilateral trading system* (pp. 13–36). Basingstoke: Palgrave Macmillan.

Milthorp, P. (2009). WTO accessions: The story so far. *The Hague Journal of Diplomacy, 4*, 103–112.

Osakwe, C. (2011). Developing countries and GATT/WTO rules. *Minnesota Journal of International Law, 20*(2), 365–436.

Pregelj, V. N. (2005a). *Normal-trade-relations (most-favored-nation) policy of the United States.* Washington, DC: Congressional Research Service.

Pregelj, V. N. (2005b). *The Jackson-Vanik amendment: A Survey.* Washington, DC: Congressional Research Service.

Snyder, F. (2001). The origins of the 'nonmarket economy': Ideas, pluralism and power in EC anti-dumping law about China. *European Law Journal, 7*(4), 369–424.

Subramanian, A., & Wei, S. (2007, May). The WTO promotes trade, strongly but unevenly. *Journal of International Economics*, 72(1), 151–175.

Williams, P. J. (2008). *A handbook on accession to the WTO.* Cambridge: Cambridge University Press.

World Bank. (2005). *Global economic prospects 2005: Trade, regionalism, and development.* Washington, DC: Author.

World Bank. (2011). *Leveraging trade for development and inclusive growth: The World Bank Group trade strategy, 2011–2021.* Washington, DC: Author.

World Bank Independent Evaluation Group. (2006). *Assessing World Bank support for trade, 1987–2004: An IEG evaluation.* Washington, DC: World Bank.

World Bank & International Finance Corporation. (2006). *Doing business 2007: How to reform.* Washington, DC: Authors.

World Bank & International Finance Corporation. (2007). *Doing business 2008.* Washington, DC: Authors.

World Bank & International Finance Corporation. (2008). *Doing business 2009.* Washington, DC: Authors.

World Bank & International Finance Corporation. (2009). *Doing business 2010: Reforming through difficult times.* Washington, DC: Authors.

World Bank & International Finance Corporation. (2010). *Doing business 2011: Making a difference for entrepreneurs.* Washington, DC: Authors.

World Bank & International Finance Corporation. (2012). *Doing business 2012: Doing business in a more transparent world*. Washington, DC: Authors.

World Bank & International Finance Corporation. (2013). *Doing business 2013: Smarter regulations for small and medium-size enterprises*. Washington, DC: Authors.

World Trade Organization. (1995a). *The results of the Uruguay round of multilateral trade negotiations: Legal texts*. Geneva: Author. (Original work published by the GATT Secretariat 1994).

World Trade Organization. (1995b). *Accession to the World Trade Organization: Procedures for negotiations under article XII—Note by the secretariat* (WT/ACC/1). Geneva: Author.

World Trade Organization. (1997). *European Communities—Regime for the importation, sale and distribution of bananas: Complaint by Ecuador—Report of the panel* (WT/DS27/R/ECU). Geneva: Author.

World Trade Organization. (2001a). *Ministerial conference, fourth session, Doha, 9–14 November 2001: Ministerial declaration—Adopted on 14 November 2001* (WT/MIN(01)/DEC/1). Geneva: Author.

World Trade Organization. (2001b). *Committee on agriculture, special session: WTO agriculture negotiations—Proposal by Jordan* (G/AG/NG/W/140). Geneva: Author.

World Trade Organization. (2001c). *Committee on agriculture, special session: Sixth special session of the committee on agriculture, 22–23 March 2001—Statement by Jordan* (G/AG/NG/W/147). Geneva: Author.

World Trade Organization. (2001d). *Committee on agriculture, special session: WTO negotiations on agriculture—Submission by Croatia* (G/AG/NG/W/141). Geneva: Author.

World Trade Organization. (2001e). *Ministerial conference, fourth session, Doha, 9–14 November 2001: European Communities—The ACP-EC partnership agreement: Decision of 14 November 2001* (WT/MIN(01)/15). Geneva: Author.

World Trade Organization. (2002a). *Negotiation group on market access: Market access for non-agricultural products—Contribution from Oman* (TN/MA/W/14). Geneva: Author.

World Trade Organization. (2002b). *Negotiation group on market access: Market access for non-agricultural products—Proposal by the People's Republic of China* (TN/MA/W/20). Geneva: Author.

World Trade Organization. (2003a). *Negotiation group on market access: Market access for non-agricultural products—Communication form Albania, Croatia, Georgia, and Moldova* (TN/MA/W/29). Geneva: Author.

World Trade Organization. (2003b). *Ministerial conference, fifth session, Cancún, 10–14 September 2003: Proposal on flexibility provisions for recently acceded members—Communication from China* (WT/MIN(03)/W/8). Geneva: Author.

World Trade Organization. (2003c). *Negotiation group on market access: Market access for non-agricultural products—Proposal by the People's Republic of China, corrigendum* (TN/MA/W/20/Corr.1). Geneva: Author.

World Trade Organization. (2003d). *Negotiating group on rules: Proposal of the People's Republic of China on the negotiation on anti-dumping* (TN/RL/W/66). Geneva: Author.

World Trade Organization. (2004a). *Doha work programme: Decision adopted by the general council on 1 August 2004* (WT/L/579). Geneva: Author.

World Trade Organization. (2004b). *Ministerial conference, sixth session, Hong Kong, 13–18 December 2005: Doha work programme—Ministerial declaration adopted on 18 December 2005* (WT/MIN(05)/DEC). Geneva: Author.

World Trade Organization. (2005a). *Negotiation group on market access: Market access for non-agricultural products—Communication form Armenia, Georgia, Kyrgyz Republic and Republic of Moldova* (TN/MA/W/56). Geneva: Author.

World Trade Organization. (2005b). *Negotiation group on market access: Market access for non-agricultural products—Communication form Armenia, Georgia, Kyrgyz Republic and Republic of Moldova—Revision* (TN/MA/W/56/Rev.1). Geneva: Author.

World Trade Organization. (2005c). *Committee on agriculture, special session: Communication form Armenia, Georgia, the Kyrgyz Republic and the Republic of Moldova* (TN/AG/GEN/10). Geneva: Author.

World Trade Organization. (2005d). *Committee on agriculture, special session: Communication form Armenia, Georgia, the Kyrgyz Republic and the Republic of Moldova—Corrigendum* (TN/AG/GEN/10/Corr.1). Geneva: Author.

World Trade Organization. (2006a). *Committee on agriculture, special session: Communication form small low-income economies in transition, recently acceded to the WTO—Proposal by Armenia, the Kyrgyz Republic and the Republic of Moldova* (TN/AG/GEN/16). Geneva: Author.

World Trade Organization. (2006b). *Committee on agriculture, special session: Communication form Armenia, the Kyrgyz Republic and the Republic of Moldova* (TN/AG/GEN/21). Geneva: Author.

World Trade Organization. (2006c). *Trade negotiations committee, negotiating group on market access: Market access for non-agricultural products—Position of the Kingdom of Saudi Arabia as a newly acceded member, communication from Saudi Arabia* (TN/C/W/45, TN/MA/W/81). Geneva: Author.

World Trade Organization. (2006d). *General council, committee on agriculture (special session), negotiating group on market access: Recently acceded members—Communication from Ecuador and Panama* (WT/GC/W/565, TN/AG/W/2, TN/MA/W/73). Geneva: Author.

World Trade Organization. (2007a). *Negotiating group on market access: Market access for non-agricultural products—Negotiating proposals by recently acceded members (RAMs)* (TN/MA/W/83). Geneva: Author.

World Trade Organization. (2007b). *Committee on agriculture special session: Negotiating proposals by recently acceded members (RAMs)* (TN/AG/GEN/24). Geneva: Author.

World Trade Organization. (2007c). *Committee on agriculture, special session: Negotiations on agriculture—Communication from Albania* (TN/AG/GEN/28). Geneva: Author.

World Trade Organization. (2008a). *Negotiating group on market access: Fourth revision of draft modalities for non-agricultural market access* (TN/MA/W/103/Rev.3). Geneva: Author.

World Trade Organization. (2008b). *Committee on agriculture, special session: Revised draft modalities for agriculture* (TN/AG/W/4/Rev.4). Geneva: Author.

World Trade Organization. (2008c). *Negotiating group on market access: Market access for non-agricultural products, non-agricultural market access (NAMA) negotiations—Communication from Albania* (TN/MA/W/99). Geneva: Author.

World Trade Organization. (2009). *Ministerial conference, seventh session, Geneva, 30 November–2 December 2009: Communication from the group of recently acceded members (RAMs)* (WT/MIN(09)/6). Geneva: Author.

World Trade Organization. (2010). *Technical note on the accession process: Note by the secretariat—Revision* (WT/ACC/10/Rev/4). Geneva: Author.

World Trade Organization. (2011). *Ministerial conference, eighth session, Geneva, 15–17 December 2011: Ministers/heads of delegations meeting of the group of recently acceded members (RAMs)* (WT/MIN(11)/22). Geneva: Author.

World Trade Organization. (2012). *WTO accessions: 2012 annual report by the Director-General* (WT/ACC/19). Geneva: Author.

World Trade Organization. (2014). *Accession to the World Trade Organization: Procedures for negotiations under article XII—Note by the secretariat* (WT/ACC/22). Geneva: Author.

World Trade Organization. (2018). *Committee on regional trade agreements: Treaty on the Eurasian Economic Union (EREA), EAEU—Accession of Armenia, EAEU—Accession of the Kyrgyz Republic—General incident calculation: Notes by the secretariat* (WT/REG358/2, WT/REG363/2, WT/REG/366/2). Geneva: Author.

CHAPTER 3

Georgia

1 Introduction

Since independence from the Soviet Union in 1991, Georgia has been pursuing transition to a market economy. Its overall economic policy, of which trade policy is an integral part, has been featured by a strong liberal orientation.[1] The country's simple average final bound tariff rate in the terms of WTO accession (7.4%) is relatively low among the RAMs, but what is even more striking is the record of autonomous liberalization. By 2009, the simple average applied tariff rate has declined to about 1% (or only 0.31% as far as industrial products are concerned), with products representing over 85% of tariff lines having been granted duty-free access. Both tariff peaks and tariff escalations are virtually non-existent. There is no apparent non-tariff barrier in place, and the country did not even have a legislation to implement any forms of trade remedies.[2] As reflected in its declining average MFN applied

[1] In this chapter, the term "liberal" is used as an adjective of "liberalization" (as in trade liberalization) to describe the market-oriented approach to the economic policy, whose ultimate form would be laissez-faire. It should not be confused with the same term that describes a political philosophy that favors state interventions (i.e., "liberal" as opposed to conservative). Georgia's liberal economic policy orientation was born out of post-Soviet transition since 1999 and the Rose Revolution in 2003.

[2] As of the time of trade policy review at the WTO in 2016, Georgia had no legislation for contingency measures. See WTO (2016).

K. Takamiya, *Recently Acceded Members of the World Trade Organization*, https://doi.org/10.1007/978-981-13-9159-0_3

tariff rate and widening "water" below the bound rate, Georgia's non-discriminatory trade liberalization has been taking on an increasingly unilateral nature. The liberal orientation of the trade policy stands out not only in global comparison but also in regional comparison with relatively disciplined policy of other middle- and low-income economies in Europe and Central Asia (Table 1). At the same time, Georgia is a small economy without any indication of strong export orientation.

Accordingly, this case study on Georgia provides an illustration of how a reforming economy with a strong unilateral liberalization focus would behave in the multilateral trading system. In terms of the analytical framework, it mainly verifies Hypothesis 1: *Reforming economies (especially, those in transition to a market economy) would make extensive market access commitments for WTO accession, while others would make little use of them.*[3] At the same time, the absence of export orientation and the large size of the economy also help verify Hypothesis 2-a: *Only export-oriented economies would stay proactively engaged in the post-accession market access negotiations of the Doha Round, while others would pursue autonomous liberalization*; and Hypothesis 2-b: *Only large economies would stay proactively engaged in the market access negotiations of the Doha Round, while others would pursue autonomous liberalization.*

The underlying assumption for these hypotheses is that market access negotiations for accession and those at the Doha Round have two completely different functions related to broad trade policy objectives, described by respective economic theories. The focus of accession negotiations is to lock in the country's own unilateral liberalization, as prescribed in the commitment theory. On the other hand, the Doha Round takes the form of reciprocal trade negotiations, whose primary objective is to open trading partner's markets (not just one's own). The former appeals generally to the governments of countries undertaking market-oriented reforms, such as economies in transition, whereas the latter would be relevant only to economies characterized by the export

[3]This chapter is organized mostly to follow the events chronologically, rather than just by hypothesis. Given Georgia's trade policy priority dedicated almost exclusively to unilateral liberalization (assumed in Hypothesis 1), the country case study inevitably places less emphasis on description of other trade policy objectives (featured in Hypotheses 2-a, 2-b, and 3). Impacts of the absence of multiple policy objectives can be analyzed only in comparison with other case study countries that possess them. Such comparison is presented in the last chapter on conclusion.

Table 1 Georgia—MFN tariff profile with international comparison (%)

	Georgia				*ECA*	*World*
	1995–1999	*2000–2004*	*2005–2008*	*2009*	*2009*	*2009*
Simple average applied rates	10.57	8.78	3.03	1.03	7.18	9.61
Agricultural products	11.93	12.16	7.74	5.85	12.47	13.12
Non-agricultural products	10.37	8.28	2.33	0.31	6.39	9.08
Trade-weighted average applied rates	10.12	9.51	3.47	1.05	5.36	8.57
Agricultural products	12	14.23	8.21	5.63	9.42	11.38
Non-agricultural products	9.52	8.37	2.60	0.21	4.98	8.22
Maximum applied rate	12	30	18	12	44.23	96.44
Dispersion (coefficient of variation)	0.27	0.57	2.41	3.25	1.19	1.20
Domestic tariff peaks (tariff lines share)	0.00	1.04	9.96	14.03	6.58	4.47
International tariff peaks (tariff lines share)	0.00	3.68	2	1.02	12.19	23.51
Tariff escalation (finished % minus raw %)	–	–	−1.65	−1.74	1.58	2.56
Duty-free tariff lines share	0.00	3.99	65.98	85.63	23.95	23.86
Non-ad valorem share (in all tariff lines)	0.18	0.46	1.21	1.89	4.91	2.54
Bound tariff lines (% of all tariff lines)	–	99.97	99.99	100	96.16	81.98
Tariff overhang (bound minus applied rate)	−3.31	−1.73	4.04	6.12	5.78	28.84

Note ECA = Europe and Central Asia, excluding high-income countries. Indicators for 1995–1999, 2000–2004, and 2005–2008 are period averages. Data on average, maximum and dispersion rates covers ad valorem tariffs only

Source World Bank. World Trade Indicators 2009/2010 Web site: http://info.worldbank.org/etools/wti/2a1.asp

orientation as per the juggernaut theory, or large size as per the terms of trade externality theory. The case study of Georgia illustrates that its long-term trade policy objective has been market opening of its own economy but, hardly being an export-oriented or large economy, the country was not keen to proactively pursue reciprocal liberalization. As such, while Georgia effectively utilized the accession process to catalyze and consolidate its domestic reform, the country got disengaged from post-accession market access negotiations of the Doha Round and pursued autonomous trade liberalization outside of the WTO. The case study also shows that, over time, the mode of disengagement from the multilateral negotiations evolved from one characterized by defensiveness to that of aloofness.

To certain extent, autonomous liberalization is featured broadly across most of the developing country members of the WTO, and the case study should provide some insights on the role of the multilateral trading system in their domestic reform initiatives. In the case of Georgia, two historical incidents of collapse of the Soviet Union in 1991 and domestic movement in pursuit of economic liberty in 2003, known as the "Rose Revolution," played important roles in underlining the overall context of the country's economic policy. Accordingly, the second and third sections of the study chronologically trace back the record of Georgia's domestic reform initiatives during the post-Soviet transition phase up to the early 2000s and those after the post-Rose Revolution phase since 2003. On the multilateral front, these two periods correspond to the country's WTO accession and the early days of the Doha Round on the one hand and conclusion of its draft 2008 modalities on the other hand. Where relevant, performances of other low-income economies in transition (that formed a negotiating coalition with Georgia) are analyzed. The fourth section provides further theoretical observations, including examination of the country's unique domestic contexts and Hypothesis 3: *Countries that face the discriminatory cost of prior non-membership would stay engaged in the relevant multilateral liberalization schemes, while others would refrain from such activities.* The fifth section concludes.

2 Post-Soviet Transition, WTO Accession, Toward the Doha Round

2.1 From the Crisis to International Economic Integration

2.1.1 Post-Soviet Transition and Stabilization

Georgia's trade policy and WTO accession should be seen in the broader context of transition to a market economy since independence from the Soviet Union in 1991. Under the previous communist regime, Georgia's economy was highly integrated with other Soviet republics, which were the destinations of a nearly whole of the country's exports and the sources of three-quarters of imports. As such, the collapse of the Soviet Union was followed by acute destabilization of the Georgian economy. The degree of its distress was more severe than in other countries of the Commonwealth of Independent States (CIS), and the outbreak of civil unrest and internal conflicts did not help the situation. By 1994, GDP declined to 17% of its pre-independence level of 1990, and the economy suffered from serious hyperinflation. The growth rate in 1992–1994 was minus 28.2%, and the average annual inflation surged to nearly 7000% in the same period. Real wages recorded 90% below the pre-independence level, and the government revenue declined sharply from 15% of GDP in 1992 to 2.3% in 1993 (World Bank, 2003, 2012; WTO, 2010a).

In the face of the acute crisis, the program of macroeconomic stabilization and transition to a market economy was launched in 1994 with support by the international financial institutions (IFIs)—namely, the IMF and the World Bank. This and successive programs comprised not only fiscal and monetary tightening on the macroeconomic policy front but also comprehensive market-oriented structural reforms at the industry level. Thus, Georgia's microeconomic policy in the 1990s was directed to privatization of state-owned enterprises (SOEs), price deregulation, and trade and investment liberalization. The external trade policy followed this broadly liberal orientation of the overall economic reform. Vladimir Papava, Georgia's Minister of Economy at the time, wrote (in his paper co-authored with Teimuraz Beridze):

> Competition is the main driving force behind any improvement in quality of goods and any cost savings. The later [sic] can also be achieved through the introduction of new technologies. This is true not only for the domestic market but also for the world market. Any barriers put up by a country for the sake of protection for domestic producers would limit the beneficial effects of the international competition which – in conjunction with introduction of new technologies – impact favourably on economic incentives and cost savings. (Papava & Beridze, 1997, p. 70)

Policy-makers were equally aware of the danger of giving into vested interests of certain domestic industries seeking active industrial policy and protection:

> (R)epresentatives of industrial sector in the government … lobby for preferential treatment for a particular branch on the domestic market… it is clear that a protectionism policy of this nature will be extremely detrimental to our industry: First of all, it is impossible in practice to select one particular industry worthy of support by way of providing preferential customs treatment it, while nearly all the industries are in equally bad "technical" and "financial" shape… Second, … This will undermine any economic incentives for them to lower their production costs and improve quality of their goods… Thirdly, one cannot ignore the fact, that the losses incurred in the course of consuming domestic goods of poor quality which become more expensive will simultaneously adversely affect the welfare of the population. In this case, the introduction of the Government of Georgia of protectionist policies based on differential customs tariffs would do disservice to our industry. (Papava & Beridze, 1997, pp. 71–72)

As per the Law on Customs Duty of 27 December 1996, tariff bands comprised 0, 5, and 12%, with a weighted average tariff rate below 12% (WTO, 1997). Later, under the Law on Customs Tariff and Duty of 20 March 1998, most imports were subjected to the 12% rate, while the 5% rate was applied to imported pharmaceuticals; capital goods, including spare parts and supplementary equipment; and specific goods used in production. According to the Working Group Report on Georgia's WTO Accession, the average trade-weighted tariff rate (inclusive of duty-free products) came down to 4.9% by 1997, signifying that Georgia had already established a relatively liberal trade regime even before WTO accession (WTO, 1999).[4] By the mid-1990s, the stabilization program appeared to have successfully contained the post-independence crisis, and the economy started to grow again. The GDP growth rate marked 10.5% in 1997, and the inflation rate was tamed down to 7.3% in the same year.[5]

[4] A trade-weighted average rate of tariffs excluding goods with duty-free access was 10.3% in 1998 (WTO, 1999).

[5] Macroeconomic data was sourced from the Asian Development Bank (ADB) (2013). For further reference on Georgia's economy of the relatively more recent past, the IMF (2004a) provides its account of the performances in 1996–2003, and the World Bank (2013) covers the subsequent period.

2.2 WTO Accession: Tying Hands to Consolidate Domestic Reforms

The record of Georgia's engagement in the WTO accession was in line with the prediction of Hypothesis 1 for the reforming economies. The commitment theory that underlies this hypothesis prescribes the government to tie its own hands by locking the domestic reforms into multilateral trade agreements.[6] It was with this reform objective in mind that Georgia applied for the GATT observer status—the first step toward the ultimate accession to the prospective WTO. After the establishment of the WTO in 1995, this move was followed by requests for the WTO observer status and, in turn, for membership in 1996. At the WTO General Council meeting that discussed Georgia's request for the observer status, on behalf of the Georgian delegation, Amiran Kavadze, Director of Department of Foreign Economic Relations of the Ministry of Foreign Affairs, stated that the decision had been "*logical consequence of Georgia's economic reforms and of its integration to the world economy*" (Kavadze, Ukleba, Katamadze, 2003, p. 51). WTO accession was envisaged to help complete the domestic reforms for post-Soviet transition to a market economy, as stated in the Government's Memorandum of the Foreign Trade Regime submitted subsequently to the membership application:

> Georgia reaffirms its strict orientation to the free trade policy… The Government of Georgia considers its accession to the World Trade Organization one of the most important steps toward integration into the world economy. Furthermore, this will help Georgia to complete reforms, to create a legislative framework corresponding to international standards and build a prosperous and democratic society. (WTO, 1997, p. 1)

To the government of Georgia, WTO accession was an attractive instrument to consolidate its unilateral trade liberalization while deterring domestic protectionist interests. Tamara Beruchashvili, then Deputy Foreign Minister of Georgia, also recalled that "*Georgia began the accession process having already made a firm decision to embrace the principle of a modern open economy*" (Beruchashvili, 2001, p. 5).[7] Subsequently in

[6] Staiger and Tabellini (1987) and Maggi and Rodriguez-Clare (1998, 2007).

[7] The paper prepared for the Sub-regional Workshop on Accession to the WTO—Economies in Transition, held in Tashkent on 25–27 July 2001. With some revisions, it is also reprinted in the United Nations (2001).

the period from 1998 to 1999, six meetings of the Working Party and eight series of bilateral market access negotiations were conducted. At its inception, the Working Party was chaired by Eveline Herfkens from Netherland, a former Executive Director of the World Bank. During market access negotiations, Georgia's policy-makers were conscious of the role of the WTO accession in consolidating preceding domestic efforts, precisely in line with the commitment theory prescription. The memoirs co-authored by Amiran Kavadze, Deputy Foreign Minister and former Permanent Representative in Geneva; Michael Ukleba, former Minister of State Property Management; and Valerian Katamadze, Senior Councilor of the Permanent Mission[8] echo its logic of tying hands of the government against future policy reverse:

> Although the trade regimes in acceding countries vary considerably, many have established regimes with relatively low tariffs and no significant formal non-tariff barriers. For these countries, membership provides the opportunity to lock in these regimes by assuming legally binding obligations regarding tariff levels. This not only permits them to enjoy the benefits of liberal trade but also gives them a first line of defense [sic] against the domestic protectionist pressures that are present in all market economies. (Kavadze et al., 2003, p. 38)

Recognizing that the lower the tariff, the larger the welfare gains to the country itself, they were conscious of the merit of not only tariff binding but also its depth. Unlike many other RAMs that bound their tariffs only within the level of their pre-accession applied rate, on simple average, Georgia's commitment on final bound rate went further beyond the pre-accession applied rate. Accordingly, they dismissed the "minimal liberalization" strategy for WTO accession:

> There are significant dangers to a "minimum liberalization" accession strategy. Individual countries, especially small developing economies, have little leverage in market access negotiations, and so the potential benefits they may be able to obtain through such strategy may be very small. At the same time, maintaining protection through relatively high tariffs and protected agriculture and services sectors imposes costs on the applicants' own economies: they forgo the benefits of a more liberal trade regime, which, in the first instance, accrue to the country itself. If the countries bind tariffs at

[8] Designations of authors are those presented in the publication as of 2003.

levels higher than those applied and assume few commitments regarding agriculture and services (both of which are possible under WTO rules), they are subject to another risk: they create an opening for domestic interest to exert political pressure for additional protection in the future … Even recognizing political difficulties involved, a strong argument can nonetheless be made that if developing countries and transition economies currently applying for WTO accession adopt a liberal trade strategy at entry, they will maximize the benefits and opportunity for integration in the international community that WTO membership offers and will accede more quickly, as well. (Kavadze et al., 2003, pp. 42–43)

However, avoidance of the minimum liberalization strategy did not mean immediate removal of all remaining tariffs. At this stage prior to WTO accession, what Georgia was pursuing was a relatively liberal trade policy, rather than nearly complete free trade.[9] The government was aware of the merit of complete removal of protection on the microeconomic grounds,[10] but was also pragmatic in securing fiscal revenues from trade-related taxes:

Zero-rated customs tariff on imports would not be justified from the fiscal problems perspective. We would then lose a certain part of budgetary revenues which otherwise should grow as the Customs Service improves enforcement… As shown by international practice, the best system of import tariffs comprise a uniform tariff applied to imported goods across the board, which should not be excessively high. (Papava & Beridze, 1997, pp. 72–73)

The country's Memorandum of Foreign Trade Regime states clearly "*Georgia would reserve the right to impose customs duties in the future, in full consistency with its concessions and commitments as a Member of the WTO*" (WTO, 1997, p. 1), implying its intention to retain some room

[9] Examples of economies that pursue nearly or completely free trade include Hong Kong and Singapore, whose simple average applied tariff rate was 0.0% as of 2017. Data was retrieved from trade profiles of the WTO Web site: https://www.wto.org/english/res_e/statis_e/tariff_profiles_list_e.htm.

[10] Papava and Beridze (1997, p. 70) wrote "*(T)he economic theory suggests that the best trade policy for the improvement of a country's competitiveness, is to have zero – rate customs tariffs on imports and exempt exports from all taxes, and to eliminate quotas and minimize restrictions and licenses of exports and imports. Only then can the domestic become part and parcel of international markets.*"

for future protection from the beginning of negotiations. Accordingly, while maintaining the overall liberal position, negotiators were still cautious against making great leap in the request and offer process of bilateral market access negotiations:

> Georgia took a fairly tough line negotiating tariffs, and was generally successful in maintaining tariffs in areas of particular interest. This was facilitated by the fact that Georgia applied a uniform tariff of 12% to most of goods at the start of the negotiations, and could thus claim to have already established a generally low-tariff policy… In general, the tariff negotiations proceeded by the presentation of "request list" by the negotiating partners, to which Georgia would then respond, usually by making a few insignificant concessions and then reiterating its positions that it had already cut tariffs to low levels, and could not do more. (Kavadze et al., 2003, pp. 145–146)

The final tariff schedule agreed as terms of WTO accession was designed to reduce the tariff rate broadly on average, but allowed for the possibility of future increase for a limited number of tariff lines in sectors with domestic production capacity, to a level up to 30%.[11] Specifically, the tariff for sensitive agricultural products was bound at 16.5% (an initial bound rate) and 15.5% (a final bound rate at the end of the transition period), and tariffs for traditional Georgian products, including some foods and beverages, were bound at 25–30%. The bound rates for cement, bricks, footwear, and some other light industry products were set at 15–20%.

Still, Georgia's accession commitments were quite liberal in many respects and, as assumed in Hypothesis 1, the country successfully utilized the WTO membership process to catalyze and consolidate its domestic reforms. Apart from the low level of the final bound tariff rates (7.4% overall on simple average, comprising 13.1% for agriculture and 6.5% for NAMA) and 100% coverage of tariff bindings for trade in

[11] Market access negotiations for WTO accession take on bargaining of tariff rates on specific products of interest to each trading partner. As such, it was probably difficult to maintain a single uniformed rate across the board and, partly for this reason and due to domestic sensitivity, the simple tariff structure that the country had introduced in the pre-accession phase had to be compromised. See Kavadze et al. (2003) for details on bilateral market access negotiations.

goods, the number of service sectors with the General Agreement on Trade in Services (GATS) commitment counted as many as 125 (out of the total number of subsectors in the order of 160).[12] Following precedents of other RAMs, the country also committed not to resort to anti-dumping, countervailing, or safeguard measures in the absence of the WTO-consistent domestic legislations. Georgia did not even request a developing country status (Kavadze et al., 2003), practically giving up the flexibility privileges that could be accorded to poor countries.

One important point to take note is that, at this stage, Georgia's liberal position in accession negotiations was not just a reflection of an autonomous decision of reformers within the government alone. For one thing, Georgia's post-Soviet reform since independence had been pursued with support by the IMF and the World Bank, and these multilateral institutions also preferred liberal trade policy as a matter of principle (In particular, IMF's Enhanced Structural Adjustment Facility for 1997–1999 required a 5% tariff for a limited number of raw materials and intermediate goods while maintaining 12% uniformly for all other goods.[13]). The Georgian delegation was aware of the prevailing practice that acceding countries start bilateral negotiations processes with an initial offer of somewhat higher tariff rates than the applied ones,[14] but such an approach did not easily get through opposition of IFIs and like-minded reformers within the government. A memoir written by policy-makers describes the government's internal policy debate as follows:

> Interministerial Commission in close cooperation with relevant ministries and organizations, including private sector representatives, had started the active preparations for bilateral market access negotiations with WTO member countries, thus drafting the initial offers on goods and services based on expert analysis provided by appropriate Georgian institutions. However, strong resistance had emerged from high level officials in Georgian administration, who were against increase in customs tariffs

[12] Adlung and Roy (2005a) of the WTO secretariat report that, as of March 2005, the average numbers of subsectors committed by LDCs, developing and transition countries, developed countries, and RAMs were 24, 53, 106, and 103 (out of the total of approximately 160), respectively. The average for all members was 52. See also Adlung and Roy (2005b).

[13] IMF (1997).

[14] Report on the Observation Mission of the Georgian Delegation to the WTO Headquarters, November 1996 (Kavadze et al., 2003, p. 409).

> when preparing the initial offers on goods. The rationale for this resistance was whether international financial institutions would not allow Georgia to make any tariff increases. (Kavadze et al., 2003, p. 53)

As expected, the tariff level for the initial offer for WTO accession soon became a contentious issue between the IFIs' Joint Mission[15] and the government's Interministerial Commission on Georgia's Accession to the WTO.[16] The opinion of the IMF on this matter is stated in its staff paper on Georgia's recent economic development and selected issues of the day:

> Georgia, like other WTO members, would be expected to accept binding limits on tariff rates. Although Georgia's low tariff rates (5 and 12 percent) imply that setting of binding rates is not likely to become a major issue, it would be still important for Georgia to accept low binding rates so as to prevent the current tariff rates against political pressures to increase them in the future. (IMF, 1998, p. 56)

Likewise, the World Bank advised to make tariff rates as uniform as possible, and generally low across the board—not higher than 12%, including 0% for some. At the special meeting with IFIs, the government side argued for the prerogative of setting the bound rate above the currently applied level, in case where needs to resort to protection arise in the future, while maintaining that the government would not necessarily take such an action. After prolonged discussions, both sides reached a compromise of an initial tariff binding offer at 17% for industrial products and 25% for agriculture.

Through bilateral market access negotiations, incumbent WTO members also played roles in further reducing the prospective bound rate. Tamara Beruchashvili recalls, for instance, that the EU took a position

[15] Shadman Valavi, the IMF coordinator for Georgia, led the Joint Mission with Cyril Muller, a trade expert of the World Bank.

[16] The Interministerial WTO Commission was established on the basis of a special Presidential Decree, issued in July 1996 for the purpose of coordinating interagency works and conducting accession negotiations. Michael Ukleba, First Deputy Minister of Foreign Affairs, Nugzar Duchidze, Deputy Minister of Foreign Economic Relations and Trade, and Amiran Kavadze, Director of International Economic Relations Department of the Ministry of Foreign Affairs were appointed as Chairman, Vice-Chairman, and Secretary, respectively.

that anything over 15% should be treated as a "tariff peak" that would require justification and sought expansion of the sectorial initiative of zero import duties. It was also of a view that protection of sensitive sectors should be addressed only through transition periods but not through high tariffs. Japan sought elimination of tariffs on information technology products and pharmaceuticals (Beruchashvili, 2001). Toward the end of the accession process, the United States insisted on tariff reduction in whiskey, and that induced the EU to argue for equivalent reductions on all other spirits of its export interests. Overall, nonetheless, broadly liberal orientation of Georgia's unilateral trade policy and accommodating stance from the beginning, as supported by IFIs' guidance, ensured smooth market access negotiations for WTO accession. According to the statement made by Michael Ukleba at the second Working Party meeting on 13 October 1998, as early as that stage, the Georgian delegation had revised the negotiated tariff schedule offer downwards to reach 9.4% on trade-weighted average (Kavadze et al., 2003).

In 1999, moves toward finalization of the accession negotiations were also stepped up by the Georgian government's desire to bring the accession package to the parliament for domestic ratification before it would adjourn for the fall election. With some delay, the negotiations were wrapped up at the last Working Party meeting on 28 July, and the WTO General Council approved terms of accession on 6 October. The parliament approved the Protocol of Accession after lengthy and heavy hearing on 20 April 2000, and Georgia became the 137th member of the WTO on 14 June 2000, in about four years from its membership application. Mike Moore, then Director-General of the WTO commended this achievement in his remark: "*I congratulate Georgia on its swift accession and the comprehensive commitments it has taken on. This accession is particularly noteworthy given Georgia's remarkable transition to a market economy.*"[17] As he observed, Georgia's accession was conducted as part of the country's own unilateral reforms aimed at transition to a market economy and was completed relatively quickly.

It should be noted that the two multilateral schemes of trade liberalization Georgia actively utilized in the late 1990s through the early 2000s, namely WTO accession and IFIs' policy-based lending, shared

[17] Cited in the WTO press release "Georgia joins the WTO," on 14 June 2000. See the WTO Web site: http://www.wto.org/english/news_e/pres00_e/pr182_e.htm.

one common feature (albeit many differences). Both commitments for WTO accession and conditionality under IFI's adjustment program address the client country's own domestic reforms, whereby the role of the respective multilateral institutions (IMF, World Bank, and WTO) is to support unilateral liberalization (rather than reciprocal market opening by other countries). Georgia's objective was essentially domestic reforms, and the government managed to make extensive market access commitments with support by these multilateral institutions. Georgia's behavior validates Hypothesis 1, with regard to WTO accession.

2.3 Setback at the Post-accession Reforms and Early Days of the Doha Round

2.3.1 Restrictive Measures of 2002

Once stabilization was achieved in the late 1990s, the momentum for domestic reforms was phased out for a short period of time.[18] The government became increasingly incapable of resisting pressure from domestic vested interests (WTO, 2010a). As Georgia's terms of WTO accession left bound tariff rates for some products above the applied level, the government was soon tempted to resort to tariff increase within these allowances. Whereas this type of protection within tariff water was permissible at the WTO on legal grounds, its legitimacy was questionable in the eyes of IFIs on economic grounds. As was the case for the initial tariff offer at the accession negotiations, the IMF cautioned against the government's move toward protectionism. Beruchashvili recalls:

> Among the obligations undertaken under WTO the most important one are [sic] the tariff changes as a result of agreed "bound tariff" schedules during the accession process. As mentioned before, Georgia's "bound

[18]Vladimir Papava, former Minister of Economy (1994–2000) wrote: "*Georgia's economic development from 1991 until the revolution, which was characterized by some successes but also several significant mistakes,... can be thought of in three phases: the years of disregarding economics (1991–94), then consistent reforms (1994–98), followed by the rise of corruption (1999–2003)*" (Papava, 2006, p. 658). The World Bank also noted deterioration of the governance conditions toward 2003, as follows: "*Georgia had an increasingly weak governance framework, corruption was rampant, selective reform efforts were not being sustained, and the country was drifting rapidly toward 'failed state' status. These conditions created a fertile environment for the peaceful Rose Revolution in late2003*" (World Bank, 2009, p. 15).

> tariffs" cover a broad range of commodities and allow the possibility of tariff growth on a number of products. Unfortunately, the implementation of such possibility encountered rather strong resistance from the International Monetary Fund (IMF). The IMF's position is based on the consideration that any increase of applied tariffs (from current 0; 5 and 12 per cent) due to the weak customs administration is not desirable. (Beruchashvili, 2001, p. 39)

On 6 December 2002, however, the Law on Customs Tariffs and Duties was amended for alignment of tariff lines with the WTO accession commitments. This amendment raised the number of tariff bands from three to 22 and their maximum tariff from 12 to 30%, for implementation from 11 January 2003. Under the revised scheme, agricultural products and processed food, mineral water, tobacco products, masonry stone and cement received higher protection by tariff rates between 20 and 30%, while tariff rates on the majority of imported goods were reduced as per the sectoral initiative of the accession package (the left columns in Table 2).

The IFIs were not pleased with this move of complicating the tariff schedule.[19] The report by IMF's Article IV Consultation mission completed on 7 July 2003 reads:

> These measures reduced the simple average tariff from 10.9 percent to 8.2 percent, but increased weighted-average tariff from 10.3 percent to 11.3 percent and the standard deviation from 3.3 to 5.6... Fund and Bank staff encouraged the authorities to reverse these protectionist measures, which were spearheaded by interest groups. More generally, ... staff proposed a shift to a low uniform import tariff, which would significantly reduce distortions and rent-seeking opportunities, while providing ample scope for curbing smuggling and raising collections... Staff encouraged them to finalize their trade liberalization strategy by year's end, so that it could become an important element of a successor Fund-supported economic program. (IMF, 2003, pp. 20–21)

[19] According to Vladimer Papava, former Minister of Economy, due to deterioration of fiscal conditions, the IMF suspended its financing in 2002 and other development partners followed the suit. The new government secured renewal of the Fund program by 2004 (Papava, 2006).

Table 2 Georgia—import tariff bands

2003		*2005*		*2009*	
Tariff rate (%)	*No. of lines*	*Tariff rate (%)*	*No. of lines*	*Tariff rate (%)*	*No. of lines*
Duty-free	668	Duty-free	2757	Duty-free	9346
2	753	4	248	5	63
3	22	5	1828	12	1303
4	1791	6	613		
5	1212	7	1		
7	433	8	415		
8	1048	10	261		
9	364	12	3741		
10	228	14	6		
12	3700	15	110		
13	80	16	6		
14	43	17	26		
15	110	18	39		
16	6	20	149		
17	26	25	86		
18	39	30	80		
20	105				
22	25				
24	19				
25	20				
27	66				
30	81				
Total	10,839		10,366		10,712

Source World Bank (2003) and WTO (2010a)

The World Bank also expressed similar concerns. Its report of the diagnostic trade integration study presented in Tbilisi on 29 September 2003 says:

> Although the new schedule is within the bounds agreed with the WTO upon accession, it is a set back from the previous, simpler schedule. The new schedule seems to have no other purpose than to serve the interests of groups lobbying for increased protection. (World Bank, 2003, p. 28)

Possible increase of dispersion in the tariff schedule may potentially bring about distortion of domestic resource allocation and higher effective protection. At the same time, the IFIs were also concerned that more complex tariff structure would give higher discretion to customs officers and may invite corruption at the border. By then, administrative corruption had become a serious issue in Georgia. Bribes were required wherever Georgian citizens and businesses had to interact with the public authority—dealing with traffic police, application for passport or drivers licenses, property registration, starting businesses, building home, paying taxes, and entrance to the university. The customs regime was not an exception, and the new tariff policy created a vicious environment where customs officials could further abuse their power and extract bribes, that would deter smooth flow of cross-border trade and revenues. In fact, customs revenues of Georgia accounted for less than 1% of GDP, recording the lowest level in the region (World Bank, 2012).

However, the overall impacts of this setback of 2002–2003 on the average tariff rates were relatively small. It should be noted that the policy reverse took place only as part of implementation of the WTO accession commitments, and the government was fully aware of what could be accommodated within multilateral tariff binding that had already been in place by then. Even in this period, the simple average tariff rate had declined, as the IMF acknowledged, while the trade-weighted average increased slightly. From the medium-term perspective, the incident did not substantially affect the downward trend of the tariff level, and it was hardly a complete turn-around of Georgia's generally liberal trade policy. Considering the fact that the state of governance significantly deteriorated in this period, it should be noteworthy that the soundness of trade policy was not completely compromised by introduction of more profound protectionist measures. Disciplines the government had imposed on itself earlier as WTO accession commitments seem to have worked effectively to prevent more concrete reversals of its trade liberalization, just as the policy-makers had originally envisioned.

2.4 *Doha Round Negotiations as a Recently Acceded Member*

Whereas Georgia effectively used the multilateral trading system to consolidate its domestic reform through accession, it ceased to do so once it joined the WTO. To the contrary, Georgia's position in the initial phase of the Doha Round was defensive from the outset. In the early days of the Doha Round, it was a coalition of relatively small transition economies from Europe and Central Asia that played a prominent role as a RAMs group (larger economies like China and Chinese Taipei were yet to join the WTO after the Doha Ministerial Conference), and Georgia took lead in coordinating positions of these newly acceded transition economies. On the eve of the Doha Ministerial Conference, Georgia and Lithuania delegations prepared a negotiating proposal on behalf of transition economies, and, in Qatar, Georgia further led the group of newly acceded countries in consolidating their position. Delegations of transition economies argued that: (i) in the course of the negotiations, measures already taken by them should be fully recognized; (ii) low tariffs should be exempted from further reduction; and (iii) negotiations should address non-tariff barriers. As a result, their call for special recognition as RAMs got reflected in paragraph 9 of the Doha Ministerial Declaration (see Chapter 2). Aside from coordinating the position of newly acceded transition economies, Georgia also called for special treatment as a RAM on its own behalf. At the Doha Ministerial Conference in 2001, Tamar Beruchashvili made the following statement:

> I would like to express the concerns of Georgia, as a newly acceded country, regarding new negotiations commitments and their interaction with the commitments undertaken just recently during the accession process. It should be a well-known fact that newly acceded countries have made really substantive market access commitments, sometimes going far beyond those made during the Uruguay Round. (WTO, 2001, p. 1)

Georgia's defensive position was particularly acute in the area of agriculture. The statement further reads:

> Georgia, being committed to comprehensive negotiations in the sphere of agriculture, would seek the extension of the special and differential treatment for the countries with economies in transition as well, and its appropriate reflection in the Ministerial Declaration. This alongside with the developing countries would enable the countries with low income and at the same time being in the transition stage, to take account of their real transformation and development needs. We do believe that small vulnerable countries in transition should be an integral part of the elements of negotiations in this field. (WTO, 2001, pp. 1–2)

During the Soviet era, Georgia was a major agricultural and food producer, accounting for over 10% of intra-Union trade in agriculture, and exporting twice as much as its imports in the sector. Back then, Georgia's agriculture production took the form of large-scale plantation of basic crops for consumption and industry use. After the collapse of the Communist regime, the land reform program of 1999 dissolved the large collective farms into over one million small farmers, with an average land size of less than one hectare. This transformation from large collective to less efficient small subsistence farming led to a decline of agricultural production and exports. The country soon became a net importer of foods and beverages by the mid-1990s. The difficulty of transition in agriculture underlay Georgia's specifically defensive position in this sector.

Georgia retained these defensive positions throughout the early phase of the Doha Round, as further elaborated in Beruchashvili's statement at the Cancún Ministerial Conference in 2003:

> I want to stress that Georgia as a small, low-income economy facing all challenges of transition is strongly in favour of progressive, balanced and equitable liberalization and consider it as a key principle for globalization; however we have a number of concerns to highlight… I would like to remind the Members that in Doha our Ministers have unanimously recognized the extensive market access commitments undertaken by recently acceded countries that often go far beyond those negotiated during the Uruguay Round… Therefore, any measure towards further tariff liberalization, which represent only means to protect our domestic producers, could harmfully affect our economy, particularly agriculture. We continue to express our strong expectation that these concerns would be adequately reflected in the new text of framework for modalities… Georgia is actively involved in tariff negotiations for non-agricultural products… We are glad that some of the Members shared our approach that the countries which have already "paid" should not be taxed again, or should pay less, and therefore the "Swiss formula" of tariff reduction is more fair than a formula independent from initial tariff rate. (WTO, 2003, pp. 1–2)

The significance of this position for the Doha Round market access negotiations is that transition was highlighted as a reason for disengagement from the multilateral liberalization. Previously for accession, the adjustment problem for transition to a market economy was the very reason for the government's engagement in the multilateral process (as per the commitment theory), but the logic was completely reversed for the Doha Round. Clearly, the government was no longer expecting the same role of catalyzing domestic reforms from the WTO. Interestingly, the last part of Beruchashvili's statement quoted above shows that Georgia itself was still involved in the DDA market access negotiations and not opposing the use of the Swiss formula. Thus, the government appeared to have been ready to accept modest liberalization commitment at this early stage of the Doha Round. Nonetheless, it was a far cry from the much more positive stance it had shown during the earlier accession negotiations.

In particular, the approach of treating liberalization commitments as “payment” or “tax,” rather than the source of economic benefits, is typical of “GATT-think” unique to reciprocal negotiations. Recall this notion comprises three simple principles: Firstly, exports are good; secondly, imports are bad; and thirdly, an increase in imports is good only if exports increase equally.[20] The juggernaut theory further says a country’s pursuit of GATT-think—export market access in particular—is driven by domestic business interests, and economies increasingly represented by exporters would tend to prefer reciprocal trade negotiations to open trading partners’ markets and, to that end, their own.[21] In this reciprocal setting, existence of substantive export interests holds the key for multilateral tariff cuts.

In the case of Georgia, however, presence of export sectors did not quite stand out. In the period of 2002–2008 (when the DDA market access negotiations were still active), Georgia recorded persistent trade deficit, and its share even increased over time to reach 30% of GDP by 2008. The share of exports stood constantly at around 20% of GDP, while that of imports grew to roughly a half of the entire economy (Table 3).

Accordingly, there is no indication that private businesses tried to lobby the government actively for the Doha Round and, in the absence of substantive export interests, the government did not have to entertain the first and third principles of GATT-think. In fact, no formal statement by the government explicitly referred to pursuit of export interests in the course of the DDA negotiations. Absence of an export orientation in the Georgian economy and irrelevance of the first and third principles of GATT-think leaves only its second principle—imports are bad—as a

[20] Krugman (1991). The purpose of this research is not to establish that GATT-think or reciprocity serves the economic interests of WTO members. Krugman himself says that GATT-think is economic nonsense, while it well suited the political reality. See Chapter 1.

[21] Richard Baldwin (2006, 2012).

Table 3 Georgia—trade performance

	2002	*2003*	*2004*	*2005*	*2006*	*2007*	*2008*
Net merchandise trade (% of GDP)	−14.4	−16.0	−17.9	−18.9	−26.0	−28.5	−30.0
Merchandise exports (% of GDP)	17.8	20.8	21.3	23.0	21.5	20.5	19.0
Merchandise imports (% of GDP)	32.1	36.8	39.2	41.9	47.5	49.0	48.9
Merchandise exports Growth (%)	21.6	37.7	31.5	34.8	13.2	25.3	16.3
Merchandise imports growth (%)	4.5	34.4	36.7	33.8	37.2	35.2	25.6

Source WTO (2010a)

relevant code of conduct. In line with this presumption, the government only tried to defend its tariff protection that had remained after WTO accession, but it was not proactively engaged in the reciprocal liberalization process of the Doha Round. Disengagement from the reciprocal market access negotiations is exactly what Hypothesis 2-a predicted, for an economy that lacks export orientation.

Apart from being a non-export-oriented economy, Georgia was also a small economy. The terms of trade externality theory says that large economies seek coordinated tariff cuts through the multilateral trading system, to avoid adverse effects of price manipulation by their unilateral trade policies.[22] With the small import market size of US$6.1 billion, accounting for only 0.04% of the global share (see Table 10, Chapter 2), however, the theoretical concern over terms of trade was never relevant to Georgia. Actually, trade negotiators were not even conscious about the terms of trade consideration. Available data shows that its terms of trade have generally been improving, regardless of tariff levels of its own and the rest of the world (Table 4), and the apparent absence of terms of trade concern seems to be empirically warranted. Small economies could not manipulate international prices of traded goods in the first place and, in line with the prediction of Hypothesis 2-b, Georgia had no reason to take part in the reciprocal negotiations of the Doha Round for containment of the terms of trade externality.

[22] Bagwell and Staiger (1999, 2002).

Table 4 Georgia—reciprocity and terms of trade

	2002	*2003*	*2004*	*2005*	*2006*	*2007*	*2008*
Applied tariff rate (incl. preferences)							
Simple average	9.93	7.78	7.52	–	8.45	1.39	1.44
Trade-weighted averages	10.74	9.52	9.54	–	4.32	1.16	1.24
Applied ROW tariff rate (incl. preferences)							
Simple average	8.14	6.22	7.49	7.00	4.43	9.71	9.49
Trade-weighted averages	5.18	2.17	2.11	3.57	0.43	0.83	0.58
Net barter terms of trade index (2000 = 100)	100.91	102.07	109.38	104.76	113.94	117.08	126.16

Note ROW = rest of the world. The net barter terms of trade index is the percentage ratio of unit export value indexes to unit import value indexes, measured against the base year of 2000

Source World Trade Indicators 2009/2010 of the World Bank Web site: http://info.worldbank.org/etools/wti/2a1.asp; World Bank Open Data retrieved from the World Bank Web site: http://data.worldbank.org/

3 Rose Revolution and Departure from the WTO Track

3.1 Resurgence of Domestic Reforms After the Rose Revolution

After a short period of stagnation, the domestic reforms of Georgia recovered the momentum from late 2003. By then, dissatisfaction with prevalent corruption, dysfunctional public services, and widespread poverty was paramount among Georgian citizens. In November 2003, tens of thousands of protesters, holding roses in their hands, went on three weeks of massive demonstrations against the government of the day and gathered in front of the parliament building in Tbilisi, the country's capital. Led by Mikhail Saakashvili, the US-educated young former Justice Minister, the street protesters criticized the results of the flawed parliamentary election and demanded resignation of President Eduard Shevardnadze, who had come from the Soviet Communist Party and ruled Georgia for over 30 years. The protesters handed roses to surrounding police and peacefully took over the parliament. Waving the rose at the parliament building, Saakashvili shouted "resign" to Shevardnadze in his face. Escorted by his bodyguard, Shevardnadze rushed out of the site. This dramatic incident, known as the Rose Revolution, ousted Shevardnadze from power. Afterward, Saakashvili was elected as the new president in January 2004, and his National

Movement-Democratic Front won the parliamentary election in March 2004. The transfer of power was completed smoothly, with no attempt of resistance from Shevardnadze's side. In fact, even the outgoing president voted for the opposition (King, 2004; MacFarlane, 2004; Papava, 2006; Saakashvili, 2004).[23]

Following the revolution, the new government pursued two interrelated objectives. One was to eradicate administrative corruption, and the other was to establish a further competitive business environment in Georgia so as to become a regional hub for trade and investment as an industrialized economy. It was envisaged that both could be achieved by scaling back state interventions and bringing in market disciplines to the economy, more concretely than in the past. Like the earlier efforts of post-Soviet transition, the overall direction of the reform was that of market orientation but, combined with the objective of ruling out corrupt state interventions, it entailed much stronger laissez-faire philosophy. Saakashvili's article of the day, titled "*Fulfilling the promise of the Rose Revolution Georgia's progress*" even refers to Milton Friedman, well illustrating the ideological orientation of the post-revolution government:

> We must now fulfill [sic] Georgia's potential. We will continue the fight against corruption... And, we will create the conditions for economic prosperity... Economically, we have initiated a privatization effort that would make Milton Friedman proud, selling everything the government had no business owning in the first place... (Saakashvili, 2004)

Since 2004, a wide range of structural reform measures were taken to foster private investment and rule out the opportunities for rent-seeking and corruption, and efforts for transition to a market economy were further accelerated. These comprised market deregulation, privatization of state assets, simplification of taxation, trade liberalization, and other forms of reducing bureaucratic barriers. The reform was most visible in the area of business licensing, whose number was reduced from 950 to 150. Mandatory industrial standardization was replaced by voluntary standards, further curtailing the scope for discretion of the state. Many government officials and civil servants from the old Soviet communist era were replaced

[23] See also "How the Rose Revolution happened," posted on the BBC Web site: http://news.bbc.co.uk/1/hi/4532539.stm.

by the younger generation exposed to the market economy. Saakashvili recalls "*(w)e cannot afford not to have liberal economics because that's our principal access*" (Brookings Institution, 2011, p. 21).[24]

The impact of reforms was clearly visible. Georgia steadily climbed up the rankings in the World Bank's Doing Business reports and was recorded as the global top reformer among all economies covered (Table 8 in Chapter 2).[25] Table 5 provides further details with breakdown of scores in various fields. There appears to be a tendency that the country scored higher in the areas that require less interventions by the state (e.g., starting businesses and licensing), rather than enhancement of its capacity (e.g., resolving insolvency and enforcing contracts). According to the 2009 enterprise survey by the World Bank Group, senior managers of Georgian firms spent only 2% of their time to deal with the government bureaucracy, recording lowest among countries of Eastern Europe and Central Asia (World Bank Group, 2009).

Ultimately, the government's liberal policy has culminated in the Economic Liberty Act, which stipulates the long-term irreversibility of the reforms undertaken since the Rose Revolution. In the words of Prime Minister Nika Gilauri, "*(t)he Economic Liberty Act seeks to limit the discretion of the executive branch of government and ensures that the government remains small and limited and taxes remain (other than through the sovereign will of the people) low and flat.*"[26] The law was adopted by the parliament in 2011.

[24] Saakashvili's speech on "From Popular Revolutions to Effective Reforms: The Georgia Experience," at the Brooking Institution, Washington, DC on 17 March 2011.

[25] Whereas the government made concerted efforts to undertake broad-based structural reforms covered by the Doing Business report, its ranking does not necessarily reflect the quality of broader public policies in the areas left out from the survey, such as enhancement of export competitiveness. The World Bank's country economic memorandum for Georgia reads: "*(w)hile Georgia benefited from a productivity spurt that is usually observed in transition economies after broad-based market reforms are launched, productivity improved primarily in the nontradable sectors, while export sophistication and quality stagnated*" (World Bank, 2013, p. xi). This observation is consistent with the view presented in this chapter, that the government prioritized import liberalization but not export promotion.

[26] Cited in news release by the Government of Georgia (2011) titled "Georgia Adopts the Economic Liberty Act," on 11 July, posted on its Web site: http://www.government.gov.ge.

Table 5 Ease of doing business in Georgia

	2005	*2006*	*2007*	*2008*	*2009*
Overall	48.44	61.48	65.83	70.41	73.72
Starting a business	79.07	84.41	89.42	95.40	95.44
Dealing with construction permits	59.29	79.67	85.37	85.46	91.44
Registering property	82.16	81.54	86.00	96.40	96.40
Getting credit	31.25	50.00	56.25	75.00	75.00
Protecting investors	40.00	40.00	60.00	60.00	60.00
Paying taxes	37.46	57.96	59.60	59.60	66.71
Trading across borders	25.69	63.84	64.88	65.47	82.70
Enforcing contracts	59.08	66.83	66.83	66.83	66.83
Resolving insolvency	22.01	29.11	24.16	29.56	29.56

Note 100 represent the highest performance observed across all countries measured
Source Doing Business Web site: http://www.doingbusiness.org/

As an integral part of the overall economic policy after the Rose Revolution, trade policy has also followed the enhanced liberal orientation, as summarized in the opening statement by the Georgia delegation at WTO's trade policy review meeting in Geneva in December 2009:

> Georgia's trade policy has to be viewed in the context of its economic policies. Our economic policies have been characterised by very active, simultaneous, and consequent efforts to reform the economy, create private sector as the driving force of economic growth, liberalise the economic environment, and increase trade and investment... Trade liberalization has been one of the main priorities of our economic reforms. We have been trying to introduce reforms that were aimed at the creation of Georgia's trade and transit hub, especially against the background that our country is located in the corridor that is the shortest route from China to Europe. Therefore facilitation of trade and investment has been the key objective of our reforms. (WTO, 2009, p. 4)

In the area of market access for trade in goods, the first move in this direction was to accept IMF's advice to rationalize the tariff regime. As agreed with the government, reversal of earlier changes in import tariffs (by end-December 2004) became part of the 2004 structural conditionality for the three-year arrangement under the Poverty Reduction and Growth Facility (IMF, 2004b). Its Memorandum of Economic and Financial Policies for 2004, attached to the letter of intent from President Saakashvili and Prime Minister Zurab Zhvania to the IMF Acting Managing Director Anne Kruger, reads:

> Georgia will continue to maintain a liberal foreign trade regime… In keeping with Georgia's outward-looking growth strategy, we will phase out the protective measures introduced in late 2002, with a view to reducing the level and dispersion of import tariffs, thereby reducing rent-seeking opportunities, by end-2004… Given the anti-smuggling efforts mentioned earlier, we believe it should be possible to liberalize the trade regime while simultaneously raising duty collections, improving resource allocation, and reducing the anti-export bias of the trade regime. (IMF, 2004b, p. 68)

By 2005, the number of tariff bands was reduced initially from 22 to 16. At this stage, 2757 tariff lines out of 10,366 were duty-free, while the level of highest tariff rate remained unchanged at 30% (the center columns in Table 2).

3.2 *Disengagement from the DDA Negotiations as a Low-Income Economy in Transition*

After the Rose Revolution in 2003, there were focused discussions on the future direction of Georgia's trade policy within the government, reflecting the debate between the two groups of parliamentarians—those pushing for immediate further trade liberalization and the others who took a more cautious position. The latter was of a view that trade liberalization should be conducted primarily under the WTO auspices and withheld until the progress is made in the Doha Round. The decision-making of the Saakashvili administration was conducted by a small number of like-minded reformers and, under the presidential leadership, the cabinet members closely coordinated their works (World Bank, 2012). Whereas senior officials of the government's economic policy team had considered both arguments of the parliamentary debate on the direction of Georgia's trade policy (i.e., WTO vs. autonomous), they were in favor of straight pursuit of the liberal economic policy. Thus, the government decided to accelerate market opening autonomously outside of the WTO. Even if the WTO members were to agree on market access liberalization eventually, it was less likely that such an agreement would be substantial enough to achieve global free trade. At the same time, trade liberalization was a critical piece of the country's overall reform agenda, and the government could not afford delaying it to wait for the progress of the Doha Round.

This decision marked a clear turning point of Georgia's trade policy. Previously, trade liberalization was anchored to the WTO. The country used WTO accession as a device for catalyzing and consolidating its unilateral reform (and even the set back in 2002–2003 was carried out as implementation of the WTO accession commitment). In contrast, launch of autonomous liberalization by the Saakashvili administration was a departure from this WTO track. At the WTO's Hong Kong Ministerial Conference in December 2005, Irakli Chogovadze, Georgia's Minister of Economic Development stated:

> Georgia's reforms in the area of trade are in full harmony with principles based on which the WTO functions and the objectives that it pursues. But I have to emphasize that we are going much further than that. As far as market access is concerned, what we are doing in Georgia can be termed as "autonomous liberalization". This reform goes far beyond the alternatives discussed in the framework of WTO talks. Our aim is to create the most liberal trade regime in the region and reach a stage where we completely abolish import duties. Such an open and liberal trade policy will help Georgia to attract more foreign investment and to fully utilize its transit and trade potential as a country located at crossroads between Europe and Asia. (WTO, 2005c, p. 1)

Reciprocal trade negotiations of the Doha Round were not a suitable vehicle for supporting its unilateral liberalization in a straightforward manner. Reciprocity assumes that the member country liberalizes its trade only if trading partners agree to do the same, and such deals need to be negotiated multilaterally. Spending time and administrative resources in reciprocal negotiations would make sense only if a country is seeking to open its trading partner's market. However, if the government's sole objective is pursuit of its own economic welfare through unilateral market opening, as in the case of Georgia, such negotiations would be simply redundant. Instead, the obviously logical course of action is to move alone outside of the multilateral trading system. Thus, Georgia launched market opening autonomously in line with the prediction of Hypotheses 2-a and 2-b.

As the government switched to autonomous market opening, it practically abandoned the WTO as a venue for its own trade liberalization. Thus, even after the recovery of the domestic reform momentum following the Rose Revolution, the new government's liberal policy orientation did not have to be immediately passed on to the position of its Geneva delegation, and the latter carried forward the previous government's stance of defensive disengagement from the Doha Round, at least till mid-2005. Apart from being a member of the RAMs group, by then, Georgia had joined another coalition of low-income economies in transition comprising a sub-group of RAMs (Armenia, Georgia, Kyrgyz Republic, and Moldova). These former Soviet republics were all pursuing transition to market economies and bound their tariffs at the low level at the time of accession. As richer newly acceded transition economies (Bulgaria, Croatia, Estonia, Latvia, and Lithuania) joined the EU and left the RAMs group, these low-income economies that stayed on took on a common identity and formed a group of its own. They stressed their status as small and poor economies and associated adjustment problems for transition to a market economy. Led by Moldova, they sought treatments equivalent to those for LDCs and other vulnerable economies, implying possible exemption from making market access commitments during the Doha Round. Their negotiating proposal to the Committee on Agriculture Special Session dated 29 June 2005 reads:

> Armenia, Georgia, the Kyrgyz Republic and the Republic of Moldova, are particularly low-income countries in terms of their level of economic development and facing great difficulties in undergoing the transitional period. Moreover, they are in the middle of economic and institutional reform process under the terms of accession to the WTO… In this respect, we request the Special Session of the Committee on Agriculture to agree that all Members which are small low-income economies in transition which recently acceded to the WTO be granted the same flexibilities with regard to agriculture as have already been agreed for LDCs and other vulnerable developing countries. (WTO, 2005b, p. 4)

The group of low-income economies in transition called for the similar treatment also for NAMA negotiations, as stated in their negotiating proposal to the Negotiating Group on Market Access dated 6 July 2005:

> Simulation of the currently discussed formulas such as the Swiss formula and the so called "Girard" formula shows that Armenia, Georgia, Kyrgyz Republic and Republic of Moldova would have to make substantial additional tariff cuts with much lower final bound rates than the vast majority of developing country Members. That would cause even more serious adjustment costs to our vulnerable economies... In this respect, we request the Negotiating Group on Market Access to agree that our countries be granted the same flexibilities with regard to the non-agricultural market access as have already been agreed for LDCs and other vulnerable developing countries. (WTO, 2005a, p. 3).

As in Georgia's previous defensive statement, the adjustment problem for transition was highlighted as a reason for disengagement from multilateral liberalization (rather than the reason for engagement, as was the case for accession), implying no intention to use the WTO as an instrument for domestic reform. In particular, the negotiating proposal clearly dismissed the application of any formula-based tariff cuts to these countries. In this sense, the collective position of low-income economies in transition appeared to have become even more defensive than the earlier stance of Georgia alone. Yet, the seemingly paradoxical contrast between the liberal orientation in autonomous reforms at home and the defensive posture at the WTO was not something completely irreconcilable at this early stage of post-revolution reform. As of 2005, unilateral liberalization was still work in progress, and some segments of Georgia's domestic products were protected by relatively low tariffs (see Table 2). Thus, in the interim, autonomous liberalization had to be insulated from exposure to multilateral negotiations, so that the government can proceed with the reform where it can at its own discretion.

3.3 Toward Free Trade: Going Alone Further with Autonomous Liberalization

In accordance with its medium-term reform strategy for economic development,[27] the government of Georgia implemented further autonomous liberalization (WTO, 2009, p. 4) through unilateral tariff cuts and

[27] See Government's *Progress Report on Economic Development and Poverty Reduction Program*, incorporated by the IMF (2006) as Georgia's poverty reduction strategy paper progress report.

rationalization in 2006. The number of tariff bands was reduced from 16 to three (0, 5, and 12%), with the maximum rate having been reduced to 12% as was the case for pre-WTO accession tariff regime. Under this reform, most of tariff lines were designated for duty-free access, rather than at 12%. By 2009, 9346 tariff lines out of 10,712 were set for duty-free (the right columns in Table 2), and the average tariff rate had declined to about 1%, in both simple and trade-weighted terms. These measures were undertaken completely outside of the WTO (and were even beyond the initial IMF conditionality[28]).

Practically speaking, import duties were eliminated for most goods, especially in the industrial sector. Georgia also accepted the technical regulations of over 30 countries, above all members of the EU and the Organisation for Economic Co-operation and Development (OECD), easing flow of imports from these countries. In line with the liberal policy orientation, the Saakashvili administration made a conscious decision of not preparing legislations for anti-dumping and safeguard, so as to freeze use of trade remedies permanently.[29] For the liberal-minded government, cheap imports were a manifestation of market efficiency rather than dumping, and it believed that domestic industries should grow in the competitive environment rather than under the protection by the state.

3.4 *Draft 2008 Modalities of the Doha Development Agenda*

After the envisaged autonomous liberalization had been fully completed in 2006, there was a sign of change in Georgia's position at the Doha Round: from defensive disengagement to aloof disengagement. For the government pursuing autonomous liberalization, rather than cultivation of export markets, there was no need to stay actively engaged in the DDA market access negotiations. At the same time, once it

[28] The IMF and the World Bank were generally supportive of the reform initiatives taken by the Saakashvili administration and barely expressed critical views (Papava, 2009).

[29] Non-use of trade remedies in itself is not necessarily unusual. For instance, only 47 WTO members reported anti-dumping initiations and 42 took anti-dumping measures for a period from 1995 to 2012. In the same period, 48 WTO members reported safeguard initiation and 30 WTO members reported safeguard measures. In the case of Georgia, the strong liberal policy orientation of the post-revolution government underlay its stance on trade remedies.

thoroughly completed such autonomous liberalization, there was also no reason to vocally insist on defensiveness in an explicit manner, as the coalition of the low-income economies in transition had been doing. In fact, the coalition's self-portrayed image as poor and vulnerable countries could not be reconciled with Georgia's goal of becoming a lively investment hub as an industrialized country. The Georgian delegation increasingly felt uneasy about rhetorical positions taken by its fellow colleagues of the low-income economies in transition in their internal discussions, and later formally withdrew from the coalition.[30] From 2006 onwards, Georgia stopped signing up for joint statements submitted by this group at the Doha Round negotiations (WTO, 2006a, 2006b). The country still remained in the RAMs group, but became less active as its member. Ultimately, Georgia decided not to sign up for the RAMs group's joint negotiating proposals on NAMA and agriculture in 2007 (WTO, 2007a, 2007b).

In the draft December 2008 modalities for NAMA (WTO, 2008a), Georgia was still listed as one of the RAMs, but not as a low-income economy in transition or VRAM completely exempted from making market access commitment. This gives ambiguity on Georgia's status under the modalities. In terms of the country's global trade share, it could still be treated as an SVE if it so wishes, but Georgia was unwilling to accept labeling as a "vulnerable" economy. A straightforward interpretation would be that Georgia voluntarily accepted the formula with minimum flexibility for the RAMs (as was the case for China, Chinese Taipei, and Croatia). However, this interpretation should be understood in light of the fact that the country did not even claim a developing country status (that was a presumption for the RAMs group) at the time of accession, and it was not clear if, at least from the official record, Georgia was actually seeking any flexibility as a RAM any longer. In fact, while keeping silence to respect solidarity of the RAMs group, Georgia was ready to accept reduction of the bound tariff rate of industrial products down

[30]The WTO Web sites describe low-income economies in transition as a group comprising Armenia, Kyrgyz Republic, and Moldova, "*(s)eeking to secure the same treatment as least-developed countries. (Georgia formally withdrew, but in the agriculture draft the full list is: Albania, Armenia, Georgia, Kyrgyz Rep, Moldova)*" (http://www.wto.org/english/tratop_e/dda_e/negotiating_groups_e.htm, accessed on 28 January 2014).

to its applied level (i.e., close to zero) or even in accordance with the developed country formula—if the reciprocal market access negotiations would ever move to that direction. However, this quietly positive attitude was not to use the Doha Round as an instrument for trade liberalization proactively, as was previously the case for accession. Rather, it was aloof non-objection to reflecting part of autonomous liberalization already undertaken outside of the WTO. After nearly removing tariffs on industrial products, there was almost nothing left to either liberalize or protect at NAMA negotiations any longer. At the end of the day, however, the Doha Round got deadlocked after 2008, and the draft modalities never materialized.

Contrary to the NAMA negotiations, the draft December 2008 modalities paper for agricultural negotiations (WTO, 2008b) still listed Georgia as a low-income economy in transition. Unlike the industry sector, agriculture was partly left out from the scope of the government's aggressive reform initiatives after the Rose Revolution. The sector continuously comprised subsistence farming by small producers, and its productivity remained one-tenth of that of the rest of the economy. Subsequently in 2012, the government launched the agricultural reform (in the areas of irrigation and drainage systems, mechanization and farm input services, consultation and information centers, access to finance, food safety, and legislative changes), but it was only after long years of neglect. Unilateral liberalization continued, but not as ambitiously as in the industry sectors. As such, as of 2008, the government chose to retain the scope for modest protection, and the sector was carved out from Georgia's potential liberalization commitments in the Doha Round.

Albeit less aggressively than Georgia, other low-income economies in transition also proceeded with their autonomous liberalization. By 2008, their simple average MFN applied tariff rate all came down to a lower single-digit level, similar to the level of high-income economies. While Georgia opted to act mostly on its own and others retained the coalition, they all undertook further market opening unilaterally, beyond their WTO accession commitments and outside of the Doha Round. As the conventional trade theory states, autonomous market opening was simply in their own interest, and they were able to pursue liberalization without spending unnecessary administrative resources on reciprocal negotiations at the Doha Round. In other words, the post-accession reform was perceived to be none of WTO's business, and simply going ahead with autonomous liberalization was their best alternative to a negotiated agreement (BATNA). Still, Armenia, Kyrgyz Republic, and Moldova retained low levels of tariffs (respectively, 2.8, 4.6, and 4.4%), possibly out of domestic sensitivity, and maintained their defensive posture at the Doha Round negotiations to guard these remaining protection.[31] All of them ran current account deficit and lacked any strong export orientation. At the same time, they are all small economies, least likely in a position to manipulate terms of trade (see Tables 9 and 10, Chapter 2).

Performance of Georgia and other low-income economies in transition broadly validates Hypothesis 1, 2-a, and 2-b. All of them are reforming economies characterized by the absence of any strong export orientation and also by their small sizes. They made substantial market access commitments at the time of accession (Hypothesis 1), but later disengaged themselves from the reciprocal DDA market access negotiations and pursued autonomous trade liberalization (Hypotheses 2-a and 2-b). Their sole policy objective was domestic reform for transition to market economies, and WTO accession served as a right instrument to lock in their unilateral trade liberalization. However, the Doha Round was not perceived as the venue to pursue the same policy objective. One import caveat to Georgia's behavior is that the shift from pre-accession engagement to post-accession disengagement did not take a simple linear process. When there were still remaining tariffs, Georgia was presenting defensive postures in the early phase of the Doha Round. As its aggressive autonomous tariff cuts in the industrial sector were completed by 2006, however, the mode of disengagement from NAMA negotiations evolved from one of defensiveness to one of aloofness. On the other hand, Georgia still maintained the stance of defensive disengagement in agriculture, where pace of the reform has been relatively modest. So did other low-income economies in transition in the period toward conclusion of the draft 2008 modalities, in both NAMA and agriculture.

[31] In this interpretation of BATNA, low-income economies in transition disengaged themselves from the Doha Round not because these countries dismissed market opening but because they opted to pursue trade liberalization by their own way, as testified by their impressive record of autonomous reforms.

4 Further Theoretical Considerations

4.1 Domestic Contexts

The key objective of Georgia's trade policy has been unilateral liberalization, and the government effectively used the WTO accession commitment to lock in this domestic policy orientation, albeit leaving some loopholes for partial departure. In line with the commitment theory, policy-makers were conscious of the merits of tying their hands. However, once the mode of the WTO negotiations took the form of reciprocity at the Doha Round, Georgia started to disengage itself from the multilateral liberalization process, first defensively as a member of the RAMs group (and, later, in the low-income economies in transition coalition). As its reform was accelerated after the Rose Revolution, the government made a decision to act more autonomously outside of the WTO, and lost interests in the Doha Round.

Georgia's performance is in line with Hypotheses 1, 2-a, and 2-b, but what it implies is that the government did not have to rely on the external support by the WTO (while the country was still under the IMF program) to proceed with reforms in the post-accession period. Then, one natural question is how the government managed to pursue its policy of unilateral market opening forcefully in the domestic policy-making environment. Saakashvili recalls: "*(w)e're not constrained by dogma or dead weight of bureaucracies and powerful interest groups*"[32] (Brookings Institution, 2011, p. 5); but weren't there oppositions from domestic stakeholders? At the trade policy review meeting in December 2009, the Korean delegation made this particular inquiry. In answering, the Georgian delegation stated:

> After the "Rose Revolution", the main key to the success of Georgia in implementing reforms in a short time period was the strong will of Georgian population and Georgian Government to overcome the old system and strengthen corruption-free market economy… Despite the fact, that opposition from interest groups existed, strong political will and will of Georgian population helped Georgian Government to successfully implement reforms. During this period, Government maintained public support, as proved by last presidential and parliamentary elections. (WTO, 2010b, pp. 50–51)

[32] Saakashvili's speech on "From Popular Revolutions to Effective Reforms: The Georgia Experience," at the Brookings Institution, Washington, DC on 17 March 2011.

Performance of the economy after the Rose Revolution has been quite robust. Since 2003, the real GDP growth rate averaged at nearly 10%, before outbreak of the war with Russia and the global financial crisis in 2008–2009 (and somewhat moderated growth from 2010 onwards), and the economic policy of the government appeared extremely successful. At its inception, the government was strongly supported by the citizens of Georgia. President Saakashvili received more than 90% of votes, and his United National Movement party won about 68% of the parliament seats. The popularity of the Rose Revolution leader in the early days of his administration created an enabling environment to push through reforms. Among the domestic constituencies, the private business community in particular supported market-oriented reform and freer trade. A report titled "*Georgia's Long-Term Economic Development Concept*" by the Business Association of Georgia—a largest union representing large and medium-sized businesses—underlines importance of the competitive business environment guided by the principles of "small state" and "free market economy" as a prerequisite for development (see Box).

Box: Economic Declaration

1. Government ensures full protection of property rights;
2. Government guarantees the rule of law and independence of courts;
3. Government is guided by the principles of free market economy in taking economic decisions, even when it implements industrial policies;
4. Government strives to establish as competitive an environment as possible, within which only natural monopolies exist;
5. Government is guided by the principles of free market in tackling market failure, and it focuses on performing the function of a coordinator in this process;
6. Government is guided by the "principles of small state"; it strives to gradually reduce the number of regulations to the necessary minimum level and rejects excessive bureaucracy;
7. Government makes state investments in the private sector, only: a) with the purpose to deal with market failures; b) in projects that cannot be financed through the private sector; c) based on the free market principles; d) within the limited

timeframe; e) with terms and conditions that are clearer and declared in advance; f) after clear mechanism of withdrawal are in place;

8. Economic decisions made by the government are consistent, support stability and comply with the long-term decisions of the government and business sector;
9. Government maintains low-tax policy in the long-term perspectives;
10. Government ensures stable and predictable investment policies, steady investment terms and conditions, and consistency of decisions made, regardless of the election cycle (and of the election outcomes);
11. Government applies predictable, transparent and stable regulatory policies toward the fields that are subject to regulations and ensures that regulatory bodies operate free of political considerations and are highly proficient;
12. Government guarantees the freedom of business, separates it from politics and considers business the main source of creating jobs.

Source: Business Association of Georgia (2013, p. 6).

Through the privatization program of small and medium state-owned enterprises (SOEs) launched in 1993 and that of larger SOEs since 2004, the share of the public sector in total output had already declined to 10% and that of the total employment to 26% by 2008. SOEs that could oppose the market-oriented reform were no longer major players in Georgia's policy-making environment. Also, there were no large import-competing enterprises that the government had to protect. This policy-making environment provided a suitable ground for the government to pursue autonomous reforms. In fact, this is consistent with part of the juggernaut theory. The earlier reforms downsized the import-competing industries who would oppose further liberalization. However, in the absence of substantial export business interests, such liberalization did not have to take the form of reciprocal market opening through the Doha Round. Instead, the government just seized the enabling policy-making environment to proceed with autonomous liberalization in line with its reform agenda.

4.2 *Absence of Substantive Discrimination*

Unlike Hypotheses 1, 2-a, and 2-b on broad trade policy objectives, Hypothesis 3 (drawn upon the domino theory[33]) relates to more specific costs of previous non-membership in the form of discriminatory trade barriers. WTO accession would be an occasion to redress these disadvantages and, if these issues are still unresolved through membership, the country would try to address them continuously in the post-accession phase. In the case of Georgia, however, the country did not have to suffer from such costs even before WTO accession (Table 6). With regard to MFN access to trading partners' market, available data shows that there were no major discriminatory barriers against Georgia's exports both before and after WTO accession (except at the time of war with Russia in 2008). The simple average rest-of-the-world tariff (including preferences) for the 5-year period before WTO accession was 6.26%, much lower than those faced by the Europe and Central Asia region (8.29%) and the world as a whole (8.86%), while it slightly deteriorated later. On the trade-weighted term, tariffs (including preferences) faced by Georgian exports prior to WTO accession (5.89%) were only less than a half of the world average (14.22%), and the rate further declined to 1.35% by 2005–2008. The share of MFN duty-free exports was 35.06% in 1995–1999, prior to the WTO accession, again representing a more favorable condition than those for the region (28.12%) and the world as a whole (26.94%). The ratio increased further after WTO accession, nearing a half of the exports by 2005–2008. Throughout pre- and post-WTO accession periods, trade remedy initiations against Georgia's exports were almost none, and terms of WTO accession imposed no discriminatory clauses, such as NME and TPS provisions.[34] No official record indicates that coping with discrimination was the country's objective at the WTO.

The favorable external environment was partly a reflection of regional and bilateral arrangements. The share of exports with preferential access was 39.59% prior to WTO accession, higher than the regional and world averages, and the ratio even increased thereafter. Georgia had a regional FTA with CIS countries in 1994. Although this FTA did not formally

[33]Baldwin (1995).

[34]Typical discrimination against transition economies, such as the NME treatment and the Jackson–Vanik Amendment, was a non-issue for Georgia.

Table 6 Georgia—external environment with international comparison

	Georgia			*ECA*	*World*
	1995–1999	*2000–2004*	*2005–2008*	*1995–1999*	*1995–1999*
Rest-of-the world applied tariffs (%)					
Simple average	6.26	7.45	7.66	8.29	8.86
Maximum	148.6	1350.1	596.4	1013.2	1088.9
Dispersion	1.86	6.61	1.67	3.31	3.27
Trade-weighted average	5.89	4.09	1.35	5.44	14.22
Trade remedy initiations faced (per year)	0.00	0.20	0.00	1.23	1.56
Share of MFN duty-free exports (%)	35.06	45.39	45.48	28.12	26.94
Share of exports to CU/FTA partners (%)	39.59	52.24	41.81	16.44	21.04
Share of imports from CU/FTA partners (%)	33.62	35.61	42.28	18.56	19.37

Note CU=customs union; ECA=Europe and Central Asia (excluding high-income countries); FTA=free trade area. Indicators for 1995–1999, 2000–2004, and 2005–2008 are period averages. Tariff data includes preferences

Source World Bank. World Trade Indicators 2009/2010 Web site: http://www.worldbank.org/

take effect, bilateral FTAs have been in place with most of CIS countries (even after Georgia's departure from the CIS in 2009), practically restoring free access among them that was prevalent previously under the Soviet Union. Even before WTO accession, Georgia was a beneficiary of the generalized system of preferences (GSP) from the EU, Canada, Japan, Czech Republic, Slovak Republic, and Switzerland. Georgia and the EU signed the Partnership and Cooperation Agreement (PCA) in 1996, to formalize the MFN treatment with each other, but there appeared to be no serious discriminatory trade barriers even before it took effect in 1999. Whereas the bilateral agreement with the EU in 1993 stipulated potential imposition of quotas on Georgia's textile exports, it was never invoked in practice. Likewise, accord of the unconditional normal trade relations with the United States (that was suspended under the Jackson–Vanik Amendment) had to wait for Georgia's WTO accession in 2000, but no strong evidence showed that its prior absence had adverse impacts on exports (see Tables 3 and 4, Chapter 2).[35] Thus, the country did not have to suffer from costs of the outsider status even before WTO accession, and there was no need to recover any after membership. Georgia did not have any major concern left to multilateral negotiations through the Doha Round, and the country has never been a party to dispute settlement at the WTO, both as a complainant and as a defendant. Concerns underlying Hypothesis 3 were never relevant to Georgia and, in line with the hypothesis, the country did not have to take part in the relevant multilateral liberalization schemes.

5 Conclusion

The key element of Georgia's trade policy was its unilateral liberalization under the country's own structural reforms, particularly in its industry sector. It first took the form of liberalization for transition to a market economy after collapse of the Soviet Union by the mid-1990s. This was supported by IFIs' adjustment programs and subsequently consolidated into terms of WTO accession, albeit with some minor deteriorations to protect certain segment of the economy. Thus, as per Hypothesis 1, Georgia successfully utilized the WTO membership in support of its preceding domestic reforms. After a short period of a small setback in 2002–2003, the next wave of domestic reforms came after the Rose Revolution in late 2003, by which time the Doha Round had been launched. Unlike accession negotiations, whose focus was unilateral liberalization of its own trade regime, reciprocal market access negotiations under the Doha Round was guided by the GATT-think of mercantilism, which is essentially driven by calls to open export market of trading partners. Hardly an export-oriented economy, Georgia's prime interests back then were not to cultivate export markets, which were quite favorable at any rate. Also, given the small size of the economy, terms of trade were not its concern. The long-term policy objective of the country remained to be the unilateral liberalization of its own economy, and that was

[35] After WTO accession, the United States included Georgia in its GSP scheme in 2001. As Western Europe and Turkey became Georgia's largest trading partners, along with CIS countries, Georgia received the GSP plus (with extended products coverage) status from the EU in 2005 and concluded the free-trade agreement (FTA) with Turkey in 2007. Georgia's exports still faced some challenges like informal customs barriers or product standards, but tariffs were almost never a major issue.

achieved more efficiently outside of the WTO. If the Doha Round negotiations had any role for the country, it was just to defend the diminishing import tariffs where they still remained, but not for proactive liberalization through the reciprocal tariff-cutting process.

In the early phase of the Doha Round, Georgia expressed its intention of some defensive disengagement from market access negotiations as a RAM and, subsequently, also as a low-income economy in transition. As the pace of its unilateral liberalization got accelerated by 2006, the country more completely departed from the WTO track and went ahead with the autonomous route. These policy behaviors followed the scenario envisaged as Hypotheses 2-a and 2-b, but with an important qualification that the mode of disengagement evolved from defensiveness to aloofness. Georgia did not have to suffer from any major cost of the previous WTO non-member status, and it refrained from taking part in the relevant multilateral schemes, such as dispute settlement, in line with Hypothesis 3.

As evidenced, the government's strategy appears to have been quite successful. As of 2012, the simple average MFN tariff rate for industrial products remained nearly zero, and the country's business environment stands most favorable among almost all economies of the world. In 2013, however, nearly a decade of Saakashvili's presidency came to an end.[36] Thereafter, the average MFN applied tariff rate was raised slightly, but an overall orientation of Georgia's trade policy remained liberal.[37]

References

Adlung, R., & Roy, M. (2005a). *Turning hills into mountains? Current commitments under the GATS and prospects for change* (Staff Working Paper ERSD-2005-01). Retrieved from WTO website: http://www.wto.org/english/res_e/reser_e/ersd200501_e.htm.

Adlung, R., & Roy, M. (2005b). Turning hills into mountains? Current commitments under the general agreement on trade in services and prospects for change. *Journal of World Trade, 39*(6), 1161–1194.

[36] See the *Economist* magazine article ("Georgia's Election," 2013).

[37] Georgia signed an Associate Agreement with the EU in June 2014, and the Deep and Comprehensive Free Trade Agreement between the two provisionally came into effect on 1 September 2014. See WTO (2016).

Asian Development Bank. (2013). *Key indicators for Asia and the Pacific 2013* (44th ed.). Manila: Author.

Bagwell, K., & Staiger, R. W. (1999). An economic theory of GATT. *American Economic Review, 89*(1), 215–248.

Bagwell, K., & Staiger, R. W. (2002). *The economics of the world trading system*. Cambridge: MIT Press.

Baldwin, R. E. (1995). A domino theory of regionalism. In R. Baldwin, P. Haaparanta, & J. Kiander (Eds.), *Expanding membership of the European Union* (pp. 25–48). Cambridge: Cambridge University Press.

Baldwin, R. E. (2006). Multilateralising regionalism: Spaghetti bowls as building blocs on the path to global free trade. *The World Economy, 29*(11), 1451–1518.

Baldwin, R. E. (2012). Preferential trading arrangements. In A. Narlikar, M. Daunton, & R. M. Stern (Eds.), *The Oxford handbook on the World Trade Organization* (pp. 632–654). Oxford: Oxford University Press.

Beruchashvili, T. (2001). *Accession to the World Trade Organization: The case of Georgia*. Retrieved from United Nations Economic and Social Commission for Asia and Pacific website: http://www.unescap.org/oes/speca/docs/Divisions/TID/Accession_to_WTO-Tashkent/Georgia-finalpaper.pdf.

Brookings Institution. (2011). *From popular revolution to effective reforms: The Georgia experience*. Retrieved from Brookings website: http://www.brookings.edu/~/media/events/2011/3/17%20saakashvili/20110317_saakashvili_transcript.pdf.

Business Association of Georgia. (2013). *Georgia's long-term economic development concept*. Tbilisi: Author.

Georgia's election: The end of Saakashvili's reign. (2013, November 2). *The Economist, 409*(8860), 56.

International Monetary Fund. (1997). *Georgia: Enhanced structural adjustment facility policy framework paper, 1997–1999*. Retrieved from IMF website: http://www.imf.org/external/np/pfp/georgia/geor-01.htm.

International Monetary Fund. (1998). *Georgia: Recent economic developments and selected issues* (IMF Staff Country Report No. 98/99). Washington, DC: Author.

International Monetary Fund. (2003). *Georgia: 2003 article IV consultation—Staff report; staff statement; and public information notice on the executive board discussion annex* (IMF Staff Country Report No. 03/346). Washington, DC: Author.

International Monetary Fund. (2004a). *Georgia: Ex post assessment of Georgia's performance under fund-supported programs—Staff report; staff supplement; public information notice on the executive board discussion; and statement by the executive director for Georgia* (IMF Staff Country Report No. 04/26). Washington, DC: Author.

International Monetary Fund. (2004b). *Georgia: Request for three-year arrangement under poverty reduction and growth facility—Staff report; staff supplement; press release on the executive board discussion; and statement by the executive director for Georgia* (IMF Staff Country Report No. 04/165). Washington, DC: Author.

International Monetary Fund. (2006). *Georgia: Poverty reduction strategy paper progress report* (IMF Staff Country Report No. 06/360). Washington, DC: Author.

Kavadze, A., Ukleba, M., & Katamadze, V. (2003). *Georgia's path to the multilateral trading system*. Tbilisi: Forma.

King, C. (2004). A rose among thorns: Georgia makes good. *Foreign Affairs, 83*(2), 13–18.

Krugman, P. (1991, November/December). The move toward free trade zones. *Economic Review—Federal Reserve Bank of Kansas City, 76*(6), 5–25.

MacFarlane, S. N. (2004). Georgia's revolution and the region: Is it catching? *The World Today, 60*(2), 14–15.

Maggi, G., & Rodríguez-Clare, A. (1998). The value of trade agreements in the presence of political pressures. *Journal of Political Economy, 106*(3), 574–601.

Maggi, G., & Rodríguez-Clare, A. (2007). A political-economy theory of trade agreements. *American Economic Review, 97*(4), 1374–1406.

Papava, V., & Beridze, T. (1997). Industrial policy and trade regime in Georgia. *Eurasian Studies, 3*(4), 65–78.

Papava, V. (2006). The political economy of Georgia's Rose Revolution. *Orbis, 50*(4), 657–667.

Papava, V. (2009). The "rosy" mistakes of the IMF and the World Bank in Georgia. *Problems of Economic Transition, 52*(7), 44–55.

Saakashvili, M. (2004, November 30). Fulfilling the promise of the rose revolution Georgia's progress. *The New York Times*. Retrieved from: http://www.nytimes.com/2004/11/30/opinion/30iht-edsaakash_ed3_.html.

Staiger, R. W., & Tabellini, G. (1987). Discretionary trade policy and excessive protection. *American Economic Review, 77*(5), 823–837.

United Nations. (2001, July 25–27). Accession to the World Trade Organization: Issues and recommendations for Central Asian and Caucasian economies in transition. In *Proceedings and papers presented at the subregional workshop on accession to the World Trade Organization, economies in transition, Tashkent*. New York: United Nations.

World Bank. (2003). *Georgia: An integrated trade development strategy* (Report No. 27264-GE). Washington, DC: Author.

World Bank. (2009). *Georgia: Poverty assessment* (Report No. 44400-GE). Washington, DC: Author.

World Bank. (2012). *Fighting corruption in public services: Chronicling Georgia's reforms*. Washington, DC: Author.

World Bank. (2013). *Georgia: Sustaining rapid economic growth—Country economic memorandum* (Report No. 79532-GE). Washington, DC: Author.

World Bank Group. (2009). *Enterprise surveys country note series: Georgia—Running a business in Georgia.* Retrieved from World Bank website: http://documents.worldbank.org/curated/en/2009/01/11143000/running-business-georgia.

World Trade Organization. (1997). *Accession of Georgia: Memorandum of the foreign trade regime* (WT/ACC/DEO/3). Geneva: Author.

World Trade Organization. (1999). *Working party on the accession of Georgia: Report of the working party on the accession of Georgia to the World Trade Organization* (WT/ACC/GEO31). Geneva: Author.

World Trade Organization. (2001). *Ministerial conference, fourth session, Doha, 9–13 November 2001—Georgia: Statement by H.E. Mrs. Tamar Beruchashvili, Deputy Minister of Foreign Affairs* (WT/MIN(01)/ST/106). Geneva: Author.

World Trade Organization. (2003). *Ministerial conference, fifth session, Cancún, 10–14 September 2003—Georgia: Statement by H.E. Mrs. Tamar Beruchashvili, Deputy Minister of Foreign Affairs* (WT/MIN(03)/ST/106). Geneva: Author.

World Trade Organization. (2005a). *Negotiation group on market access: Market access for non-agricultural products—Communication form Armenia, Georgia, Kyrgyz Republic and Republic of Moldova—Revision* (TN/MA/W/56/Rev.1). Geneva: Author.

World Trade Organization. (2005b). *Committee on agriculture, special session: Communication form Armenia, Georgia, the Kyrgyz Republic and the Republic of Moldova* (TN/AG/GEN/10). Geneva: Author.

World Trade Organization. (2005c). *Ministerial conference, 6th session, Hong Kong, 13–18 December 2005: Georgia—Statement by H.E. Mr. Irakli Chogovadze, Minister of Economic Development* (WT/MIN(05)/ST/156). Geneva: Author.

World Trade Organization. (2006a). *Committee on agriculture, special session: Communication form small low-income economies in transition, recently acceded to the WTO—Proposal by Armenia, the Kyrgyz Republic and the Republic of Moldova* (TN/AG/GEN/16). Geneva: Author.

World Trade Organization. (2006b). *Committee on agriculture, special session: Communication form Armenia, the Kyrgyz Republic and the Republic of Moldova* (TN/AG/GEN/21). Geneva: Author.

World Trade Organization. (2007a). *Negotiating group on market access: Market access for non-agricultural products—Negotiating proposals by recently acceded members (RAMs)* (TN/MA/W/83). Geneva: Author.

World Trade Organization. (2007b). *Committee on agriculture special session: Negotiating proposals by recently acceded members (RAMs)* (TN/AG/GEN/24). Geneva: Author.

World Trade Organization. (2008a). *Negotiating group on market access: Fourth revision of draft modalities for non-agricultural market access* (TN/MA/W/103/Rev.3). Geneva: Author.
World Trade Organization. (2008b). *Committee on agriculture, special session: Revised draft modalities for agriculture* (TN/AG/W/4/Rev.4). Geneva: Author.
World Trade Organization. (2009). *Trade policy review body, 8 and 10 December 2009: Trade policy review, Georgia—Record of the meeting* (WT/TPR/M/224). Geneva: Author.
World Trade Organization. (2010a). *Trade policy review body: Trade policy review report by the secretariat, Georgia—Revision* (WT/TPR/S/224/Rev.1). Geneva: Author.
World Trade Organization. (2010b). *Trade policy review body, 8 and 10 December 2009: Trade policy review, Georgia—Record of the meeting, addendum* (WT/TPR/M/224/Add.1). Geneva: Author.
World Trade Organization. (2016). *Trade policy review body: Trade policy review report by the secretariat, Georgia—Revision* (WT/TPR/S/328/Rev.1). Geneva: Author.

CHAPTER 4

People's Republic of China

1 Introduction

The preceding chapter looked into the case of Georgia whose sole trade policy objective was the pursuit of unilateral liberalization, conceived as an integral part of its domestic reforms for transition to a market economy. By shedding light on People's Republic of China (PRC), this chapter takes a departure of extending the observations also to the RAMs' other possible trade policy objectives. As a transition economy, China clearly pursued catalyzing its market-opening policy through the WTO accession. At the same time, as reflected in its substantial current account surplus, China is an economy with a strong export orientation, and its products have long been targets of discriminatory protectionist measures by the trading partners, both before and after WTO accession. These economic features would make not only prescriptions of the commitment theory (on enhancing credibility of unilateral liberalization) but also other motivations illustrated in the juggernaut (pursuit of export interests through reciprocity) and the domino (joining trade agreements to overcome the cost of non-membership) theories potentially relevant reasons for the country's engagement in the multilateral trading system. Inference from the theories predicts that, given these multiple policy objectives, China would not only make the extensive market access commitments in its terms of WTO accession but also stay engaged in the post-accession WTO activities, such as the Doha Round and dispute settlement. Another important feature of the Chinese

K. Takamiya, *Recently Acceded Members of the World Trade Organization*, https://doi.org/10.1007/978-981-13-9159-0_4

economy is its huge size. As the world's second largest economy, China is probably in a position to be able to manipulate the international prices of traded goods and, in theory, this uniqueness may potentially give rise to containment of the terms of trade externality as a possible policy objective for engagement in reciprocal trade negotiations at the WTO. Large economies may be induced to raise tariffs for its terms of trade gains. However, if other counties retaliate, such gains would be lost, leaving only the efficiency loss as a result of tariff hikes. Reciprocal tariff cuts would impose disciplines for the large countries to stay away from such a destructive course of actions and allow them to reap only the efficiency gains of trade liberalization. However, as this case study on China illustrates, this does not necessarily mean that the country actually conceives such a motivation.

Following the theoretical framework and on account of these unique country contexts, the rest of this chapter examines China's trade policy objectives and behaviors at the WTO, in light of the hypotheses. The second section establishes that consolidation of the domestic reforms was the prime objective of China's WTO accession, and outlines the record of China's market access commitments for WTO membership. Observations verify Hypothesis 1 for transition economies: *Reforming economies (especially, those in transition to a market economy) would make extensive market access commitments for WTO accession, while others would make little use of them.* The third and fourth sections review China's positions at the market access negotiations of the Doha Round. China has been actively engaged in the reciprocal negotiations at the background of rising trade and current account surplus, and the episode helps validate Hypothesis 2-a: *Only export-oriented economies would stay proactively engaged in the post-accession market access negotiations of the Doha Round, while others would pursue autonomous liberalization.* At the same time, a number of important qualifications were found to have limited China's proactiveness at the Doha Round. Apart from the strong export orientation, the Chinese economy is also characterized by its huge size, and the country acted consistently with the prediction of Hypothesis 2-b: *Only large economies would stay proactively engaged in the market access negotiations of the Doha Round, while others would pursue autonomous liberalization.* Yet, the case found no qualitative evidence showing that the terms of trade consideration had any role in actual policy-making by China. Finally, the fifth section identifies various forms of discrimination China faced as the cost of the non-member status prior to the WTO accession and traces how the country has been redressing them. Its record of engagement in the WTO, most notably through accession negotiations and its dispute settlement mechanism, is in conformity with Hypothesis 3: *Countries that face the discriminatory cost of prior non-membership would stay engaged in the relevant multilateral liberalization schemes, while others would refrain from such activities.* The last section concludes.

2 Pushing Domestic Reforms Through WTO Accession

The process of China's accession to the multilateral trading system had been closely linked to its reform and opening policy launched by Deng Xiaoping[1] in the late 1970s. Under the strong leadership from within the Communist Party at the time, the old economic regime characterized by the central planning and industrial inefficiency had been gradually replaced by a relatively more market-oriented system. China's socialist market economy accommodated coexistence of both state-owned enterprises (SOEs) and private enterprises, including foreign-invested enterprises (FIEs), and was characterized by the staged and progressive form of transition in accordance with the so-called gradualist approach (in contrast to the "shock therapy" supported by the IMF elsewhere).[2] From 1979 onwards, the initial scope of reform was the agriculture sector whereby interventions by the local governments were reduced and the household contract system linked to production was extended in the rural areas. The pricing system was gradually liberalized, and the rural economy was substantially commercialized. Subsequently, with the adoption of Decisions on Reform of the Economic Structure by the Communist Party's Central Committee in 1984, the reform was rolled out to urban areas. The role of the government in the overall economy was altered from the direct production to indirect coordination and planning, and commercial decision-making powers were delegated to

[1] Statement by Assistant Minister Long Yongtu, head of the Chinese delegation at the third session on the Working Party on China on 6 March 1997, contained in WTO Department, Ministry of Commerce (MOFCOM) (Ed.) (2013, p. 691), Volume 10 (Multilateral 5).

[2] Godoy and Stiglitz (2006) acknowledge merit of the gradualist approach of transition to a market economy. Another term "state capitalism" is often used to describe China's economic model, as in the US representative's statement at the meeting on the trade policy review of China in the WTO in 2012, but China argued against use of such a terminology (WTO, 2012b).

enterprises. Since then, the custom legislation had been revised, with an objective of opening the economy to the outside world (GATT, 1987), and China cut import tariffs unilaterally (while also participating in the Uruguay Round as an observer) (GATT, 1991, 1994a).[3] Yet, its simple average applied tariff rate in the pre-accession period prior up to 2001 (a multi-year average of 18.55%) was still higher than in the post-accession period (Table 1). The other available data of China's tariff rates also indicates that their simple average as of 1996 (23.70%) was more than the double of that of East Asia and the Pacific region (11.02%) back then.[4]

The commitment theory states that the government may enhance credibility of its policy through binding trade agreements[5] and, as assumed in Hypothesis 1 for reforming economies, China's prime motivation for accession to the multilateral trading system was to catalyze its unilateral trade liberalization. With this objective in mind, China had filed a request for the GATT observer status in 1984 (GATT, 1984) and another request to resume the contracting party statues in 1986 (GATT, 1986). While China was a founding party of the GATT 1947, the PRC lost its status after the government in Taiwan announced China's withdrawal from the multilateral trading system (in ignorance of the government in Beijing) subsequently to the revolution in 1949. In 1987, the multilateral body tasked to examine China's return to the old GATT system was initially established as the Working Party on China's status as a Contracting Party, which met on 20 occasions. After the establishment of the WTO in 1995, China filed a new request for accession under Article XII of the Marrakesh Agreement, so as to convert the GATT Working Party to the WTO Working Party (WTO, 1995b), which met 18 times thereafter. In line with its opening-up policy, the main objective for accession to the multilateral trading system was consistently to support domestic reforms, as clearly stated in the remark by Long Yongtu, then Assistant Minister, Ministry of Foreign Trade and Economic

[3] Statements by Fan Guoxiang, Ambassador and Permanent Representative of China at the 47th session of GATT contracting parties, and by Yufeng Tang, Minister Counsellor, Deputy Permanent Representative at the 49th session of the GATT contracting parties.

[4] Data is retrieved from World Bank's *World Trade Indicators 2009/2010* Web site: http://info.worldbank.org/etools/wti/2a1.asp.

[5] Staiger and Tabellini (1987) and Maggi and Rodriguez-Clare (1998, 2007).

Table 1 People's Republic of China—MFN tariff profiles with international comparison (%)

	People's Republic of China				*EAP*	*World*
	1995–2000	*2001–2004*	*2005–2008*	*2009*	*2009*	*2009*
Simple average applied rates	18.55	12.58	9.80	9.57	10.46	9.61
Trade-weighted average applied rates	16.06	8.85	4.64	4.14	7.21	8.57
Maximum applied rate	121.5	85.87	65.00	65.00	103.4	96.44
Dispersion (coefficient of variation)	0.74	0.75	0.74	0.75	0.93	1.20
Domestic tariff peaks (tariff lines share)	1.41	1.90	2.44	2.16	1.77	4.47
International tariff peaks (tariff lines share)	45.95	28.83	15.42	14.80	15.95	23.51
Tariff escalation (finished % minus raw %)	–	2.38	2.01	2.23	0.83	2.56
Duty free tariff lines share	2.31	5.36	8.98	9.51	16.06	23.86
Non-Ad valorem share (in all tariff lines)	0.35	0.22	0.48	0.69	1.50	2.54
Bound tariff lines (% of all tariff lines)	100	100	100	100	83.96	81.98
Tariff overhang (bound minus applied rate)	−8.54	−2.61	0.09	0.00	15.22	28.84

Note EAP = East Asia and the Pacific. Indicators for 1995–2000, 2001–2004, and 2005–2008 are period averages. Data on average maximum and dispersion rates covers ad valorem tariffs only
Source World Bank. World Trade Indicators 2009/2010. Retrieved from the World Bank Web site: http://info.worldbank.org/etools/wti/2a1.asp

Cooperation (MOFTEC) at the fifth session of GATT Contracting Parties, dated 22 December 1994[6]:

> 'The decision' of China to return to the multilateral trading system has been made first of all, out of the need of China to promote its policy of reform and opening to the outside world. The decision is also an evidence to demonstrate China's support to the multilateral trading system and its firm commitment to undertake the international responsibility and obligations in handling the international economic and trade relations'. (GATT, 1994b, p. 1)

China used the WTO accession to leverage and enhance the credibility of reforms among its domestic constituencies. Long Yongtu recalls that China purposefully utilized external pressure from the accession negotiations to further push its domestic reforms:

> The important thing is that we in China have successfully and skilfully handled the domestic side of the accession process and have transformed the pressure generated by these negotiations, both at home and abroad, and turned them into a promoter, a catalyst for China's historic process of economic reforms and opening up to the outside world – a process started by Deng Xiaoping 23 years ago. That is the most significant lesson we can draw from the negotiations: that we have involved not only dozens of negotiators but also millions of ordinary Chinese in the process. (Yongtu, 2002, p. 26)

Institutionally, China's accession process was managed by top-down decision making and driven by the leadership of the Communist Party and the government (Feng, 2006). Both President Jiang Zemin and Premier Zhu Rongji, who seized power toward the conclusion of China's accession negotiations, succeeded Deng Xiaoping's reform path and forcefully proceeded with further market opening through the multilateral process. Hans-Friedrich Beseler, former Director-General of Trade of

[6]Another testimony of China's domestic reform objective of the WTO accession is Long Yongtu's statement at the Fifth Session of the Working Party on 1 August 1997, that reads "*China has taken major steps regarding market access, which not only represent the new efforts made by the Chinese government for the purpose of accelerating the WTO accession process, but more importantly they are necessitated by China's own objective to further expand the opening-up process.*" Statement contained in WTO Department, MOFCOM (Ed.) (2013, p. 23), Volume 11 (Multilateral 6).

the European Commission who served as chief of its China Negotiating Team until May 2000, notes involvement of the top leadership in the accession process:

> It soon became evident that all final decisions were taken at the highest level. In particular, Prime Minister Zhu Rongji was extremely well informed, even about minor details, and highly committed personally, especially since the experience of his visit to Washington in April 1999. In the end, it was Zhu Rongji's final negotiation with Mr Lamy which led to the conclusion of negotiations on May 19, 2000. (Beseler, 2002, p. 8)

Under the reform-minded top leadership, China's negotiating team was led by Long Yongtu, MOFTEC's chief negotiator (particularly in the period after the conclusion of the Uruguay Round). With the orders from and direct reporting to Zhu Rongji, Long Yongtu managed to cope with resistance from other ministries (in particular, the Ministry of Information Industry) and industries (such as SOEs and state-owned commercial banks) with vested protectionist interests ("China and the WTO," 1999).[7] Unlike the typical profile of trade negotiators, who tend to be either diplomats or trade lawyers, Long Yongtu was an international economist trained at the London School of Economics.[8] While diplomats and trade lawyers tend to treat liberalization commitments negatively as "concessions," reformers and economists take them positively as instruments for economic welfare and growth (VanGrasstek, 2001).[9] This was exactly what Long Yongtu had been claiming in his consultation with domestic constituencies in proceeding with the accession process (Yongtu, 2002). In his words, "*tariff-cut is not an [sic] one-sided concession, but rather it is our initiative to make up for a 'missed lesson', in a certain sense, it is a progress.*"[10] In fact, as the time went by,

[7]Feng (2006) assesses that the government restructuring launched by Zhu Rongji in 1998 empowered MOFTEC vis-à-vis domestic protectionist stakeholders and facilitated implementation of reforms by the top leadership.

[8]"Long Yongtu: China's chief negotiator," dated 19 March 2012, in CCTV Web site: http://english.cntv.cn/program/upclose/20120319/118542.shtml.

[9]Krugman (1997) states that the economists' case for free trade is essentially unilateral, but that is a virtue not usually shared by trade negotiators. China's WTO accession presents an interesting case of an economist acting as a negotiator.

[10]"Interview: Long Yongtu on China's WTO Entry," dated 12 November 2001, in *People's Daily* Web site: http://english.peopledaily.com.cn/200111/10/eng20011110_84267.shtml.

private domestic enterprises took the WTO accession as an opportunity to improve the business environment and seek the level-playing field with SOEs, and supported reforms and market opening through the membership process. By and large, foreign investors had similar pro-reform perspectives.[11]

Given the gradualist approach of economic transition, China did not fully open its economy through WTO accession right away. Nonetheless, negotiations by these reformers led to substantive market access commitments for a country that still retained socialism under the communist regime. In the finally agreed terms of accession, China bound all tariff lines, at the final average bound rate of nearly 10% (9.0% for non-agriculture, with a range of 0–47%, and 15.3% for agriculture, with a range of 0–65%). Most of the tariff reductions were to be implemented by 2005, and the rest no later than 2010. Apart from market access, China accepted the pricing reform and liberalization of trading rights, whereas the service sectors with GATS commitments counted 93. However, some of the discriminatory measures against China's exports adopted by its trading partners prior to WTO accession were still to be retained, for varying periods of time (more on this issue in the fifth section). Negotiations on these terms of accessions were concluded at the 18th Working Party meeting on 17 September 2001. There, Long Yongtu reiterated the top-down domestic reform objective:

> Just as President Jiang Zemin pointed out recently that WTO accession is a strategic decision made by the Chinese Government under economic globalization and is in line with China's reform and opening-up policy and the goal of establishing a socialist market economic system. The achievements made in China's reform and opening-up process have provided conditions and possibilities for China's participation into the multilateral

[11]According to the survey conducted by the United States General Accounting Office (GAO), almost 80% of 191 US companies that responded indicated their expectations that China's WTO commitments would have a very positive or positive impact on their businesses (USGAO, 2002). Michael Gadbaw, Vice President and Senior Counsel, General Electric Company, stressed the importance of WTO accession as an opportunity to improve China's business environment at the policy level (Gadbaw, 1998).

trading system. And on the other hand, the efforts made by China for its WTO accession have greatly accelerated the reform and opening-up process in China.[12]

This statement accurately summarizes China's objective for WTO accession and its achievements in line with Hypothesis 1. China's primary motivation for membership was to catalyze its domestic reforms and, albeit within its gradualist approach, the country made substantive market access commitments. At the same time, as part of the same statement, he also said "*China will, in light of the WTO principle of market opening on reciprocal basis, strength its economic and technological cooperation with all the WTO Members including developing members.*" It appeared that China was already geared to proceed with reciprocal market opening among WTO members—an issue that the next section on the Doha Round sheds light on. On 10 November, China's accession was approved at the Doha Ministerial Conference that launched the new round of trade negotiations. Subsequently, on 11 December 2001, the country became the 143rd member of the WTO.[13]

3 Pursuit of Export Interests in the Doha Development Agenda

Unlike many other RAMs that defensively disengaged from the DDA market access negotiations, China proactively participated in the reciprocal liberalization process even after WTO accession. At the same time, the country was not completely committed to assume the strong leadership role at the Doha Round. As an export-oriented economy, China had substantive interests in seeking reciprocal market opening vis-à-vis trading partners, but a close observation also reveals that there were other factors that constrained pursuit of mercantilism in the post-accession period.

[12]WTO news "Meeting of the Working Party on accession of China: Statement by H.E. Vice Minister LONG Yongtu, Head of the Chinese Delegation, at the eighteenth session of the Working Party on China," Geneva, 17 September 2001, retrieved from the WTO Web site: http://www.wto.org/english/news_e/news01_e/wpchina_longstat_17sept01_e.htm.

[13]For further information on China's WTO accession, insights on the negotiation process are shared in writing by Jeffrey L. Gertler, Legal Affairs Division of the WTO secretariat and former Secretary of the Working Party on Accession of China, WTO. See Gertler (1998, 2002, 2003, 2004). There are also a substantial amount of secondary research works conducted on China's WTO accession, as referenced in the literature review in Chapter 1.

3.1 Export Orientation and Engagement in Market Access Negotiations

After WTO accession in 2001, China's trade expanded rapidly. While imports increased sharply, exports always exceeded them. By 2007, the current account surplus had reached 10.1% of GDP and trade balance 9% (Table 2). This was part of the phenomenon referred to as "global imbalances" whereby, by and large, developing countries (mainly from East Asia, plus oil-producing countries) recorded a huge current account surplus to some developed economies. In fact, the imbalance was partly a reflection of domestic savings accumulated in surplus countries, or what Ben Bernanke called "global savings glut,"[14] resulting from various structural and macroeconomic factors. Thus, the impact of trade policy on the rising imbalances, if any, might have not been significant. Nonetheless, what emerged as a result of excessive savings was a policy-making environment potential ripe for multilateral market opening assumed by the juggernaut theory—an expanded export sector and a shrunk import sector of the economy.[15]

Hypothesis 2-a predicts that such an environment enables the government to proceed with reciprocal trade liberalization in reflection of rising export interests and, in line with this prediction, China actually remained proactively engaged in the DDA market access negotiations. Even after accession, catalyzing domestic reforms remained to be the country's main objective at the WTO, but it was solely on the premise of reciprocity that other WTO members would also contribute to multilateral tariff cuts. While China rarely talks about pursuit of commercial interests officially, presumably due to sensitivity with deficit countries, the export-oriented strategy of reciprocal trade negotiations at the WTO is stated in private writing by a senior government official. Commenting on the future direction of China's post-accession trade policy, Zhihai Zheng, President of MOFTEC's Chinese Academy of International Trade Economic Cooperation, argued as follows (Zheng, 2003, pp. 9–11):

[14] "The Global Saving Glut and the U.S. Current Account Deficit," remarks by Governor Ben S. Bernanke at the Sandridge Lecture, Virginia Association of Economists, Richmond, Virginia on 10 March 2005, retrieved from the Federal Reserve Board Web site: http://www.federalreserve.gov/boarddocs/speeches/2005/200503102/.

[15] Richard Baldwin (2006, 2012).

Table 2 People's Republic of China—state of global imbalances and rebalancing

	2001	*2002*	*2003*	*2004*	*2005*	*2006*	*2007*	*2008*	*2009*	*2010*
GDP growth rate	8.3	9.1	10.0	10.1	11.3	12.7	14.2	9.6	9.2	10.4
Current account balance (% of GDP)	1.5	2.8	3.2	4.2	7.1	9.2	10.1	9.1	5.2	5.2
Merchandize trade balance (% of GDP)	2.9	3.5	3.1	3.6	5.9	8.0	9.0	8.0	5.0	4.3
Merchandize exports (% of GDP)	22.6	25.6	30.9	35.9	33.8	35.7	34.9	31.7	24.1	26.7
Merchandize imports (% of GDP)	19.7	22.2	27.8	32.3	27.8	27.7	25.9	23.7	19.1	22.4
Merchandize export growth (%)	6.8	22.4	34.6	35.4	28.5	27.2	25.8	17.6	−16.1	31.4
Merchandize import growth (%)	8.1	21.3	39.8	35.8	17.6	19.7	20.3	18.7	−11.1	39.1

Source ADB (2013) and WTO (2008b, 2010a, 2012a)

> Its new strategy of opening-up should be like this: Development of an export-oriented economy by grasping the opportunity from its participation in the WTO ... China's range of opening-up, for instance, will be extended... from self-opening of a mainly unilateral character to mutual opening between China and all WTO members...Shaping the competitive edge of its export commodities will be the key for China to participate in economic globalization and the basis for it to take part in international division of work and competition.

This statement appears to reflect China's shift in the emphasis from unilateral trade liberalization, as was mainly the case for WTO accession, to reciprocal trade liberalization that characterizes the Doha Round in the post membership period.[16] Pursuit of export interests was one important motivation for China's participation in the Doha Round and, unlike most of the other RAMs that disengaged themselves from the multilateral liberalization process and increasingly acted autonomously after WTO accession, China retained the position that reciprocal DDA market access negotiations were a prime venue for its trade liberalization. The government's report submitted for the 2008 trade policy review claimed centrality of WTO and the Doha Round as China's top trade policy agenda.

> The Chinese Government always supports the multilateral trading system and puts it on top of its trade policy agenda. China emphasizes the importance of maintaining and strengthening the central role of WTO in coordinating trade policies of Members and supports the advancement of trade and investment liberalization and facilitation worldwide through multilateral trade negotiations... As a top priority in its trade policy, China has committed to pushing forward the Doha Round negotiations to an early and successful conclusion. In this regard, China has actively participated in all the negotiations under Doha Development Agenda and played a constructive role. China has submitted a large number of proposals on agriculture, NAMA, services, rules, trade facilitation etc.... (WTO, 2008a, pp. 5–18)

While China still claimed the right for some flexibility on market access commitments as a developing country and RAM (in particular,

[16] Sally (2008) also notes this change in China's trade policy focus, from unilateral liberalization to reciprocal hard bargaining.

seeking the longer staging period for further tariff cuts) (Lim & Wang, 2010; WTO, 2002c, 2002d), the country retained the positive stance in the tariff-cutting negotiations of the Doha Round.[17] Unlike other RAMs that had expressed strong reservation against further market access commitments on the grounds that they had previously made extensive commitments as part of the accession process, China made it clear that, notwithstanding its substantive accession commitments, the country would still contribute to the Doha Round even beyond these earlier achievements. The country's intention to stay engaged in the Doha Round is clearly stated in the introductory remarks made by the Chinese representative at the WTO trade policy review in 2006:

> Despite China's extensive accession commitments and the numerous difficulties in fulfilling them, it was fully committed to the DDA and was willing to work with others to make appropriate contributions in the negotiation process, compatible with its own capacity. (WTO, 2006a, p. 6)

In particular, China's relatively positive attitude toward the DDA market access negotiations was most strongly reflected in its 2002 proposal to adopt the formula-based tariff cuts for NAMA across all members of the WTO (see Chapter 2). Part of China's original proposal reads as follows:

> China proposes that non-agricultural market access negotiations shall be conducted in accordance with the mandate embodied in the Doha Ministerial Declaration with a view to balancing the interests of the WTO Members at different levels of development... The newly-acceded Members shall take the simple average rate of their applied rates in 2000 and their final bound rates committed in their accession negotiations as their base rates... To facilitate the negotiations and meet the requirement of eliminating tariff peaks and tariff escalations as embodied in the Doha Ministerial Declaration, China proposes to adopt a uniform formula for tariff reduction. (WTO, 2002a, p. 1)

Clearly, China's negotiating proposal assumed prospective commitments by the RAMs. Negotiations on the Swiss formula subsequently became a core element of the NAMA negotiations, and it was the very proposal of

[17] Lawrence (2006) noted that China was the most active developing country member of the WTO in terms of the number of written submission at the WTO ruling bodies and in the DDA negotiations in 2003.

China that helped constitute this backbone of the Doha Round. In fact, at the meeting by the Negotiating Group on Market Access on 26–28 May 2003, Chair P. L. Girard said that his proposed formula was partly inspired by China's proposal, intended to eliminate tariff peaks and escalations (WTO, 2003b). Unlike most of the other newly acceded countries that used the status as the RAMs only for the defensive cause at the WTO, China appeared to have taken a positive spin of "GATT-think" (an increase in imports is good as long as exports also increase[18]), aiming at forward-looking reciprocal liberalization among the WTO members.[19]

Ultimately in the draft December 2008 modalities, China accepted a prospective commitment in NAMA that far exceeded those of many other RAMs and major emerging market economies. Table 3 presents estimates of the tariff cuts envisaged through application of the draft modalities, calculated by the staff of international organizations.[20] Unlike the case of most of the low-income economies in transition and the VRAMs that completely refused to make market access commitments, China agreed to cut tariffs on the basis of the Swiss formula, albeit with allowance of a 3-year staging period. This positive stance stood out in contrast also to the defensiveness of other large developing countries. Since the formula of the final draft 2008 NAMA modalities incorporated the bound rate as the basis of tariff-cutting commitments, other large developing countries with tariff overhang (water beyond the applied rate) would not be required to make any substantial tariff cuts for industrial products. For instance, India's applied tariff rate would be

[18]Krugman (1991).

[19]To be precise, in this proposal, China claimed to retain flexibility for the RAMs in the sectoral initiatives (additional liberalization for designated sectors on top of the formula-based tariff cuts), but the latter was not its priority for NAMA negotiations. China also retained the defensive stance at the market access negotiations in agriculture throughout the duration of the Doha Round. For instance, the Chinese delegation stated "*China also underlined the contribution it had already made through its WTO accession commitments. Implementation of, and adjustment to, these commitments needed time. Therefore, China required an exemption from further modalities for market access*" at negotiations held on 6 September 2002 (WTO, 2002b, p. 5).

[20]While estimates presented in this paper by Laborde, Martin, and Mensbrugghe (2012) are not official calculations by the WTO, they are presented in its World Trade Review journal and referenced in the interim report commissioned by a number of WTO members and co-chaired by Bhagwati and Sutherland (2011).

Table 3 Prospective tariff cuts by WTO members under the draft 2008 modalities

	Non-agriculture			*Agriculture*		
	Base	*Formula*	*Flex*	*Base*	*Formula*	*Flex*
Selected economies						
Brazil	8.5	7.4	7.8	4.8	4.7	4.8
Canada	0.9	0.5	0.5	10.7	5.1	8.6
China	5.6	3.9	4.4	7.8	5.3	7.5
EU-27	1.8	1.0	1.0	15.9	6.6	10.2
India	12.9	11.7	12.0	59.2	54.6	59.2
Japan	1.3	0.7	0.7	29.8	14.0	20.4
United States of America	1.5	0.8	0.8	4.8	2.1	3.0
All countries	2.9	2.0	2.3	14.6	9.0	11.9
Developed	1.7	1.0	1.0	15.4	7.0	10.4
Developing (non-LDCs)	4.8	3.6	4.2	13.7	11.2	13.6
LDCs	10.9	8.0	10.9	12.5	12.2	12.5
Normal developing	3.9	3.1	3.4	15.1	12.3	15.0
RAMs	9.5	7.1	9.5	13.4	12.8	13.4
SVEs	5.3	3.9	4.4	10.7	7.8	10.5

Note EU= European Union; LDCs = leased-developed countries; RAMs= recently acceded members; SVEs= small, vulnerable economies. Rates under Flex columns reflect various flexibility provisions allowed for certain groups of members

Source Laborde et al. (2012)

reduced only marginally from a high base of 12.9 to 12.0%, while Brazil would cut its rate from 8.5 to 7.8%. On the other hand, China's average tariff rate would be reduced from an already low level of 5.6% down to 4.4%. For agriculture, China strongly argued for retaining flexibility, and offered only limited tariff cuts, but this was actually the case for all developing countries (whose applied tariff rate would barely change after application of the formula). Unlike the low-income economies in transition and the VRAMs, China still accepted minor agricultural tariff cuts, and additional flexibility retained as a RAM vis-à-vis other developing countries was rather small. In any case, the average tariff level of China's agricultural sector was much lower than those of the entire WTO membership (including both developed and developing countries), and it would remain so even after the application of the modalities.

Table 4 People's Republic of China—average bound and applied tariff rates (%)

	2001	*2002*	*2003*	*2004*	*2005*	*2007*	*Final bound (2010)*
WTO bound rate							
Simple average	n.a.	12.4	11.3	10.4	10.0	9.9	9.9
Agriculture	n.a.	18.2	16.9	15.6	15.3	15.3	15.3
Non-agriculture	n.a.	11.5	10.4	9.6	9.1	9.0	9.0
MFN applied rate							
Simple average	15.6	12.2	11.1	10.2	9.7	9.7	n.a.
Agriculture	23.1	18.2	16.8	15.5	15.3	15.3	n.a.
Non-agriculture	14.4	11.2	10.1	9.3	8.8	8.8	n.a.

Note MFN = most-favored nation; n.a. = not applicable; WTO = World Trade Organization
Source WTO (2006b, 2008b)

While retaining a proactive stance at the Doha Round on the one hand, China nearly ceased to proceed with autonomous trade liberalization on the other hand. As presented in Table 4, China's liberalization of applied tariffs closely followed the reduction in the bound rates committed in terms of WTO accession, and the simple average of the applied rate has nearly reached the level of final binding by the end of 2004. However, unlike the case of many other RAMs (or developing countries at large), China barely cut its applied tariffs in excess of the WTO accession commitments (that had been set at around 10% on average). China continuously carried on domestic reforms in the areas other than trade liberalization (see Tables 8, Chapter 2) but, as far as its trade policy was concerned, the government almost completely froze its autonomous actions in the post-accession period.

Clearly, China opted to go down the path of multilateral liberalization through reciprocal negotiations, rather than pursuing immediate economic benefits straightforwardly through autonomous liberalization. Where the needs for further tariff liberalization arose, China has only selectively cut its so-called interim rates (temporary duty rates), without affecting the main MFN applied rates. According to the 2006 trade policy review report by the WTO Secretariat, the authority stated that, by not reducing the MFN rate below the bound rate for the majority of the tariff lines, China tried to retain bargaining chips in the WTO negotiations (WTO, 2006b).[21] The stance shows China's priority placed upon

[21] China initially proposed an average of applied and bound tariff rates as the basis for tariff cuts by developing countries at the Doha Round (WTO, 2002b).

WTO negotiations over autonomous liberalization, even at the cost of forgoing potential gains from the latter. Clearly, China has been consistently sticking to multilateralism as the main vehicle for MFN-based trade liberalization.[22]

3.2 Still Falling Short of Prominent Leadership

3.2.1 "Partial Stakeholder" at the WTO

The research presented above thus far validates Hypothesis 2. As an export-oriented economy, compared with most of the other RAMs or developing countries at large, China exhibited more proactive attitudes in market access negotiations of the Doha Round. At the same time, it was also true that the country was not aspiring to play the prominent leadership role to drive the entire multilateral negotiations forward. In the eyes of some observers with high expectations, China's level of engagement in the multilateral liberalization process was not necessarily very satisfactory. For instance, James Bacchus, a former US congressman and former chair of the WTO Appellate Body, noted:

> Although China has embraced its obligations as a member of the World Trade Organization, the continuing reluctance of Beijing to press for lower barriers to trade risks the very future of the WTO as the central forum and fulcrum for world trade… Since joining the WTO in 2001, China has been a constructive WTO member. Always polite and patient, it has participated diligently in WTO proceedings. China has complied increasingly with WTO rules and consistently with WTO rulings. It has done everything it should do as a member—except show the leadership to help sustain the centrality of the global trading system overseen by the WTO.[23]

[22]China has also become increasingly active in reciprocal trade negotiations on the bilateral and regional fronts. According to the data available from the 2014 trade policy review, China has concluded 12 FTAs with over 20 regions and states (WTO, 2014a). However, no free trade agreement has been reached with large trading partners, such as the EU and the United States. China was not a party to the Trans-Pacific Partnership (TPP) negotiations.

[23]"The WTO Needs China to Lead: Beijing ought to show the leadership needed to help sustain the global trading system," by James Bacchus, posted in the *Wall Street Journal* Web site: http://online.wsj.com/news/article_email/bacchus-the-wto-needs-china-to-lead-1401381136-lMyQjAxMTA0MDEwOTExNDkyWj.

This view that China did not exercise the expected leadership role in the global trade talks has been widely shared in the trade policy circle. In the words of Pascal Lamy, WTO's former Director-General, China was still nothing more than a "partial stakeholder" of the global economic governance:

> As an increasingly heavy weight in the global economy, China definitely has a huge stake in making sure that multilateral systems work effectively. So far, China has actively participated in various configurations of global economic governance. But it has not yet taken a proactive role. China is still a "partial stakeholder" in global governance... As a key stakeholder, China should take a more proactive role in international economic governance...[24]

By 2004, China had become the world's third largest trader (accounting for 6.7% of the global total) among WTO members, after the EU (14.5%) and the United States (13.6%), overtaking Japan (5.9%) (WTO, 2006b), and there was a high expectation for China's more prominent leadership role in the Doha Round, especially from these major economies in the developed world.[25] However, China's engagement was falling short of these expectations.

3.2.2 Qualifiers on Pursuit of Post-accession Multilateral Liberalization

As the juggernaut theory states, the dominance of export industries should potentially enable the government to proceed with reciprocal negotiations. However, to what extent the government actually seizes such an advantage for advancing multilateral trade liberalization

[24]Speech by Pascal Lamy at the China Development Forum in Beijing on 24 March 2013, in the news release titled "China should be more active in global economic governance, Lamy tells Beijing forum," posted in the WTO Web site: http://www.wto.org/english/news_e/sppl_e/sppl274_e.htm.

[25]At the trade policy review meeting in 2010, the US representative stated: "*The WTO process that needs China's participation most urgently is the Doha Development Agenda. Since the Doha Round was launched in 2001, China's power and influence in the world economy have expanded dramatically. It is vital for China, like other major emerging economies, to accept the responsibility that goes along with its power and influence*" (WTO, 2010b, p. 26). At the same meeting, the EU representative also called for China's "leadership in the DDA negotiations" (WTO, 2010b, p. 21).

could ultimately be up to its own discretion. In other words, if the government does not accord utmost priority to the pursuit of exports alone and there are conflicting policy objectives, the existence of business interests may not necessarily let the juggernaut roll forcefully. A close look at China's country context reveals that there were a number of factors that constrained China's more proactive engagement in the Doha Round. Priority on pursuit of export interests was qualified by the unique international economic contexts (of rebalancing China's growth model and the rise of the global value chains) of the day. At the same time, there were also other factors that restrained the straightforward pursuit of trade liberalization, both domestically (inward-looking domestic policy orientation) and internationally (foreign policy consideration vis-à-vis other developing countries), elaborated as follows.

Rebalancing the Growth Model. As the current account surplus of China reached its unprecedented level in the lead to the global financial crisis of 2008–2009, there had been international calls to shift the source of its growth[26] from exports and investments (especially in the manufacturing sector) to domestic consumption (partly through expansion of the service sector). In fact, even before the crisis, the government had already been gradually shifting away from the export-oriented growth strategy and its efforts have been continued even thereafter (IMF, 2006, 2011, 2012, 2013). The most visible demonstration of the policy shift was revaluation of the renminbi (RNB) against the US dollar and adoption of the managed float exchange rate regime in July 2005, but it was also reflected in China's intensified use of export restrictions (WTO, 2010a).[27] The authority was well aware that there was a limit to the growth strategy depending on exports alone and began to give a lesser emphasis on it, as stated in the government's report for the 2008 trade policy review at the WTO:

[26] See the IMF (2007) on the multilateral consultation on global imbalances.

[27] The 2008 trade policy review report by the WTO secretariat notes that the number of tariff lines subject to interim export duties had almost doubled in the past two years by then (WTO, 2008b). The subsequent report in 2010 says that the simple average export tariff rate was around 13.5% (WTO, 2010a), and the figure appears to have increased to around 14.5% by 2011 (WTO, 2012a).

> It is worth noting that while China is in trade surplus vis-à-vis some WTO Members, China also has major trade deficit with a number of other WTO Members. The Chinese Government always believes that excessive trade surplus would bring about adverse impact on China's economy... Therefore, the Chinese Government has never single-mindedly pursued trade surplus and has been doing everything possible to reduce trade surplus through comprehensive measures including those to boost domestic demand. (WTO, 2008a, p. 15)

Thus, while rising external surplus provided the potentially enabling ground to advance export interests through reciprocal trade liberalization (as per the juggernaut theory), it also brought about the authority's resolve to stay away from further exploitation of the export-oriented growth strategy. Pursuit of export interests still carried weight in policy-making, but it would be fair to say that such mercantilism did not turn out to be the sole motivation for China's continued engagement in the WTO. After the global financial crisis, its current account surplus actually began to shrink (Table 2), partly because of cyclical factors.

Rise of the Global Value Chains. Another important factor was the rise of global value chain. Today's global trade is highly characterized by international value chains, comprising a flow of intermediary inputs for assembling elsewhere, from one country to the other,[28] and a large portion of such commercial transactions is undertaken by multi-national corporations (MNCs), rather than domestic enterprises. The Chinese economy is certainly not an exception, and over 80% of its processed exports (and over 50% of the total exports) originated from FIEs in around 2008 (Table 5). It is plausible that, under China's unique form of economic governance, commercial interests of SOEs affected the government's trade policy. However, they did not represent a majority of exporters that, according to the juggernaut theory, hold the key to move reciprocal liberalization forward. As outsiders, FIEs may not have a strong leverage to affect the government's trade policy (and domestic private enterprises do not appear to have any high expectations on the Doha Round). In such circumstances, there is a disconnect between

[28] For further references on the global value chains, see the WTO webpage on "Made in the World," Web site: http://www.wto.org/english/res_e/statis_e/miwi_e/miwi_e.htm.

Table 5 People's Republic of China—state of global value chains (%)

	2007	*2008*	*2009*
Share of processing trade in total exports	50.6	47.2	48.8
FIEs' share in total exports	57.0	55.3	55.9
Share of processed exports in FIEs' total exports	75.0	72.4	73.4
Share of FIEs processed exports in total processed exports	84.4	84.8	84.1

Note FIEs = foreign invested enterprises
Source WTO (2010a)

exporters' interests and the government's trade policy, and the former could not serve as a primary driving force of the latter.[29]

As argued above, there is a limit to the applicability of the juggernaut theory as an explanation of engagement in the reciprocal trade negotiations for transition and developing economies integrated into the global value chains. The basic assumption of the juggernaut theory is that export businesses are domestic constituencies and the governments negotiate trade deals to cultivate their overseas markets. This model would fit well for home countries of MNC headquarters that are typically developed countries. However, the same conditions would not necessarily prevail in transition and developing economies that tend to be the host of MNCs, rather than home.[30] There are also domestic exporters in

[29] Impacts of global value chains on various modes of trade liberalization are yet to be fully researched. Baldwin (2006) argues that the policy of facilitating trade in the global supply chains led to race-to-the-bottom unilateralism of MFN-based tariff cuts among developing countries, particularly in East Asia. Manger (2009) found that the need to attract FDI led to proliferation of preferential trade agreements. At the multilateral level, however, global value chains do not appear to have had any positive impacts on the DDA market access negotiations. Baldwin (2014) comments that the present WTO does not cater to the needs of today's supply-chain trade, and the new institution ("WTO 2.0") should be created.

[30] In the world of global value chains, what nominally looks as one country's export may not be produced completely by the same country's producers. By 2009, the foreign contents of China's exports in value-added terms had increased to about one-third of the total from about 12% in 1995 (data was sourced from the OECD-WTO Database on Trade in Value-Added, Web site: http://www.oecd.org/industry/ind/measuringtradeinvalue-addedanoecd-wtojointinitiative.htm). Reciprocal trade negotiations assume clear distinction of one country's exports from others', but such a basic presumption of mercantilism that drove the past multilateral trade rounds may not be valid in today's highly integrated global economy. In the words of Pascal Lamy, "*(t)he high level of import intensity in export production has created an unprecedented level of inter-dependency among countries*

Table 6 People's Republic of China—presence of state-owned enterprises

	2001	*2002*	*2003*	*2004*
Number of SOEs	173,504	158,712	149,988	137,753
Employment (million)	48.2	44.6	42.3	39.8
Profits realized (Y billion)	281.1	378.6	495.1	752.5
Asset values (% of the total)	64.9	60.9	56.0	n.a.
Value added (% of the total)	51.7	48.3	44.9	n.a.

Note n.a. = not available; SOEs = state-owned enterprises. Data are only for SOEs with sales over Y5 million
Source WTO (2006b)

developing and transition economies but, in circumstances where their presence in the entire exporting sector is rather limited, the power of juggernaut as a catalyst of the reciprocal trade liberalization would have to be moderated.

Domestic Orientation in Public Policy. There were also other domestic factors that directed China's trade policy away from straightforward pursuit of export interests through engagement in the market access negotiations. In the post-accession period, the leaders in China who had previously driven the reforms through the WTO membership were succeeded by the new generation (Sally, 2011). Its economic policy was relatively more domestically oriented, featuring use of industrial policies and SOEs to promote home-grown technologies.[31] As of 2001, the year of WTO accession, more than a half of China's value added, was created by relatively large SOEs that accounted for nearly 65% of asset values and slightly less than a half of the total employment. Available data shows that SOEs maintained significant presence, and their realized profits more than doubled within a few years after WTO membership (Table 6).

engaged in supply chains. It is no longer just about exports. Imports are essential to export. It is no longer just about 'them'. It is about 'us'." See WTO news "Lamy: Global value chains are 'binding us together'," dated 19 September 2012, retrieved from the WTO Web site: http://www.wto.org/english/news_e/sppl_e/sppl245_e.htm.

[31] Long Yongtu's comments on China's post-WTO accession policy cited in *The Economist* magazine ("All Change," 2011).

Foreign policy considerations vis-à-vis other developing countries. On the international front, China felt obliged to retain some defensive postures at the WTO so as to be aligned with other developing countries. It was a long-standing position of China, since pre-accession years (when it was a much smaller player in international trade), that the perspective of the developing countries should be respected at the multilateral trading system, and this stance has not changed after its WTO membership.[32] For instance, at the Cancún Ministerial Conference on 10–14 September 2003, Lu Fuyuan, Minister of Commence, stated:

> We believe that all Members should have equal participation in the WTO negotiations with their interests fully respected and reflected. The overwhelming majority of WTO Members are developing ones. Therefore enabling developing Members to genuinely benefit from the negotiations essentially safeguards the success of the DDA. Disregarding such an important basic fact will only result in a more zigzag and lengthy DDA process. (WTO, 2003c, p. 2)

At the Doha Round, some of the large developing countries, including those in NAMA-11,[33] have been exhibiting a strong protectionist stance. If China takes a leadership role to move reciprocal liberalization forward at the Doha Round, as called for by developed countries, that would directly conflict with the position of these protectionist countries from the developing world. This foreign policy consideration of preserving

[32] China's development focus in the old GATT period is stated in the remarks by Qian Jiadong, Ambassador, Permanent Representative at the 44th session of Contracting Parties dated 25 November 1988 (GATT, 1988a) and by Gu Yongjiang, Vice-Minister for Foreign Trade and Economic Cooperation at the Trade Negotiations Committee meeting in Marrakesh, Morocco on 12–15 April 1994 (GATT, 1994c). After establishment of the WTO, the priority on development was emphasized in statements by Shi Guangsheng, Minister of Foreign Trade and Economic Cooperation at the Seattle Ministerial Conference on 30 November–3 December 1999, Bo Xilai, Minister of Commerce at the Hong Kong Ministerial Conference on 13–18 December 2005 (WTO, 2005), and Chen Deming at the Geneva Ministerial Conference on 15 December 2011 (available from the WTO Web site: http://www.wto.org/). Another statement by Lu Fuyuan, Minister of Commence at the Cancún Ministerial Conference on 10–14 September 2003, is cited above.

[33] NAMA-11 is a group of developing countries opposing liberalization of trade in industrial goods, including Argentina, Brazil, Egypt, India, Indonesia, Namibia, Philippines, South Africa, Tunisia, and Venezuela. See the WTO Web site: http://www.wto.org/english/tratop_e/dda_e/negotiating_groups_e.htm.

coherence with other developing countries underlay part of China's middle-ground stance at the WTO.

In summary, the record of China's engagement in the Doha market access negotiations broadly confirms Hypothesis 2 derived from the juggernaut theory, but a closer review also revealed important qualifications. It was certainly true that as the economy became more export-oriented after WTO accession, China firmly engaged itself in the reciprocal trade negotiations toward conclusion of the draft December 2008 modalities. The negotiating position of China was relatively stronger than those of many other RAMs and other large developing countries. However, for the reasons highlighted in this case study, China did not fully exploit this potentially enabling environment to take a more prominent leadership role in reciprocal negotiations to the satisfaction of more traditional players like the United States and the EU. In this sense, the episode showed that there were some limits to the practical role of export interests as a decisive driving force of reciprocal trade liberalization.

4 Potential Relevance of Terms of Trade for a Large Economy

For a large economy like China, in theory, containment of the terms of trade externality (and thus avoidance of tariff wars with trading partners) could become another potential motivation for engagement in the reciprocal negotiations in the multilateral trading system.[34] Accordingly, Hypothesis 2-b assumes that large economies remain engaged in the reciprocal trade negotiations of the Doha Round to contain terms of trade externality. Table 7 shows the trend of terms of trade and the average tariff rates of China and the rest of the world, roughly for the period when the country implemented tariff cuts as per the WTO accession commitments. China's tariff cuts were partly reciprocated by other WTO members (see the fifth section), but the degree of liberalization was much larger on the part of China. In this sense, China's tariff cuts in this period were more of a unilateral nature with limited elements of reciprocity. Interestingly, the data shows that China's terms of trade were constantly deteriorating in this period.[35] Obviously, this should

[34] Bagwell and Staiger (1999, 2002).

[35] Available data for the 19 RAMs shows that, on average, their terms of trade improved by about 20% by 2008, compared with the record of 2000. To the contrary, China's terms

Table 7 People's Republic of China—reciprocity and terms of trade

	2000	*2001*	*2002*	*2003*	*2004*	*2005*	*2006*
China applied tariff rate (incl. preferences)							
Simple average	16.40	15.39	–	10.69	9.81	–	9.77
Trade weighted averages	14.67	14.11	–	6.48	5.96	–	4.30
ROW applied tariff rate (incl. preferences)							
Simple average	11.60	11.65	12.42	10.33	10.30	9.82	9.16
Trade weighted averages	4.77	5.29	5.62	4.03	4.29	3.41	3.61
Net barter terms of trade index (2000=100)	100.00	102.25	102.48	98.47	93.37	87.20	83.53

Note ROW = rest of the world. The net barter terms of trade index is the percentage ratio of unit export value indexes to unit import value, measured against the base year of 2000
Source World Trade Indicators 2009/2010 of the World Bank Web site: http://info.worldbank.org/etools/wti/2a1.asp; World Bank Open Data retrieved from the World Bank Web site: http://data.worldbank.org/

not be a result of trade liberalization alone but, arguably, it may also be interpreted as a rough indication that terms of trade may be partly affected by China's trade policy.

In cases where an economy is sufficiently large to be able to affect international prices through trade liberalization, as seems to be the case possibly for China, it is also plausible that, in reverse, the country could pursue terms of trade gains by raising tariffs, at the risk of triggering retaliations by trading partners. Multilaterally coordinated trade liberalization would serve as international disciplines on such mutually destructive moves, and the resort to reciprocity would also prevent terms of trade deterioration that may arise from unilateral tariff cuts.

In fact, the hypothesis that large economies would stay actively engaged in the reciprocal trade liberalization seems to be verified strictly on the basis of limited available data. China is the world's second largest

of trade deteriorated by about 25% in the same period, and the degree of deterioration was largest among the RAMs. Statistics were sourced from World Bank Open Data Web site: http://data.worldbank.org/.

economy (and the largest among the RAMs) and, as already reviewed in this chapter, the country has been exhibiting a relatively more pro-active stance compared with other RAMs. However, it is hard to find any qualitative evidence that this correlation resulted from China's conscious intention to use the multilateral trading system to contain terms of trade externality. There was no negotiating proposal, statements, or any other forms of documentation referring to the terms of trade rationale for engagement in the reciprocal trade liberalization and, in fact, China's trade negotiators themselves were not even conscious of this notion.

While the statistical evidence supports Hypothesis 2-b, there is no direct indication that China's engagement in the Doha Round was actually motivated by the terms of trade considerations.[36] The terms of trade externality are a theoretically interesting proposition, but the qualitative observation does not support its practical relevance in the real world of trade negotiations.

[36]Yet, skeptics may still claim relevance of terms of trade consideration on the basis of disciplines on export taxes inserted as Paragraph 11.3 of China's Protocol of Accession (WTO, 2001c, p. 7), that reads "*China shall eliminate all taxes and charges applied to exports unless specifically provided for in Annex 6 of this Protocol or applied in conformity with the provisions of Article VIII of the GATT 1994.*" Just as the large country may manipulate the terms of trade in its favor through imports tariffs, they should be able to affect the international price also through export tariffs, and this WTO-plus provision on export restrictions could be interpreted as a sign of China's intent to use the multilateral trading system to self-discipline the pursuit of terms of trade gains. However, in disputes filed by a number of trading partners with regard to various raw materials and rare earth in 2009 and 2012 (WTO, 2009d, 2009e, 2009f, 2011f, 2012d, 2014b, 2014c), China claimed that its export taxes and restrictions were aimed at natural resources conservation and environment protection, rather than manipulation of trade (WTO, 2012c), implying that the country did not have the intent to affect terms of trade through these measures in the first place. It should be noted that China was also expressing an objection to inclusion of disciplines on export taxes as an agenda for the DDA negotiations. The minutes of the meeting of the Negotiating Group on Market Access on 14–16 April 2003 (WTO, 2003d, p. 60) read "*(t)he representative of China stated that his delegation strongly opposed the inclusion of export duties and restrictions in the discussion of NTBs…*" If China had hypothetically wanted to rely on the WTO to discipline terms of trade manipulation among members (including China itself), it should have welcomed the introduction of a new multilateral rule on export taxes, but what the country actually sought at the negotiating table was quite the opposite.

5 Long-Standing Pursuit of Non-discrimination

As reviewed in the first section, China's prime objective of WTO accession was to catalyze its own reform, but it does not necessarily mean that there was no other motivation. The domino theory presents recovery of the cost of the previous non-member status as a motivation to join the international trade agreement.[37] In the context of the WTO, these costs take the form of discrimination by older members of the multilateral trading system, and China has actually been suffering from a very extensive range of these obstacles since the pre-accession period. The specific discrimination against China included the absence of the unconditional MFN status, textile quota constraints and targeted safeguard, the non-market economy (NME) status in anti-dumping, and the transitional product-specific safeguard (TPS) by the incumbent members. The WTO accession provided an opportunity for China to redress some of these discriminatory measures, but others remained even long after its membership to the multilateral trading system. Hypothesis 3 assumes that countries remain engaged in the relevant multilateral schemes as far as such costs of the previous non-membership still prevail, so as to redress them. China's long-standing endeavors to counter these problems since the pre-accession period are broadly in line with this hypothesis, as elaborated below.

5.1 *Unconditional MFN Treatment*

China's memorandum of the foreign trade regime submitted to the GATT in 1987 states that the country had already concluded MFN-based bilateral trade agreements with more than 90 trading partners, including the European Economic Community (EEC) back then. Thus, broadly speaking, China had already gained the bilateral MFN status well ahead of the WTO accession. However, these treaties were not anchored in the multilateral agreement, and their existence did not necessarily guarantee that China was completely free from selective discriminative measures, that still existed in a more targeted and specific form (as elaborated further below). As an indication, with regard to market access, the simple average rate of tariffs that the rest of the world imposed on China's exports was higher than the global average by over 3% in the

[37] Baldwin (1995).

Table 8 People's Republic of China—external environment with international comparison

	People's Republic of China			*EAP*	*World*
	1995–2000	*2001–2004*	*2005–2008*	*1995–2000*	*1995–2000*
Rest-of-the world applied tariffs (%)					
Simple average	12.17	11.18	9.73	9.57	8.83
Maximum	2703.3	3000	1450.1	1016.1	1066.8
Dispersion	2.26	3.56	1.76	2.68	3.16
Trade weighted average	9.88	4.81	3.75	11.25	12.78
Trade remedy initiations faced (per year)	35.50	54.75	70.25	2.77	1.64
Share of duty free exports (%)	26.21	38.28	54.81	26.49	27.97
Number of CU/FTA partners	–	–	7.33	–	–
Share of exports to CU/FTA partners (%)	47.10	42.89	35.43	32.91	21.04

Note CU= customs union; EAP = East Asia-Pacific, excluding high-income countries; FTA = free trade area. Indicators for 1995–2000, 2001–2004, and 2005–2008 are period averages. Tariff data includes preferences

Source World Bank. World Trade Indicators 2009/2010. Retrieved from the World Bank Web site: http://info.worldbank.org/etools/wti/2a1.asp

pre-accession period (while China appears to have enjoyed the better access on the trade-weighted term) (Table 8).

To eliminate selective discriminatory measures, in the GATT/WTO accession negotiations, China claimed non-discrimination as a matter of the natural right in the multilateral trading system. In particular, the unconditional MFN in accordance with GATT Article I was perceived as the foundation of the multilateral trading system, as clearly stated in its note attached to a letter dated 12 February 1993, from Tong Zhiguang, Vice-Minister, Ministry of Foreign Economic Relations and Trade to Pierre-Louis Girard, Chairman of the Working Part on China's status as a Contracting Party[38]:

[38]Contained in WTO Department, MOFCOM (Ed.) (2013, p. 184), Volume 8 (Multilateral 3).

> The unconditional Most-Favoured-Nation treatment is the corner stone of the GATT. In view of the complex web of discriminatory treatment against China inconsistent with the MFN principle, China's protocol should guarantee that all contracting parties should accord China unconditional MFN treatment as provided for in Article I of the General Agreement.

Among targeted discriminatory measures against China, one contentious issue related to the accord of the unconditional MFN treatment by the United States, known as the permanent normal trade relations (PNTR) status. Under the US Jackson–Vanik Amendment, provision of the normal trade relations to China (and some other transition economies) had been subjected to annual reviews, leaving uncertainty for business decisions on trade and investment. This was a source of serious concerns to the authority in China. The letter from Wu Yi, Minister of Foreign Trade and Economic Cooperation to Michael Kantor dated 11 April 1995,[39] well illustrates China's anxiety when the United States once indicated possibility of opting out from the WTO relations (an option available under the Article XIII of the Marrakesh Agreement when accord of the MFN to a new member is not feasible):

> I am writing to express my serious concerns over your recent remarks that the United States will not apply the WTO Agreements to China. Your statement will preclude our two countries from establishing WTO-based trade relations. This creates a major obstacle in our negotiations towards China's GATT/WTO membership and is detrimental to our bilateral trade relations... China is always ready to respond positively to any gesture from the U.S. side for building closer economic ties. We have made tremendous efforts to meet the U.S. concerns in respect of market access, IPR, trade in services, investment and many other areas. Now, I need some reciprocal actions from the U.S. side to build my confidence on further development of our economic relations.

Jeffrey Gertler, former Secretary of the WTO Working Party on the Accession of China, also recalls that the accord of PNTR by the United States was a quid pro quo for China's market access commitments

[39] Contained in WTO Department, MOFCOM (Ed.) (2013, p. 731), Volume 15 (Bilateral 1).

(Gertler, 2003, 2004). Toward the conclusion of China's accession process, the US Congress ultimately passed the PNTR status in September 2000.

In fact, it was not just the United States that retained the discriminatory measures against the exports from China prior to its WTO accession, albeit in a much less contentious manner. Table 9 lists WTO-inconsistent quantitative restrictions and trade remedies imposed by the incumbent members, which were still in place at the time of China's accession, known as "reservations." In a sense that these measures were directed only against China, they were inconsistent with the non-discrimination principle of the multilateral trading system. At the same time, by not observing part of the general multilateral rules (such as prohibition of quantitative restrictions under GATT Article XI), the incumbent members were also making departure from the single undertaking practice of the WTO.[40] Article XVI of the WTO Agreement prohibited any reservation in its respects, and reservations for individual multilateral trade agreements could be made only exceptionally to the extent provided by them. Thus, legality of leaving these reservations in terms of accession was rather questionable (Tyagi, 2012).

In the accession negotiations, China sought elimination of these discriminatory measures maintained inconsistently with the MFN principle. As a counter, incumbent members took a position that restrictions should be phased out only in parallel with China's own trade liberalization, as recorded in the Working Party report:

> The representative of China stated that WTO Members should eliminate all discriminatory non-tariff measures maintained against Chinese exports from the date of China's accession. In response, some members of the Working Party stated that, in their view, such measures did not need to be phased out until such time as China's foreign trade regime fully conformed to WTO obligations. (WTO, 2001b, p. 47)

Accordingly, the Protocol of Accession reflected mutual reduction in trade barriers between China and the incumbent members. The remaining trade restrictions were scheduled to be phased out by 2005, by which

[40]The WTO members are deemed to have accepted all multilateral trade agreements annexed to the Marrakesh Agreement, while the plurilateral agreements are outside of the scope of single undertaking.

Table 9 People's Republic of China—reservations by WTO members

WTO members	*Products*	*Transition arrangements*
Argentina	Textile and clothing; footwear not used for sporting activities; and toys	Quotas to be eliminated by 31 July 2002 and duties in excess of 35% ad valorem rate to be phased out over the 5-year transition period
European Community	Footwear (with exceptions); tableware, kitchenware of porcelain or china; and ceramic tableware or kitchen ware	Phasing out industrial (non-textiles) quotas by 2005
Hungary	Footwear; overwear; and other clothing and ready-made clothing products	Quantitative restrictions to be phased out by 2005
Mexico	Bicycles; footwear and parts thereof; brass padlocks; baby carriages; door knob locks; malleable iron connections; non-refillable pocket lighters, gas-fuelled; fluorite; furazolidone; tools; textiles (yarns and fabrics of artificial and synthetic fiber); toys; pencils; bicycle tyres and inner tubes; electrical machines, appliances and equipment and parts thereof, parathion-methyl; clothing; organic chemicals; ceramic and porcelain dishware and loose articles; iron and steel valves; and candles	Anti-dumping measures to be maintained against imports from China, during 6 years of the accession (without being subjected to the WTO agreement and the protocol of accession)
Poland	Pocket lighters	Continuation of anti-dumping measures not consistent with the WTO agreement till end-2002
	Footwear; and electronic smoothing irons	Continuation of safeguard measures, to be phase out by end-2004
Slovak Republic	Footwear	Quantitative restrictions to be phased out by 2005
Turkey	Footwear (with exceptions); tableware, kitchenware of porcelain or china; and ceramic tableware or kitchenware, other than of Porcelain or China	Elimination of quantitative restrictions for non-textile products by 2005

Source WTO (2001a)

time China was also to complete most of tariff cuts to the final bound level. The terms of accession state:

> All such prohibitions, quantitative restrictions and other measures shall be phased out or dealt with in accordance with mutually agreed terms and timetables as specified. (WTO, 2001c, p. 10)

Thus, through WTO accession, China managed to resolve the issue related to the general MFN treatment (albeit with reservations made by some other members just for a few years of the transition period), that was the cost of the outsider status before joining the multilateral trading system. Interestingly, these episodes also show that China's market access commitments were made partially in exchange for removing discrimination by trading partners. In this sense, there were some limited elements of reciprocity in China's accession negotiations (unlike the case of most of the other RAMs), and the country was already familiar with this prevailing practice of the WTO. On this account, it is probably not so surprising that China started to engage in reciprocal negotiations of the Doha Round even in its early phase, right after the country's accession in 2001.

However, resolution of these general MFN issues through WTO accession did not completely remove other forms of selective discrimination. These include measures related to textile and clothing, the NME status for anti-dumping, and TPS. They remained as sources of concerns for the Chinese government in the post-accession period,[41] as stated in its report for the WTO trade policy review in 2006:

> Currently, China has been subject to the greatest number of anti-dumping actions among all WTO Members... Chinese enterprises and exporters also have grave concern over all kinds of technical barriers and their adverse impact on trade. Interests of a lot of them were also seriously damaged by the restrictive measures against Chinese textiles and clothing.

[41] Looking back at China's experiences for the first two years as a new WTO member, Yuqing Zhang, Director-General of the Department of Treaty and Law, MOFCOM, and Guohua Yang, Director for WTO Legal Affairs of the Department of Treaty and Law, MOFCOM, raised concerns on TPS and textile safeguard measures in their writing (Zhang & Yang, 2004).

> The Chinese Government holds the view that discriminatory measures against a particular member is [sic] contrary to the spirit of free trade and the principle of non-discrimination enshrined in the multilateral trading system. The abuse of such measures damages the creditability of the multilateral trading system and is harmful for its further development. (WTO, 2006c, p. 18)

Among these, restrictive measures on textile and clothing were to last only for a relatively limited period of time, while NME and TPS had much longer-term implications. The remainder of this section reviews the record of how China has dealt with them in the multilateral trading system, chronologically tracing back its performance from the pre-accession period to early years of WTO membership.

5.2 *Textile Quotas and Special Safeguard*

Exclusion of non-WTO members from multilateral trade liberalization through implementation of the Uruguay Round Agreement on Textiles and Clothing (ATC) was one major concern for China. The ATC stipulates phased elimination of bilateral quotas on textiles and clothing negotiated under the Multifibre Arrangement (MFA) by 1 January 2005. While the quota arrangements under the MFA were applicable to the concerned non-members of the WTO, including China, their removal under ATC was to be limited exclusively to the WTO members (Chuanshui & Yang, 2000). Thus, staying outside of the multilateral trading system would have left some competitive disadvantage to China, and the WTO accession was an obvious avenue to redress such discrimination. Ian Dickson of Australia's Department of Foreign Affairs and Trade[42] observed that the ATC implementation was one of the drivers of accelerating China's WTO accession process:

> Between 1995 and 1998, work on China's WTO accession essentially stalled... But by late 1998 China's leaders were renewing their interest in the Organization. This renewed interest stemmed from a range of political,

[42] The designation is as of the time of his writing. Ian Dickson later moved from the China Economic and Trade Section of the Department of Foreign Affairs to the Department of Treasury.

> economic and strategic considerations, one of which may have been the threatened loss of competitiveness of China's clothing and textile exporters if China did not join the WTO soon. Under this situation, competitors with WTO membership would benefit from quota integration and acceleration while China would not. (Dickson, 2003, p. 196)

Ultimately, through WTO membership, China secured elimination of the textile quotas as stipulated in ATC. However, the terms of accession also preserved the possibility of recourse to the special safeguard action by trading partners in the early phase of the ATC implementation, for a period up to 31 December 2008. The relevant text of the Working Group report reads:

> In the event that a WTO Member believed that imports of Chinese origin of textiles and apparel products covered by the ATC as of the date the WTO Agreement entered into force, were, due to market disruption, threatening to impede the orderly development of trade in these products, such Member could request consultations with China with a view to easing or avoiding such market disruption... Upon receipt of the request for consultations, China agreed to hold its shipments to the requesting Member of textile or textile products in the category or categories subject to these consultations to a level no greater than 7.5 per cent (6 per cent for wool product categories) ... If no mutually satisfactory solution were reached during the 90–day consultation period, consultations would continue and the Member requesting consultations could continue the limits... No action taken under this provision would remain in effect beyond one year, without reapplication, unless otherwise agreed between the Member concerned and China. (WTO, 2001b, pp. 46–47)

Since 1995, China had been the world's largest textiles and clothing exporter (WTO, 2006b) and, as expected, its exports triggered special safeguard investigations and measures by the trading partners. Against these moves, China responded by conclusion of memoranda of understanding (MOU) with trading partners to restrain its exports, soon after ATC came into effect, rather than filing disputes at the WTO. For instance, an MOU with the EU was signed on 10 June 2005 to restrict annual export growth rates of ten product categories of textile and clothing between 3 and 12.5% until 31 December 2007, and a similar agreement was signed with the United States on 8 November 2005 to restrict the growth rates of exports, that were to increase only progressively from 8 to 17% in the period from 1 January 2006 to 31 December 2008 (WTO, 2006b).[43] In return, both the EU and the United States were to refrain from import restrictions from their side. Unlike the case of tariff protection by importing countries, whereby the rents generated accrue to their own governments as fiscal revenues, quota rents under voluntary exports restraints (VERs) (due to higher prices) are captured by the exporting country.[44] Thus, resort to bilateral VERs was probably the second best policy for China.

One feature of the textile safeguard provision in China's terms of accession was its relatively limited duration of possible recourse by trading partners, only for a period up to end-2008. In fact, ATC multilaterally allowed similar safeguard actions against imports from all WTO members during its transitional period until the beginning of 2005 and, practically speaking, the WTO-minus constraint specifically imposed upon China was an extension of this arrangement for additional four years. During this period, China was still in the learning stage of the WTO dispute settlement system following its accession, and its involvement was mostly as the third party, rather than as a primary disputant (Jiang, 2005). Apart from the economic rationale, the necessary learning period of the WTO dispute settlement mechanism probably explains China's resort to bilateral settlement rather than multilateral litigation in the inception years soon after returning to the multilateral trading system.

Interestingly, in a writing published in 2005, Liyong Jiang, a diplomat of the Permanent Mission of China to the WTO, argued that China had accumulated sufficient knowledge on the WTO dispute settlement mechanism by then, and should start utilizing it to cope with abuse of WTO-plus and WTO-minus trade remedy provisions by trading partners in the future:

> Those articles are concessions made by China for its accession to the WTO. However, the articles are exceptions of WTO general rules and are relatively ambiguous, subject to different interpretations. It is possible that other countries could take advantage of the ambiguous provisions

[43] Despite these restraints, China's share in the global textile exports increased from the pre-accession record of 10.3% in 2000 to 26.1% in 2008, and that of clothing exports from 18.2 to 33.2% in the same period. Data is sourced from the WTO (2009a).

[44] For theoretical illustration of differences in impacts of various trade policy instruments, see Krugman and Obstfeld (1997).

> and abuse them deliberately. If resorting to the dispute settlement mechanism, China may achieve the goal of clarifying the true meaning of relevant articles and restricting abuse... China has become quite familiar with the dispute settlement procedure and trained some capable officials through participation as the third party... The WTO dispute settlement mechanism is relatively fair and independent, and therefore trustworthy. Under certain circumstances, the dispute settlement mechanism may achieve better results than bilateral consultation. The Chinese government should use the WTO dispute settlement mechanism more actively. (Jiang, 2005, pp. 311–314)

As revealed below, this is exactly what China actually did through trade remedy disputes related to NME and TPS with the United States and the EU in later years.

5.3 Non-market Economy Status in Anti-dumping

For anti-dumping investigations, China has been treated as an NME by its trading partners. The NME treatment assumes that prices prevailing in transition economies are distorted by state interventions, and these may not be used as a legitimate basis to determine dumping and its margins. Going further, domestic anti-dumping legislations of WTO members like the United States and the EU stipulate use of prices in their chosen surrogate market economy country as normal values, and other measures that may inflate calculated anti-dumping duty rates. For instance, in the EU's anti-dumping investigations on exports of bicycles from China initiated in 1991,[45] Chinese Taipei and Mexico had been considered as analogue countries.[46] By far, China was the world's largest target of anti-dumping actions by trading partners. Out of 4519 anti-dumping initiations and 2894 measures taken by WTO members in the period of 1995–2013, 989 and 717, respectively were against China (followed by others that lagged behind, such as Korea at 331 and 199,

[45] *The Official Journal of the European Communities* No. C 266/6 of 12 October 1991: Notice of initiation of anti-dumping proceeding concerning imports of bicycles originating in Taiwan and the People's Republic of China (91/C 266/07).

[46] *The Official Journal of the European Communities*: Council Regulation (EC) No. 1524/2000 of 10 July 2000.

the United States at 255 and 150, and Chinese Taipei at 251 and 162). Even in the pre-accession period of 1995–2000, 209 anti-dumping initiations and 152 measures were targeted against China.[47]

Data on more than 200 anti-dumping cases initiated by the United States and the EU between 1995 and 1998 clearly shows that the average dumping margins calculated by the NME methodology (40.0% by the United States and 45.6% by the EU) were much higher than those based on normal price comparison alone (3.2 and 22.7%, respectively) (Messerlin, 2004). Thus, the discriminatory designation as an NME by trading partners was a concern to China, and the country had been arguing for respect of the non-discriminatory treatment during the WTO accession negotiations. In its view, targeted protectionism against transition economies would not be reconciled with the non-discrimination principle of the multilateral trading system and, on top of that, China was allegedly no longer an NME in the first place. At the third session of the GATT Working Party on China in Geneva on 26 April 1988, Shen Jueren, Vice-Minister of Foreign Economic Relations and Trade, Head of the Chinese delegation, stated:

> There are no such provisions in GATT regarding so-called "obligation of non-market economy." Therefore, it is not appropriate to ask China to undertake such obligations. Over the past nine years, China has substantially restructured its economy, and much progress has been achieved in the establishment of a new system of commodity economy. Recently, it further decided to intensify the reform, develop the market mechanism and speed up the implementation of the export-oriented economic strategy. If China is required to assume obligation as a non-market economy, it would be inconsistent not only with China's actual situation, but also with general policy of further reform and wider opening to the outside world. (GATT, 1988b, p. 7)

Despite China's resistance, the NME clause was eventually inserted in the Working Party report and the Protocol of Accession. Paragraph 15. (a)(ii) of the latter reads:

[47] Data is sourced from the WTO Web site: http://www.wto.org/english/tratop_e/adp_e/adp_e.htm.

> The importing WTO Member may use a methodology that is not based on a strict comparison with domestic prices or costs in China if the producers under investigation cannot clearly show that market economy conditions prevail in the industry producing the like product with regard to manufacture, production and sale of that product. (WTO, 2001c, p. 9)

The language of the terms of accession is rather vague, simply allowing to "*use a methodology that is not based on a strict comparison with domestic prices or costs in China*" without prescribing the limits on the alternative methodologies permissible. One may argue that such a method can accommodate use of the surrogate country prices but, other than that, the general multilateral disciplines on anti-dumping (GATT Article VI and the Anti-Dumping Agreement) should be strictly applicable. Others may say that any methodology should be allowed as far as it is not based on prices found in China. The terms of accession stipulate that this NME status lasts for 15 years after China's membership, unless its trading partners agree otherwise—a time span much longer than the transition arrangement on textiles and clothing.

After WTO accession, China continuously redressed the NME practice through a number of multilateral channels. Firstly, with regard to the use of the surrogate country prices, the country criticized such practices as artificially creating dumping in the rules negotiations of the Doha Round. Part of its 2003 negotiating proposal reads:

> Under the above-mentioned "non market economy" clauses, some Members use domestic prices of third countries instead of domestic prices of targeted Members in the comparison with the export price. Past experiences show that these Members, in most cases suggested by complaining industries, tend to choose those third countries at more advanced development levels, with higher labour costs and therefore with much higher domestic prices. Using this methodology, an artificial "dumping" is easily created and an anti-dumping measure is therefore "justified". With wide discretion in choosing the third country, an importing member is free to choose any other country as the third country as long as the latter produces the same or like products. (WTO, 2003a, p. 3)

At the same time, China was well aware that it would not be easy to rewrite the multilateral rule itself at the WTO, and sought non-discrimination also through bilateral trade agreements (Green, 2004). The trade policy review report by the WTO Secretariat comments that, apparently, most of the trading partners that concluded bilateral or regional trade agreements with China recognized the country as a market economy (WTO, 2006b).[48]

Secondly, to cope with possible abuse of the NME treatment by major trading partners beyond their use of the surrogate country prices, China resorted to the WTO dispute settlement mechanism in recent years. From 2008 onward, China filed a number of cases against the EU and the United States. Disputes against the EU related to its anti-dumping regulations and application to exports of fasteners (EC—Fasteners) and footwear (EU—Footwear) from China (WTO, 2009b, 2010c). While these were two separate disputes, domestically initiated by the fastener industry association on the one hand and the footwear association on the other hand, China's complaint was commonly directed to EU's Basic Anti-Dumping Regulation, whose relevant provisions imposed two kinds of examinations against imports from alleged NMEs, known as the market economy treatment (MET) test [Article 2(7)] and the individual treatment (IT) test [Article 9(5)]. Under the MET test, exporters from NMEs are screened by certain criteria, and anti-dumping duties are calculated on the basis of the surrogate country prices when they cannot demonstrate as operating in the market economy environment. On top of that, these exporters who failed to pass the MET test are screened also by the IT test, based on similar criteria. Exporters that failed to pass the IT test could not claim individual calculation of dumping margins for their products and would have to accept a common duty rate assigned by the EU to each country. The IT test assumed that, in NMEs, a single entity of "the State" controlled the entire economy, and calculation of dumping margins for individual enterprises was not valid. Vermulst and Graafsma (2006), who were involved in over 200 EC anti-dumping proceedings, comment that the EU had increasingly become more protectionist in its use of the NME methodology comprising these two tests (essentially, against China and Viet Nam).

[48]As opposed to typical characterization that bilateral trade agreements are discriminatory and the WTO is not, in this particular case, it was bilateral agreements that assured non-discriminatory market economy treatment to China, against the discrimination inscribed in the terms of WTO accession (Green, 2004). Also, unlike the case of WTO accession process (where applicant countries are placed in disadvantaged positions), bilateral negotiations provided China with a better standing as an equal signatory of the treaties.

In the EC—Fasteners case initiated in 2009, China took a position that, while Paragraph 15 of the Protocol of Accession may accommodate the MET test, the IT test is not allowed and should not be imposed discriminately upon NMEs, while also maintaining that China had already become a market economy. For closing of the first meeting of the panel, the Chinese delegation stated:

> During the last two days, the EU has argued that the EU's "individual treatment" regime is somehow justified by a common understanding contained in China's Protocol of Accession that China is a "non-market economy". When questioned, the EU was, however, unable to point to any specific wording in the Protocol which would confirm the existence of such an understanding which would be common to the WTO membership... Paragraph 15 of China's Protocol of Accession only deals with one very limited issue, namely the possibility for some WTO members to determine normal value on the basis of data other than the domestic prices and costs in China. Nothing more, nothing less.... Whatever the situation may have been in the past, China can no longer be considered as a so-called non-market economy country. In any event, this question is irrelevant since neither Article 6.10 nor Article 9.2 distinguish between any such different categories of WTO Members. (WTO, 2010d, p. C-18).[49]

China argued that the relevant provision of the EU's Basic Anti-Dumping Regulation, both as such and as applied to fasteners and footwear, was beyond the scope of its terms of accession and hence should be subjected to Articles 6.10 and 9.2 of the normal WTO Anti-Dumping Agreement, which primarily called for individual calculation of anti-dumping duties. On the other hand, the EU took a position that China's status as NME was relevant, and the terms of accession allowed any '*methodology that is not based on a strict comparison with domestic prices or costs in China*', including the IT test.[50]

[49] A similar argument was made by China for the EU—Footwearcase (WTO, 2011a).

[50] The executive summary of the EU's opening statement at the second meeting of the panel on fasteners reads "*China argues that 'whether China is a market economy country or not is totally irrelevant for this dispute'. The European Union strongly disagrees. If anything the uncontested fact that China is a non-market economy country is the only reason we are here today discussing this 'as such' claim... All imports from non-market economy countries are therefore considered to emanate from a single producer, the State. Article 9(5) is also in line with China's Protocol of Accession... A methodology for the purpose of determining the existence of dumping which considers the State as the actual producer of the product concerned*

In the end, both the panel (for fasteners and footwear) and the Appellate Body (for fasteners alone, as the footwear case was not appealed) broadly supported China's claim with regard to the IT test (WTO, 2010d, 2011a, 2011b). Importantly, since China's claim related to the relevant provision of the EU's Basic Anti-Dumping Regulation "as such" (in addition to "as applied" to specific products),[51] compliance with the Dispute Settlement Body (DSB) recommendation required altering the basic European rule itself, leaving implications far beyond the resolution of these particular disputes. While the EU reported completed implementation of the DSB recommendation on both cases in 2012, China was not satisfied with regard to fasteners and filed a recourse to the compliance panel under Article 21.5 of the Dispute Settlement Understanding (DSU)[52] in 2013. Subsequently, the compliance panel on the faster case was established in 2014, and the dispute continued.[53]

A different dispute that China filed against the United States in 2008 concerned simultaneous use of anti-dumping and countervailing duties (United States—Anti-Dumping and Countervailing Duties), known as a "double remedy," on certain imported products (pipes, tubes, woven sacks, and off-the-road tyres) (WTO, 2008c).[54] As explained above, the special NME methodology of allowing for departure from the standard calculation of dumping margins is based on the premise that prices in transition economies are distorted by state interventions. At the same time, countervailing duties are aimed at offsetting the impacts of

and uses information available to compare export prices of the actual producer with an analogue country normal value is also 'a methodology that is not based on a strict comparison with domestic prices or costs in China'" (WTO, 2010d, pp. F-10-F-11).

[51] The "as such" claim was not included in the initial industry petition and added by MOFCOM.

[52] Article 21.5 of DSU reads "*(w)here there is disagreement as to the existence or consistency with a covered agreement of measures taken to comply with the recommendations and rulings such dispute shall be decided through recourse to these dispute settlement procedures, including wherever possible resort to the original panel*" (WTO, 1995a, p. 421).

[53] WTO (2011b). In 2013, China filed another dispute, United States—Anti-Dumping Methodologies (China) that also related to a similar issue of single rate presumption for NME. See WTO (2013).

[54] In 2012, China also filed a similar dispute, United States—Countervailing and Anti-Dumping Measures (China) that also related to double remedy for NME. See WTO (2012e).

subsidies, that are one form of state interventions. China claimed that these two different kinds of duties are both addressing the same state subsidies, based on their double-counting in violation of the WTO Agreement on Subsidies and Countervailing Measures (SCM). Given that the double remedy arises when the importing country uses the discriminatory NME methodology (that is not applicable to non-NMEs), China also claimed that it is inconsistent with the MFN principle under GATT. The executive summary of China's first written submission for the panel at the WTO reads:

> China considers that a double remedy arises in all cases in which Commerce applies its NME methodology in conjunction with countervailing duties… the United States has denied imports from China most-favoured nation treatment under Article I: 1 of the GATT 1994 by failing to extend to these imports the same unconditional entitlement to the avoidance of double remedies that it extends to imports from countries that it designates as market economies. This treatment not only deprives Chinese imports of most-favoured nation treatment under Article I: 1 of the GATT, but it also serves to underscore Commerce's consistent recognition of the impermissibility of offsetting the same subsidies twice. (WTO, 2010e, p. A-9)

Just as the EU argued in their disputes, the United States responded that the NME-related provisions in China's terms of WTO accession allow discriminatory actions against China—in this case, the double remedy.[55] Again, the issue was where to draw a legally legitimate line to justify NME-related reasoning for triggering targeted trade remedies against China. Whereas the panel initially did not support China's claim, including the one based on the MFN principle (WTO, 2010e),

[55]The executive summary of the opening statement by the United States at the first panel meeting reads: "*China's Accession Protocol was negotiated against this backdrop of the well-established right to apply both anti-dumping and countervailing duties concurrently. The Protocol affirms Members' right to apply NME anti-dumping duties to imports from China, and their right to apply countervailing duties to imports from China. Nowhere in the Protocol is there any limitation on the resort to either of these remedies… In addition, the alleged discrimination underlying China's MFN claim stems from the fact that imports from China, unlike those form market economies, are subject to an NME methodology. This differential treatment, however, is necessitated by the nature of China's economy itself, as recognized in the explicit authority given under China's Protocol to employ such a methodology*" (WTO, 2010e, p. D-10).

the Appellate Body reversed the finding and ultimately concluded that the double remedy was inconsistent with the SCM Agreement (WTO, 2011c). Thus, China successfully challenged the abuse of the NME provision inserted in terms of accession by major trading partners through the WTO dispute settlement mechanism.

5.4 *Transitional Product-Specific Safeguard*

Among WTO-minus provisions inscribed in China's terms of accession, the arguably most discriminatory rule relates to possible resort to TPS by trading partners. Unlike the normal multilateral safeguard rule (GATT Article XIX and the Agreement on Safeguard), that requires the MFN treatment and compensatory tariff cuts by the country imposing import protection, the TPS provision inserted in China's terms of WTO accession allows trade restrictions against China alone and compensations are not required. Also, the recourse to TPS does not require the context that increase in imports represents "unforeseen circumstances," and the level of injury to justify protection of the domestic industry is just "material," not "serious" as in the normal safeguard rules. Weaker disciplines may make it more likely to bring about costs on not only importing countries (due to welfare loss from their own protection) but also exporting countries (due to potential loss of export opportunities), and China opposed the concept of discriminatory safeguard in the course of accession negotiations. Back then, Shen Jueren remarked:

> Selective safeguard clause is in contravention of GATT basic principles. There is already a large number of Chinese export products subject to discriminatory safeguard measures. Such measures restrict the export of Chinese products of high international competitiveness, limit the increase of export earning and the expansion of China's import capacity, consequently, affect trade expansion between China and other contracting parties ..... It is contrary to the basic principle of the General Agreement and the objective of the Uruguay Round to request China to accept a selective safeguard clause. (GATT, 1988b, p. 8)

However, as in the case of the NME designation for anti-dumping, the TPS clause was inserted in terms of accession against China's opposition. Paragraph 16 of the Protocol of Accession reads:

> In cases where products of Chinese origin are being imported into the territory of any WTO Member in such increased quantities or under such conditions as to cause or threaten to cause market disruption to the domestic producers..., the WTO Member so affected may request consultations with China... If consultations do not lead to an agreement..., the WTO Member affected shall be free, in respect of such products, to withdraw concessions or otherwise to limit imports only to the extent necessary to prevent or remedy such market disruption... Market disruption shall exist whenever imports of an article, like or directly competitive with an article produced by the domestic industry, are increasing rapidly, either absolutely or relatively, so as to be a significant cause of material injury, or threat of material injury to the domestic industry. (WTO, 2001c, p. 9)

The TPS was allowed for 12 years after China's WTO accession, for a relatively long time span. Unlike anti-dumping, safeguard was not part of the Doha Round mandate for rules negotiations, and the dispute settlement mechanism was the only possibly effective multilateral instrument to cope with the actual use of TPS by trading partners. Thus, in response to the domestic petition by the rubber industry association (that was also involved in the double remedy case), China filed a dispute at the WTO against the United States on its recourse to the TPS measure on certain passenger vehicle and light truck tyres (United States—Tyres) in 2009 (WTO, 2009c). Its main argument was that the TPS provision in terms of accession should be interpreted in light of disciplines under normal safeguard rules applicable to all WTO members (China even claimed that the TPS provision assumed tighter disciples). In counter, the United States stated that China's request for non-discriminatory treatment on safeguard had already been refused at the time of accession negotiations. In its view, the provision in the Protocol of Accession should be applied on its own right, and the normal safeguard rules are not relevant. The executive summary of the oral statement by the United States at the second meeting of the panel reads:

> According to China, the negotiating history of the Protocol provides no meaningful interpretive guidance, but confirms the relationship between the Safeguards Agreement and the transitional mechanism. On the contrary, a quick review of the documents in the WT/ACC/SPEC/CHN series confirms our reading of the Protocol. China alleges that these documents only demonstrate that the result was a "hybrid" or compromise. Those documents show China sought, but failed, to have the Safeguards Agreement apply to the Protocol, except as otherwise provided in the Draft Protocol. (WTO, 2010f, pp. F-11-F12)

In fact, the panel and the Appellate Body straightforwardly rejected all arguments made by China (WTO, 2010f, 2011d), signifying the difficulty of challenging the safeguard measure within the framework of the loose TPS disciplines. The ruling also represented the first ever occasion since the establishment of the WTO that the respondent's argument completely prevailed in safeguard disputes. While the US delegation declared this to be a historic victory, China expressed its deep concerns at the DSB meeting on 5 October 2011. In its view, the WTO's mandate is to promote free trade, and the multilateral trading system should have never sided with protectionism:

> (t)he WTO was an international organization that had been dedicated to improving global free trade, resisting trade protectionism, and eliminating discriminatory treatment in international trade relations. However, under the current uncertainties and difficulties of the global economy, China was concerned that the findings of the Appellate Body and the Panel Reports in this dispute, upholding trade protectionist measures, conveyed the wrong signal to WTO Members. The Chinese industry had suffered for over two years of the punitive duties imposed by the US measures. China continued to urge the United States to discard the measures promptly and to maintain a market of fair competition for Chinese enterprises'. (WTO, 2011e, pp. 3–4)

The medium-term record of China's engagement in the WTO verifies Hypothesis 3. China successfully redressed part of the cost of the earlier non-member status by securing the less discriminatory treatment through its accession to the WTO, as reflected in the accord of PNTR by the United States and phasing out of restrictions by some other trading partners. However, certain forms of trade remedy discrimination remained for some time even after China's WTO membership. Among them, the textile safeguard was short-lived, triggered by the trading partners during China's learning phase of the WTO dispute settlement system, and the government addressed them through bilateral VER agreements. However, the NME and TPS provisions had longer durations of effectiveness, and China decided to counter some of discriminatory trade restrictions at the multilateral trading system, mainly through dispute settlement with the United States and the EU. Its challenge against the abuse of the NME status was broadly successful, whereas the one on TPS was not. The loose discipline on the latter provided in terms of accession placed China in an extremely disadvantageous position.

6 Conclusion

China's performance in trade liberalization in the multilateral trading system reviewed in this chapter is in line with Hypothesis 1 for transition economies: *Reforming economies (especially, those in transition to a market economy) would make extensive market access commitments for WTO accession, while others would make little use of them*; as well as Hypothesis 2-a: *Only export-oriented economies would stay proactively engaged in the post-accession market access negotiations of the Doha Round, while others would pursue autonomous liberalization.* As in the case of Georgia reviewed in Chapter 3, China's prime objective for WTO accession was to support its domestic reform, as per the commitment theory prescription. Thus, the country made extensive market access commitments in its terms of WTO accession, albeit within its gradualist reform approach. However, China also had other policy objectives and followed a unique path in the post-accession period. Unlike Georgia that pursued autonomous trade liberalization, China continuously tried to stay engaged in the DDA market access negotiations, especially with regard to NAMA. As per the juggernaut theory, the strong export orientation of the Chinese economy provided an enabling environment for the government to pursue reciprocal liberalization through the multilateral process. However, the extent to which the government actually seized this contextual advantage was moderated by other factors. Thus, while China showed much more positive engagement in the Doha Round than many other RAMs (and some large emerging market economies), the country did not meet expectations to take the more prominent "leadership" role at the Doha Round.

In fact, part of China's middle-ground position was also reflected in its other negotiations at the WTO on expansion of product coverage for tariff elimination under the Information Technology Agreement (ITA). Unlike multilateral agreements mandatory to all WTO members (such as GATT), the ITA is a plurilateral agreement only among its voluntary signatories. Nonetheless, China joined not only the original ITA Agreement in 2003[56] but also recent negotiations on its expansion, showing the

[56]WTO news "China, Egypt join WTO's Information Technology Agreement," dated 24 April 2003, retrieved from the WTO Web site: http://www.wto.org/english/news_e/news03_e/news_china_egypt_25apr03_e.htm.

positive sign of engagement.[57] On the other hand, China once showed the defensive attitude by requesting removal of more than 100 products from the expanded ITA coverage, putting the entire negotiations on hold in July 2013 ("Special Report," 2013),[58] before reaching an understanding with the United States toward the prospective conclusion of the expanded ITA subsequently in November 2015.[59]

Further in relation to the reciprocal market access negotiations, this chapter also examined Hypothesis 2-b: *Only large economies would stay proactively engaged in the market access negotiations of the Doha Round, while others would pursue autonomous liberalization*, by shedding light on the theory of terms of trade externality. As the world's second largest economy, China exhibited a more positive stance at the market access negotiations of the Doha Round than many other RAMs, and the hypothesis was verified arguably by the data gathered. However, no qualitative evidence was found to establish the relevance of terms of trade externality in actual policy-making.

A number of episodes covered in this chapter confirmed part of Hypothesis 3: *Countries that face the discriminatory cost of prior non-membership would stay engaged in the relevant multilateral liberalization schemes, while others would refrain from such activities.* Unlike the case of some other RAMs including Georgia, China has been long suffering from targeted discrimination by its trading partners. Thus, China tried to remove the discriminatory measures through accession to

[57] The ITA requires involvement of members representing 90% of the global trade (so-called critical mass) and participation by China as a large trading nation was inevitable. The country has benefitted from the original ITA and sought to take part in its expansion with major trading partners.

[58] This negative stance frustrated developed country trading partners, which made a resolve not to welcome China to other plurilateral negotiations, such as the Trade in Services Agreement (TiSA) initiative any longer. Panel discussions on "Looking beyond MC9: how to deal with reciprocity and flexibility in moving forward on the Doha Development Agenda?" at the 2013 WTO Public Forum on 1–3 October. See the WTO Web site: http://www.wto.org/english/forums_e/public_forum13_e/public_forum13_e.htm.

[59] See WTO news "Information Technology Agreement: Azevêdo hails breakthrough on the WTO's Information Technology Agreement," dated 11 November 2014, posted in the WTO Web site: http://www.wto.org/english/news_e/news14_e/ita_11nov14_e.htm.

international agreements, as inferred from the domino theory. However, some forms of trade remedy discrimination still remained as WTO-minus provisions in its terms of accession. Among them, the NME status for anti-dumping and TPS had relatively long time horizons, and China continuously tried to redress them, partly through the rules negotiations of the Doha Round and also through the dispute settlement mechanism.[60]

References

All Change: China's Economy and the WTO. (2011, December 10). *The Economist, 401*(8763), 45–46.

Asian Development Bank. (2013). *Key indicators for Asia and the Pacific 2013* (44th ed.). Manila: Author.

Bagwell, K., & Staiger, R. W. (1999). An economic theory of GATT. *American Economic Review, 89*(1), 215–248.

Bagwell, K., & Staiger, R. W. (2002). *The economics of the world trading system.* Cambridge: MIT Press.

Baldwin, R. E. (1995). A domino theory of regionalism. In R. Baldwin, P. Haaparanta, & J. Kiander (Eds.), *Expanding membership of the European Union* (pp. 25–48). Cambridge: Cambridge University Press.

Baldwin, R. E. (2006). Multilateralising regionalism: Spaghetti bowls as building blocs on the path to global free trade. *The World Economy, 29*(11), 1451–1518.

Baldwin, R. E. (2012). Preferential trading arrangements. In A. Narlikar, M. Daunton, & R. M. Stern (Eds.), *The Oxford handbook on the World Trade Organization* (pp. 632–654). Oxford: Oxford University Press.

Baldwin, R. E. (2014). WTO 2.0: Governance of 21st century trade. *Review of International Organizations, 9*(2), 261–283.

Beseler, H. F. (2002). The EU-China negotiations: Breaking the deadlock. In H. Holbig & R. Ash (Eds.), *China's accession to the World Trade Organization: National and international perspectives* (pp. 3–13). London: RoutledgeCurzon.

[60]As a recent development, on 12 December 2016, China filed new disputes against the EU and the United States pertaining to their continuous determination of normal value for NMEs in anti-dumping proceedings claiming that the relevant provision in the protocol of accession expired on 11 December 2016, 15 years after the country's WTO accession. Unlike previous dispute settlement cases, China's present claims relate the NME methodology itself, not its abuse, and would have more profound implications. See WTO (2016a, 2016b, 2017).

Bhagwati, J., & Sutherland, P. (Co-chairs). (2011). *The Doha round: Setting a deadline, defining a final deal—Interim report*. Retrieved from the Graduate Institute Geneva website: http://graduateinstitute.ch/files/live/sites/iheid/files/sites/ctei/shared/CTEI/Baldwin/Publications/Chapters/Regionalism/The_Doha_round_Setting_a_deadline,defining_a_final_deal.pdf.

China and the WTO: Long March. (1999, April 1). *The Economist*. Retrieved from: http://www.economist.com/node/320544/print.

Chuanshui, Z., & Yang, Y. (2000). China's textile and clothing exports in the post Uruguay round. In P. Drysdale & L. Song (Eds.), *China's entry to the WTO: Strategic issues and quantitative assessments* (pp. 175–193). London: Routledge.

Dickson, I. (2003). China's interest in the World Trade Organization's deregulation in international textiles trade. In D. Z. Cass, B. G. Williams, & G. Barker (Eds.), *China and the world trading system: Entering the new millennium* (pp. 175–201). Cambridge: Cambridge University Press.

Feng, H. (2006). *The politics of China's accession to the World Trade Organization: The dragon goes global*. London: Routledge.

Gadbaw, M. (1998). WTO accession: A private sector view. In F. M. Abbott (Ed.), *China in the world trading system: Defining the principles of engagement* (pp. 81–86). Cambridge, MA: Kluwer Law International.

General Agreement on Tariffs and Trade. (1984). China—Request for observer status (L/5712). Geneva: Author.

General Agreement on Tariffs and Trade. (1986). China's status as a contracting party: Communication from the People's Republic of China (L/6017). Geneva: Author.

General Agreement on Tariffs and Trade. (1987). *China's status as a contracting party: Memorandum on China's foreign trade regime* (L/6125). Geneva: Author.

General Agreement on Tariffs and Trade. (1988a). *Contracting parties, forty-fourth session: China—Statement by Qian Jiadong, ambassador, permanent representative (speaking as an observer)* (SR. 44/ST/28). Geneva: Author.

General Agreement on Tariffs and Trade. (1988b). Working party on China's status as a contracting party: Communication from China (Spec(88)37). Geneva: Author.

General Agreement on Tariffs and Trade. (1991). *Contracting parties, forty-seventh session: China—Statement by H.E. Mr. Fan Guoxiang, ambassador and permanent representative (speaking as an observer)* (SR. 47/ST/6). Geneva: Author.

General Agreement on Tariffs and Trade. (1994a). *Contracting parties, forty-ninth session: China—Statement by Yufeng Tang, Minister-Counsellor, Deputy Permanent Representative (speaking as an observer)* (SR. 49/ST/18). Geneva: Author.

General Agreement on Tariffs and Trade. (1994b). *Contracting parties, fiftieth session: China—Statement by Mr. Long Yongtu, Assistant Minister, Ministry of Foreign Trade and Economic Cooperation (speaking as an observer)* (SR. 50/ST/19). Geneva: Author.

General Agreement on Tariffs and Trade. (1994c). *Multilateral trade negotiations, the Uruguay round, trade negotiations committee, Meeting at ministerial level, Marrakesh (Morocco), 12–15 April 1994: China—Statement by Gu Yongjiang, Vice-Minister for Foreign Trade and Economic Cooperation* (MTN. TNC/MIN(94)/ST/45). Geneva: Author.

Gertler, J. L. (1998). The process of China's accession to the World Trade Organization. In F. M. Abbott (Ed.), *China in the world trading system: Defining the principles of engagement* (pp. 65–74). Cambridge, MA: Kluwer Law International.

Gertler, J. L. (2002). Negotiating China's protocol of accession. In S. Ostry, A. S. Alexandroff, & R. Gomez (Eds.), *China and the long march to global trade: The accession of China to the World Trade Organization* (pp. 22–29). London: Routledge.

Gertler, J. L. (2003). China's WTO accession—The final countdown. In D. Z. Cass, B. G. Williams, & G. Barker (Eds.), *China and the world trading system: Entering the new millennium* (pp. 55–67). Cambridge: Cambridge University Press.

Gertler, J. L. (2004). What China's WTO accession is all about. In D. Bhattasali, S. Li, & W. Martin (Eds.), *China and the WTO: Accession, policy reform, and poverty reduction strategies* (pp. 21–28). Washington, DC: World Bank.

Godoy, S., & Stiglitz, J. E. (2006). *Growth, initial conditions, law and speed of privatization in transition countries: 11 years later* (Working Paper No. 11992). Retrieved from National Bureau of Economic Research website: http://www.nber.org/papers/w11992.

Green, S. (2004). *China's quest for market economy status* (Chatham House Briefing Note). Retrieved from Royal Institute of International Affairs website: https://www.chathamhouse.org/sites/files/chathamhouse/public/Research/Asia/bnmay04.pdf.

International Monetary Fund. (2006). *People's Republic of China: 2006 article IV consultation—Staff report; staff statement; and public information notice on the executive board discussion* (IMF Staff Country Report No. 06/394). Washington, DC: Author.

International Monetary Fund. (2007). *Staff report on the multilateral consultation on global imbalances with China, the Euro area, Japan, Saudi Arabia, and the United States.* Washington, DC: Author.

International Monetary Fund. (2011). *People's Republic of China: 2011 article IV consultation* (IMF Country Report No. 11/192). Washington, DC: Author.

International Monetary Fund. (2012). *People's Republic of China: 2012 article IV consultation* (IMF Country Report No. 12/195). Washington, DC: Author.
International Monetary Fund. (2013). *People's Republic of China: 2013 article IV consultation* (IMF Country Report No. 13/211). Washington, DC: Author.
Jiang, L. (2005). The WTO dispute settlement mechanism and China's participation. In H. Gao & D. Lewis (Eds.), *China's participation in the WTO* (pp. 303–314). London: Cameron May.
Krugman, P. (1991, November/December). The move toward free trade zones. *Economic Review—Federal Reserve Bank of Kansas City, 76*(6), 5–25.
Krugman, P. (1997). What should trade negotiators negotiate about? *Journal of Economic Literature, 35*(1), 113–120.
Krugman, P. R., & Obstfeld, M. (1997). *International economics: Theory and policy* (4th ed.). Reading, MA: Addison-Wesley.
Laborde, D., Martin, W., & Mensbrugghe, D. V. D. (2012). Implications of the Doha market access proposals for developing countries. *World Trade Review, 11*(1), 1–25.
Lawrence, R. Z. (2006). *China and the multilateral trading system* (Working Paper No. 12759). National Bureau of Economic Research website: http://www.nber.org/papers/w12759.
Lim, C. L., & Wang, J. Y. (2010). China and the Doha development agenda. *Journal of World Trade, 44*(6), 1309–1331.
Maggi, G., & Rodríguez-Clare, A. (1998). The value of trade agreements in the presence of political pressures. *Journal of Political Economy, 106*(3), 574–601.
Maggi, G., & Rodríguez-Clare, A. (2007). A political-economy theory of trade agreements. *American Economic Review, 97*(4), 1374–1406.
Manger, M. S. (2009). *Investing in protection: The politics and proliferation of preferential trade agreements between north and south*. Cambridge: Cambridge University Press.
Messerlin, P. A. (2004). China in the WTO: Antidumping and safeguards. In D. Bhattasali, S. Li, & W. Martin (Eds.), *China and the WTO: Accession, policy reform, and poverty reduction strategies* (pp. 29–47). Washington, DC: World Bank.
Sally, R. (2008). *Trade policy, new century: The WTO, FTAs and Asia rising*. London: Institute of Economic Affairs.
Sally, R. (2011). *Chinese trade policy after (almost) ten years in the WTO: A post-crisis stocktake* (ECIPE Occasional Paper No. 2/2011). Brussels: European Centre for International Political Economy.
Special Report—World Economy: In My Backyard—Trade. (2013, October 12). *The Economist, 409*(8857), 16.
Staiger, R. W., & Tabellini, G. (1987). Discretionary trade policy and excessive protection. *American Economic Review, 77*(5), 823–837.

Tyagi, M. (2012). Flesh on a legal fiction: Early practice in the WTO accession protocols. *Journal of International Economic Law, 15*(2), 391–441.

United States General Accounting Office. (2002). *World Trade Organization: Selected U.S. company views about China's membership*. Washington, DC: Author.

VanGrasstek, C. (2001). Why demands on acceding countries increase over time: A three-dimensional analysis of multilateral trade diplomacy. In United Nations Conference on Trade and Development, *WTO Accession and Development Policies* (UNCTAD/DITC/TNCD/11) (pp. 78–95). Retrieved from United Nations Conference on Trade and Development website: http://unctad.org/en/Docs/ditctncd11_en.pdf.

Vermulst, E., & Graafsma, F. (2006). Recent EC anti-dumping practice towards China and Vietnam: The great leap backward? *International Trade Law and Regulation, 12*(5), 124–129.

World Trade Organization. (1995a). *The results of the Uruguay round of multilateral trade negotiations: Legal texts*. Geneva: Author. (Original work published by the GATT Secretariat 1994).

World Trade Organization. (1995b). *Accession to the World Trade Organization: Procedures for negotiations under article XII—Note by the secretariat* (WT/ACC/1). Geneva: Author.

World Trade Organization. (2001a). *Working party on the accession of China: Report of the working party on the accession of China* (WT/ACC/CHN/49). WTO: Author.

World Trade Organization. (2001b). Ministerial conference, fourth session, Doha, 9–13 November 2001: Report of the working party on accession of China (WT/MIN/01/3). Geneva: Author.

World Trade Organization. (2001c). Accession of the People's Republic of China: Decision of 10 November 2001 (WT/L/432). Geneva: Author.

World Trade Organization. (2002a). Negotiation group on market access: Market access for non-agricultural products—Proposal by the People's Republic of China (TN/MA/W/20). Geneva: Author.

World Trade Organization. (2002b). Committee on agriculture, special session: Summary report on the thirteen meeting of the committee on agriculture special session held on 6 September 2002—Note by the secretariat (TN/AG/R3). Geneva: Author.

World Trade Organization. (2002c). *Negotiating group on market access: Minutes of the meeting held in Centre William Rappard on 2 August 2002* (TM/MA/M2). Geneva: Author.

World Trade Organization. (2002d). *Negotiating group on market access: Minutes of the meeting held in Centre William Rappard on 30 October 2002* (TN/MA/M/3). Geneva: Author.

World Trade Organization. (2003a). *Negotiating group on rules: Proposal of the People's Republic of China on the negotiation on anti-dumping* (TN/RL/W/66). Geneva: Author.

World Trade Organization. (2003b). *Negotiating group on market access: Minutes of the meeting, held in the Centre William Rappard on 26–28 May 2003—Chairman: Ambassador P-L. Girard (Switzerland)* (TN/MA/M/8). Geneva: Author.

World Trade Organization. (2003c). *Ministerial conference, fifth session, Cancún, 10–14 September 2003—China: Statement by H.E. Lu Fuyuan, Minister of Commence* (WT/MIN(03)/ST/12). Geneva: Author.

World Trade Organization. (2003d). *Negotiating group on Market access: Minutes of the meeting held in the Centre William Rappard on 14–16 April 2003* (TN/MA/M7). Geneva: Author.

World Trade Organization. (2005). *Ministerial conference, sixth session, Hong Kong, 13–18 December 2005: China—Statement by H.E. Bo Xilai, Minister of Commerce* (WT/MIN(05)/ST/59). Geneva: Author.

World Trade Organization. (2006a). *Trade policy review body, 19 and 21 April 2006: Trade policy review—People's Republic of China: Minutes of meeting* (WT/TPR/M/161). Geneva: Author.

World Trade Organization. (2006b). *Trade policy review body: Trade policy review report by the secretariat—People's Republic of China, revision* (WT/TPR/S/161/Rev.1). Geneva: Author.

World Trade Organization. (2006c). *Trade policy review body: Trade policy review report by the People's Republic of China* (WT/TPR/G/161). Geneva: Author.

World Trade Organization. (2008a). *Trade policy review body: Trade policy review—Report by China* (WT/TPR/G/199). Geneva: Author.

World Trade Organization. (2008b). *Trade policy review: Report by the secretariat—China, revision* (WT/TPR/S/199/Rev.1). Geneva: Author.

World Trade Organization. (2008c). *United States—Definitive anti-dumping and countervailing duties on certain products from China: Request for consultations by China* (WT/DS379/1). Geneva: Author.

World Trade Organization. (2009a). *International trade statistics 2009*. Geneva: Author.

World Trade Organization. (2009b). *European Communities—Definitive anti-dumping measures on certain iron or steel fasteners from China: Request for consultations by China* (WT/DS397/1). Geneva: WTO.

World Trade Organization. (2009c). *United States—Measures affecting imports of certain passenger vehicle and light truck tyres from China: Request for consultations by China* (WT/DS399/1). Geneva: Author.

World Trade Organization. (2009d). *China—Measures related to the exportation of various raw materials: Request for consultations by the United States* (WT/DS394/1). Geneva: Author.

World Trade Organization. (2009e). *China—Measures related to the exportation of various raw materials: Request for consultations by the European Communities* (WT/DS395/1). Geneva: Author.

World Trade Organization. (2009f). *China—Measures related to the exportation of various raw materials: Request for consultations by Mexico* (WT/DS398/1). Geneva: Author.

World Trade Organization. (2010a). *Trade policy review: Report by the secretariat—China, revision* (WT/TPR/S/230/Rev.1). Geneva: Author.

World Trade Organization. (2010b). *Trade policy review body, 31 May and 2 June 2010: Trade policy review—People's Republic of China: Minutes of meeting* (WT/TPR/M/230). Geneva: Author.

World Trade Organization. (2010c). *European Union—Anti-dumping measures on certain footwear from China: Request for consultations by China* (WT/DS405/1). Geneva: Author.

World Trade Organization. (2010d). *European Communities—Definitive anti-dumping measures on certain iron or steel fasteners from China: Report of the panel* (WT/DS397/R). Geneva: Author.

World Trade Organization. (2010e). *United States—Definitive anti-dumping and countervailing duties on certain products from China: Report of the panel* (WT/DS379/R). Geneva: Author.

World Trade Organization. (2010f). *United States—Measures affecting imports of certain passenger vehicle and light truck tyres from China: Report of the panel* (WT/DS399/R). Geneva: Author.

World Trade Organization (2011a). *European Union—Anti-dumping measures on certain footwear from China: Report of the panel* (WT/DS4065/R). Geneva: Author.

World Trade Organization. (2011b). *European Communities—Definitive anti-dumping measures on certain iron or steel fasteners from China: Report of the appellate body* (WT/DS397/AB/R). Geneva: Author.

World Trade Organization. (2011c). *United States—Definitive anti-dumping and countervailing duties on certain products from China: Report of the appellate body* (WT/DS379/AB/R). Geneva: Author.

World Trade Organization. (2011d). *United States—Measures affecting imports of certain passenger vehicle and light truck tyres from China: Report of the appellate body* (WT/DS399/AB/R). Geneva: Author.

World Trade Organization. (2011e). *Dispute settlement body, 5 October 2011: Minutes of the meeting* (WT/DSB/M/304). Geneva: Author.

World Trade Organization. (2011f). *China—Measures related to the exportation of various raw materials: Report of the panel* (WT/DS394/R, WT/DS395/R, WT/DS398/R). Geneva: Author.

World Trade Organization. (2012a). *Trade policy review body: Trade policy review report by the secretariat, Ecuador—Revision* (WT/TPR/S/254/Rev.1). Geneva: Author.

World Trade Organization. (2012b). *Trade policy review body, 12 and 14 June 2012: Trade policy review, China—Record of the meeting* (WT/TPR/M/264). Geneva: Author.

World Trade Organization. (2012c). *Dispute settlement body, 23 July 2012: Minutes of the meeting* (WT/DSB/M/320). Geneva: Author.

World Trade Organization. (2012d). *China—Measures related to exportation of various raw materials: Reports of the appellate Body* (WT/DS394/AB/R, WT/DS395/AB/R, WT/DS398/AB/R). Geneva: Author.

World Trade Organization. (2012e). *United States—Countervailing and anti-dumping measures on certain products from China: Request for consultations by China* (WT/DS449/1, G/L/1001, G/SCM/D92/1, G/ADP/D95/1). Geneva: Author.

World Trade Organization. (2013). *United States—Certain methodologies and their application to anti-dumping proceedings involving China: Request for consultations by China* (WT/DS471/1, G/L/1060, G/ADP/D100/1). Geneva: Author.

World Trade Organization. (2014a). *Trade policy review body: Trade policy review report by the secretariat, China* (WT/TPR/S/300). Geneva: Author.

World Trade Organization. (2014b). *China—Measures related to the exportation of rare earth, tungsten, and molybdenum: Reports of the panel* (WT/DS431/R, WT/DS432/R, WT/DS433/R). Geneva: Author.

World Trade Organization. (2014c). *China—Measures related to the exportation of rare earth, tungsten, and molybdenum: Reports of the appellate body* (WT/DS431/AB/R, WT/DS432/AB/R, WT/DS433/AB/R). Geneva: Author.

World Trade Organization. (2016a). *United States—Measures Related to Price Comparison Methodologies: Request for consultations by China* (WT/DS515/1, G/L/1169, G/ADP/D115/1). Geneva: Author.

World Trade Organization. (2016b). *European Union—Measures Related to Price Comparison Methodologies: Request for consultations by China* (WT/DS516/1, G/L/1170, G/ADP/D116/1). Geneva: Author.

World Trade Organization. (2017). *United States—Measures Related to Price Comparison Methodologies: Request for consultations by China—Addendum* (WT/DS515/1/Add.1, G/L/1169/Add.1, G/ADP/D115/1/Add.1). Geneva: Author.

WTO Department, Ministry of Commerce (Ed.). (2013). *Basic Instruments and selected documents on the negotiations for China's accession to the World Trade Organization*. Beijing: China Commerce and Trade Press.

Yongtu, L. (2002). Negotiating entry: Key lessons learned. In C. A. Magariños, L. Yongtu, & F. C. Sercovich (Eds.), *China in the WTO: The birth of a new catching-up strategy* (pp. 25–35). New York: Palgrave Macmillan.

Zhang, Y., & Yang, G. (2004). China as a WTO member in the first two years. In M. Matsushita & D. Ahn (Eds.), *WTO and East Asia: New perspectives* (pp. 313–325). London: Cameron May.

Zheng, Z. (2003). Economic globalization and development of China's foreign economic cooperation and trade. In D. Lu, G. J. Wen, & H. Zhou (Eds.), *China's economic globalization through the WTO* (pp. 5–12). Aldershot: Ashgate.

CHAPTER 5

Viet Nam

1 Introduction

Viet Nam's WTO Accession in 2007 should be seen in the context of the process of its Doi Moi, transition to a market economy since 1986. On the trade policy front, tariff liberalization took place primarily after its membership to the Association of Southeast Asian Nations (ASEAN) in 1995 through its Common Effective Preferential Tariff (CEPT) regime implemented since 1996, and conclusion of the 2000 bilateral trade agreement (BTA)[1] with the United States, that came into effect in 2001. WTO accession was an important multilateral milestone to build further upon these preceding regional and bilateral market-opening efforts. Nonetheless, the pace of the overall reform was even more gradual than that of China, and the government was not enthusiastic about the WTO accession in the early phase of accession negotiations. However, its efforts for accession were accelerated later on, especially after 2001—the year of China's entry to the WTO and launch of the Doha Round. Yet, reflecting the country's utmost gradualist reform approach, its market access commitments (in terms of the average final bound tariff rate) were

[1] Hereafter, the 2000 bilateral trade agreement with the US is expressed as "BTA," for distinction from the bilateral market access agreement with the US for Viet Nam's WTO accession that is fully spelled out in this chapter. The text of BTA closely resembles those of WTO's multilateral trade agreements, but it was negotiated outside of the WTO auspices. Market access commitments on the side of Viet Nam in terms of WTO accession were deeper than those in BTA (WTO, 2013a).

K. Takamiya, *Recently Acceded Members of the World Trade Organization*, https://doi.org/10.1007/978-981-13-9159-0_5

less extensive than those of some other recently acceded transition economies, including China. Subsequently, Viet Nam's WTO accession was followed by acute macroeconomic destabilization, including deterioration of the external account, and the country almost entirely disengaged from the DDA market access negotiations until the time of macroeconomic recovery later on, resorting to cautious autonomous liberalization instead. Like the case of China, Viet Nam's terms of accession imposed the non-market economy (NME) designation for anti-dumping actions by trading partners, while the country managed to redress other forms of targeted discrimination through WTO membership. After WTO accession, Viet Nam filed NME-related anti-dumping disputes on shrimps at the WTO against the United States, its largest trading partner, exhibiting proactive engagement in this particular scheme of multilateral trade liberalization.

The second section of this case study shows that Viet Nam's somewhat moderate WTO accession commitments reflect its cautious gradualist reform approach, in line with Hypothesis 1 on the commitment theory: *Reforming economies (especially, those in transition to a market economy) would make extensive market access commitments for WTO accession, while others would make little use of them.* By looking into the link between deterioration of the external accounts and engagement in reciprocity, the third section mainly examines Hypothesis 2-a based on "GATT-think" and the juggernaut theory: *Only export-oriented economies would stay proactively engaged in the post-accession market access negotiations of the Doha Round, while others would pursue autonomous liberalization.* Whereas the statistical data verifies this hypothesis, the qualitative analysis reveals that additional factors (other than lack of substantive export interests, as inferred from the juggernaut theory) were also at play in the country's disengagement from the reciprocal liberalization at the WTO. The study also found no sign of conscious pursuit of the terms of trade objective assumed in Hypothesis 2-b: *Only large economies would stay proactively engaged in the market access negotiations of the Doha Round, while others would pursue autonomous liberalization.* The fourth section reveals that the country tried to recover part of the previous costs of the non-member status through WTO accession, and the NME related dispute settlement case, in line with Hypothesis 3 inferred from the domino theory: *Countries that face the discriminatory cost of prior non-membership would stay engaged in the relevant multilateral liberalization schemes, while others would refrain from such activities.* The fourth section concludes.

2 WTO Accession Under Cautious Gradualism of Doi Moi

Viet Nam clearly had the reform objective in mind when it applied for WTO membership on 12 January 1995, and the accession process was designated as an extension of the overall reform to the market economy called Doi Moi. Hypothesis 1 assumes that the country utilizes market access commitments for WTO accession in accordance with its own domestic needs, by tying hands as per the commitment theory.[2] Thus, the more reform-oriented government would make more extensive commitments, while the less enthusiastic reformers would make less use of them. Before the launch of the reform, Viet Nam's international trade was monopolized by a small number of foreign trading corporations, with quantitative controls on exports and imports (Auffret, 2003), but this restrictive regime was incrementally liberalized. However, as was the case of China, Viet Nam's transition to a market economy since 1986 was characterized by gradualism (Godoy & Stiglitz, 2006), as opposed to a shock therapy, but its approach was even more cautious than China's. In the period from 1995 (the year of WTO membership application) to 2007 (the year of WTO accession), the simple average MFN tariff rate remained about 16% with no major change, at levels relatively high in the liberal East Asian standard (Table 1). In this period, substantive tariff liberalization was undertaken only regionally through ASEAN and bilaterally with the United States, rather than on the broader MFN basis. Under the CEPT scheme for the ASEAN Free Trade Area (AFTA), Viet Nam committed reducing the tariff rates for intra-ASEAN imports (of non-sensitive products) to below 20% by 2003 and 5% by 2006, with the goal of further eliminating tariffs by 2015 (with some flexibilities allowed until 2018). The BTA with the United States was light on market access commitments for trade in goods on Viet Nam's part, only requiring a tariff cut on a limited range of industrial products by 30–50% within three years. In the broader areas of economic reforms, Viet Nam almost constantly lagged behind China, according to World Bank's Doing Business ranking and, unlike China, the country had not been rated as one of the top 50 reformers across the globe in the medium term (see Table 8, Chapter 2).

[2] Staiger and Tabellini (1987) and Maggi and Rodriguez-Clare (1998, 2007).

Table 1 Viet Nam—MFN tariff profiles [pre-WTO accession] (%)

	Viet Nam			*EAP*	*World*
	1995–1999	*2000–2004*	*2004–2007*	*2007*	*2007*
Simple average applied rates	16.52	16.63	16.82	9.34	9.10
Trade-weighted average applied rates	18.95	15.74	14.86	7.89	8.18
Maximum applied rate	100.00	125.00	112.50	68.45	90.07
Dispersion (coefficient of variation)	1.13	1.25	1.17	0.95	1.10
Domestic tariff peaks (tariff lines share)	10.56	6.71	3.11	5.67	6.41
International tariff peaks (tariff lines share)	40.25	40.40	41.72	16.20	22.05
Tariff escalation (finished % minus raw %)	–	–	7.54	1.70	1.62
Duty free tariff lines share	34.29	30.54	28.80	17.89	23.24
Non-ad valorem share (in all tariff lines)	0.66	0.09	0.05	0.76	3.38
Bound tariff lines (% of all tariff lines)	0.00	0.00	25.00	83.96	81.98
Tariff overhang (bound minus applied rate)	–	–	−5.47	26.98	25.78

Note EAP = East Asia-Pacific, excluding high-income countries. Indicators for 1995–1999, 2000–2004, and 2004–2007 are period averages. Data on average, maximum and dispersion rates covers ad valorem tariffs only

Source World Bank. World Trade Indicators 2009/2010 Web site: http://www.worldbank.org/

This cautious approach of transition to a market economy was reflected in Viet Nam's negotiating stance for WTO accession. On the one hand, the country had a clear intention to utilize market access commitments to leverage its domestic reforms. The 1996 memorandum of foreign trade regime Viet Nam submitted to the WTO clearly articulates the government's intention to proceed with international economic integration as a departure from the past centrally planning regime, and the WTO accession was envisaged as a means to that end:

> Since 1986, Vietnam has embarked on its socio-economic renewal reform (known as "doi moi") aiming at dismantling the old centrally-planned economic mechanism and shifting progressively therefrom [sic] to a market-oriented mechanism, in which the rule of law is performed by the State. One of the key parts of the economic reform is the re-organization and structural adjustment of Vietnam's foreign trade. The success of the economic reform in Vietnam is much dependent on trade development and the successful integration of the latter into international trade... The State has employed uses economic leverage and legal instruments to administer all activities in socio-economic life; to gradually integrate in the process of gradual integration into the world economy... For the afore-mentioned objectives, the Government of Vietnam has observed fundamental principles and practices of the international trading system and requested accession to the WTO.... (WTO, 1996a, pp. 1–2)

On the other hand, Viet Nam retained cautiousness in its trade liberalization. As the above-cited statement indicates repeatedly, what the authority sought was "gradually" integrating to the global economy through "gradual" accession to the WTO. With regard to market access, tariffs were first introduced in 1988 (replacing direct financial contributions by state-trading entities) under the Law on Export and Import duties, but the scope of import liberalization had been quite limited. The government preferred leaving protection to domestic industries largely untouched, especially where state-owned enterprises were dominant (IMF, 1998). This cautious attitude had been translated into Viet Nam's somewhat defensive position at the WTO accession negotiations. At the Seattle Ministerial Conference in 1999, Truong Dinh Tuyen, Minister of Trade, said[3]:

[3]The memorandum of the foreign trade regime also says "*The Government of Vietnam appreciates roles of the world trade system in promoting reforms in Vietnam. The Government of Vietnam, however, would like to note some shortcomings in unilateral liberalization*" (WTO, 1996a, p. 2).

> Acknowledging significant progress in new Members' admission, the comparison, however, has shown that their commitments are substantially higher than those of former WTO Members having the same level of development. Viet Nam would like to share proposals from many WTO Members that the Members should sympathize with developing countries, especially those in transition and with low-income. WTO Members should request developing countries to make market access commitment only at appropriate level and pace in accordance with their needs of development and capacity. (WTO, 1999b, p. 1)

Throughout the accession process, Viet Nam repeatedly called for sympathy from incumbent members for not imposing excessive requirements, including WTO-plus commitments.[4] As was inevitably the case for the very recently acceded members (VRAMs), a substantial part of Viet Nam's accession negotiations period overlapped with that of the Doha Round and, in a way, the country had been taking on the RAMs' defensive cause even before it joined the WTO. The statement by Luong van Tu, Vice-Minister of Trade, at the Doha Ministerial Conference in 2001 echoes its long-held position as a prospective RAM:

> Vietnam is also concerned about the fact that acceding countries are in some cases requested to make commitments which are higher than those of WTO Members having the same level of development. Vietnam, therefore, supports the proposals by some Members to accord acceding developing countries, in particular those with very low income, with flexibility needed to meet their development objectives. In our view, WTO Members should only request from developing countries such commitments that are in accordance with their development priorities and implementation capabilities. (WTO, 2001, p. 1)

By the time of the Working Party meeting on 10–11 December 2003, its delegation made the third offer of average tariff reduction to 22%, but that was on the high end on account of precedents by other

[4] For instance, the report of the accession Working Party reads "*(r)eferring to Viet Nam as a low-income and highly indebted developing country, he hoped and believed that Members would show sympathy and flexibility in the elaboration of the terms and conditions for Viet Nam's membership*" (WTO, 2006, p. 2).

Table 2 Viet Nam—WTO accession commitments on trade in goods (%)

	2006 MFN applied	*WTO 2007 bound*	*WTO final bound*	*WTO implementation*
Simple average	17.3	17.2	13.4	2007–2019
Agricultural products	25.7	27.3	21.7	2007–2012
Non-agricultural products	16.3	15.8	12.2	2007–2019
Textiles and clothing	36.4	13.6	13.5	2007
Footwear	43.9	35.8	27.2	2007–2012
Cars and other motor vehicles	55.5	84.8	58.7	2009–2019
Maximum tariff				
Agricultural products	100	100–150	85–135	
Non-agricultural products	90–100	100	75–100	

Note Agricultural products include fisheries, and non-agricultural products exclude used motor vehicles
Source IMF (2007)

RAMs (against the benchmark of around 10%).[5] At the time of the next Working Party meeting on 15 June 2004, the offer was cut to 18%,[6] still relatively high, and above its own pre-accession applied rate. Eventually, bilateral negotiations on market access were finally completed (with the United States and Mexico) in May 2006, and the agreement was reached at 13.4% as the final bound rate (Table 2)—above the RAMs' average but below the country's own applied rate. The Working Party process was completed on 26 October 2006, and the terms of accession were approved by the WTO General Council on 7 November. After domestic ratification, the country joined the WTO as its 150th member on 11 January 2007. The final bound rate was relatively high compared with many other RAMs in transition, and implementation of tariff cuts was envisaged to be phased over the period up to 2019. Thus, the country achieved the objective of catalyzing the domestic reform, but only in line with its cautious gradualism.

[5]WTO news release "Viet Nam Membership Negotiations 10-11 December 2003: Viet Nam starts its 'quantum jump' but still some way to go," dated 12 December 2003, posted at the WTO Web site: http://www.wto.org/english/news_e/news03_e/acc_vietnam_12dec_e.htm.

[6]WTO news release "Viet Nam Membership Negotiations 15 June 2004: Members praise Viet Nam's new offers, but seek improvements and more clarification," posted at the WTO Web site: http://www.wto.org/english/news_e/news04_e/acc_vietnam_15june04_e.htm.

The record of Viet Nam's market access commitments for WTO membership is in conformity with Hypothesis 1. As prescribed in the commitment theory, Viet Nam's WTO accession was partly motivated by the objective of catalyzing the domestic reforms under Doi Moi. In fact, at the final session of the Working Party on accession on 26 October 2006, Truong Dinh Tuyen stated "*Viet Nam's negotiations process had always gone hand in hand with the reforms.*"[7] At the time of General Council's accession approval on 7 November 2006, Pascal Lamy also commented "*WTO membership will help Viet Nam firmly anchor these reforms and use trade opening as an engine for economic growth and development.*"[8] However, the level of accession commitments was moderated by its cautious gradualist reform approach. At the same time, it should be noted that the market access commitment to catalyze the unilateral reform was not the sole motivation that drove Viet Nam's engagement in the accession process. The fourth section of this case study reveals that there was another factor of the cost of the non-member status at play.

3 Doha Round Negotiations Under Macroeconomic Instability

3.1 Side-Lined from the Post-accession Market Access Negotiations

After WTO accession in 2007, Viet Nam temporarily disengaged itself from further multilateral market access negotiations at the Doha Round. Hypothesis 2-b inferred from "GATT-think"[9] and the juggernaut theory[10] assumes pursuit of export interests as the objective for a country's

[7] Statement by H.E. Mr. Truong Dinh Tuyen, Minister of Trade, Viet Nam at the 14th and final session of the Working Party on the Accession to the WTO in Geneva on 26 October 2006, presented in WTO news release "Viet Nam membership negotiations 26 October 2006: Working party completed Viet Nam's membership talks," available at the WTO Web site: http://www.wto.org/english/news_e/news06_e/acc_vietnam_26oct06_e.htm.

[8] "Accession: Welcome Address by the Director-General to Viet Nam at the General Council meeting on 7 November 2005," available at the WTO Web site: http://www.wto.org/english/news_e/news06_e/gc_dg_stat_07nov06_e.htm.

[9] Krugman (1991).

[10] Richard Baldwin (2006, 2012).

engagement in reciprocal trade liberalization, and less export-oriented economies that lack such motivation would stay away from the DDA market access negotiations. On this account, it may be noteworthy that Viet Nam's external account exhibited contrasting developments before and after WTO membership. In the years preceding WTO accession in 2007, Viet Nam's current account deficit had been narrowing, moving toward nearly balancing at 0.2% of GDP in 2006. The country's policy statement refers to its reform since the 1980s as the "export-led growth strategy" (WTO, 2013b, p. 3) and, by 2006, exports accounted for 60% of GDP and grew at the rate of 22.7%. However, Viet Nam's characteristic as an export-oriented economy was severely compromised due to macroeconomic instability after the WTO membership. Following the WTO accession, the economy began to get severely overheated, as reflected in the skyrocketing inflation that reached 23.1% by 2008 (from the pre-accession level of 7.1% in 2006), and the external sector also showed the sign of deterioration. The current account turned to a huge deficit of 9.2% of GDP in 2007 and 10.9% in 2008. In the same years, the trade deficit reached 13.5 and 12.9%. In fact, export growth was robust, and these developments were mainly a reflection of rising imports (Table 3).

Arguably, deterioration of the external account was partly a reflection of an unprecedented amount of capital inflow that followed Viet Nam's entry to the multilateral trading system. The WTO membership enhanced the credibility of Viet Nam as an investment destination and that led to a flood of foreign capital. FDI inflow to Viet Nam increased sharply, from the pre-accession level of about US$2.3 billion in 2006 to $6.5 billion in 2007 and 9.2 billion in 2008. In the same year, portfolio investment also skyrocketed from US$1.3 billion to 6.2 billion in 2007, before reverse of capital flight in the face of economic destabilization in 2008 (Table 3). According to the 2006 business environment sentiment survey of 202 respondent enterprises (of which 76% were foreign enterprises) conducted by the Viet Nam Business Forum secretariat, reforms enacted under the WTO were one of the main reasons for planned expansion of their businesses in the coming years (International Finance Corporation, Ministry of Planning and Investment, & World Bank, 2006). Using the gravity model, Hanh (2011) also found empirically that WTO accession had significant impacts on the FDI inflow.

Inward investment, especially FDI, was envisaged to have positive development impacts such as productivity growth and employment, but its macroeconomic consequences were not necessarily positive

Table 3 Viet Nam—selected macroeconomic indicators

	2005	*2006*	*2007*	*2008*	*2009*	*2010*	*2011*	*2012*
Growth rate of GDP (% per year)	7.5	7.0	7.1	5.7	5.4	6.4	6.2	5.2[a]
Inflation (CPI, % per year)	8.3	7.1	8.3	23.1	5.9	10.0	18.6	9.2[a]
Change in money supply (M2, % per year)	29.7	33.6	46.1	20.3	29.0	33.3	12.1	12.6
Fiscal balance (% of GDP)	−1.0	1.2	−0.9	0.6	−3.6	−2.1	−3.0	−4.0
Merchandize exports (% of GDP)	56.3	60.0	62.7	63.2	53.9	62.3	71.4	73.5[a]
Growth of merchandize exports (% per year)	22.5	22.7	21.9	29.1	−8.9	26.5	34.2	18.2[a]
Merchandize imports (% of GDP)	−60.5	−64.2	−76.2	−76.1	−61.0	−66.7	−71.8	−67.2[a]
Growth of merchandize imports (% per year)	15.0	22.1	39.8	28.6	−13.3	21.3	25.8	6.6[a]
Trade balance (million US dollars)	−2439	−2776	−10,438	−12,783	−7607	−5147	−450	9884[a]
Trade balance (% of GDP)	−4.2	−4.2	−13.5	−12.9	−7.2	−4.4	−0.3	6.3[a]
Current account balance (% of GDP)	−1.0	−0.2	−9.2	−10.9	−6.2	−3.7	0.2	5.8[a]
Direct investment (million US dollars)	1889	2315	6516	9279	6900	7100	6569	7168[a]
Portfolio investment (million US dollars)	865	1313	6243	−578	−71	2370	1460	1990[a]

Note [a]Provisional as of mid-year 2013
Source ADB (2013)

(Menon, 2009).[11] The inflation in 2008 was partly due to high commodity prices, but sudden influx of capital after WTO accession and an accommodating policy stance of the central bank probably played some roles, too. The capital inflow was directed to hotels and restaurants, and real estate and renting business activities (rather than manufacturing and social services), creating bubbles in the asset markets. On the external front, anything else being equal, an increase of capital inflow leads to a widening current account deficit, just as observed in Viet Nam. While the external deficit itself does not necessarily represent an undesirable state of the economy, the level reached by 2008 for Viet Nam was rather high and the move was drastic.

The very fact that these phenomena occurred immediately following the WTO accession to an otherwise soundly growing economy bought about negative perceptions even among observers within the government. For instance, the assessment of three years of WTO membership by the government's institute provided an at least partially negative account on its impacts on the external sector in general and FDI in particular:

> As can be seen, international economic integration made balance of payments and sub-balances vary more drastically in an unpredictable way. The most evident impact of international economic integration on balance of payments in the years 2007-2009, relative to that before the WTO accession period, was the widening of trade deficit, current account deficit and increase in capital flows, in both absolute terms and relative to GDP. (Central Institute for Economic Management [CIEM], 2010, p. 78)

> When massive FDI flows into Vietnam, the economy cannot fully absorb them effectively (in 2008). In other words, the inflow of FDI contains risks and challenged in terms of investment structure by industry, the commitment as compared to investors' ability, and the compatibility with advantages of the economy and national benefits, and sustainable development goals. (CIEM, 2010, p. 42)

Furthermore, in 2009, the global economy entered into a period of the financial crisis. On a positive note, the worldwide great recession had an effect of cooling down the previously overheated Vietnamese

[11] Menon (2009) comments that, in a dollarized economy such as Viet Nam, the authority has a limited means of sterilizing liquidity growth, and capital inflow tends to be translated directly into rise of inflation.

economy and, thanks to fiscal and monetary stimulus measures introduced at the time, the country coped with the crisis relatively well. However, the late exit of these expansionary measures posed risks of another round of destabilization to the economy in the post-crisis period (IMF, 2010), which again might have been perceived as related to WTO accession. The government's report[12] launched at the workshop on five years of WTO experience in Hanoi on 3 April 2013 indicated that WTO membership was a major factor in driving up inflation[13] and failed to stimulate economic growth.[14]

Against the backdrop of rising current account and trade deficit, Viet Nam did not act as an aggressive demander at the DDA market access negotiations and showed no sign of positive engagement in the reciprocal negotiations in Geneva. While export performance was still robust, it was more than taken over by imports. Thus, relative presence of export businesses in the entire economy was diminishing. During the Doha Round, the Vietnam Chamber of Commerce and Industry (VCCI)—a nationwide organization representing the business community of the country—made suggestions to the government on issues like trade facilitation and technical barriers to trade (TBT) including product labeling, but not on tariffs. The state sector, that tends to cater domestic markets rather than exports, accounted for 35.9% of GDP in 2007, and SOEs still represented a substantial part of the economy (WTO, 2013a).

At the Doha Round, Viet Nam did not submit any negotiating proposal on NAMA and agriculture (and its remark has not been recorded in the minutes) and, as a VRAM, the country was exempted from making further market access commitments in the draft December 2008 modalities. The silence in this period was also a reflection of the fact that there was only a short period of time between accession in 2007 and conclusion of the draft December 2008 modalities. In such a context,

[12] The full report by CIEM (2013) on "Assessing the overall economic situation—Vietnamese society after 5 years of joining WTO," was initially available only in Vietnamese. See the Web site of CIEM, Ministry of Planning and Investment: http://ciem.org.vn/en/xuatban/sach.aspx.

[13] "Five-year WTO membership review—not as good as expected," posted in the Voice of Vietnam Web site updated on 10 September 2012: http://english.vov.vn/Economy/Fiveyear-WTO-membership-review-not-as-good-as-expected/229236.vov.

[14] "WTO membership fails to stimulate economic growth," posted in the Vietnam News Web site updated on 5 April 2013: http://vietnamnews.vn/economy/237792/wto-membership-fails-to-stimulate-economic-growth.html.

Table 4 Viet Nam—MFN tariff profiles [post-WTO accession] (%)

	MFN applied		*Final bound*
	2007	*2013*	
Simple average applied rates	18.5	10.4	13.4
Agriculture	27.0	17.4	20.9
Non-agriculture	17.4	9.3	12.4
Dispersion (coefficient of variation)	1.2	1.2	1.1
Domestic tariff peaks (tariff lines share)	3.1	4.1	3.6
International tariff peaks (tariff lines share)	41.7	25.6	31.2
Share of duty free tariff lines	28.8	32.9	14.5
Share of non-ad valorem tariffs (in all tariff lines)	0.0	0.9	0.1
Bound tariff lines (% of all tariff lines)	100.0	100.0	100.0
Tariff overhang (bound minus applied rate)	−5.1	3.0	–

Source WTO (2013a)

Viet Nam's efforts of post-accession trade liberalization took place outside of the Doha Round, while maintaining its gradual pace of cautious reforms. By 2013, the simple average MFN applied tariff rate has declined to 10.4% (17.4% for agriculture and 9.3% for NAMA), below the level of the final bound rate of 13.4% (20.9% for agriculture and 12.4% for NAMA) envisaged in terms of WTO accession (Table 4). Liberalization was meant to improve the country's investment climate by facilitating inputs to sectors like machinery and other industrial goods. As far as the MFN-based market opening was concerned, the government preferred autonomous liberalization, based on its own assessment of development needs rather than demands by trading partners, and it was reluctant to rely on the multilateral negotiations of the Doha Round.

Strictly on the basis of available macroeconomic data, Viet Nam's behavior is found to be consistent with Hypothesis 2-a. The country had been running the current account and trade deficits, and these increased sharply after WTO accession. Then, Viet Nam side-lined itself from reciprocal market access negotiations of the Doha Round. However, episodes observed in this case study cast some doubt that abatement of export interests was the sole reason for Viet Nam's inaction at the DDA market access negotiations. What Viet Nam was actually concerned about may well be the state of the overall macro-economy, and the widening deficit was one manifestation of such worsening economic conditions. It was probably the very fact that such macroeconomic instability emerged immediately after Viet Nam's WTO accession, as reiterated in the assessment below, which raised skepticism on the merit of further engagement in the multilateral trading system in the mind of policy-makers:

> WTO accession and greater integration may bring about great advantages for the country. However, the economy may be vulnerable upon external shocks, especially when there is lack of policies/measures to actively address these… These facts have led to an increase in macroeconomic instabilities and financial risks, especially in the first three quarters of 2008. (CIEM, 2010, pp. 126–127)

While staying disengaged from the DDA market access negotiations, Viet Nam announced the decision to fully take part in the Trans-Pacific Partnership (TPP) negotiations (with Australia, Brunei Darussalam, Chile, Malaysia, New Zealand, Peru, Singapore, Viet Nam, and the United States) in November 2010, so as to proceed with further liberalization of trade and investment. It appears that the country did not totally discredit the merit of reciprocal trade liberalization outside of the WTO. To the contrary, Viet Nam's active engagement in TPP talks showed its confidence in the merit of reciprocal trade negotiations. It was just that, in the eyes of some, the WTO in particular was perceived to have failed to deliver favorable consequences.[15]

3.2 Irrelevance of Term of Trade Externality for a Medium-Sized Economy

Apart from the pursuit of export interests, containment of terms of trade externality could be another motivation to participate in the reciprocal trade liberalization, provided that the size of the economy is sufficiently large to be able to manipulate international prices of traded goods. Accordingly, Hypothesis 2-b based on the theory of terms of trade externality[16] states only large economies would stay engaged in market access negotiations of the Doha Round, and smaller ones would not. With the market size of less

[15] See CIEM (2010). However, there was also awareness that trade liberalization for WTO accession was not a direct cause of macroeconomic instability, which could have been prevented through prudent financial regulation and governance.

[16] Bagwell and Staiger (1999, 2002).

Table 5 Viet Nam—reciprocity and terms of trade

	2004	*2005*	*2006*	*2007*
Viet Nam applied tariff rate (incl. preferences)				
Simple average	13.89	–	15.85	19.31
Trade weighted averages	13.55	–	12.25	11.73
ROW applied tariff rate (incl. preferences)				
Simple average	9.30	8.75	7.44	9.95
Trade weighted averages	6.49	5.49	5.38	5.83
Net barter terms of trade index (2000=100)	94.57	97.28	96.18	93.21

Note ROW = rest of the world. The net barter terms of trade index is the percentage ratio of unit export value indexes to unit import value, measured against the base year of 2000
Source World Trade Indicators 2009/2010 of the World Bank Web site: http://info.worldbank.org/etools/wti/2a1.asp; World Bank Open Data retrieved from the World Bank Web site: http://data.worldbank.org/

than 0.5% of the global economy (see Table 10, Chapter 2), Viet Nam was not necessarily a very small economy (compared with, e.g., Georgia), but it was not extremely large (compared with, e.g., China), either. It is difficult to determine correctly how large the country would have to be to affect international market prices through its trade policy, but a casual observation of available statistics seems to indicate that Viet Nam may not qualify to be a large country in this respect. Table 5 presents Viet Nam's terms of trade in the period of 2004–2007, when the country raised its tariff rates (including preferences) whereas the rest of the world maintained a relatively stable tariff level. In such a case, terms of trade should improve if the country is sufficiently large to be able to affect international prices of its imports, but Viet Nam's terms of trade were rather stable in this period. Arguably, this limited data seems to suggest that Viet Nam might have not been a large country from the terms of trade perspective.[17] In fact, no official documents submitted by Viet Nam to the WTO had any mention of the terms of trade

[17] Given that trade policy is not the only factor that can affect terms of trade, this finding should be treated as only indicative. Yet, interviews with trade negotiators also revealed that terms of trade consideration played no role in actual policy-making.

consideration, and containment of terms of trade externality was never stated as the country's policy objective. Being a relatively small economy, Viet Nam was not proactively engaged in the reciprocal DDA market access negotiations, and this observation is consistent with Hypothesis 2-b.

4 Recovering the Cost of Previous Outsider Status

Hypothesis 3 assumes that RAMs' engagement in the WTO is driven by the objective of recovering the cost of previous non-member status. The theoretical presumption is the domino theory that countries join trade agreements one after the other to overcome disadvantages of staying outside of the system.[18] China's WTO accession in 2001 and resulting competitive concerns particularly in the textile and clothing exports set such domino expansion of multilateralism in East Asia (particularly among transition economies of the Greater Mekong Subregion [GMS],[19] including Cambodia, Laos, and Viet Nam). Acceleration of Viet Nam's WTO accession negotiations in the late phase could be best understood in light of such domino effects of China's preceding membership. Viet Nam also suffered from its designation as an NME by the trading partners since the pre-accession period, as was the case for China, and its endeavor to redress this specific discrimination continued in the post-accession period, particularly through anti-dumping disputes with the United States in the fisheries sector (the United States—Shrimp case).

4.1 Restoring MFN Access in the Textile and Clothing Sector

4.1.1 Domino in Motion—Acceleration of Accession Negotiations Since 2001

The initial stage of Viet Nam's WTO accession negotiations proceeded at a moderate pace. However, the accession process steadily gained momentum on the part of Viet Nam in 2001. On 27 November of the year, the Communist Party of Viet Nam issued its resolution on

[18] Baldwin (1995).

[19] GMS comprises China (Yunnan Province and Guangxi Zhuang Autonomous Region), Cambodia, Laos, Myanmar, Thailand, and Viet Nam. See the ADB Web site: http://www.adb.org/countries/gms/main.

Table 6 WTO timetable for 2001 and 2005

	2001	*2005*
China's WTO Accession	China's membership (December), following the Doha Ministerial Conference	Substantial completion of trade liberalization commitments, by both China and trading partners
ATC	Phased partial elimination of textile quotas (ongoing)	Complete elimination of textile quotas among WTO members (January)
Doha Round	Launch of DDA (November) at the Doha Ministerial Conference	The initial deadline to complete DDA negotiations (January)

Note ATC = Agreement on Textile and Clothing; DDA = Doha Development Agenda

international economic integration,[20] and domestic preparatory works for accession began to be accelerated thereafter (Van, Thanh, & Sa, 2005). The government's program for implementation of the resolution was issued in the name of Prime Minister Phan Van Khai on 14 March 2002, with specific guidance to proceed with legislative reforms for compliance with the WTO requirements,[21] and the target date for accession was set for 1 January 2005. While the deadline eventually had to be missed, Viet Nam still sought membership "as soon as possible"[22] even after that. The change in Viet Nam's stance reflected important developments that took place at the WTO between 2001 and 2005.

As summarized in Table 6, these two milestone years of 2001 (when Viet Nam's accession gained momentum) and 2005 (Viet Nam's target date for accession) had special connotations at the multilateral trading system. 2001 was the year of the Doha Ministerial Conference, which launched the DDA and approved China's accession to the WTO. The year 2005 was when the DDA was initially scheduled to be completed

[20] Resolution 07/NQ-TW dated 27 November 2001.

[21] Decision no. 37 2002/QD-TTg of 14 March 2002 on the Government's Program of Action for Implementation of Politburo Resolution No. 07/NQ-TW of 27 November 2002 on International Economic Integration, available at the Vietnamese ministry of justice Web site: http://moj.gov.vn/vbpq/en/Lists/Vn%20bn%20php%20lut/View_Detail.aspx?ItemID=9532.

[22] A remark by Vice Trade Minister Luong Van Tu at the Working Party meeting on 15 June 2004.

(as per the 2001 Doha Ministerial Declaration) and elimination of import quotas was to be completed among WTO members under the Uruguay Round Agreement on Textile and Clothing (ATC). Also, by 2005, trade liberalization commitments stated in China's terms of accession were to be substantially completed, by both China itself and the incumbent WTO members.

From the experience of other RAMs, Viet Nam was aware that those who joined the multilateral trading system after the conclusion of the Uruguay Round had to accept more stringent terms than others (see Chapter 2) and, out of this concern of becoming a latecomer, the government aimed at gaining membership before the Doha Round was scheduled to be completed in 2005 (Ministry of Planning and Investment, 2003[23]). At the same time, China's accession in 2001 was also an important trigger for Viet Nam to become more serious about WTO accession. The two countries shared a similar reform path toward a socialist-oriented market economy. In a way, the experience of China was one role model for transition, and its WTO accession showed the way to proceed with further international economic integration.[24] A statement by Luong van Tu at the Doha Ministerial Conference indicated Viet Nam's intention to accelerate the efforts of accession exercises (following China's membership), first through making initial market access offer:

> Vietnam warmly welcomes the significant progress in the admission of the new Members, and particularly welcomes the accession of China into this Organization… Vietnam is in the process of accelerating its accession to the WTO. With the support and constructive engagement of all Members of the Working Party, we have basically concluded the first stage of the

[23]Presented by Nguyen Bich Dat, Vice-Minister of Planning and Investment at the forum on "Viet Nam: Readiness for WTO accession," in Hanoi and Ho Chi Minh City in June 2003.

[24]In fact, China's trade negotiators visited Viet Nam and shared the accession experience with Vietnamese policy-makers. See presentations by Long Yongtu, former Vice-Minister of MOFTEC and Chief negotiator for China's WTO Accession in Hanoi and in Ho Chi Minh City in June 2003, available from the World Bank Web site: http://siteresources.worldbank.org/INTRANETTRADE/Resources/WBI-Training/wtoaccessionimact-chinaexp_Yongtu.pdf and Ma Xiaoye, China's former trade negotiator, in Ho Chi Minh City in December 2005, available also from the World Bank's Web site: http://siteresources.worldbank.org/INTRANETTRADE/Resources/WBI-Training/288464-1139428366112/Session1-MA-revised2.pdf.

> accession process. Following this Conference, we will soon submit our initial offers in goods and services for substantive negotiations on market access. (WTO, 2001, p. 1)

At the same time, China was also a competitor as an export-oriented economy in East Asia, and there was a concern that, after WTO accession, China will seize global export markets (and investment) in manufacturing and drive away regional rivals. This general concern was particularly valid in the context of full ATC implementation by 1 January 2005. As a WTO member, Chinese exports would no longer be subjected to quota restraints (unless the special safeguard stated in its terms of WTO accession is triggered, as eventually happened—see Chapter 3), while non-WTO members would be still constrained by quotas. In the estimates by World Bank's economists, developing economies in Asia were to be adversely affected by resulting trade diversion and, as a discriminated outsider of the multilateral trading system, Viet Nam was thought to be a largest victim on per-capita terms (Table 7).

As the domino theory states, once China joined the WTO, other East Asian economies that were still non-members would be induced to join the multilateral trading system, in their attempts to recover the level-playing field (so as to compete in the export market on the equal footing). In particular, the threat of trade diversion envisaged to arise from China's WTO accession and ATC implementation was one important driver for such domino expansion of multilateralism, particularly among other GMS transition economies including Cambodia, Laos, and Viet Nam. Following China's membership in 2001, Cambodia joined the WTO in 2004, Viet Nam in 2007, and Laos in 2013. For Viet Nam, the general MFN access to its trading partners was not necessarily a major issue in other sectors, particularly after the BTA with the United States became effective in the same year. Even before WTO accession, the simple average of rest of the world applied tariff rate against Viet Nam's exports had come down at around the level of world and regional average (Table 8). However, the textile and clothing sector had been carved out from the general MFN treatment, and non-members of the WTO were not deemed entitled to benefit from elimination of quotas under ATC from 2005 onwards.

The recovery of the competitive ground in textile and clothing trade vis-à-vis incumbent WTO members (including China since late 2001) was a major motivation for the GMS transition economies that joined the multilateral trading system, one after another. The following statements by

Table 7 Economic Impacts of China's WTO Accession

Country or group	*Welfare change 1995–2007*			*Welfare change 2001–2007*
	Quota reduction impact (1997 US$ million)	*Total impact (1997 US$ million)*	*Per capita utility change (%)*	*Total impact (1997 US$ million)*
North America	2713	6072	0.0	5259
Western Europe	8285	18,189	0.2	14,200
Australia/New Zealand	−47	136	0.0	152
Japan	291	5694	0.1	2553
China	2389	40,552	2.2	9563
Chinese Taipei	338	2985	0.6	1376
Other newly industrialized countries	−82	6831	0.7	1456
Indonesia	−216	−408	−0.2	−310
Viet Nam	−395	−453	−1.4	−405
Other Southeast Asia	−464	−585	−0.1	−268
India	−2338	−3357	−0.4	−2999
Other South Asia	−1427	−1622	−0.8	−1619
Brazil	3	−76	0.0	359
Other Latin America	−171	−32	0.0	−36
Turkey	−295	−338	−0.1	−327
Other Middle East and North Africa	−467	368	0.0	−365
Economies in Transition	−321	19	0.0	−185
South African Customs Union	−18	78	0.0	13
Other Sub-Saharan Africa	−159	−45	0.0	−78
Rest of world	−210	155	0.0	−78
World	7409	74,166	–	28,261

Source E. Ianchovichina and W. Martin (2004)

Sok Siphana, former State Secretary of Cambodia's commerce ministry; Vu Duc Thinh, deputy director-general of a textile and garment corporation of Viet Nam's industry ministry; and Banesaty Thephavong, deputy director-general and others from the foreign trade department of the Lao commerce ministry, are testimony of this domino effect in motion:

Table 8 Viet Nam—external environment with international comparison

	Viet Nam			*EAP*	*World*
	1995–2000	*2001–2006*	*2007*	*2007*	*2007*
Rest-of-the world applied tariffs (%)					
Simple average	12.33	9.25	9.95	10.23	9.87
Maximum	2382.8	2647.9	1000	1000	1000
Dispersion	3.29	2.97	1.59	1.60	1.63
Trade weighted average	54.51	6.98	5.83	4.33	3.34
Trade remedy initiations faced (per year)	0.50	3	2	4.43	1.23
Share of duty free exports (%)	21.28	37.27	42.72	47.20	44.79
Share of exports to CU/FTA partners (%)	18.16	16.49	38.08	22	37.91
Share of imports from CU/FTA partners (%)	25.60	25.31	64.24	30.57	37.39

Note EAP = East Asia-Pacific, excluding high-income countries. Indicators for 1995–2000, 2001–2007, and 2007 are period averages. Tariff data includes preferences
Source World Bank. World Trade Indicators 2009/2010 Web site: http://www.worldbank.org/

> Cambodia targeted a rapid accession to WTO. The need for a rapid accession was driven mainly by the 1st of January 2005 deadline facing the garment industry, when the international quota regime governing trade in garments finally ended. After that date all WTO members in principle should have unrestrained access to the markets of other members. Being outside of the WTO would have meant that Cambodian garment exporters risked facing continued quotas on their exports, something that would have had a strongly negative impact on FDI into the industry. (Siphana, 2005, pp. 3–4)

> In Asia, there are also large textile and garment exporters, such as China, India, and Pakistan, and are competing with ASEAN. These are very tough competitors of ASEAN textile and garment industry. Vietnam's accession to WTO will bring significant opportunity to developing countries in general and textile and garment exporters in particular. Once in the WTO, after 2005 Vietnam will not have to be imposed export quota, will be able to access the world market without quantitative restriction. WTO will bring in opportunity to access market of all countries. (Thinh, 2003, p. 3)[25]

[25] Presentation at the forum on "Viet Nam: Readiness for WTO accession," in Hanoi and Ho Chi Minh City in June 2003. See: http://web.worldbank.org/WBSITE/EXTERNAL/TOPICS/TRADE/0,,contentMDK:20604456~menuPK:2644066~pagePK:64020865~piPK:51164185~theSitePK:239071,00.htmlhttp://web.worldbank.org/WBSITE/EXTERNAL/TOPICS/TRADE/0,,contentMDK:20604456~menuPK:2644066~pagePK:64020865~piPK:51164185~theSitePK:239071,00.html.

> The Lao textile and clothing industry will face fierce competition in its export markets, particularly the European Union (EU), its main market for garments. Laos is not yet a member of the WTO and thus its textile and clothing trade is dependent on bilateral trade arrangements with its trading partners; membership of the WTO would give Laos its necessary predictable market access to major markets. (Thephavong, Iemsouthi, & Vilavong, 2005, p. 318)

In particular, the 2000 BTA between Viet Nam and the United States exempted textile and clothing from its disciplines on quotas and safeguard actions and, due to the domestic protectionist concern in the United States, import quotas on textiles and apparel were a contentious issue for bilateral market access negotiations for Viet Nam's WTO accession.[26] In hindsight, whether or not this concern substantially materialized is somewhat questionable. Data shows that Viet Nam's clothing exports increased in 2005 (WTO, 2007), even when Viet Nam could not achieve the WTO membership by that target year.[27] However, as testified by the statement above, there were at least perceptions on the possible risk of non-membership, and avoiding such potential competitive disadvantage was one important objective of joining the multilateral trading system. The forecast by the credible source (the World Bank) on the potential adverse impacts of China's WTO accession in 2001 also helped justify these concerns,[28] and there emerged a strong sense of urgency to secure membership by 2005. Viet Nam's WTO accession was motivated partly by this defensive cause, consistently with the domino theory prediction.[29]

[26]Viet Nam also had an export quota arrangement with the EU and a number of other industrialized economies (WTO, 2006).

[27]One possible reason is that the US and the EU triggered a special safeguard against China. See Chapter 4.

[28]The findings by the World Bank were conveyed to the Vietnamese authority. Will Martin's presentation on "China's WTO Accession: Some Lessons for Vietnam," in Hanoi on 3 June 2003 was posted at the World Bank Web site: http://web.worldbank.org/WBSITE/EXTERNAL/TOPICS/TRADE/0,,contentMDK:20604456~menuPK:2644066~pagePK:64020865~piPK:51164185~theSitePK:239071,00.html. Another presentation he made in Hanoi on 9 May 2006 was posted at the World Bank Web site: http://siteresources.worldbank.org/INTRANETTRADE/Resources/WBI-Training/288464-1152217173757/Session6b_WillMartin.pdf.

[29]Interestingly, these GMS transition countries (Cambodia, China, Laos, and Viet Nam) all signed BTA with the US ahead of their WTO accession. Viet Nam had concluded the BTA that took effect in 2001. While the BTA accorded Viet Nam's non-permanent MFN

With the WTO accession subsequently in 2007, Viet Nam secured the rights under ATC and the general MFN access to WTO member countries. Unlike the case of China for which its textile exports were subjected to special safeguard provision for possible re-imposition of quotas in case of market disruption (see Chapter 4), Viet Nam's terms of accession did not impose any departure from the non-discrimination principle as far as textile and clothing are concerned. The only condition for removal of textile quotas by trading partners was elimination of WTO-prohibited subsidies on Viet Nam's part, as negotiated bilaterally with the United States for accession (Office of the United States Trade Representative [USTR], 2006),[30] but it was simply a commitment to comply with the existing WTO rules (rather than WTO-plus or WTO-minus requirement additionally imposed upon Viet Nam). Para 286 of the accession Working Party Report reads:

> Viet Nam would eliminate all prohibited subsidies (i.e., subsidies contingent upon export performance or the use of domestic over imported goods) to the textile and garment industries, including but not limited to investment incentives contingent upon export performance for domestic businesses, investment incentives contingent upon export performance for foreign-invested enterprises, export promotion subsidies contingent upon export performance and trade promotion subsidies contingent upon export performance, as of the date of accession. The Working Party took note of these commitments. (WTO, 2006, p. 73)

In fact, this paragraph does not fully reflect what was negotiated with the United States in their bilateral market access negotiations for WTO accession. In the bilateral agreement, both sides concurred to

access to the US market, it did not eliminate the textile and clothing quotas in particular. On 6 November 2006, Truong Dinh Tuyen, Vietnamese trade minister, said "*(i)f the US doesn't grant PNTR to Viet Nam, our textile-garment exports will be still imposed with quotas.*" See the American Chamber of Commerce Viet Nam Web site: http://www.amchamvietnam.com/975/update-and-background-on-wto-accession-and-implementation-and-apparel-trade/. WTO accession, that would require provision of the permanent normal trade relations (PNTR) on the part of the US, was the next ultimate goal to secure full MFN access to Viet Nam's export market without quota constraints.

[30]See the Web sites of the American Chamber of Commerce in Viet Nam at: http://www.amchamvietnam.com/1052/u-s-vietnam-wto-bilateral-market-access-agreement-textiles-apparel/ and the US Vietnam Trade Council at: http://www.usvtc.org/trade/wto/coalition/URTR-VietnamTextileBenefits05Sep06.pdf.

establish a unique monitoring and enforcement mechanism, whereby the United States can re-impose quotas in the event that Viet Nam is found, by the WTO dispute settlement process, to have failed eliminating prohibited subsidies.[31] Yet, the applicable rule is that of the normal WTO agreement and the compliance would be judged only by the formal dispute settlement mechanism common to all members. Thus, there was actually no element of targeted discrimination specifically disadvantageous to Viet Nam. The condition was far more favorable to Viet Nam than what was inscribed in terms of WTO accession for China, in line with the claim made by the industry lobby that Viet Nam's share of apparel exports to the United States was much smaller than China's (U.S.-Vietnam Trade Council, 2006)[32]:

> The Vietnam textile sector therefore poses little threat to the most sensitive U.S. domestically produced textile products… Unlike China, Vietnam is not a major producer or exporter of textile (nonapparel) products (yarn, fabric, fiber, carpet, sheets, towels, etc.) to the U.S. – or to other countries… In addition, unlike China, Vietnam is also not a major producer of cotton. In contrast, Vietnam's textile industry depends on imported cotton inputs from the U.S.… We urge that the U.S. – Vietnam quota regime end with Vietnam's accession to the WTO. (U.S.-Vietnam Trade Council, 2006, pp. 2–3)

Relatively little threat of Vietnamese exports to the US market served as justification for the non-discriminatory treatment in terms of WTO accession.

4.1.2 The US Import Monitoring Program for Textiles and Apparel

The record of Viet Nam's policy behavior in the textile and clothing sector broadly validates Hypothesis 3. Viet Nam's WTO membership was partly motivated by the threat of competitive disadvantage that would

[31] USTR's Trade Facts "U.S.-Vietnam Bilateral WTO Accession Agreement: Ensuring a Level Playing Field for U.S. Textile and Apparel Industries," dated May 2006, downloaded from the U.S. Vietnam Trade Council Web site: http://www.usvtc.org/trade/wto/coalition/USTR-VietnamTextileBenefits05Sep06.pdf

[32] The US-Viet Nam Trade Council explains its status as follows: "*The U.S.-Vietnam Trade Council is a nonprofit membership organization founded in 1989 under the leadership of Ambassador William H. Sullivan and Foreign Minister Nguyen Co Thach to build a new future relationship between former enemies.*" See its Web site: http://www.usvtc.org/aboutus/index.htm.

arise out of China's accession, and the government accelerated negotiations to avoid this particular cost of staying outside of the multilateral trading system. The country successfully achieved the objective of removing quotas through WTO accession, on a term better than China's, and there is no record showing that Viet Nam pursued the textile and clothing issues further at the WTO, either through the DDA negotiations or dispute settlement.[33]

However, confirmation of Hypothesis 3 must be accompanied by a caveat on one development that took place outside of the WTO. On 18 September 2006, toward the completion of Viet Nam's WTO accession process, US Senators Elizabeth Dole and Lindsey Graham placed holds on the PNTR legislation for Viet Nam and wrote a letter to USTR Susan Schwab, conveying their concerns over adverse impacts on textile jobs in North and South Carolina.[34] In response dated 28 September, USTR and the US Department of Commerce (USDOC) indicated introduction of a monitoring scheme,[35] whereby USDOC's Office of Textiles and Apparel (OTEXA) was to conduct biannual review of imports from Viet Nam until the end of the Bush administration. If dumping and material injury to domestic industries were to be found, USDOC would self-initiate anti-dumping investigation, using the NME methodology. This mechanism was essentially about discriminatory anti-dumping against Viet Nam and was distinctly different from the scheme only addressing the general WTO rule on prohibited subsidies incorporated in the bilateral market access agreement.

The government of Viet Nam swiftly reacted to this move. In a letter to Carlos Gutierrez, US Commerce Secretary dated 13 December 2006, Truong Dinh Tuyen expressed his concern, while welcoming

[33] As to other GMS transition economies, neither Cambodia nor Laos filed any disputes on textiles and clothing at the WTO, too. These two countries are classified as LDCs and have been acting as members of the LDC group at the Doha Round. See the WTO Web site: http://www.wto.org/english/tratop_e/dda_e/negotiating_groups_e.htm.

[34] "Letter to USTR Schwab from Senators Dole and Graham, 18 September 2006," in the American Chamber of Commerce Vietnam Web site: http://www.amchamvietnam.com/1043/letter-to-ustr-schwab-from-senators-dole-and-graham-18-sep-06/.

[35] "Letter to Senator Dole and Graham from USTR Schwab and Commerce Secretary Gutierrez, 28 September 2006," whose summary and key points are posted in the American Chamber of Commerce Viet Nam Web site: http://www.amchamvietnam.com/1050/letter-to-senators-dole-and-graham-from-ustr-schwab-and-commerce-secretary-gutierrez-28-sep-06/.

efforts directed to passage of the PNTR.[36] Subsequently, the trade ministry sent another letter to USDOC dated 22 December 2006 that reads:

> A unique and separate monitoring program on imports of textile and apparel products from Viet Nam which is completely different from monitoring regimes applied by the U.S. to cover imports from other WTO Members constitutes an overt discrimination against Viet Nam and runs contrary to the WTO's most fundamental principle of non-discrimination. This Program is violation of Article XXIII of the GATT 1994 as it causes nullification and serious prejudice to the interests of Viet Nam as a WTO Member. Furthermore, this Program is also inconsistent with the Bilateral Agreement between Viet Nam and the United States on Viet Nam's accession to the WTO signed on 31 May 2006.[37]

At the hearing in Washington, DC on 24 April 2007, a representative of the Vietnamese trade ministry commented that the monitoring mechanism discriminately targeting Viet Nam was in violation of the MFN principle under GATT Article I, among other WTO rules, and stated:

> This is the first and clear loss for Vietnam upon becoming a WTO member. Vietnam made many significant and difficult concessions to the US and other WTO members in all aspects of its trade rules, with the hope that people of Vietnam could enjoy the benefit of exporting textiles and apparel products to the U.S. market freely, with their goods being treated as all other normal goods. But because of the monitoring system, Vietnam is not realizing this expectation.[38]

[36] Downloaded from the US-Vietnam Trade Council Web site: http://www.usvtc.org/trade/wto/textile/LetterVNTrade13Dec06.pdf.

[37] Downloaded from the US-Vietnam Trade Council Web site: http://www.usvtc.org/trade/wto/textile/LetterVNTrade22Dec06.pdf.

[38] "Statement of the representative from Ministry of Trade of Vietnam at hearing on the DOS's [sic] Monitoring Program on Textile and apparel import from Viet Nam, 24 April 2007 at Washington DC," downloaded from the US-Vietnam Trade Council Web site: http://www.usvtc.org/trade/wto/textile/MOT.pdf.

The Vietnam Textile and Apparel Association (VITAS) also made negative comments in its letter dated 20 December 2006 to David M. Spooner, US assistant commerce secretary.[39]

Simultaneously with Viet Nam's WTO accession in January 2007, the US government initiated the import monitoring program for textile and apparel from Viet Nam. In exchange for adoption of the monitoring program, Senators Dole and Graham had already withdrawn their holds on PNTR. On 29 December, the United States accorded the PNTR status to Viet Nam, converting the previously provisional MFN treatment (that came into force earlier under the 2000 BTA) into a permanent status. USDOC conducted three times of biannual review of imports from Viet Nam before expiry of the monitoring mechanism at the end of the Bush administration on 19 January 2009. However, USDOC found only insufficient evidence of dumping to self-intimate investigation,[40] and Viet Nam did not pursue dispute settlement at the WTO. Thus, UCDOC did not initiate any related anti-dumping actions in practice.

4.2 Anti-dumping Disputes as an NME in the Fishery Sector

4.2.1 Pre-accession Dispute on United States—Catfish

Even before WTO accession, Viet Nam had been a frequent target of anti-dumping actions by its trading partners, and the country had to face them in a disadvantageous status as an NME. According to the WTO database, there were 18 anti-bumping initiations (and 12 measures) against Viet Nam in the period from 1995 (establishment of the WTO) to 2006 (the year preceding Viet Nam's entry to the WTO).[41]

[39] "Comments on Import Monitoring Program on Textile and Apparel Products from Vietnam, 71 Fed. Reg. 70364 (4 December 2006)," downloaded from the US-Vietnam Trade Council Web site: http://www.usvtc.org/trade/wto/textile/LetterVietnamTextileApparelAssociation27Dec06.pdf.

[40] News release "Commerce Completes First Review of Vietnam Import Data: Commerce Finds Insufficient Evidence of Dumping," dated 26 October 2007, "Commerce Completes Second Review of Viet Nam Import Data: Commerce Finds Insufficient Evidence to Self-Initiate," dated 6 May 2008, and "Commerce Finds Insufficient Evidence to Self-Initiate Vietnam Apparel Dumping Case: Completes Final Review of Import Data," dated 21 November 2008, all downloaded from the OTEXA Web site of USDOC: http://web.ita.doc.gov/tacgi/eamain.nsf/6e1600e39721316c852570ab0056f719/46e285131a-24fa9b8525753d006edfca?OpenDocument.

[41] See the WTO Web site: http://www.wto.org/english/tratop_e/adp_e/adp_e.htm.

Table 9 Viet Nam—pre-WTO accession anti-dumping lawsuits (industrial goods)

Year	*Number of cases*	*Type of goods*	*Country of petition/ petitioner*
1994–2004	18	Surfboards, fluorescent lamps, stainless steel latch, bicycles, steel pipes, tyres	EU, Peru, Turkey, US, Korea, Canada. Poland, Columbia
2005	3	Bicycle spokes, fluorescent lamps, leather shoes	Argentina, Egypt, EU
2006	2	Shoes, cloth, hat, belt	Peru, Turkey

Source Central Institute of Economic Management (2010)

In anti-dumping cases, trading partners have been treating Viet Nam as an NME, and their discretion to adopt the price of any surrogate third countries for calculation of the fair price placed Viet Nam in a vulnerable position. Table 9 lists anti-dumping lawsuits against Viet Nam's exports of industrial products from 1994 onwards. Among them, for instance, the EU selected Mexico as a surrogate country in anti-dumping investigations on bicycles in 2005 (EU, 2005)[42] and Brazil on footwear in 2006 (EU, 2006).[43] On top of that, the incumbent WTO members applied a discretionally calculated single duty rate to multiple numbers of Vietnamese exporters on the premise that all of them belong to a single state entity, further raising the hurdles for them to compete in foreign markets.

The most contentious case, however, occurred with the United States on a fishery product—catfish.[44] Following conclusion of the BTA in 2000, catfish imports from Viet Nam to the United States increased rapidly. According to the USDOC data, the volume of imports from Viet Nam increased from 3,260,000 kg in 1999 to 8,624,000 kg

[42] *The Official Journal of the European Union*: Council Regulation (EC) No. 1095/2005 of 12 July 2005.

[43] *The Official Journal of the European Union*: Council Regulation (EC) No. 1472/2006 of 5 October 2006.

[44] A report by the US Congressional Research Service says "*Catfish have been a regular source of trade friction between the United States and Vietnam for the past decade*" (Martin, 2012, p. 12), singling out disputes over this fishery product.

in 2000, 13,475,000 kg in 2001 and 20,965,000 kg in 2002. On value terms, imports grew from $13,371,000 in 1999 to $29,667,000 in 2000, $38,286,000 in 2001 and $62,778,000 in 2002 (USDOC, 2003a). These flux of imports triggered protectionist moves by the US producers. Since 2001, the Catfish Farmers of America (CFA), an industry association, lobbied to persuade the congress to amend a number of product labeling-related legislations (in particular, through the Farm Security and Rural Investment Act of 2002) to block the Vietnamese imports from being marketed as "catfish." Initially, these Vietnamese catfish products were sold with labeling such as "Delta Fresh Raised Catfish," "Harvest Fresh Catfish," "Farm Select Catfish," and "Cajun Delight Catfish" (US International Trade Commission [USITC], 2003). CFA claimed that Vietnamese catfish were raised in unsanitary third-world rivers and should not be treated and labeled equally with home-grown "catfish" ("Vietnam and the United States," 2002).

After amendment of the US legislation, Vietnamese catfish were marketed as "basa" and "tra" (Vietnamese common names for catfish species), but merely changing the labeling did not stop imports. On 28 June 2002, unsatisfied CFA and a number of US catfish producers filed an anti-dumping petition to the USDOC and USITC as the next move (USITC, 2003). Subsequently, USDOC made final determination, confirming dumping by Viet Nam based on the constructed value reflecting Bangladesh prices (supplemented by data from India) (USDOC, 2003b[45]; "Viet Nam and the WTO," 2006). The direct stakeholder in this dispute from the Vietnamese side was the Vietnam Association of Seafood Exporters and Producers (VASEP), which acted as a respondent of the dispute, supported by the government. From the early stage of this dispute, VASEP had been resisting the NME treatment, arguing that the commercial dispute should be resolved based on the objective economic criteria, rather than the Cold War legacy of NME, as stated in the letter from its lawyer to the US Commerce Secretary:

> On behalf of the Vietnam Association of Seafood Exporters and Producers ("VASEP") and its individual members, we respectfully submit this rebuttal to the October 2, 2002 comments regarding Vietnam's status as either a market economy or non-market economy country,

[45] Federal Register 68(120), 23 June 2003.

filed on behalf of the Catfish Farmers of America and individual U.S. catfish processors ("Petitioners")... Petitioners attempt in their October 2, 2002 comments on Viet Nam's economic status to make up in Cold War rhetoric what their arguments lack in substance... VASEP submits that the Department's consideration of the appropriate treatment of Viet Nam's economy should focus solely on the level of Vietnam's economic development... The seafood export industry has been one of the most dynamic components of sustained private sector growth in Viet Nam. The Foundation for this growth and vigor was laid a few years ago when Vietnam aggressively restructured the industry and state influence was minimized... The American Chamber of Commerce in Vietnam ("Amcham") submitted comments supporting treatment of Viet Nam as a market economy on behalf of its 7000 plus members... VASEP urges the Department to take into account the testimony of American business in Viet Nam.[46]

In the final determination by USDOC, differentiated dumping margins were calculated for different categories of Vietnamese exporters: 44.76–36.84%, individually calculated for mandatory respondents of this anti-dumping investigation; "separate rates" of 44.66% (based on the weighted average margin of the mandatory respondents) for voluntary respondents of the investigation; and the Vietnam-wide rate of 63.88% for all other Vietnamese produces and exporters (USDOC, 2003a).[47] The Vietnam-wide rate was the highest rate calculated in the initiation stage of investigation, based on "adverse facts available"[48] provided in the petition (USDOC, 2003b, p. 37120).

This was followed by another determination by the USITC that the domestic industry was materially injured by Vietnamese imports

[46]A White & Case letter on "Certain Frozen Fish Fillets from the Socialist Republic of Viet Nam," from counsels to VASEP and its individual members to Donald L. Evans, Secretary of Commerce dated 15 October 2002, pp. 1–4, downloaded from the USDOC Web site: http://enforcement.trade.gov/download/vietnam-nme-status/comments/wc-vasep/wc-vasep-vietnam-nme-status-rebuttal.pdf.

[47]Fact Sheet: Final Determination in the Antidumping Duty Investigation of Certain Frozen Fillets from Viet Nam. Available from the international trade administration Web site of the US Commerce Department: http://www.ita.doc.gov/media/FactSheet/0603/catfish_final_061703.html. See also Federal Register. Vol. 68, No. 120. Monday, 23 June 2003. Notices.

[48]Further details on what constitutes adverse facts available could not be found in official documentation on final dumping determination.

(USITC, 2003),[49] giving an ultimate go signal for imposition of anti-dumping duties. Toward the conclusion of this investigation, VASEP expressed its deep dissatisfaction through the Vietnamese embassy in the United States:

> In an effort to find a positive solution to the dumping dispute regarding frozen tra and basa fish fillets imported into the United States, the Government of Vietnam sent a delegation of officials from responsible ministries to negotiate with the U.S. Department of Commerce (DOC) in Washington, D.C. last week. The Vietnam Association of Seafood Exporters and Producers (VASEP) is however very disappointed that the efforts and reasonable proposals of the Vietnamese side were not received in a constructive spirit of good faith… VASEP, as well as American organizations and individuals, have time and again proved that the success of tra and basa fish fillets in the U.S. market is not at all attributable to dumping, but is the result of Vietnamese businesses providing high quality products at reasonable prices that appeal to the tastes of U.S. consumers.[50]

As an NME, Viet Nam was severely disadvantaged in the anti-dumping disputes. The Tariff Act of 1930 gives ample latitude of possible discretion for determination of dumping by NMEs (Startup, 2005), and the dispute was handled solely on the basis of the US law in CFA's favor. At the same time, as a non-member of the WTO, the country lacked the means for litigation at the multilateral level (Davis, 2006). While the BTA was in place, it lacked the bilateral dispute settlement mechanism. On top of that, the BTA even carved out disciplines on anti-dumping actions from the scope (Cong, 2010). Viet Nam had learned a hard lesson from this pre-WTO accession dispute on catfish. Davis (2006) reports that this incident renewed the government's resolve to join the WTO, so that the country could cope with the future disputes better through its multilateral litigation.

4.2.2 Post-accession Disputes on United States—Shrimp

Viet Nam's terms of accession included the NME provision for anti-dumping actions by trading partners, like the case of China (see Chapter 4) but unlike the case of many other transition economies

[49] USITC. *Certain frozen fish fillets from Vietnam: Investigation No. 731-TA-1012 (Final)*. Washington, DC: USITC.

[50] Retrieved from the Web site of the Vietnamese embassy in the United States at: http://vietnamembassy-usa.org/relations/press-release-catfish-dispute.

that had joined the WTO since 1995 (including Georgia—see Chapter 3). The NME designation allows importing countries to exercise certain discretions on their part in calculation of the normal value to determine dumping margins (see Chapter 2 on a general description of the NME). Wording given in the accession Working Party Report for Viet Nam was quite similar to what was stated in China's Protocol of Accession:

> In determining price comparability under Article VI of the GATT 1994 and the Anti-Dumping Agreement, ... The importing WTO Member may use a methodology that is not based on a strict comparison with domestic prices or costs in Viet Nam if the producers under investigation cannot clearly show that market economy conditions prevail in the industry producing the like product with regard to manufacture, production and sale of that product. (WTO, 2006, p. 66)

Viet Nam had tried to remove its NME status through the WTO accession process, but could not achieve this particular objective. To the contrary, its accession terms multilateralized the discriminatory treatment against Viet Nam.[51] Out of the recognition that the NME issue is outside of the Doha Round mandate, the government of Viet Nam did not pursue this issue in the rules negotiations. Instead, the government had been trying to revoke the NME status bilaterally outside of the WTO. Some major trading partners, such as Australia, China, India, Japan, Korea, Russia, and Switzerland, among others, came to recognize Viet Nam as a full market economy (WTO, 2013b).

In the meantime, the next major anti-dumping investigation against VASEP came up, again in the fishery sector with the United States. This time, the target was shrimps. In 2003, the ad hoc Shrimp Trade Action Committee and some other US shrimp producers filed an anti-dumping petition to USDOC and USITC, against a number of countries including Viet Nam. Subsequently to USITC's determination of material injury to domestic industries,[52] USDOC published the anti-dumping order for Viet Nam in February 2005,[53] including imposition of

[51] This provision shall expire on 31 December 2018 (WTO, 2006).

[52] USITC determined material injury on only non-canned shrimps, and canned shrimps were excluded from the scope of anti-dumping. See USITC (2005).

[53] Initial announcement of USDOC's final determination was published in Federal Register 69(235) dated 8 December 2004 (USDOC, 2004).

differentiated anti-dumping margins as in the case for catfish, comprising: the individual rates of 4.30–5.24% for three mandatory respondents; a separate rate of 4.57% to voluntary respondents ("all others" rate); and the Vietnam-wide rate of 25.76% based on the adverse facts available ("facts available" rate). As in the catfish case, Bangladesh was designated as a surrogate country.

While this original investigation and the first review by USDOC were about imports prior to Viet Nam's accession to the WTO in January 2007, the succeeding reviews covered those after the country's membership. Thus, Viet Nam was in a position to be able to use the WTO dispute settlement mechanism to cope with this problem. In March 2009, VASEP requested the Vietnamese government to file a suit at the WTO, claiming that access to the dispute settlement mechanism was a natural right of Viet Nam as a WTO member. VCCI joined the force with VASEP later on, and Viet Nam filed a request for consultation with the United States on 1 February 2010 (WTO, 2010a) and establishment of the dispute settlement panel on 7 April 2010 (WTO, 2010b).

In fact, VASEP had been confident that there was a high likelihood of winning the shrimp case at the WTO. Apart from the NME methodology, the US anti-dumping measures entailed a practice of so-called zeroing, whereby a zero value was used in calculating the average dumping margin when the export price was higher than the normal value. Zeroing artificially inflates the calculated dumping margin, and the Appellate Boding had ruled against it in a number of previous dispute settlement cases, including United States—Zeroing (Japan), United States—Stainless Steel (Mexico), and United States—Softwood Lumber V (Canada). Thus, VASEP had a promising "winning argument" (VASEP, 2011, p. 7) at its hand, as commented by Nguyen Huu Dung, VASEP Deputy Chairman:

> The WTO has concluded that the U.S. was wrong in applying the zeroing method in precedent cases. I can see high possibility of Viet Nam winning the case. (VASEP, 2010)[54]

The zeroing argument did not address the NME issue directly, but was instrumental in winning the case. Probably for this reason, Viet Nam

[54] Retrieved from: http://www.vietfish.org/20100420110657640p49c64/viet-nam-brings-shrimp-case-against-us-to-wto.htm.

joined the forces with 18 other WTO members (Brazil, Chile, China, Columbia, Costa Rica, Hong Kong, Indonesia, Israel, Japan, Korea, Malaysia, Mexico, Norway, Pakistan, Singapore, Switzerland, Chinese Taipei, and Thailand) to oppose the attempt to legalize zeroing at the rules negotiations of the Doha Round. Their statement dated 8 July 2008 reads:

> We recall that the chairman's first draft text on anti-dumping last November (TN/RL/W/213) lacked balance and raised serious concerns. One of the reasons for such concerns was the legalization of zeroing, a method that unfairly inflates anti-dumping duties. As stated in the document TN/RL/W/214/Rev.3: "Zeroing is a biased and partial method for calculating the margin of dumping and inflates anti-dumping duties. If the use of such practice prevails in the future, it could nullify the results of trade liberalization efforts. The Chair's text must serve the spirit of the Doha Development Agenda, which we understand to be to increase trade flows, enhance predictability, and provide more transparency". (WTO, 2008, p. 1)

Since Viet Nam's NME status had already been codified in its terms of WTO accession, the country could not challenge this designation itself (and use of the surrogate country). Instead, as China also did in anti-dumping cases with the United States and the EU, Viet Nam addressed what it regarded as abuse of the NME designation by the trading partner. Among three groups of anti-dumping margins, the single rate assigned to the Vietnam-wide entity was based on the alleged presumption on the US side that, since Viet Nam was an NME, fishery companies collectively belonged to the State, which was a single entity. Referring to the accession negotiations on the NME treatment, the United States claimed that all Vietnamese companies that could not sufficiently demonstrate independence from the government should be treated as a Vietnam-wide entity and subjected to dumping margins determined on the basis of adverse facts available. Thus, the highest rate of 25.76%, based on the information on adverse facts provided in the petition, was applied to them (USDOC, 2004).[55] Referring to the preceding catfish case and WTO accession negotiations, the United States argued that it had legitimate discretion on how to treat companies

[55] Further details on what constitutes adverse facts available could not be found in official documentation on final dumping determination.

of NME in the anti-dumping investigation (WTO, 2011).[56] In response, Viet Nam claimed that the terms of accession did not justify such a complete lack of disciplines.

> At the time of accession, Viet Nam understood that certain concessions would be necessary to assuage the concerns of market economy countries that Viet Nam's economy was not sufficiently market based to allow for application of the antidumping remedy. Accordingly, Viet Nam agreed to the specific instances in which an administering authority could treat Vietnamese entities differently than entities from other Member countries. These specific instances are detailed in paragraph 527 of the Working Party Report and in Viet Nam's Protocol of Accession. Neither document provides that an investigating authority may impose a rebuttable presumption that all exporters or producers operate under the control of the government. There is simply no basis by which the USDOC can impose additional commitments in the form of discriminatory and unjustified presumptions towards Vietnamese producers or exporters not likewise applied to the producers of other Member countries. (WTO, 2011, p. C-6)

More specifically, Vu Dung, Vietnamese Ambassador and permanent representative to the WTO stated "*(t)here is no such authority for this so-called Vietnam wide rate in either the Antidumping Agreement or Vietnam's Protocol of Accession.*"[57]

In the final ruling of the dispute, as Viet Nam had expected, the panel ruled against zeroing, both "as such" and "as applied" to second and third administrative reviews of US anti-dumping investigation. It also found that Viet Nam's terms of accession allowed special treatment as an NME only in relation to price comparability, and application of the facts available rate to the Vietnam-wide entity was inconsistent with relevant provisions of the WTO Agreement on Anti-Dumping (WTO, 2011). The United States did not appeal this ruling, and the panel report was adopted on 2 September 2011. At the meeting of the WTO Dispute Settlement Body on 27 September 2011, the United States indicated that it would implement the ruling.[58] Thus, unlike the case of initial pre-WTO accession catfish dispute, Viet Nam successfully overcame part of its disadvantage as an NME.

[56] The US appeared to have dropped this argument later on (WTO, 2011).

[57] Web site of the Vietnamese Embassy in the US: http://vietnamembassy-usa.org/relations/vietnam-requests-wto-panel-us-shrimp-duties.

[58] WTO Web site: http://www.wto.org/english/tratop_e/dispu_e/cases_e/ds404_e.htm.

This episode is consistent with Hypothesis 3. Taking the advantages of access to the dispute settlement mechanism and with the zeroing argument at hand, Viet Nam filed a suit on its shrimp exports to the United States at the WTO. While the NME designation remained even after the WTO accession, as stated in its terms of accession, the membership gave the country access to the dispute settlement mechanism and Viet Nam successfully challenged the abuse of the WTO-minus provision by the trading partner. Also, it is noteworthy that VASEP—a private business entity—played a very active role in bringing the case to the WTO.

5 Conclusion

Viet Nam's WTO membership in 2007 was partially motivated by its domestic reform under Doi Moi, and the accession commitments served as an instrument to pursue its progressive transition to a market economy. However, this domestic reform was characterized by the cautious gradualist approach, and pre-WTO accession trade liberalization was conducted only selectively through preferential trade agreements (AFTA with ASEAN countries and BTA with the United States, in particular), rather than broadly on the MFN basis with all trading partners. Thus, Viet Nam's average MFN applied tariff rate remained high in the pre-accession period. The cautious approach to transition was translated into Viet Nam's negotiating stance for WTO accession, which led to tariff binding slightly higher than other RAMs in transition. Still, the final bound tariff rate was lower than the pre-accession applied rate on average. Thus, Viet Nam managed to advance its unilateral trade liberalization through WTO accession commitments, in accordance with its cautious gradualist approach. This episode is in conformity with Hypothesis 1 on the commitment theory that a country makes WTO accession commitments in line with its reform needs.

In the early post-accession period, macroeconomic destabilization caused suspicion on the merit of further engagement in the WTO among some policy-makers, and Viet Nam stayed away from the DDA market access negotiations and pursued further MFN-based market opening autonomously outside of the WTO. In a sense that Viet Nam's disengagement from market access negotiations coincided with deterioration of the current account and trade balance, Hypothesis 2-a on the juggernaut theory seems to be verified on statistical grounds. However, the qualitative observation revealed that lack of exporters' interest may not be the sole reason for Vet Nam's silence at the Doha Round. There was also a concern over broader macroeconomic instability. At the same time, Viet Nam is arguably not a large economy, and the country's behavior was also consistent with Hypothesis 2-b on terms of trade externality.

Viet Nam previously faced a number of specific disadvantages as the outsider of the WTO, including partial lack of MFN access to trading partners' market, particularly in the textile and clothing sector, and the designation as NME in anti-dumping disputes, particularly in the fishery sector. The impact of the former was thought to be multiplied by China's accession to the WTO in 2001 and full implementation of ATC among WTO members in 2005, which triggered domino expansion of multilateralism in GMS. Partly for this reason, Viet Nam's accession efforts were accelerated after 2001, with the target of achieving membership by 2005. With WTO accession, Viet Nam gained the full MFN access in this respect. However, Viet Nam still suffered from the NME designation for anti-dumping investigations continuously, as its terms of accession spelled out. From the lessons learned in the pre-accession catfish dispute, Viet Nam proactively utilized the newly gained access to WTO's dispute settlement mechanism to counter the abuse of the NME designation by its trading partner. These episodes broadly confirm validity of Hypothesis 3 that a country takes part in the relevant multilateral scheme of trade liberalization to redress the cost of the previous outsider status, as inferred from the domino theory.

A few years after the global financial crisis, Viet Nam's macroeconomic conditions showed signs of recovery. In February 2011, the government announced a program of macroeconomic stabilization (Resolution 11) (World Bank, 2012). By 2012, inflation had been reduced to a single-digit level, and both current account and trade balance recorded surplus in 2013. In the 2013 Article IV consultation, the IMF acknowledged that the economic stability had been regained over the past year.[59] In the words of Christine Lagarde, its Managing Director:

> We had productive discussions on the progress Vietnam has made in regaining macroeconomic stability over the past year, and on policies to

[59]See press release "IMF Executive Board Concludes 2013 Article IV Consultation with Vietnam," dated 9 August 2013 Web site: http://www.imf.org/external/np/sec/pr/2013/pr13304.htm.

> consolidate these achievements and further Vietnam's commendable track record of reducing poverty. I welcomed the authorities' efforts to sustain fiscal consolidation and achieve the budget deficit target this year, which along with maintaining the current monetary policy stance, will be instrumental to containing inflation.[60]

This recovery of macroeconomic standing seems to have brought Viet Nam back as an active player at the WTO. The government's policy statement at the time of Viet Nam's trade policy review in 2013 indicates the country's renewed engagement in the WTO[61]:

> In the WTO framework, despite the deadlocks of the Doha negotiations, we remain committed to continue to work towards success in all negotiating groups, including on Agriculture, NAMA, Rules and Services, as we wish to achieve commercially-meaningful global improvements in market access conditions to which we are willing to contribute. (WTO, 2013b, p. 20)

Viet Nam's increasingly proactive stance was most clearly demonstrated in its entry to the Cairns Group on 20 November 2013, in the lead to the WTO Bali Ministerial Conference.[62] The Cairns Group is a negotiating group calling for ambitious trade liberalization in agriculture.[63] Its liberal orientation makes a sharp contrast to the defensive posture of the RAMs.

[60] See press release "Statement by IMF Managing Director Christine Lagarde on the Socialist Republic of Viet Nam," date 26 September 2012 Web site: http://www.imf.org/external/np/sec/pr/2013/pr13363.htm.

[61] A remark by Vu Van Ninh, Deputy Prime Minister and Chairman of National Committee for International Economic Cooperation (NCIEC), also seems to indicate that Viet Nam is geared to pursue export growth, not just import liberalization that was the focus of the past policy: "*The country's rapid trade growth during the past two decades has been built on international economic integration process -- lower barriers to trade and participation in agreements with trade partners. However, with this progress in international commitments well advanced, the advantages of trade liberalization in contributing to the growth of trade are reaching their limits. It is time to have a new approach to improve trade competitiveness and export growth*" (Ninh, 2013, p. vii).

[62] Communiqué, 38th Cairns Group Ministerial Meeting in Bali, Indonesia dated 2 December 2013, posted in Cairns Group Web site: http://www.cairnsgroup.org/Pages/131202-communique.aspx#moving-forward.

[63] See the WTO Web site: http://www.wto.org/english/tratop_e/dda_e/negotiating_groups_e.htm.

Clearly, Viet Nam's engagement at the WTO changed after its macroeconomic recovery,[64] and this development took place along with the rise of the country's export orientation. Determination of to what extent Viet Nam's renewed engagement in multilateralism reflected rising export interests, as envisaged by Hypothesis 2-a, requires further study.

With regard to anti-dumping actions related to NME, Viet Nam recently filed the second dispute on shrimps against the United States (United States—Shrimp II), raising similar issues of zeroing and the Vietnam-wide duty rate. Building upon the earlier successful challenge against second and third administrative reviews, Viet Nam requested consultation on fourth, fifth, sunset and subsequent reviews on 22 February 2012 (WTO, 2012) and establishment of the dispute settlement panel on 17 January 2013 (WTO, 2013c). The panel was established on 27 February 2013, and its final report upholding some of Viet Nam's arguments was issued on 17 November 2014 (WTO, 2014).[65] Subsequently, the appellate body report was issued on 7 April 2015 (WTO, 2015a, 2015b). Viet Nam's continuous challenge at the WTO dispute settlement is in line with Hypothesis 3.[66]

References

Asian Development Bank. (2013). *Key indicators for Asia and the Pacific 2013* (44th ed.). Manila: Author.

Auffret, P. (2003). *Trade reform in Viet Nam: Opportunities with emerging challenges*. Washington, DC: World Bank.

Bagwell, K., & Staiger, R. W. (1999). An economic theory of GATT. *American Economic Review, 89*(1), 215–248.

Bagwell, K., & Staiger, R. W. (2002). *The economics of the world trading system*. Cambridge: MIT Press.

[64] Nguyen Trung Thanh, Ambassador of Viet Nam to the UN and the WTO, also expressed the country's willingness to engage further with multilateral trade liberalization, at the session on the global value chains of the WTO Public Forum in Geneva on 3 October 2014. See the WTO Web site: http://www.wto.org/english/forums_e/public_forum14_e/programme_e.htm.

[65] See the WTO Web site: http://www.wto.org/english/tratop_e/dispu_e/cases_e/ds429_e.htm.

[66] As a recent development, Viet Nam filed another despite settlement case, US—Fish Fillet (Viet Nam), related to the Viet Nam-wide entity and zeroing on 8 January 2018. See WTO (2018).

Baldwin, R. E. (1995). A domino theory of regionalism. In R. Baldwin, P. Haaparanta, & J. Kiander (Eds.), *Expanding membership of the European Union* (pp. 25–48). Cambridge: Cambridge University Press.

Baldwin, R. E. (2006). Multilateralising regionalism: Spaghetti bowls as building blocs on the path to global free trade. *The World Economy, 29*(11), 1451–1518.

Baldwin, R. E. (2012). Preferential trading arrangements. In A. Narlikar, M. Daunton, & R. M. Stern (Eds.), *The Oxford handbook on the World Trade Organization* (pp. 632–654). Oxford: Oxford University Press.

Central Institute for Economic Management. (2010). *Impacts of international economic integration on Vietnam's economy after three years of WTO membership*. Hanoi: Author.

Central Institute for Economic Management. (2013). *Đánh giá tổng thể tình hình kinh tế - xã hội Việt Nam sau 5 năm gia nhập tổ chức Thương mại Thế giới* [Assessing the overall economic situation—Vietnamese society after 5 years of joining WTO]. Hanoi: Financial Publisher.

Cong, D. T. (2010). Catfish, shrimp, and the WTO: Vietnam loses its innocence. *Vanderbilt Journal of Transnational Law, 43*(5), 1235–1264.

Davis, C. L. (2006). Do WTO rules create a level playing field? Lessons from the experience of Peru and Vietnam. In J. S. Odell (Ed.), *Negotiating trade: Developing countries in the WTO and NAFTA* (pp. 219–256). Cambridge: Cambridge University Press.

European Union. (2005, July 14). Council regulation (EC) No. 1095/2005 of 12 July 2005, imposing a definitive anti-dumping duty on imports of bicycles originating in Vietnam, and amending regulation (EC) No. 1524/2000 imposing a definitive anti-dumping duty on imports of bicycles originating in the People's Republic of China. *The Official Journal of the European Union* (L183/1-L183/36).

European Union. (2006, October 6). Council regulation (EC) No. 1472/2006 of 5 October 2006, imposing a definitive anti-dumping duty and collecting the provisional duty imposed on imports of certain footwear with uppers of leather originating in the People's Republic of China and Vietnam. *The Official Journal of the European Union* (L275/1-L275/41).

Godoy, S., & Stiglitz, J. E. (2006). *Growth, initial conditions, law and speed of privatization in transition countries: 11 years later* (Working Paper No. 11992). Retrieved from National Bureau of Economic Research website: http://www.nber.org/papers/w11992.

Hanh, P. T. H. (2011). Does WTO accession matter for the dynamics of foreign direct investment and trade? Vietnam's experience. *Economics of Transition, 19*(2), 255–285.

Ianchovichina, E., & Martin, W. (2004). Economic impacts of China's accession to the WTO. In D. Bhattasali, S. Li, & W. Martin (Eds.), *China and the*

WTO: Accession, policy reform, and poverty reduction strategies (pp. 211–236). Washington, DC: World Bank.
International Finance Corporation, Ministry of Planning and Investment, & World Bank. (2006, December 13). *Vietnam Business Forum: Vietnam consultative group meeting 2006*. Hanoi: Vietnam Business Forum Secretariat.
International Monetary Fund. (1998). *Vietnam: Selected issues and statistical annex* (IMF Staff Country Report No. 98/30). Washington, DC: Author.
International Monetary Fund. (2007). *Vietnam: 2007 article IV consultation—Staff report; staff supplement and statement; and public information notice on the executive board discussion; and statement by the executive director for Vietnam* (IMF Staff Country Report No. 07/387). Washington, DC: Author.
International Monetary Fund. (2010). *Vietnam: 2010 article IV consultation—Staff report and public information notice* (IMF Staff Country Report No. 10/281). Washington, DC: Author.
Krugman, P. (1991, November/December). The move toward free trade zones. *Economic Review—Federal Reserve Bank of Kansas City, 76(6)*, 5–25.
Maggi, G., & Rodríguez-Clare, A. (1998). The value of trade agreements in the presence of political pressures. *Journal of Political Economy, 106*(3), 574–601.
Maggi, G., & Rodríguez-Clare, A. (2007). A political-economy theory of trade agreements. *American Economic Review, 97*(4), 1374–1406.
Martin, M. F. (2012). *U.S.-Vietnam economic and trade relations: Issues for the 112th congress*. Washington, DC: Congressional Research Service.
Menon, J. (2009). Managing success in Viet Nam: Macroeconomic consequences of large capital inflows with limited instruments. *ASEAN Economic Bulletin, 26*(1), 77–95.
Ministry of Planning and Investment. (2003). *Foreign investment policy of Vietnam in the process of international economic integration*. Retrieved from World Bank website: http://siteresources.worldbank.org/INTRANETTRADE/Resources/WBI-Training/vietFIP_dat.pdf.
Ninh. (2013). Foreword. In D. M. Pham, D. Mishra, K. Cheong, J. Arnold, A. M. Trinh, H. T. N. Ngo, & H. T. P. Nguyen, *Trade facilitation, value creation, and competitiveness: Policy implications for Vietnam's economic growth—Summary report* (p. vii). Washington, DC: World Bank.
Office of the United States Trade Representative. (2006). *Trade facts—May 2006: U.S.-Viet Nam bilateral WTO accession agreement—Ensuring a level-playing field for U.S. textile and apparel industries*. Retrieved from U.S.-Vietnam Trade Council website: http://www.usvtc.org/trade/wto/coalition/URTR-VietnamTextileBenefits05Sep06.pdf.
Siphana, S. (2005). *Cambodia enters the WTO: Lessons learned for least-developed countries*. Retrieved from Asian Development Bank Institute website: http://www.adbi.org/research-policy-brief/2005/10/11/1430.cambodia.wto.lessons/.

Staiger, R. W., & Tabellini, G. (1987). Discretionary trade policy and excessive protection. *American Economic Review, 77*(5), 823–837.
Startup, J. (2005). From catfish to shrimp: How Vietnam learned to navigate the waters of "free trade" as a non-market economy. *Iowa Law Review, 90*(5), 1963–1990.
Thephavong, B., Iemsouthi, K., & Vilavong, B. (2005). Laos: The textile and garment industry in the post-ATC era. In P. Gallagher, P. Low, & A. L. Stoler (Eds.), *Managing the challenges of WTO participation: 45 case studies* (pp. 316–325). Cambridge: Cambridge University Press.
Thinh, D. V. (2003). *Tariff reduction and NTB removal roadmap during WTO accession: A state-owned company.* Retrieved from World Bank website: http://siteresources.worldbank.org/INTRANETTRADE/Resources/WBI-Training/viet-tariffreduc_thinh.pdf.
United States Department of Commerce. (2003a). *Fact sheet: Final determination in the antidumping duty investigation of certain frozen fish fillets from Vietnam.* Retrieved from International Trade Administration website: http://www.ita.doc.gov/media/FactSheet/0603/catfish_final_061703.html.
United States Department of Commerce. (2003b). Notice of final antidumping duty determination of sales at less than fair value and affirmative critical circumstances: Certain frozen fish fillers from the Socialist Republic of Viet Nam. *Federal Register, 68*(120), 37116–37121. Retrieved from United States International Trade Commission website: http://www.usitc.gov/trade_remedy/731_ad_701_cvd/investigations/2002/frozen_fish_fillets_from_vietnam/final/PDF/fr_commerce_determination.pdf.
United States Department of Commerce. (2004). Final determination of sales at less than fair value: Certain frozen and canned warmwater shrimp from the Socialist Republic of Vietnam. *Federal Register, 69*(235), 71005–71010. Retrieved from International Trade Commission website: http://www.usitc.gov/trade_remedy/731_ad_701_cvd/investigations/2004/shrimp/final/PDF/fr_commerce_determination_vietnam.pdf.
United States International Trade Commission. (2003). *Certain frozen fish fillets from Vietnam* (Investigation No. 731-TA-1012 [Final]). Washington, DC: Author.
United States International Trade Commission. (2005). *Certain frozen or canned warmwater shrimp and pawns from Brazil, China, Equador, India, Thailand, and Vietnam* (Investigation Nos. 731-TA-1063-1068 [Final]). Washington, DC: Author.
U.S.-Vietnam Trade Council. (2006). *Vietnam WTO accession issues in brief: Textile safeguards.* Retrieved from the U.S.-Vietnam Trade Council website: http://www.usvtc.org/trade/other/textiles/TextileMemo04may06.pdf.
Van, D. N., Thanh, P. C., & Sa, L. K. (2005). Vietnam. In S. J. Evenett (Ed.), *Preparing for WTO accessions: Insights from developing countries.* Retrieved from

World Bank website: http://siteresources.worldbank.org/INTRANETTRADE/Resources/WBI-Training/PreparingforWTOAccessions.pdf.

Vietnam Association of Seafood Exporters and Producers. (2010). Viet Nam brings shrimp case against U.S. to WTO. *Vietfish International, 7*(2). Retrieved from: http://www.vietfish.org/20100420110657640p49c64t52/viet-nam-brings-shrimp-case-against-us-to-wto.htm.

Vietnam Association of Seafood Exporters and Producers. (2011). Despite shrimp dumping "zeroing" victories at WTO, Vietnam sees continuing trade challenges. *VASEP News, 1*(28), 7. Retrieved from: http://www.vasep.com.vn/pic/VasepNew/swfEbook/VASEP_News_No-28_2011.swf.

Vietnam and the United States: Case of the Ghostly Catfish. (2002, December 14). *The Economist, 365*(8303), 35.

Viet Nam and the WTO: Market Maker. (2006, November 2). *The Economist, 381*(8502), 100.

World Bank. (2012). *Taking stock: An update on Vietnam's recent economic development*. Hanoi: Author.

World Trade Organization. (1996a). *Accession of Vietnam: Memorandum on the foreign trade regime* (WT/ACC/VNM/2). Geneva: Author.

World Trade Organization. (1999b). *Ministerial conference, third session, Seattle, 30 November–3 December—Viet Nam: Statement by H.E. Mr. Truong Dinh Tuyen, Minister of Trade* (WT/MIN(99)ST/81). Geneva: Author.

World Trade Organization. (2001). *Ministerial conference, fourth session, Doha, 9–13 November 2001—Viet Nam: Statement by H.E. Mr. Luong van Tu, Vice-Minister of Trade* (WT/MIN(01)/ST/149). Geneva: Author.

World Trade Organization. (2006). *Working party on the accession of Viet Nam: Accession of Viet Nam—Report of the working party on the accession of Viet Nam to the World Trade Organization* (WT/ACC/VNM/48). Geneva: Author.

World Trade Organization. (2007). *International trade statistics 2007*. Geneva: Author.

World Trade Organization. (2008). *Negotiating group on rules: Statement on anti-dumping negotiations—Communication from Brazil; Chile; China; Columbia; Costa Rica; Hong Kong, China; Indonesia; Israel; Japan; Korea, Rep. of; Malaysia; Mexico; Norway; Pakistan; Singapore; Switzerland; the Separate Customs Territory of Taiwan, Penghu, Kinmen and Matsu; Thailand; and Viet Nam* (TN/RL/W/233). Geneva: Author.

World Trade Organization. (2010a). *United States—Anti-dumping measures on certain shrimp from Viet Nam: Request for consultations by Viet Nam* (WT/DS404/1). Geneva: Author.

World Trade Organization. (2010b). *United States—Anti-dumping measures on certain shrimp from Viet Nam: Request for the establishment of a panel by Viet Nam* (WT/DS404/5). Geneva: Author.

World Trade Organization. (2011). *United States—Anti-dumping measures on certain shrimp from Viet Nam: Report of the panel* (WT/DS404/R). Geneva: Author.

World Trade Organization. (2012). *United States—Anti-dumping measures on certain shrimp from Viet Nam: Request for consultations by Viet Nam* (WT/DS429/1). Geneva: Author.

World Trade Organization. (2013a). *Trade policy review body: Trade policy review report by the secretariat, Viet Nam—Revision* (WT/TPR/S/287/Rev.1). Geneva: Author.

World Trade Organization. (2013b). *Trade policy review body: Trade policy review—Report by Viet Nam* (WT/TPR/G/287). Geneva: Author.

World Trade Organization. (2013c). *United States—Anti-dumping measures on certain shrimp from Viet Nam: Request for the establishment of a panel by Viet Nam* (WT/DS429/2/Rev.1). Geneva: Author.

World Trade Organization. (2014). *United States—Anti-dumping measures on certain shrimp from Viet Nam: Report of the panel* (WT/DS429/R). Geneva: Author.

World Trade Organization. (2015a). *United States—Anti-dumping measures on certain shrimp from Viet Nam: Report of the appellate body* (WT/DS429/AB/R). Geneva: Author.

World Trade Organization. (2015b). *United States—Anti-dumping measures on certain shrimp from Viet Nam: Report of the appellate body*—Corrigendum (WT/DS429/AB/R/Corr.1). Geneva: Author.

World Trade Organization. (2018). *United States—Anti-dumping measures on fish fillets from Viet Nam—Request for consultations by Viet Nam* (WT/DS536/1 G/L/1208 G/ADP/D122/1). Geneva: Author.

CHAPTER 6

Ecuador

1 Introduction

Unlike the RAMs covered by other case studies in the preceding chapters, Ecuador's objective for WTO accession in 1996 was not to catalyze domestic reforms through market access commitments. In the cases of Georgia, China and Viet Nam, consolidation of unilateral trade liberalization in support of their transition to a market economy was either the whole or at least part of their reasons to start engagement in the multilateral trading system, and they used the accession process to that end, albeit in different degrees. Unlike these countries covered by the preceding chapters (or indeed a majority of the RAMs), Ecuador was not an economy in transition, and domestic economic reform was not its priority. Accordingly, Ecuador did not make substantive market access commitments to undertake tariff cuts at the time of accession. Also, in the absence of the reform objective, the country did not fully observe part of its relatively modest accession commitments in the post-membership period. Rather, its prime objective for membership to the WTO was to defend export interests in the agricultural sector, especially bananas. Prior to (and even after) WTO membership, Ecuador's banana exports were subjected to discriminatory trade barriers from the European Union (EU)[1]—the

[1] For the purpose of consistency of presentation, the contemporary term "EU" is used even where it actually refers to EC (European Communities) or EEC (European Economic Community).

K. Takamiya, *Recently Acceded Members of the World Trade Organization*, https://doi.org/10.1007/978-981-13-9159-0_6

main export market. The trade policy of most of the European countries, both individually and collectively as the EU, was to accord preference to its former colonies in the African, Caribbean and Pacific (ACP) regions at discrimination against rival Latin American exporters. This preference triggered the so-called banana wars (Josling & Taylor, 2003) between the EU and Latin America (subsequently joined by the United States) since the early 1990s. As an outsider of the multilateral trading system back then, Ecuador could not join this war formally through the dispute settlement mechanism under the old GATT 1947 system (that existed prior to establishment of the WTO in 1995).[2] As a result, the country had to face disadvantage compared with not only ACP countries but also some other Latin American countries. Ecuador's accession to the WTO was aimed at redressing this long-standing cost of discrimination. After WTO accession, Ecuador fiercely fought the banana war with the EU through dispute settlement. At the same time, the country advocated ambitious agricultural trade liberalization among WTO members at the Doha Round, particularly in tropical products including bananas (especially when its external balance has been improving toward 2008).

Accordingly, this case study on Ecuador reveals that a country suffering from the cost of previous non-member status stays actively engaged in the post-accession multilateral trade liberalization process, even if it had no interest in consolidating the domestic reforms through accession. To that end, the second section reviews Ecuador's accession commitment on market access liberalization and the status of post-membership implementation and establishes the fact that support to domestic reforms was not a major objective of the WTO membership. The analysis confirms part of Hypothesis 1 for non-reforming economies: *Reforming economies (especially, those in transition to a market economy) would make extensive market access commitments for WTO accession, while others would make little use of them.* The third section describes Ecuador's proactive engagement in dispute settlement on bananas, to demonstrate the validity of Hypothesis 3: *Countries that face the discriminatory cost of prior non-membership would stay engaged in the relevant multilateral liberalization schemes, while others would refrain from such activities.* The fourth

[2]With the establishment of the WTO in 1995, the dispute settlement rule under the old GATT system was replaced with the new Dispute Settlement Understanding (DSU), whose main features include adoption of the ruling based on the negative consensus, as explained in this chapter.

section shows that Ecuador was actively engaged in the Doha Round market access negotiations in agriculture when the country's export orientation had been enhanced. On the one hand, the latter episode statistically proves the validity of Hypothesis 2-a: *Only export-oriented economies would stay proactively engaged in the post-accession market access negotiations of the Doha Round, while others would pursue autonomous liberalization.* On the other hand, however, the case study shows that what determined Ecuador's position was not the increasing presence of the export businesses in the overall economy, as the underlying juggernaut theory assumes. Rather, for Ecuador, the Doha Round negotiations were partly an extension of the banana disputes (and thus more relevant to Hypothesis 3). It also reveals that, given the small size of the economy, Ecuador's signs of engagement in the reciprocal market access negotiations are at odds with Hypothesis 2-b: *Only large economies would stay proactively engaged in the market access negotiations of the Doha Round, while others would pursue autonomous liberalization.* The last section concludes.

2 WTO Accession Commitment and Implementation

2.1 Tariff Binding Detached from Domestic Reforms

Ecuador's economic reform had taken place since the mid-1980s, following the then prevailing trend of adopting the liberal economic policy prescription, or "Washington consensus" (Williamson, 1990, p. 20), after the debt crisis in Latin America. The government intensified market-oriented economic adjustment measures, such as cutback of price controls and energy subsidies, elimination of export taxes, import liberalization, FDI promotion, and slowing of the credit expansion (World Bank, 1987). In the area of trade policy, market access liberalization was launched in 1989, with an objective of simplifying the tariff structure and reducing protection, and the average tariff rate declined from 29% in 1989 to 11% in 1994. The number of tariff bands was reduced from 14 to seven, and the maximum rate declined from 290 to 40% in 1992 (WTO, 2005a).[3] However, the momentum of structural reform did not

[3] The 1993 memorandum of foreign trade regime and the 1995 Working Party Report for WTO accession record the simple average tariff rate of 9.3% and the trade weighted average at 6.8% back then (GATT, 1993a; WTO, 1995b).

last long through the 1990s. Also, compared with other Latin American countries, Ecuador's reform and macroeconomic performances have been rather modest. While the absence of data makes cross-country comparison of overall structural reforms difficult, the IMF's report provides some explanations of Ecuador's modest performances:

> The Ecuadorian economy has recorded a poor performance over the past decade. Trend growth has been negative since before 1990... Many factors have contributed to this unfortunate outcome. Structural rigidities have distorted resource allocation and left the economy highly vulnerable to shocks... The tax system has been dominated by the dual weaknesses of tax legislation and regulations that contain distortive provisions, such as high and dispersed import tariff rates ... The trading system retains, in addition to moderately high tariff rates, a number of nontariff barriers. In general, Ecuador has been slower in liberalizing its trade system than many of its neighbours... The difference between Ecuador and the other countries in growth performance is striking... Ecuador's failure to pursue sound financial policies in combination with the lack of structural reforms has been another important factor behind the disappointing performance, especially in the 1980s. (IMF, 2000, pp. 7–12)

In the IMF's assessment, the progress in Ecuador's reform was moderate in comparison with those of some other Latin American countries that sustained liberal policies; combined with unfavorable external factors (such as a decline in oil prices in the 1980s), this poor policy performance led to a poor economic performance. Whereas more active reformers like Argentina, Bolivia, Chile, and Peru achieved an economic recovery by the 1990s, Ecuador continued to record a negative average annual per capita GDP growth (Table 1). Thus, Ecuador was a poor reformer even in comparison with these other non-transition economies in the region.

Table 1 Average annual per capita GDP growth (%)

	Chile	*Ecuador*	*Bolivia*	*Argentina*	*Peru*
1970–1980	0.7	5.4	2.3	1.1	1.1
1980–1990	1.9	−0.5	−1.8	−2.6	−3.3
1990–1999	5.0	−0.4	1.8	3.5	2.5

Note GDP = gross domestic product
Source IMF (2000)

Hypothesis 1 based on the commitment theory[4] predicts that non-reforming countries make less extensive market access commitments in their terms of WTO accession and, in line with this prediction, Ecuador actually made little use of tariff binding as a commitment device for unilateral trade liberalization. While the GATT accession process (launched before the WTO was yet to be in place) was perceived to be "*a logical step based on the past accomplishment*" (GATT, 1993a, p. 6) as stated in the country's memorandum of foreign trade regime, the government did not proactively use the market access commitment to leverage the pace of tariff liberalization or to lock in the status quo. The memoir of the former trade negotiator indicates that Ecuador regarded the bound tariff simply as a legal ceiling and did not adjust its applied tariff rate for the purpose of WTO accession (Cañizares, 1995). Thus, the final bound rate under terms of WTO accession (21.0% on simple average) was designated at the level far above the pre-accession applied rate (around 12.86%[5]) (Table 2). In fact, Ecuador and Panama were the only RAMs that bound the average tariff rate at the high level exceeding 20%. Unlike a majority of the RAMs, these two small, vulnerable economies (SVEs) from Latin America are not transition countries, and the motivation to use WTO for the purpose of the domestic reform was not necessarily strong. At the same time, their accession took place right after establishment of the WTO in 1995 (Ecuador in 1996 and Panama in 1997), and most of the membership negotiations had already been completed under the less rigorous old GATT practice (see Chapter 2). These factors led to the moderate level of tariff bindings in comparison with other RAMs.

In fact, Ecuador's tariff binding was deliberately set to stay above the applied rate. During the Uruguay Round, other Latin American countries bound their tariffs at an average of around 30–40%, and the government's first objective for accession negotiations was to achieve the

[4] Staiger and Tabellini (1987), and Maggi and Rodriguez-Clare (1998, 2007).

[5] This average tariff rate (12.86%) in the World Bank's database is slightly higher than the rates presented in the WTO's database (11.27% as per the tariff line average method and 11.87% as per the HS sub-heading average method). One plausible reason for the gap is exclusion of non-dutiable items in the former. See Web site: http://tariffanalysis.wto.org/report/TariffAverages.aspx.

Table 2 Ecuador—MFN tariff profiles with international comparison (%)

	Ecuador				*LAC*	*World*
	1995 (pre-WTO)	*2000–2004*	*2005–2008*	*Final bound*	*1995*	*1995*
Simple average rates	12.86	11.89	11.63	21.0	12.48	11.89
Dispersion (coefficient of variation)	0.43	0.54	0.61	0.4	0.76	1.07
Domestic tariff peaks (tariff lines share)	0.00	0.22	0.26	0.2	1.79	3.37
International tariff peaks (tariff lines share)	24.82	24.60	24.84	67.3	22.40	26.82
Bound tariff lines (% of all tariff lines)	–	99.82	99.92	100.0	94.40	69.28
Tariff overhang (bound minus applied rate)	8.74	9.96	10.16	–	27.47	22.29

Note LAC = Latin America and Caribbean excluding high-income countries. Indicators for 2000–2004 and 2005–2008 are period averages. Data covers ad valorem tariffs only
Source World Bank. World Trade Indicators 2009/2010 Web site: http://info.worldbank.org/etools/wti/2a1.asp; WTO (2012b)

equivalent level of tariff binding.[6] This request was not acceptable to the United States, and instead, an alternative tariff rate incorporated in a preceding regional agreement was used as a benchmark. By the time of the WTO accession, Ecuador had already become a member of the Andean Community—a regional customs union initiative with Bolivia, Colombia, Peru, and Venezuela, and the WTO bound rate was set at the level around 10% higher than its common external tariff, with some variations for sensitive products (Cañizares, 1995). The common external tariff regime was adopted with certain exceptions with implementation delay, and thus Ecuador's average MFN applied rate was even lower. In effect, the WTO tariff binding was designed so as not to affect

[6]The final bound rates of other Andean Community countries—Bolivia, Colombia, Peru, and Venezuela—were 40.0, 41.9, 29.3, and 36.5%, respectively. See the WTO Web site: http://stat.wto.org/CountryProfile/WSDBCountryPFReporter.aspx?Language=E.

the country's actual trade policy of the day, as formally recorded in the IMF's report:

> The tariff rate binding with WTO is at general ceiling which is about 10 percentage points higher than the Common External Tariff (CET) applied by the countries of the Andean Community. The CET was determined by the Andean Community as part of the renewed Cartagena Agreement and is part of Ecuadorian law. The national tariff of Ecuador, as effectively applied, is somewhat lower than the CET, whereas the ceiling for tariff rates agreed under the WTO thus lies higher than the CET. This has provided Ecuador with a substantial margin of maneuver to impose tariff measures, such as higher tariffs or tariff surcharges, when deemed necessary. (IMF, 2000, p. 84)

2.2 *Modest Implementation Record of Accession Commitment*

Apart from the initial accession commitment, non-use of WTO tariff binding for the purpose of market access liberalization was also reflected in Ecuador's post-accession policy performance.[7] The very essence of using the terms of the WTO accession as a device for market access liberalization (assumed in Hypothesis 1 for reforming economies) rests with the country's sustained commitment to not raising the applied tariff rates above the bound level. However, Ecuador often adopted the applied tariff above the level of its accession commitment. For instance, according to the trade policy review reports of the WTO secretariat (WTO, 2005b, 2012a), the MFN applied rates were higher than the bound rates for four ten-digit lines in 2005 and those for 19 ten-digit lines exceeded the bound rates by 5–15 percentage points in 2011 (Table 3). Even for other tariff lines whose applied rates were identical to bound rates, certain charges[8] on imports were imposed on top of nominal tariffs (that, in effect, made the entire tariff equivalent higher than the bound rate) (WTO, 2005b). For WTO accession, Ecuador committed to abolish the

[7]Evenett and Gage (2005) found that Ecuador's applied MFN tariff rates rose in 81% of tariff lines reported in the trade analysis information system (TRAINS) database of the United Nations Conference on Trade and Development (UNCTAD) in the period from 1993 to 1997 and commented that WTO accession did not necessarily lead to lower applied tariff rates.

[8]These include the redeemable quota and the contribution to the Children's Development Fund.

Table 3 Ecuador—products with adverse tariff overhang

Short description of products	*Number of tariff lines*	*Applies MFN rate (%)*	*Bound rate (%)*	*Differences (%)*
In 2005				
Live bovine animals	1	10	5	5
Finishing agents, dye carrier to accelerate the dying or fixing of dye stuffs and other products and preparations	1	10	5	5
Motor vehicles for the transport of ten or more persons, including the driver	1	35	20	15
Motor vehicles for the transport of ten or more persons, including the conductor	1	35	20	15
In 2011				
Other meat and edible meat offal, fresh, chilled or frozen	1	30	20	10
Residual products of the chemical industries	9	15	10	5
Semi-chemical/straw fluting paper	2	15	10	5
Other uncoated paper and paperboard	1	15	10	5
Ceramic pipes, conduits, guttering and pipe fittings	1	30	25	5
Other tubes and pipes	1	20	15	5
Other structures and parts of structures	1	20	15	5
Motor vehicles for the transport of ten or more persons, including the driver	2	35	20	15
Other cartridges and parts thereof	1	30	25	5

Note For concise presentation, descriptions of the products are shortened and a number of HS codes are covered under a single heading
Source WTO (2005b, 2012b)

price band system (that set variable import tariffs depending on international market prices, for about 140 agricultural products) by end-2001, but this measure was continued. In the IMF's assessment, possible departure from the WTO commitment was extended also to non-tariff measures. For instance, import authorizations lasted for 1424 out of 6707 tariff items (mostly for agriculture), a departure from the WTO agreement, and GATT-inconsistent import bans on used automobiles, clothes, shoes, and tyres were maintained even after the end of transition period for compliance in 1996. SPS measures were applied for the protectionist purpose[9] (IMF, 2000, 2003).

The most visible departure from disciplines of market access commitment took the form of recourse to the balance-of-payments (BOP) safeguard in 2009. GATT Article XVIII: B allows developing countries' resort to trade restrictions to protect foreign reserve at the time of BOP difficulty. As a result of the global financial crisis in 2008–2009, Ecuador's external balance suffered from a decline in oil export earnings (due to lower international crude oil prices), non-oil exports, and remittances (due to economic downturns) (WTO, 2009c). Trade balance, that had been recording surplus till August 2008 (or on the annual basis for the entire year), turned to deficit from September 2008 onward. The government estimated that both trade balance and current account would record deficit in 2009 (as actually materialized for the current account, but not for the trade balance—see Table 4) and resorted to import restrictions for a one-year period effective from 23 January 2009. BOP restrictions were subsequently notified to the WTO on 18 February 2009 (WTO, 2009a). While recourse to Article XVIII: B used to be a popular way of justifying trade protection among developing countries under the old GATT system, such cases dramatically reduced after establishment of the WTO, especially in the 2000s.[10] By 2001, remaining

[9]Another testimony of lack of reliance on accession tariff bindings is uses of trade remedies. By 2012, Ecuador undertook 8 safeguard initiations and 4 measures, as well as 3 anti-dumping initiations. See WTO Web site: http://www.wto.org/english/tratop_e/safeg_e/safeg_e.htm; and http://www.wto.org/english/tratop_e/adp_e/adp_e.htm.

[10]The list of WTO members that invoked GATT articles XII and XVIII: B (both on BOP safeguard) can be found in the Analytical Index: GATT 1994 of the WTO Web site: http://www.wto.org/english/res_e/booksp_e/analytic_index_e/gatt1994_06_e.htm#article18D6b.

Table 4 Ecuador—selected macroeconomic indicators

	2005	*2006*	*2007*	*2008*	*2009*	*2010*
Growth rate of GDP (% per year)	5.7	4.8	2.0	7.2	0.4	3.6
Inflation (CPI, % per year)	2.1	3.3	2.3	8.4	5.2	3.6
Fiscal balance (% of GDP)	−0.5	−0.2	−0.1	−1.1	−5.1	−2.4
Merchandize exports (% of GDP)	28.3	31.6	32.7	35.9	27.7	31.2
Growth of merchandize exports (% per year)	31.4	25.9	12.9	30.9	−25.9	25.3
Merchandize imports (% of GDP)	26.3	27.4	28.7	33.0	27.4	33.9
Growth of merchandize imports (% per year)	26.4	17.5	14.4	37.3	−20.3	37.7
Merchandize trade balance (% of GDP)	2.1	4.2	4.0	2.9	0.3	−2.7
Current account balance (% of GDP)	1.3	4.2	3.7	2.5	−0.3	−3.3

Source WTO (2012b)

BOP restrictions by a number of countries (by Pakistan, Romania, and the Slovak Republic) had been lifted, except for one case (by Bangladesh that was eventually concluded in 2007) (Independent Evaluation Office [IEO] of the IMF, 2009).

The restrictive measures adopted by Ecuador in January 2009 covered 8.7% of the total tariff lines and comprised: increase of ad valorem tariffs (from bound levels and applied levels) for over 1% of tariff lines; application of a specific tariff applied on top of the ad valorem rate in place for 3.9% of tariff lines; and quantitative restrictions for 3.7% of tariff lines. The ad valorem tariff increase was up to 35%, and the specific rate was US$12 per kilo for textile and clothing products and US$10 per pair for footwear. Quotas were in the amount equivalent of up to 70% of 2008 import value, and distributed not by country (hence on the MFN basis) but by importer. The measures applied affected some 23% of the total imports (WTO, 2009b, 2009c). As far as the ad valorem tariffs were concerned, the initial increase in the simple average was small, from 10.1% (as of 1 January 2009) to 10.2%, but this does not count equivalent of specific tariffs and quotas (Table 5). Thus, the effect of the entire set of restrictions would be much larger. In response to comments made by other WTO members at the Committee on BOP Restrictions, Ecuador later replaced the quantitative restrictions with price-based measures (WTO, 2009d).

Table 5 Ecuador—impact of the balance of payments restrictions

	January 2009		*March 2009*	
	Number of lines	*Share/rate(%)*	*Number of line*	*Share/rate(%)*
Duty-free lines	3637	50.3	3633	50.3
Non ad valorem tariff	0	0.0	284	3.9
Non ad valorem tariff with no AVEs	0	0.0	284	3.9
Lines subject to quota	0	0.0	271	3.7
Simple average tariff rate	7229	10.1	7229	10.2
Agriculture	950	17.3	950	17.3
Non-agriculture (excl. petroleum)	6233	9.0	6233	9.0
First stage processing	830	10.3	830	10.3
Semi-processed	2410	5.8	2410	5.8
Fully processed	3989	12.7	3989	12.7
Domestic peaks	54	0.7	54	0.7
International peaks	2143	29.6	2143	29.6
Overall standard deviation	7229	12.1	7229	12.1

Note AVEs = ad valorem equivalents
Source WTO (2009d)

The BOP restrictions were the government's initiative taken in pursuit of its two policy objectives. First, the priority of the government was to stick to the maintenance of its monetary policy regime called "dollarization" introduced in 2000 as a response to a serious macroeconomic and banking crisis of the late 1990s. By 1999, inflation reached 61%, and GDP declined by an estimated rate of 7.5%. For a period of 1998–1999, the real effective exchange rate dropped by a total of nearly 50%. Faced with hyperinflation at the backdrop of the collapse of exchange rate, in January 2000, the government announced a complete reform of the monetary policy framework as a means to restore its credibility (IMF, 2000). Since then, Ecuador officially abandoned its previous national currency (sucre) and adopted the US dollar as legal tender. This dollarization policy helped stabilize the economy, as subsequently reflected in the low level of inflation (see Table 4), but it came at the cost of giving up the autonomous monetary (and exchange rate) policy as an instrument to manage business cycles. Thus, the government had to resort to other policy options to counter downturn of the real economy at the time of the global financial crisis from late 2008 to 2009, including import restrictions (together with fiscal policy that had its own constraint). One reason for the diminishing use of GATT Article XVIII: B by other developing countries at large was the prevalence of the export-led development strategy,[11] including dismissal of an unrealistic exchange rate backed by trade controls (Finger & Winters, 1998), and Ecuador's adoption of the rigid currency regime and invocation of the BOP safeguard was a rare event that contradicted the prevailing trend among developing countries.

On the monetary side, "*In a dollarized economy, the external sector becomes the source that generates the money supply*" as stated by the government (WTO, 2009c, p. 2), and import restrictions were used as a tool to prevent drain of liquidity out of the country. In a document submitted to the WTO Committee on BOP Restrictions dated 16 April 2009, the government provided the further technical background as follows[12]:

> For a dollarized Ecuador, it is extremely important to monitor the trend in its external sector closely so as to make appropriate use of the few policy tools still available to it and thus offset the harmful effects of possible external shocks that may alter the levels of liquidity in the economy and thus affect the normal development of economic activities. For a small and open economy such as Ecuador's, with limited capacity for reaction, controlling liquidity is greatly complicated if the balance-of-payments position is negative… The external account position for the last months of 2008 and forecasts for 2009, in the midst of this marked decline in the international economy, are of concern to the Government of Ecuador and have obliged it to take measures to deal with a liquidity squeeze in the economy, the result of a deficit in the trade balance, so as to ensure that the country does not lose the macroeconomic benefits it has gained since dollarization. (WTO, 2009c, pp. 26–27)

[11] Nonetheless, it should be noted that adoption of the export-led development strategy by the governments of developing countries does not necessarily entail active participation of export business entities in policy-making, as seen in the case study on China in Chapter 4.

[12] In a plainer language of Paul Krugman, "*Ecuador is dollarized — no currency of its own, just US dollars. And this leaves the country with very limited room for maneuver during the current crisis… Can you really say that Ecuador was wrong to do this, given its lack of other policy tools? At the very least, you have to say that there's a pretty good second-best case for the policy — and the WTO has reached a compromise allowing Ecuador to keep the measures in place at least for now.*" See "Fixed rates and protectionism, 2009 edition" dated 26 October, in Paul Krugman's *The Conscience of a Liberal* blog Web site: http://krugman.blogs.nytimes.com/?s=Ecuador.

Second, from 2009 onward, the government began to pursue a policy of import substitution. The new policy came out of recognition that the previous market-oriented reforms (albeit having been very modest) had not borne tangible fruit, and to the contrary, people's living standard could be raised only through state planning, rather than market forces (National Secretariat of Planning and Development, 2013).[13] Thus, the government's new National Plan for Good Living (PNBV)[14] called for greater state interventions by reversing the previous policy, as stated in Ecuador's statement for the trade policy review at the WTO in 2011.

> The proposals contained in the PNBV 2009-2013 raise major technical and political challenges and involve substantial methodological and instrumental innovations. Nonetheless, the Plan's deeper significance stems from the conceptual break it makes with classical liberalization models and more orthodox approaches to the concept of development… This change is based on a selective import-substitution model, rather than productive development and export orientation. (WTO, 2011, pp. 22–23)

Ecuador had been one of the world's worst performers in advancing structural reforms but, under the renewed policy that favored state interventions, the operating environment for private businesses deteriorated even further (as reflected in the World Bank's Doing Business ranking of 138th out of 183 countries in 2009, sliding from 123rd in 2006, 128th in 2007, and 136th in 2008[15]—see Table 8, Chapter 2). The import restrictions introduced in 2009, albeit temporary, partly represented such an interventionist policy orientation of the government.

Business entities were against the restrictive measures adopted by the government. Both the Chamber of Industry and Production (that represents Ecuador's large enterprises accounting for 24% of the country's income tax) and the National Association of Exporters (representing

[13]This rather unconventional policy shift was a reflection of the ideological orientation of Rafael Correa, the country's then new president who took office in 2007.

[14]The guiding principle of PNBV reads "*Good Living cannot be improvised—it must be planned. Good Living is the style of life that enables happiness and the permanency of cultural and environmental diversity; it is harmony, equality, equity and solidarity. It is not the quest for opulence or infinite economic growth*" (National Secretariat of Planning and Development, 2013, p. 14).

[15]World Bank and International Finance Corporation (2007, 2008, 2009, 2010).

exporters) expressed their objections to import restrictions, arguing that the current account deficit should be contained by cutting public expenditures that crowded out private investment.[16] However, the government proceeded with its own decision of import restrictions. Interestingly, this episode casts doubt on one assumption underlying the juggernaut and other theories, that domestic business interests influence policy decision of the government. Rather, as outlined here, it was the priorities of the government itself (such as dollarization and import substitution) that dictated the trade policy, even if it was against business interests.

Ecuador's policy performances with regard to WTO membership and post-accession policy implementation are consistent with Hypothesis 1 for non-reforming countries, including non-transition economies. As a sluggish reformer, the government did not have a clear intention to use the terms of WTO accession as a commitment device for its own unilateral market access liberalization. The bound tariff rate for WTO accession was deliberately set at a level far above the applied rate at the time of the membership. After accession, Ecuador did not fully observe even that high level of bound tariffs (and other accession commitments) in its regular trade policy performances and response during the period of the global financial crisis. These behaviors make a sharp contrast with the performance of the other RAMs that tried to stick to their accession commitments. For instance, Viet Nam (a partially dollarized economy that also faced macroeconomic destabilization in recent years) had been implementing tariff liberalization following (or even faster than) the accession commitment (see Chapter 5). Thus, commitment through tariff binding was not Ecuador's objective for WTO membership. The next two sections on the banana disputes and the Doha Round negotiations reveal that the country joined the WTO mainly to redress discrimination against its key export product—the cost it had to bear as a previous non-member of the multilateral trading system. Ecuador pursued this objective consistently throughout its post-accession performances.

[16]Other things being equal, cut in public expenditure advocated by businesses reduces the aggregate demand. On the one hand, it reduces imports and thus rebalances the current account, which was one concern of the government. On the other hand, it may lead to further downturn of the domestic economy, which was government's another concern. Thus, the fiscal tightening may relieve the problem of external balance but may exacerbate the problem of the domestic economy.

3 Banana Disputes[17]

3.1 *Toward the Doha Ministerial Conference*

The banana war dates back to the time even before completion of a single market in Europe at the end of 1992. Under the Lomé IV Convention signed by the EU and ACP countries in 1989, exports from the latter had privileged access to the former. The convention had a specific protocol on bananas (WTO, 1997a), and most of the European countries (other than Germany) with colonial links to ACP countries individually accorded duty-free access to their bananas and regulated trade also with quantitative restrictions. This policy constituted discrimination against the Latin American countries and, in June 1992, five affected GATT contracting parties (Columbia, Costa Rica, Guatemala, Nicaragua, and Venezuela) requested consultations with the EU. This and other successive attempts for resolution through GATT Director-General's good offices and the Uruguay Round could not bear fruit. In June 1993, the five Latin American countries then requested the establishment of a panel ("Bananas I" case) for dispute settlement under the old GATT system, that eventually ruled that import restrictions applied by several EU members had violated GATT Articles I (on MFN) and XI (on quantitative restrictions), and could not be justified by GATT Article XXIV (on free trade areas and customs unions) (GATT, 1993b). Article XXIV allows exception to Article I in the case of reciprocal free trade agreements, but unilateral and non-reciprocal accord of preference was outside of its scope. The panel also advised that PART IV of GATT (on trade and development) could not be invoked as it does not overrule GATT Article I (and the 1979 Enabling Clause [on differential and more favorable treatment, reciprocity and fuller participation of developing countries] does not envisage accord of preferences other than through the Generalized System of Preferences). Thus, non-reciprocal preference targeted to ACP countries was judged to have constituted violation of GATT rules.

[17]The Factual Chronology and Procedural Overview of Banana Disputes Are Presented in Salas and Jackson (2000) and the WTO Web site: https://www.wto.org/english/news_e/pres09_e/pr591_e.htm; https://www.wto.org/english/news_e/news12_e/disp_08nov12_e.htm; and https://www.wto.org/english/tratop_e/dda_e/negotiating_groups_e.htm.

However, under the old GATT system of dispute settlement, any contracting party (including the defendant) could block the panel report and, accordingly, the ruling on the Banana I case was never adopted. At the same time, as of 1 July 1993, the EU had launched the new region-wide discriminatory import regime adapted for its single market, and GATT panel findings on the older national regimes by individual member states soon became irrelevant. Thus, the five Latin American countries sought establishment of the new panel against the unified new EU policy ("Bananas II" case), and again, it found the EU's violation of GATT Articles I, II (on tariff bindings), III (on national treatment), and inconsistency with GATT Article XXIV (GATT, 1994a).

After the issue of the Banana II panel report, the EU negotiated and offered an increase in the country-specific tariff quotas, reduction of in-quota tariffs (ECU75 per tonne), and allowance for export licenses management to Latin American parties to the disputes, in exchange for the latter's concession of not pursuing adoption of the Bananas II panel report at the GATT. Out of five complainants, Columbia, Costa Rica, Venezuela, and Nicaragua agreed on this deal, known as the Framework Agreement on Bananas (BFA), while Guatemala protested and did not join. BFA was incorporated into the EU's Uruguay Round schedule in March 1994 and came into force at the time of establishment of the WTO on 1 January 1995 (WTO, 1997a). Again, the panel report remained un-adopted. In 1994, the EU also secured multilateral waiver from GATT Article I obligation to continue implementation of the Lomé IV Convention with ACP countries (justifying preferences for banana imports) until 29 February 2000 (GATT, 1994b). As a non-contracting party to GATT, Ecuador (and Panama) could not be formally engaged in these multilateral processes among the EU, ACP, and other Latin American countries on the equal footing, and it was left in a disadvantageous position in relation to Europe's other former colonies,[18] including regional competitors. In his essay on banana disputes, a senior diplomat of Ecuador recalls that the country had no right to claim on Bananas I and Bananas II cases and did not take part in the BFA (Huerta, 2010). Another former diplomat wrote that Ecuador could not

[18]When Spain and Portugal joined the EU in 1986, their ties with most of their former colonies in Latin America were not strong enough to grant preferences to them. Also, Spain and Portugal sought to preserve interests in their own bananas and other agricultural products, rather than those of Latin America (Guth, 2012).

negotiate with other countries due to its outsider status in the GATT (Cañizares, 1995).

Against this background, Ecuador joined the WTO with a clear objective of redressing discrimination in banana trade to its satisfaction. By far, Ecuador had been the world's largest exporter of bananas, accounting for about one-third of the global total, and the EU had been the largest importer (Table 6). Thus, there were obvious commercial interests in the dispute between the two parties.

In fact, Ecuador's memorandum of foreign trade regime lists support to the unrestricted application of the MFN principle and opposition to any discrimination in international trade as purposes of GATT accession (GATT, 1993a).[19] After joining the WTO, the country's delegation also remarked "*Ecuador had joined the WTO with a view to obtain MFN treatment for one of its major agricultural products*" (WTO, 2005c, p. 4) at the Special Session of the Committee on Agriculture. It also stated "*Ecuador had joined the WTO in 1996 and since then it had used up its resources in an effort to make the EC fulfil its obligations and commitments and to end the discrimination against its banana exports*" (WTO, 1999a, p. 11) at the Dispute Settlement Body (DSB). Thus, the pursuit of non-discrimination for bananas was a major motivation for the country's membership and post-accession engagement in the multilateral trading system.

In the case of bananas, due to the EU's consistent violation of GATT rules, membership alone did not solve the problem of discrimination. Thus, Ecuador joined the banana disputes to challenge the EU's discriminatory import regime through WTO's litigation, immediately after its accession on 21 January 1996. Domestically, the local banana industry (in particular, the banana exporters association and Noboa, the country's largest banana export company) played the leading role in initiating the process. Together with Guatemala, Honduras, Mexico, and the United States, Ecuador requested consultation with the EU on 5 February 1996 (WTO, 1996a) and, subsequently, establishment of a panel on 11 April 1996 (WTO, 1996b). The four Latin American countries were banana exporters excluded from BFA with the EU, and the United States was

[19]Other stated objectives include: contribution to the strengthening of the multilateral trading system; promotion of access to new markets and defending existing markets; and increasing the country's export capacity through export promotion and diversification (GATT, 1993a).

Table 6 Major banana exporters and importers (thousand tonnes)

	1999	*2000*	*2001*	*2002*	*2003*	*2004*	*2005*	*2006*	*2007*	*2008*
Exports										
World	11,825.8	11,922.1	11,621.8	12,251.4	12,981.0	12,898.2	13,294.0	14,276.8	15,025.5	15,092.0
Ecuador	3935.2	3939.5	3990.4	4199.2	4671.2	4537.0	4653.9	4797.8	5057.1	5132.8
Costa Rica	2112.6	1883.3	1739.3	1622.6	1901.3	1792.5	1614.5	1961.1	2159.2	1872.6
Columbia	1818.3	1680.2	1516.3	1570.4	1423.2	1470.9	1621.5	1697.4	1749.2	1798.3
Philippines	1319.6	1599.4	1600.7	1685.0	1829.4	1797.3	2024.3	2311.5	2217.7	2192.6
Guatemala	623.4	801.3	873.8	971.7	933.3	1013.8	1046.3	982.6	1330.4	1576.4
Imports										
World	11,173.9	11,523.1	10,966.5	11,200.6	11,827.4	12,148.1	12,907.7	13,676.5	14,469.0	15,087.7
EU 27	3908.2	3890.1	3771.8	3886.8	4023.0	4001.0	3923.0	4367.6	4682.4	4873.8
United States	3872.6	3630.4	3433.8	3490.2	3451.1	3424.2	3373.3	3395.0	3543.3	3453.4
Japan	983.2	1078.7	990.6	936.3	986.6	1026.0	1066.9	1043.6	970.6	1092.7

Note Listing WTO members whose annual export or import amount of bananas exceeded one million tonnes in the period 1999–2008
Source Food and Agriculture Organization of the United Nations (FAO) (2011)

a party to the dispute mainly because of its multinational corporations involved in production and trading of Latin American bananas.[20] They claimed that the EU unfairly restricted banana imports in violation of various multilateral rules. After establishment of the WTO in 1995, complainants were able to file their claims on the basis of not only GATT (as in the cases of Bananas I and Bananas II)[21] but also other multilateral trade agreements, including the General Argument on Trade in Services (GATS), the Agreement on Import Licensing Procedures, the Agreement on Agriculture, and the Agreement on Trade-Related Investment Measures (TRIMS). In addition, the most important change from the old GATT system in relation to dispute settlement was introduction of the negative consensus scheme stipulated in the new Dispute Settlement Understanding (DSU). Under this scheme, the panel (or Appellate Body) finding is adopted unless there is a consensus among WTO members no to do so. Thus, unlike Banana I and Banana II cases, the EU could no longer block adoption at its own discretion.

For this Banana III case, the panel again found the EU's violation of GATT, as well as GATS and Agreement on Import Licensing (WTO, 1997a). The EU appealed, but the Appellate Body broadly upheld the panel opinion on the illegality of the EU's banana import regime (WTO, 1997b). It was found that the Lomé Waiver addressed departure from GATT Article I only but not GATT Article XIII (non-discriminatory administration of quantitative restrictions), and the EU's tariff quota allocation for ACP countries was a violation of the latter. At the same time, country shares stipulated in BFA, which in turn were incorporated in the EU's tariff schedule, were also in violation of GATT Article XIII, on the grounds that the tariff schedule could not overrule GATT rules. Thus, multilateral instruments the EU had previously adopted for granting preference to ACP countries (Lomé Waiver) and BFA countries (tariff schedule) were both dismissed. In addition, the EU's licensing system was found to be inconsistent with MFN and national treatment rules for both goods and services (GATT Article I, GATT Article III, GATS Article II, and GATS Article XVII). The panel decision, as modified by Appellate

[20] For further assessment on the US involvement in the banana disputes, see Stovall and Hathaway (2003).

[21] Technically, GATT effective prior to the establishment of the WTO was GATT 1947, while current GATT is GATT 1994 that incorporates GATT 1947.

Body findings, was adopted by DSB on 25 September 1997, and the EU was advised to modify its banana import regime in conformity with the WTO rules within a reasonable period of time. In the absence of agreement on the duration of such a reasonable period of time, as per Article 21.3(c) of DSU,[22] the Arbitrator determined 1 January 1999 as the deadline for implementation by the EU (WTO, 1998a).

After the ruling at the WTO, the EU amended its banana import regime, but in a manner that did not eliminate the inconsistency with the multilateral trade agreements. In fact, throughout the 20 years of banana disputes, the EU constantly made changes whenever the WTO repeatedly ruled against its discriminatory policy, but not in a manner to fully meet its obligations. Eckart Guth, a former EU ambassador to the WTO, acknowledges:

> As a result of the various WTO proceedings, the EU modified for several times the details of the banana import regime, but the EU did not make the necessary substantive changes, which would have brought the banana import regime in conformity with the WTO rules. (Guth, 2012, p. 6)

Against the move in preparation for retaliation by the unsatisfied United States, the EU claimed such an action should be preceded by another panel finding confirming that its amended trade regime was still in violation of WTO rules as per Article 21.5 of DSU. Thus, the EU filed a request for establishment of the compliance panel (WTO, 1998b). Ecuador followed suit,[23] but with a special request for the panel to suggest how the EU might implement its recommendations in accordance with Article 19 of DSU[24] (WTO, 1998c). The United States initiated

[22] Article 21.3(c) of DSU reads "*In such arbitration, a guideline for the arbitrator should be that the reasonable period of time to implement panel or Appellate Body recommendations should not exceed 15 months from the date of adoption of a panel or Appellate Body report. However, that time may be shorter or longer, depending upon the particular circumstances*" (WTO, 1995a, p. 421). Footnotes to the original legal text are deleted.

[23] After filing the initial complaint, the United States and Ecuador played two separate leading roles from the complainants' side. Unlike other Latin American banana exporting countries with heavy US multinational investments (and hence piggy-backed to the US position for dispute settlement), Ecuador's banana businesses were run mostly by domestic enterprises. Thus, Ecuador acted somewhat independently from the US (Smith, 2006).

[24] Article 19 of DSU reads "*In addition to its recommendations, the panel or Appellate Body may suggest ways in which the Member concerned could implement the recommendations*" (WTO, 1995a, p. 420).

the process to seek DSB's immediate authorization for retaliation under Article 22 (on compensation and suspension of concessions) of DSU (WTO, 1999b, 1999c), whereas the EU countered by request for arbitration on the level of suspension proposed by the United States with recourse to Article 22.6 of DSU (WTO, 1999d).[25] In April 1999, the Banana III panel reconstituted for arbitration found that the EU's banana import regime continued to be inconsistent with WTO rules and made suggestion for implementation measures for compliance, including the shift to a tariff-only regime (such as preferential tariffs to ACP countries, but with waiver or in compliance with GATT Article XXIV) (WTO, 1999e). The panel's suggestion formed a framework for subsequent discussions among parties involved (Josling, 2003). In April 1999, the WTO granted authorization to the United States to impose sanctions.

In November 1999, Ecuador also requested DSB's authorization for suspending concessions, including cross-retaliation in the areas covered by GATS and the Agreement on Trade-Related Aspects of Intellectual Property Rights (TRIPS).[26] The EU again requested arbitration under Article 22.6 of DSU (WTO, 1999f). Retaliation under WTO's dispute settlement takes the form of imposing trade restrictions against imports from the respondent. Like any other forms of trade restrictions, such measures inevitably bring welfare loss to the country imposing retaliation (to the contrary, the country supposedly suffering from such sanctions may receive welfare gain through amendment of its policy). Ecuador claimed that the potentially resulting losses would amount to over 50% of its imports from the much larger EU, including essential capitals goods and raw materials (WTO, 1999g). To avoid such losses, the cross-retaliation in the area of TRIPS was proposed as an innovative non-trade solution (Huerta, 2010). An economist Kym Anderson who served as a Panelist and Arbitrator for the banana disputes wrote, in his paper titled "Peculiarities of retaliation in WTO dispute settlement":

> (W)hen the remedy chosen is a withdrawal of concessions by the complainant towards the respondent's exports, the complainant's economy is not helped but harmed by retaliation (the standard cost of protectionist

[25] Article 22.6 of DSU reads "*if the Member concerned objects to the level of suspension proposed, … the matter shall be referred to arbitration*" (WTO, 1995a, p. 424).

[26] For further arguments in support of the use of TRIPS as a feasible, effective, and legal enforcing device, see Subramanian and Watal (2000).

> barriers). For small or developing economies confronting a much larger trader, that may well deter them from seeking recourse through the DSU or, should the Arbitrator rule in their favour, from adopting retaliatory measures (as was the case with Ecuador following the decision reported in WTO, 2000)... why not allow the possibility of cross retaliation so as to maximize the opportunity to encourage policy reform by the respondent, and to minimize the limitation that within-sector retaliation poses where the economies of the two parties are vastly different in size? While there are strict conditions attached to cross retaliation, that possibility is not completely ruled out. The conditions under which it is allowed are laid out in DSU Article 22.3. And already it has been used: in the case of the EC banana import regime, it was recognized by the Arbitrator that Ecuador imported too few goods from the EC to be able to retaliate in just goods, or even goods plus services, and so a suspension of concessions relating to TRIPS was allowed. (Anderson, 2002, pp. 129–131)[27]

The Arbitrator accepted the cross-retaliation proposal (albeit in the revised amount) (WTO, 2000a). In accordance with Article 22.7 of DSU, Ecuador further sought DSB's authorization for retaliation based on Arbitrator's decision (WTO, 2000b), that was subsequently granted in May 2000.

Thus, both of the United States and Ecuador secured authorization and means for potential retaliation at hand and proceeded with further negotiations with the EU. Ecuador's negotiating position was to

[27] Smith (2006) also comments that, despite being a small country, Ecuador managed to exercise these legal tactics to its advantage in the banana disputes against a much larger trading partner. See Narlikar (2011) on involvement of small states in multilateral economic negotiations. Odell (2010) argues that being small is not necessarily disadvantageous. In fact, one potentially unique advantage in pursuit of broader trade policy objectives is that the small size of the economy allows the government to undertake tariff cuts without concerns over terms of trade deterioration. As such, the small country can reap the gains from trade simply by its own unilateral liberalization even without going through complex reciprocal negotiations with trading partners. However, it appears that Ecuador did not exploit such an advantage. On the other hand, once in the multilateral trade negotiations, being small could be disadvantageous. The countries with the small market size tend to receive less attentions from larger trading partners and could just free-ride the MFN market access negotiated by them, making it difficult for the government to use external pressures to leverage domestic reforms (Finger & Winters, 1998). Consistently with this explanation, Ecuador did not fully utilize the Doha Round to advance its trade liberalization. Despite proactive engagement in the market access negotiations, the draft December 2008 modalities would only reduce Ecuador's bound tariffs, but not applied tariffs.

introduce the element of competition to the EU's banana importing regime without losing the current market share. In essence, it sought to transform the tariff quota regime (characterized by both preferential tariffs and quotas) to the new "tariff-only" (i.e., quota-free) system, as recorded in the minutes of the DSB meeting on 23 October 2000:

> He reiterated that his country's preference was for a banana import regime that eliminated tariff quotas and was based on a single tariff. Such a tariff-only system involved fewer distortions and injustices and allowed access for better-quality bananas on a more competitive basis to the benefit of producers and consumers... (WTO, 2000c, p. 4)

Ecuador was the world's least cost supplier of bananas (Smith, 2006), and relief from the quota constraints would allow it to compete solely on the basis of prices. Meanwhile, the EU sought continuation of preferences through extension of waiver (Guth, 2012). Under the pressure of banana disputes, in 2000, the EU and ACP agreed to replace the Lomé IV Convention with a new Cotonou Agreement. The latter set the framework to alter the WTO-inconsistent Lomé regime into a WTO-consistent trading arrangement over time, but its implementation was not to take effect immediately (Abass, 2004).

In April 2001, major agreements were reached between the EU, the United States, and Ecuador. The solution agreed to comprise the following terms: the EU's shift to the tariff-only regime by no later than 1 January 2006 and, for transition to the new regime, continuation of tariff quotas on the basis of historical licensing in the interim. In exchange, the United States and Ecuador were to lift their reservation on the renewal of waiver from GATT Article I and to work toward accord of waiver from GATT Article XIII until 31 December 2005 (WTO, 2001b). Even after reaching these agreements, however, European businesses lobbied to preserve rents generated by quotas, and there were moves to amend the deal on the part of the EU (Guth, 2012). Thus, negotiations were not closed and continued toward the Doha Ministerial Conference in November 2001. Ecuador's dissatisfaction with the EU's performance in this period is reflected in the minutes of the DSB meeting on 5 November 2001.

> Ecuador had concluded an understanding with the EC, which could serve as a good basis for a solution to the dispute, and was ready to agree to the granting of the waivers. However the EC, despite the fact

that it had the time and resources available to modify its regime, was still looking for a way to evade and only partially fulfil its obligations. (WTO, 2001c, p. 2)

During the Doha Ministerial Conference, a compromise was reached, culminating into adoption of the two key decisions on: waiver for the EU-ACP Partnership Agreement on banana and broader trade (WTO, 2001d) and the EU transitional regime for banana imports (WTO, 2001e). These decisions were built upon earlier agreements on the EU's transition to the tariff-only system and stipulated that the prospective tariff rates under the new regime (to be rebound after negotiations based on GATT Article XXVIII on modification of schedules) "*should result in at least maintaining total market access for MFN banana suppliers*" (WTO, 2001d, p. 2). Any disagreements on the prospective tariff levels were to be brought to the WTO arbitration process. At the same time, these decisions confirmed waivers to the EU from: GATT Article I until 31 December 2007, in transition to conclusion of a new trading arrangement between the EU and ACP, and GATT Article XIII until 31 December 2005, in transition to the tariff-only banana import regime. After the expiration of Article I waiver, the conclusion of the GATT Article XXIV-consistent reciprocal trade agreements would become the only way for the EU to treat ACP countries differently from other developing countries, and the non-reciprocal preference was to be terminated. Accordingly, the EU launched economic partnership agreement negotiations with ACP countries in 2003.

3.2 Toward Geneva Agreement on Trade in Bananas

The Doha Ministerial decisions still left the level of tariff rebinding applicable for non-ACP banana exporters (in effect, mainly from Latin America) under the new tariff-only regime unresolved, and the early phase of subsequent negotiations focused on this matter. On 31 January 2005, the EU announced its revised banana tariff (to €230 per tonne). Unsatisfied Latin American banana exporting countries including Ecuador requested WTO arbitration, and the panel ruled that the tariff rate would not maintain existing market access for MFN banana suppliers (required by the Doha Ministerial decisions). In September, the EU further revised its tariff offer (to €187 per tonne), but could not reach agreement with MFN banana suppliers from Latin America. The EU resorted to WTO arbitration, but the panel again concluded that the EU failed to meet its obligation. In the meantime, the EU adopted a new banana regime, to take effect on 1 January 2006, comprising a tariff of €176 per tonne on MFN bananas and duty-free access for ACP bananas up to 775,000 tons. Against sustained concerns expressed by Latin American countries at the Hong Kong Ministerial Conference in December 2005, Director-General Pascal Lamy nominated Jonas Store from Norway as a facilitator under a good offices process, but this attempt could not bridge the gap.

Along with a number of Latin American countries, Ecuador and the United States separately filed recourse to Article 21.5 of DSU in 2006–2007 and, as usual, the WTO compliance panel found the EU's violation with GATT rules (WTO, 2008b, 2008c). The EU appealed, but the Appellate Body broadly upheld the panel findings (WTO, 2008d). By then, the Doha waiver had expired, and duty-free access and the tariff quota for ACP bananas were found to be inconsistent with GATT Articles I and XIII. Also, the applied tariff rate on MFN bananas was found to have exceeded the level bound in the EU's tariff schedule, in violation of GATT Article II (on schedules of concessions). Further negotiations proceeded on the sidelines of the July 2008 package negotiations of the Doha Round (Guth, 2012; Huerta, 2010), and Pascal Lamy intervened through the good offices process. However, the gap in positions remained, and Ecuador persistently claimed its right against the EU's repeated attempts to preserve violation of WTO rules. At the DSB meeting on 11 December 2008, the Ecuadorian delegation commented, as recorded in the minutes:

> The WTO, once again, had upheld Ecuador's claims regarding the EC's failure to comply with its obligations with respect to its bananas import regime. He noted that one had lost count as to how may [sic] times the EC bananas import regime had been found to be inconsistent with WTO rules. In spite of repeated rulings under the GATT/WTO panels and decades of discrimination, in particular against Latin American developing countries, the EC continued to maintain its bananas import regime, which violated its WTO obligations. (WTO, 2009e, p. 3)

By the end of 2009, the agreement was finally reached between the EU and banana suppliers from Latin America, including Ecuador. This Geneva Agreement on Trade in Bananas (WTO, 2009f), initialed on 15

December,[28] stipulated the maintenance of the MFN tariff-only regime by the EU and annual decline of the EU's tariff in stages down to €114 per tonne.[29] The EU was to seek WTO Director-General's certification of the revised tariff schedule, and with completion of such certification, disputes filed by Latin American MFN banana suppliers to date were to be settled. The agreement constituted the EU's final market access commitment on bananas in the next multilateral trade negotiations, including the Doha Round (while tariff reduction took effect upon completion of signing). Upon certification of the EU's revised commitment by Pascal Lamy on 27 October 2012, the EU and ten Latin American countries reached mutual agreement on 8 November, bringing the 20-year banana dispute to final closure (WTO, 2012b).

Ecuador's behavior on the banana disputes validates Hypothesis 3. As an outsider to the multilateral trading system prior to WTO accession in 1996, Ecuador was not able to participate in Bananas I and Bananas II disputes through the GATT system to defend its export interests in Europe. This disadvantage induced the country to seek accession to GATT. After gaining WTO membership, it sought to recover this cost of the previous outsider status by repeatedly challenging the EU's banana import regime. The country not only filed the original request for establishing the Bananas III panel, but also had recourse to twice of compliance panels and several arbitrations. As a result, the country (together with other complainants) managed to change the EU's import regime from the one characterized by discriminatory tariff quotas to the more competitive tariff-only system, combined with the acceptable level of MFN tariff reductions.

4 Proactive Engagement in the Doha Development Agenda

4.1 *Agriculture Negotiations as Extension of Banana Disputes*

If there was a principle underlying Ecuador's position since its accession to the WTO, it was the notion that all developing countries should be treated equally in the multilateral trading system. This was the backbone

[28]The EU and the United States initialed a separate bilateral agreement to settle the dispute (Guth, 2012).

[29]The tariff reduction was scheduled to be completed by 1 January 2017. However, in the case of possible absence of the agreed modalities in the DDA agriculture negotiations, the annual tariff cuts could be delayed for up two years.

of its long engagement in banana disputes to challenge the EU's preferences to ACP countries (at discrimination against Ecuador and other Latin American countries). The same position was taken also during the Doha Round negotiations. For instance, Ecuador once expressed an objection to the idea of creating a new SVE subgroup for differential treatments within the developing countries, as recorded in the minutes of the market access negotiations on 9–11 June 2004:

> Ecuador thought that to establish this category of vulnerable and weak countries would not contribute to a better systemic operation as well as substantive operation of the ongoing NAMA negotiations. (WTO, 2004, p. 10)

Due to a small share in global trade, Ecuador was subsequently categorized as an SVE in the draft 2008 modalities (especially for agriculture) (WTO, 2008a), but it did not act as a member of the SVE negotiating group at the Doha Round.[30] The country took this position of calling for equal treatment of all developing countries to stay consistent with its own claim at the banana disputes.

Likewise, in line with this position of non-differentiation among developing countries at the banana disputes, Ecuador was initially not even in favor of granting differentiated treatments to newly acceded members. In the early phase of the Doha Round, the RAMs group mainly comprised transition economies that joined the multilateral trading system in the lead to or after the Doha Ministerial Conference in 2001, but others that had acceded soon after the establishment of the WTO in 1995 were excluded. Paragraph 9 of the Doha Ministerial Declaration, which was the first textual acknowledgment of the RAMs, referred to the new members that had joined the WTO since the Seattle Ministerial Conference in 1999 (Albania, China, Chinese Taipei, Croatia, Georgia, Jordan, Lithuania, Moldova, and Oman), as well as their extensive market access commitments already made for accession (WTO, 2001a). However, Ecuador and Panama were not listed.[31] Ecuador took

[30] In fact, the WTO Web site does not list Ecuador as a member of the SVE groups that sponsored its proposal for agriculture, NAMA, and rules negotiations Web site: http://www.wto.org/english/tratop_e/dda_e/negotiating_groups_e.htm.

[31] Croatia (that played the leading role in the core RAMs group among transition economies) long refused to accept Ecuador.

a position that all countries that acceded with extensive obligations under the new WTO rule should be treated equally regardless of the year of membership; or, otherwise, privileges to the RAM should be completely forgone, as reflected in its remark in the DDA agriculture negotiations on 1 July 2003:

> Ecuador considers it important to examine the nature and the extent of the commitments made, as well as the status of compliance by countries that have acceded to the WTO since the entry into force of its constitutive agreements, before fixing a period that would be wholly arbitrary giving countries that are in this situation additional flexibility as regards reductions in market access, export subsidies and domestic support. Countries that acceded immediately after the entry into force of the WTO have been subject to the same commitments and disciplines in relation to tariff reductions, quotas, subsidies, domestic support and all the commitments arising out of the Agreement on Agriculture. Consequently, flexibility regarding the time-limits for compliance should be granted to all countries in the same situation or to none. (WTO, 2003a, p. 46)

This issue of composition of the RAMs group was raised again after the chair of the DDA agriculture negotiations referred to the necessity to clarify this matter on 4 May 2006. By this time, the need to take special account of the RAMs' extensive accession commitment for the Doha Round negotiations had already been agreed upon among WTO members, as stated in the 2005 Hong Kong Ministerial Declaration (see Chapter 2), and treating the RAMs equally with other developing countries was no longer an option. Thus, Ecuador and Panama sought their inclusion to the RAMs group, for equal treatment vis-à-vis the rest of the post-1995 entrants:

> Ecuador and Panama strongly consider that the criteria to define the list of Recently Acceded Members is determined by the broad levels of commitments assumed in the accession processes to which these Members were subjected and that are clearly outlined in the charts prepared by the WTO Secretariat. It cannot be justified in any way that developing countries such as Ecuador and Panama be excluded from this list since our commitments are higher than those of many Members that participated in the Uruguay Round negotiations. (WTO, 2006, p. 2)

In fact, the statistical evidence attached to this statement by Panama and Ecuador showed that their average bound tariff rates were higher than the other RAMs, and one may question to what extent their argument was really convincing. Nonetheless, their bound rates were lower than those of other developing countries, and the two countries were eventually acknowledged as RAMs later in the Doha Round.

Interestingly, Ecuador's negotiating position was uniquely different from that of a large number of RAMs (notably, the low-income economies in transition and the very recently acceded members [VRAMs]), at least in two respects. Firstly, whereas a majority of the RAMs sought relief from tariff cutting commitments, Ecuador claimed that the special treatment for the RAMs, if any, should be limited to length of the transition period for implementing commitments but not the tariff levels, consistently with its overarching position of non-differentiation among developing countries. It took a stance that the Doha Round's goal of tariff liberalization itself should not be compromised. At NAMA negotiations on 26–28 May 2003, the Ecuadorian delegation remarked:

> If newly acceded Members were granted longer periods for tariff reduction Ecuador wondered what the situation would be for other developing countries. Granting longer implementation periods to newly acceded Members would be the right option rather than higher coefficients in the formula since tariff reduction was the goal of the negotiations. (WTO, 2003b, p. 33)

Secondly, rather than just being defensive, Ecuador had been actively engaged in the Doha Round and sought its ambitious results, especially in agriculture. In the opening statement of the trade policy review meeting in 2005, the delegation of Ecuador led by Cristian Espinosa Cañizares remarked:

> Ecuador attached great importance to the Doha Round. However, its expectations, like those of other developing countries, had been frustrated by slow progress in the negotiations. Ecuador stood ready to adopt ambitious liberalization commitments, as long as the willingness of other WTO Members was commensurate. Ecuador was concerned that agriculture negotiations, aimed at increasing market access, eliminating export subsidies, and substantially reducing domestic support, had come to a halt due to lack of commitment by Members that most distorted agricultural trade. (WTO, 2005a, p. 7)

Obviously, Ecuador was frustrated by, rather than welcoming, the lack of progress in the negotiations. The country was also willing to accept the Swiss formula (that most of the RAMs did not accept) for market opening. Its statement for the agriculture negotiations reads:

> Ecuador attaches particular importance to the elimination of tariff escalation and tariff peaks, remnants of the commitments made during the Uruguay Round. It therefore supports the "Swiss Formula" inasmuch as it allows more uniform bound ceilings, consistent with fullest liberalization of markets, and at the same time permits a significant lowering of the high levels of protection… (WTO, 2003a, p. 44)

The final draft 2008 modalities for NAMA and agriculture negotiations designated Ecuador as an SVE, requiring modest cuts in its bound tariffs,[32] unlike the case of most of other RAMs completely exempted from any market access commitments during the Doha Round.

Ecuador's proactive engagement in the Doha Round was a reflection of its unique interests in agricultural exports. At the Hong Kong Ministerial Conference on 13–15 December 2005, Jorge Illingworth, Ecuador's Minister for Foreign Trade, Industrialization, Fisheries and Competitiveness stated: "*In view of the importance of agriculture for the developing countries and for Ecuador in particular, we hope that this Round will result in real access for our exports*" (WTO, 2005d, p. 1). This is in line with GATT-think of mercantilism[33] but was not entirely a result of growing influence of the broader export sector within the entire economy, as assumed in the juggernaut theory[34] underlying Hypothesis 2-a. In the years leading toward the conclusion of the December 2008 modalities of the Doha Round, its external balance had improved. In particular, both trade balance and current account recorded surplus in 2005–2008 (Table 4). However, a closer look reveals that the surplus in this period was a result of robust oil exports, and the non-oil trade balance still recorded deficit, that even increased from US$729 million

[32] However, such cuts of the bound tariff rate do not necessarily lead to reduction of the applied tariff rate. In fact, unlike China's case, Ecuador's acceptance of the draft 2008 modalities would still leave some water.

[33] Krugman (1991).

[34] Richard Baldwin (2006, 2012).

in 2000 to US$6914 billion in 2008 (WTO, 2009c).[35] To date, trade in oil has not been a subject of WTO negotiations and, as such, export business interests of this particular sector could not be a driving force for Ecuador's proactive engagement in the reciprocal trade negotiations.[36] In fact, both of the Chamber of Industry and Production and the National Association of Exporters were not enthusiastic about market access negotiations of the Doha Round. It was the government, rather than the private sector, that raised its ambition as the external balances improved.[37]

More importantly, Ecuador's negotiating position was an extension of the endeavor to redress discrimination against the country's agricultural exports, in particular, bananas. At the Seattle Ministerial Conference on 30 November–3 December 1999, José Luis Ycaza Pazmiño, Ecuador's Minister of Foreign Trade, Fisheries, and Tourism, stated before the launch of the then prospective trade round:

> Ecuador proposes the following basic objectives for the next round of negotiations... To discuss, calmly and objectively, the topic of agriculture, which is highly sensitive because of its potential economic and social impact in the light of the results achieved through the Agreement on Agriculture and Committee on Agriculture... The European Union's banana import regime is a clear example of quotas, which, under the protection of the WTO rules, is used discretionally to discriminate against Latin American bananas. (WTO, 1999h, p. 1)

Following the 2001 agreements on bananas and subsequent Doha Ministerial decisions on the EU's shift to the new tariff-only regime, tariff negotiations for bananas were partly extended to the Doha Round. In the multilateral negotiations, Ecuador pursued the objective of redressing discrimination in banana trade in two ways. Firstly, the country argued for prioritizing non-discriminatory liberalization of tropical agricultural products. The Uruguay Round Agreement on Agriculture called

[35] Data for 2008 covers a period from January to November only.

[36] At the same time, the share of agriculture in the total exports declined from 32.6% in 2005 to 28.3% in 2008 (WTO, 2012a).

[37] Private businesses were always pro-liberalization, even at the time of deficit. It was the government itself that sought export interests. Even for the DDA agriculture negotiations on bananas, the government (rather than domestic exporters that took initiatives in launching the dispute with the EU) took lead in policy-making.

for taking special account of the need for "*fullest liberalization of trade in tropical agricultural products*" (WTO, 1995a, p. 39) for developing countries' export diversification from illicit narcotic crops, and Ecuador appealed to this norm during the Doha Round. At the Hong Kong Ministerial Conference, Jorge Illingworth remarked:

> We have emphasized that an essential issue for Ecuador is the fullest liberalization of trade in tropical products and products to replace illicit crops, which should not be included among the sensitive products nor be subject to the minimum cut that would also allow for a pivot that would limit a wider cut. (WTO, 2005d, p. 1)

Obviously in line with this objective, it was essential to ensure that bananas were recognized as the tropical products designated for prioritized liberalization. Thus, Ecuador opposed any moves to exclude bananas from the list of tropical products, as stated in its repeated remarks at the DDA agriculture negotiations.

> It is unacceptable to Ecuador that a tropical fruit such as bananas was excluded from the category of "tropical fruit". (WTO, 2003a, p. 46)

> Ecuador considers it unacceptable that a tropical fruit such as the banana should be excluded from classification as a tropical product. (WTO, 2003c, p. 39)

Secondly, Ecuador opposed moves on the part of the EU and ACP countries aimed at circumscribing so-called preference erosion. The term describes the state whereby the preferential tariff margins granted to specific groups of countries (such as the EU's preference to ACP countries) would diminish as a result of the decline of the MFN tariffs applicable to other trading partners. In the context of banana disputes, insertion of any DDA negotiation texts suggesting prevention of preference erosion (in favor of ACP) might have taken on the risk of nullifying the 2001 agreements and Doha decisions on bananas. These hard-won deals stipulated the EU's shift to less-discriminatory banana import regime, and continuation of preferential arrangements between the EU and ACP (other than GATT-consistent reciprocal free trade agreements) was not acceptable to Ecuador. At the agriculture negotiations on 1 July 2003, the Ecuadorian delegation stated:

> for Ecuador the inclusion of the words "preferential arrangements" in the third line of the Spanish text of the Chairman's proposal is totally unacceptable because these words could cover free trade agreements as well as the exemptions approved in Doha, which are specific rules that govern trade in products of particular interest to some developing countries. This is the case for the waivers on bananas, which brought to an end a long-running dispute, and under no circumstances can the terms and conditions laid down therein be modified by such a general provision (WTO, 2003a, p. 46).

Reflecting diverse stances taken by the WTO member countries, the DDA agriculture negotiations addressed both fullest liberalization of trade in tropical products on the one hand and circumscribing preference erosion on the other hand. Given the overlap of relevant products (bananas, in particular) covered by these two opposing themes, conflicts between countries that pushed for ambitious liberalization and others that tried to protect preference were inevitable. Ecuador's position was that the solution to preference erosion should be sought only in a manner not to divert exports from other developing countries competing on the MFN basis. At the Hong Kong Ministerial Conference, Jorge Illingworth stated:

> Furthermore, a solution to the issue of preference erosion is attainable, provided that it does not include trade solutions that prejudice other developing countries, so that we would see our market access restricted. A clear example of that is the banana question. (WTO, 2005d, p. 2)

In 2008, negotiations on this matter were continued for the conclusion of the draft agriculture modalities. Its final text dated 6 December had incorporated a provision to accelerate liberalization of trade in tropical and diversification products including bananas (at the level beyond the general tariff cuts to agriculture based on the tiered formula). Options proposed therein included, among others, complete elimination of tariffs where the current tariff rates were no more than 10% or 25%. At the same time, it indicated slower liberalization of trade in products with long-standing preferences, again including bananas. The draft modalities further stated that, where there were overlaps between the two (as was obviously the case for bananas), the provision on tropical products should prevail, except for products stated in an appendix that was to stipulate the rule on liberalization for such items. However, the said appendix never materialized by the end of DDA agriculture negotiations in 2008, due to inconclusiveness of parallel negotiations among parties to the banana disputes. In the final draft December 2008 modalities paper, the chair of the Special Session of the WTO Committee on Agriculture indicated:

> On tropical and diversification products and preference erosion.... I had wanted to record in a separate paper the considerable progress that had been made in July. As of yesterday I had drafted that on the basis that, if everything fell into place – and bananas was key to that – there was a deal there for the taking. And it would have been useful for everyone to see how close we were to that. But I was advised yesterday that, on bananas certain material changes had occurred which, in the view of at least one set of Members, vitiated any assumptions abut [sic] what might even be hypothetically possible. I cannot ignore such a strongly held view so, yet again, all we get for the time being is the 10 July text. It is a pity, in my view, but I cannot intrude on a bilateral negotiations [sic] of this intensity. All I would add is that the parties have been working on their bilateral lists as well. (WTO, 2008a, p. 2)

The banana-specific negotiations continued among direct stakeholders in the next year, leading to the conclusion of the 2009 Geneva Agreement on Trade in Bananas (see the third section).

On crude statistical grounds, Ecuador's behavior during the Doha Round is consistent with Hypothesis 2-a. Toward the conclusion of the draft 2008 modalities, the economy enhanced its export orientation, as reflected in the external balance that turned to surplus, and Ecuador expressed its willingness for proactive engagement in the Doha Round negotiations. However, exports' growth was not a reflection of expansion of WTO-relevant sectors of the economy, and the country's business communities were not so keen to exert influence on Ecuador's negotiating position. In fact, the government also had no intention to use export business interests to leverage its trade liberalization through reciprocity. Rather, a closer look at Ecuador's negotiating positions in the Doha Round revealed the validity of Hypothesis 3. The DDA agriculture negotiations were positioned as extension of the banana disputes, and they were part of Ecuador's long-standing endeavor to recover the cost of the previous outsider status to the multilateral trading system.

4.2 *Irrelevance of Terms of Trade Externality for a Small Economy*

Hypothesis 2-b based on the theory of terms of trade externality[38] predicts that a small country that could not affect terms of trade would stay away from reciprocal market access negotiations of the Doha Round and act autonomously but, as reviewed above, Ecuador acted inconsistently with this inference. Whereas its market size accounted for only about 0.1% of the world total (see Table 10, Chapter 2), this small country proactively engaged in the market access negotiations on the one hand and refrained from unilateral trade liberalization on the other hand. Given that Ecuador's trade policy has been consistently restrictive over time and exhibited no significant change (in terms of the simple average tariff rate), it is not possible to asses if it affected terms of trade in one way or the other. However, it may be noteworthy that the country's terms of trade have been steadily improving during the period of the Doha Round up to 2008, despite relative stability of its trade policy (Table 7). By implication, it could be gathered that terms of trade might have been determined by other factors (such as commodity prices and macroeconomic conditions), rather than trade policy.

Table 7 Ecuador—reciprocity and terms of trade

	2002	*2003*	*2004*	*2005*	*2006*	*2007*	*2008*
Applied tariff rate (incl. preferences)							
Simple average	12.02	–	11.60	–	11.40	11.39	10.95
Trade weighted averages	10.67	–	8.95	–	6.56	6.51	5.94
Applied ROW tariff rate (incl. preferences)							
Simple average	9.38	8.30	6.55	7.39	4.03	9.63	9.49
Trade weighted averages	11.78	9.47	2.76	7.54	1.30	2.41	2.40
Net barter terms of trade index (2000 = 100)	86.81	89.77	91.48	102.39	109.90	112.99	123.98

Note ROW = rest of the world. The net barter terms of trade index is the percentage ratio of unit export value indexes to unit import value, measured against the base year of 2000

Source World Trade Indicators 2009/2010 of the World Bank Web site: http://info.worldbank.org/etools/wti/2a1.asp; World Bank Open Data retrieved from the World Bank Web site: http://data.worldbank.org/

[38] Bagwell and Staiger (1999, 2002).

As per the hypothesis, a small country that could not affect terms of trade through its trade policy should be disengaged from reciprocal trade negotiations, but Ecuador remained an active player in the Doha Round. As was the case for other case study countries, the policy-makers were not conscious about terms of trade rationale for reciprocal trade negotiations, and the small size of the economy was not a factor that affected its policy behaviors. Rather, Ecuador had another important reason to stay engaged in the DDA agriculture negotiations, which was to protect its banana interests against the EU and ACP countries. Thus, whereas the case study rejected Hypothesis 2-b on terms of trade externality, it verified Hypothesis 3 on recovery of the cost of the previous non-membership.

5 Conclusion

Unlike transition economies covered by the preceding case studies, Ecuador was not an active reformer and had little interest in using tariff binding through WTO accession as a commitment device for domestic reforms. This was observed in the high level of bound tariff rates deliberately set above the prevailing applied rates at the time of accession, as well as occasional departures from commitments in the post-accession period, including through the adoption of BOP safeguard in 2009. Thus, Hypothesis 1 was verified for a non-reforming economy. To Ecuador, WTO accession was a means to join the banana disputes with the EU and recover the cost of its previous outsider status, as envisaged by Hypothesis 3. After gaining membership to the WTO, Ecuador had consistently challenged the EU's discriminatory banana import regime through dispute settlement, and the country demanded equal treatment among developing countries also through the Doha Round. In the lead to the conclusion of draft 2008 modalities of the Doha Round, Ecuador's trade balance and current account turned to surplus, and unlike most of the other RAMs, Ecuador sought ambitious outcome of the negotiations. This was in line with Hypothesis 2-a, that assumes a positive correlation between the economy's export orientation and the level of engagement in the reciprocal negotiations. However, a closer look in this case study showed that it was not necessarily a dominant presence of exporting businesses at large that pushed for ambitious negotiations. For Ecuador, the Doha Round was an extension specifically of the banana disputes. Despite its smallness, Ecuador stayed in the reciprocal negotiations to protect its banana interests, and Hypothesis 2-b on term of trade externality was rejected.

Overall, the case study revealed that the pursuit of non-discrimination in banana trade was at the backbone of every aspect of Ecuador's engagement in the multilateral trading system, from accession to the dispute settlement and the Doha Round. The 2009 Geneva Agreement on Trade in Bananas placed an end to the GATT-inconsistent banana import regime of the EU, through its replacement with the tariff-only regime. However, it did not preclude the possibility of forming GATT-consistent[39] preferential trade agreements reciprocally between the EU on the one hand and ACP countries and Latin American countries on the other hand. By 2012, the EU had already signed a partnership agreement with the Forum of Caribbean Group of ACP States and initialed or provisionally applied arrangements with other ACP countries (Guth, 2012). Colombia and the Central American countries also concluded bilateral trade agreement with the EU in 2010 and received a preferential tariff rate of €75 per tonne, creating a preference margin of €39 vis-à-vis the final MFN rate under the Geneva Agreement on Trade in Bananas. Against this background, Ecuador's trade negotiator engaged in the banana disputes commented "*the agreement was the first step on the need to maintain access of Ecuador as a major export of bananas to the European Union*" but, again, "*Ecuador is in danger of losing the European market*"[40] (Huerta, 2010, p. 15). Keeping up with this domino expansion of renewed preferences, Ecuador acceded to a trade agreement with the EU, Columbia, and Peru on 11 November 2016, that provisionally came into effect between the EU and Ecuador on 1 January 2017 (WTO, 2017).

References

Abass, A. (2004). The Cotonou trade regime and WTO law. *European Law Journal, 10*(4), 439–462.

Anderson, K. (2002). Peculiarities of retaliation in WTO dispute settlement. *World Trade Review, 1*(2), 123–134.

Bagwell, K., & Staiger, R. W. (1999). An economic theory of GATT. *American Economic Review, 89*(1), 215–248.

[39]Consistency of proliferating free trade agreements with GATT Article XXIV may be somewhat questionable. The GATT rule on free trade areas assumes elimination (not just some reduction) of tariffs on substantially all the trade, which may not necessarily be the case for many agreements.

[40]Translated from the original Spanish text by Google Translate Web site: https://translate.google.com/

Bagwell, K., & Staiger, R. W. (2002). *The economics of the world trading system*. Cambridge: MIT Press.

Baldwin, R. E. (2006). Multilateralising regionalism: Spaghetti bowls as building blocs on the path to global free trade. *The World Economy, 29*(11), 1451–1518.

Baldwin, R. E. (2012). Preferential trading arrangements. In A. Narlikar, M. Daunton, & R. M. Stern (Eds.), *The Oxford handbook on the World Trade Organization* (pp. 632–654). Oxford: Oxford University Press.

Cañizares, C. P. (1995). el ingreso del ecuador a la organización mundial de comercio [Entry of Ecuador to the World Trade Organization]. *AFESE, 25*. Retrieved from the AFESE website: http://www.afese.com/img/revistas/revista40/artCristianEspinoza.pdf.

Evenett, S. J., & Gage, J. (2005). Evaluating WTO accessions: The effect of WTO accession on national trade flows. In M. Kennett, S. J. Evenett, & J. Gage. *Evaluating WTO accessions: Legal and economic perspectives* (pp. 194–220). Retrieved from World Bank website: http://siteresources.worldbank.org/INTRANETTRADE/Resources/WBI-Training/EvaluatingWTOAccessions_partI.pdf.

Finger, J. M., & Winters, L. A. (1998). What can the WTO do for developing countries? In A. O. Kruger (Ed.), *The WTO as an international organization* (pp. 365–392). Chicago: University of Chicago Press.

Food and Agriculture Organization of the United Nations. (2011). *Banana Statistics 2011*. Rome: Author.

General Agreement on Tariffs and Trade. (1993a). *Accession of Ecuador: Memorandum of the foreign trade regime* (L/7202). Geneva: Author.

General Agreement on Tariffs and Trade. (1993b). *EEC—Member states' import regime for Bananas: Report of the panel* (DS/32/R). Geneva: Author.

General Agreement on Tariffs and Trade. (1994a). *EEC—Import regime for bananas: Report of the panel* (DS/38/R). Geneva: Author.

General Agreement on Tariffs and Trade. (1994b). *The fourth ACP-EEC convention of Lomé: Decision of 9 December 1994* (L/7604). Geneva: Author.

Guth, E. (2012). The end of the banana saga. *Journal of World Trade, 46*(1), 1–31.

Huerta, C. M. (2010). *Ecuador y el caso del banano* [Ecuador and the banana disputes]. *AFESE, 57*, 133–149.

Independent Evaluation Office of the International Monetary Fund. (2009). *Evaluation report: IMF involvement in international trade policy issue*. Washington, DC: International Monetary Fund.

International Monetary Fund. (2000). *Ecuador: Selected issues and statistical annex* (IMF Staff Country Report No. 00/125). Washington, DC: Author.

International Monetary Fund. (2003). *Ecuador: Selected issues and statistical appendix annex* (IMF Staff Country Report No. 03/91). Washington, DC: Author.

Josling, T. (2003). Bananas and the WTO: Testing the new dispute settlement process. In T. E. Josling & T. G. Taylor (Eds.), *Banana wars: The anatomy of a trade dispute* (pp. 169–194). Oxford: CABI.

Josling, T. E., & Taylor, T. G. (Eds.). (2003). *Banana wars: The anatomy of a trade dispute*. Oxford: CABI.

Krugman, P. (1991, November/December). The move toward free trade zones. *Economic Review—Federal Reserve Bank of Kansas City, 76*(6), 5–25.

Maggi, G., & Rodríguez-Clare, A. (1998). The value of trade agreements in the presence of political pressures. *Journal of Political Economy, 106*(3), 574–601.

Maggi, G., & Rodríguez-Clare, A. (2007). A political-economy theory of trade agreements. *American Economic Review, 97*(4), 1374–1406.

Narlikar, A. (2011). Editorial: Small states in multilateral economic negotiations. *The Roundtable, 100*(413), 135–139.

National Secretariat of Planning and Development. (2013). *Good living national plan 2013–2017: A better world for everyone—Summarized version*. Quito: Author.

Odell, J. S. (2010). Negotiating from weakness in international trade relations. *Journal of World Trade, 44*(3), 545–566.

Sales, M., & Jackson, J. H. (2000). Procedural overview of the WTO EC—Banana dispute. *Journal of International Economic Law, 3*(1), 145–166.

Smith, J. M. (2006). Compliance bargaining in the WTO: Ecuador and the banana dispute. In J. S. Odell (Ed.), *Negotiating trade: Developing countries in the WTO and NAFTA* (pp. 257–288). Cambridge: Cambridge University Press.

Staiger, R. W., & Tabellini, G. (1987). Discretionary trade policy and excessive protection. *American Economic Review, 77*(5), 823–837.

Stovall, J. G., & Hathaway, D. E. (2003). US interests and the banana trade controversy. In T. E. Josling, & T. G. Taylor (Eds.). *Banana wars: The anatomy of a trade dispute* (pp. 151-167). Oxford: CABI.

Subramanian, A., & Watal, J. (2000). Can TRIPS serve as an enforcement device for developing countries in the WTO? *Journal of International Economic Law, 3*(3), 403–416.

Williamson, J. (1990). What Washington means by policy reform. In J. Williamson (Ed.), *Latin American adjustment: How much has happened?* (pp. 7–20). Washington, DC: Institute for International Economics.

World Bank. (1987). *Ecuador: Country economic memorandum* (Report No. 6592-EC). Washington, DC: Author.

World Bank & International Finance Corporation. (2007). *Doing business 2008*. Washington, DC: Authors.

World Bank & International Finance Corporation. (2008). *Doing business 2009*. Washington, DC: Authors.

World Bank & International Finance Corporation. (2009). *Doing business 2010: Reforming through difficult times*. Washington, DC: Authors.

World Bank & International Finance Corporation. (2010). *Doing business 2011: Making a difference for entrepreneurs*. Washington, DC: Authors.

World Trade Organization. (1995a). *The results of the Uruguay round of multilateral trade negotiations: Legal texts*. Geneva: Author. (Original work published by the GATT Secretariat 1994).

World Trade Organization. (1995b). *Report of the working party on the accession of Ecuador* (WT/L/77). Geneva: Author.

World Trade Organization. (1996a). *European Communities—Regime for the importation, sale and distribution of bananas: Request for consultation by Ecuador, Guatemala, Honduras, Mexico and the United States* (WT/DS27/1). Geneva: Author.

World Trade Organization. (1996b). *European Communities—Regime for the importation, sale and distribution of bananas: Request for establishment of the panel* (WT/DS27/6). Geneva: Author.

World Trade Organization. (1997a). *European Communities—Regime for the importation, sale and distribution of bananas: Complaint by Ecuador—Report of the panel* (WT/DS27/R/ECU). Geneva: Author.

World Trade Organization. (1997b). *Appellate body: European Communities—Regime for the importation, sale and distribution of bananas: Report of the appellate body* (WT/DS27/AB/R). Geneva: Author.

World Trade Organization. (1998a). *European Communities—Regime for the importation, sale and distribution of bananas: Arbitration under Article 21.3(c) of the understanding on rules and procedures governing the settlement of disputes—Award of the arbitrator Said El-Naggar* (WT/DS27/15). Geneva: Author.

World Trade Organization. (1998b). *European Communities—Regime for the importation, sale and distribution of bananas: Request for the establishment of a panel by the European Communities* (WT/DS27/40). Geneva: Author.

World Trade Organization. (1998c). *European Communities—Regime for the importation, sale and distribution of bananas: Recourse to article 21.5 of the DSU* (WT/DS27/41). Geneva: Author.

World Trade Organization. (1999a). *Dispute settlement body: 19 November 1999* (WT/DSB/M/71). Geneva: Author.

World Trade Organization (1999b) *European Communities—Regime for the importation, sale and distribution of bananas: Recourse by the United States to article 22.2 of the DSU* (WT/DS27/43). Geneva: Author.

World Trade Organization (1999c) *European Communities—Regime for the importation, sale and distribution of bananas: Recourse by the United States to article 22.7 of the DSU* (WT/DS27/47). Geneva: Author.

World Trade Organization. (1999d). *European Communities—Regime for the importation, sale and distribution of bananas: Request by the European*

Communities for arbitration under article 22.6 of the DSU (WT/DS27/46). Geneva: Author.

World Trade Organization. (1999e). *European Communities—Regime for the importation of sale and distribution of bananas: Recourse to article 21.5 of the DSU by Ecuador—Report of the panel* (WT/DS27/RW/ECU). Geneva: Author.

World Trade Organization. (1999f). *European Communities—Regime for the importation, sale and distribution of bananas: Request by the European Communities for arbitration under article 22.6 of the DSU* (WT/DS27/53). Geneva: Author.

World Trade Organization. (1999g). *European Communities—Regime for the importation, sale and distribution of bananas: Recourse by Ecuador to article 22.2 of the DSU* (WT/DS27/52). Geneva: Author.

World Trade Organization. (1999h). *Ministerial conference, third session, Seattle, 30 November–3 December—Ecuador: Statement by H.E. Mr. José Luis Ycaza Pazmiño, Minister of Foreign Trade, Fisheries, and Tourism* (WT/MIN(99) ST/35). Geneva: Author.

World Trade Organization. (2000a). *European Communities—Regime for the importation, sale and distribution of bananas: Request by the European Communities for arbitration under article 22.6 of the DSU—Decision by the arbitrators* (WT/DS27/ARB/ECU). Geneva: Author.

World Trade Organization. (2000b). *European Communities—Regime for the importation, sale and distribution of bananas: Recourse to article 22.7 of the DSU by Ecuador* (WT/DS27/54). Geneva: Author.

World Trade Organization. (2000c). *Dispute settlement body: 30 November 2000* (WT/DSB/M/91). Geneva: Author.

World Trade Organization. (2001a). *Ministerial conference, fourth session, Doha, 9–14 November 2001: Ministerial declaration—Adopted on 14 November 2001* (WT/MIN(01)/DEC/1). Geneva: Author.

World Trade Organization, (2001b). *European Communities—Regime for the importation, sale and distribution of bananas: Notification of mutually agreed solution* (WT/DS27/58). Geneva: Author.

World Trade Organization. (2001c). *Dispute settlement body: 5 November 2001* (WT/DSB/M/112). Geneva: Author.

World Trade Organization. (2001d). *Ministerial conference, fourth session, Doha, 9–14 November 2001: European Communities—The ACP-EC partnership agreement: Decision of 14 November 2001* (WT/MIN(01)/15). Geneva: Author.

World Trade Organization. (2001e). *Ministerial conference, fourth session, Doha, 9–14 November 2001: European Communities—Transitional regime for the EC autonomous tariff rate quotas on imports of bananas: Decision of 14 November 2001* (WT/MIN(01)/16). Geneva: Author.

World Trade Organization. (2003a). *Committee on agriculture, special session: Summary report on the nineteenth meeting of the committee on agriculture special session held on 1 July 2003—Note by the secretariat* (TN/AG/R9). Geneva: Author.

World Trade Organization. (2003b). *Negotiating group on market access: Minutes of the meeting, held in the Centre William Rappard on 26–28 May 2003—Chairman: ambassador P-L. Girard (Switzerland)* (TN/MA/M/8). Geneva: Author.

World Trade Organization. (2003c). *Committee on agriculture, Special session: Summary report on the seventeenth meeting of the committee on agriculture special session held on 28 February 2003—Note by the secretariat* (TN/AG/R7). Geneva: Author.

World Trade Organization. (2004). *Negotiating group on market access: Minutes of the meeting, held in the Centre William Rappard on 9–11 June 2004—Chairman: Ambassador S.H. Jóhannesson (Iceland)* (TN/MA/M/13). Geneva: Author.

World Trade Organization. (2005a). *Trade policy review body: Trade policy review, Ecuador—Draft minutes of meeting* (WT/TPR/M/148). Geneva: Author.

World Trade Organization. (2005b). *Trade policy review body: Trade policy review report by the secretariat, Ecuador—Revision* (WT/TPR/S/148/Rev.1). Geneva: Author.

World Trade Organization. (2005c). *Committee on agriculture, special session: Summary report on the thirty-first and thirty-second formal special sessions of the committee on agriculture, held on 19 April and 3 June 2005* (TN/AG/R/20). Geneva: Author.

World Trade Organization. (2005d). *Ministerial conference, sixth session, Hong Kong, 13–18 December 2005: Ecuador—Statement by H.E. Mr. Jorge Illingworth, Minister of Foreign Trade, Industrialization, Fisheries and Competitiveness* (WT/MIN(05)/ST/148). Geneva: Author.

World Trade Organization. (2006). *General council, committee on agriculture (special session), negotiating group on market access: Recently acceded members—Communication from Ecuador and Panama* (WT/GC/W/565, TN/AG/W/2, TN/MA/W/73). Geneva: Author.

World Trade Organization. (2008a). *Committee on agriculture, special session: Revised draft modalities for agriculture* (TN/AG/W/4/Rev.4). Geneva: Author.

World Trade Organization. (2008b). *European Communities—Regime for the importation, sale and distribution of bananas: Second recourse to article 21.5 of the DSU by Ecuador—Report of the panel* (WT/DS27/RW2/ECU). Geneva: Author.

World Trade Organization. (2008c). *European Communities—Regime for the importation, sale and distribution of bananas: Recourse to article 21.5 of the*

DSU by the United States—Report of the panel (WT/DS27/RW/USA). Geneva: WTO.

World Trade Organization. (2008d). *European Communities—Regime for the importation, sale and distribution of bananas: Second recourse to article 21.5 of the DSU by Ecuador; European Communities—Regime for the importation, sale and distribution of bananas: Recourse to article 21.5 of the DSU by the United States—Reports of the appellate body* (WT/DS27/AB/RW2/ECU, WT/DS27/AB/RW/USA). Geneva: Author.

World Trade Organization. (2009a). *Committee on balance-of-payments restrictions: Notification under paragraph 9 of the understanding on the balance-of-payments provisions of the general agreement on tariffs and trade 1994—Communication from Ecuador* (WT/BOP/N/65). Geneva: Author.

World Trade Organization. (2009b). *Committee on balance-of-payments restrictions: Consultations with Ecuador—Background document by the secretariat, revision* (WT/BOP/S/15/Rev.1). Geneva: Author.

World Trade Organization. (2009c). *Committee on balance-of-payments restrictions: Consultations with Ecuador—Basic document supplied by Ecuador: Overview of the situation and outlook for the balance-of-payments taking into account internal and external factors that affect the situation* (WT/BOP/G/15). Geneva: Author.

World Trade Organization. (2009d). *Committee on balance-of-payments restrictions: Report (2009) of the committee on balance-of-payments restrictions* (WT/BOP/R/96). Geneva: Author.

World Trade Organization (2009e). *Dispute settlement body: 11 December 2008* (WT/DSB/M/260). Geneva: Author.

World Trade Organization. (2009f). *Geneva agreement on trade in bananas: Communication from Brazil, Columbia, Costa Rica, Ecuador, European Union, Guatemala, Honduras, Mexico, Nicaragua, Panama, Peru and the Bolivarian Republic of Venezuela* (WT/L/784). Geneva: Author.

World Trade Organization. (2011). *Trade policy review body: Trade policy review—Report by Ecuador* (WT/TPR/G/254). Geneva: Author.

World Trade Organization. (2012a). *Trade policy review body: Trade policy review report by the secretariat, Ecuador—Revision* (WT/TPR/S/254/Rev.1). Geneva: Author.

World Trade Organization. (2012b). *European Communities—Regime for the importation, sale and distribution of bananas (Guatemala; Honduras; Mexico; United States) (DS16); European Communities—Regime for the importation, sale and distribution of bananas (Ecuador; Guatemala; Honduras; Mexico; United States) (DS27); European Communities—Regime for the importation, sale and distribution of bananas (Panama)(DS105); European Communities—Regime for the importation, sale and distribution of bananas (Guatemala; Honduras; Mexico, Panama; United States) (DS158); European*

Communities—Regime for the importation of bananas (Colombia) (DS361); European Communities—Regime for the importation of bananas (Panama) (DS364); European Communities—The ACP-EC partnership agreement—Recourse to arbitration pursuant to the decision of 14 November 2001 (Brazil; Colombia; Costa Rica; Ecuador; Guatemala; Honduras; Nicaragua; Panama and Venezuela) (WT/L/616); European Communities—The ACP-EC partnership agreement—Second recourse to arbitration pursuant to the decision of 14 November 2001 (Brazil; Colombia; Costa Rica; Ecuador; Guatemala; Honduras; Nicaragua and Panama) (WT/L/625): Notification of a mutually agreed solution (WT/DS27/98). Geneva: Author.

World Trade Organization. (2017). *Committee on regional trade agreements, Council for trade in services: Notification of regional trade agreement—Protocol of Accession of Ecuador to the trade agreement between the European Union and its member states, of the one part, and Columbia and Peru, of the other part* (WT/REG380/N/1, S/C/N/876). Geneva: Author.

CHAPTER 7

Conclusion

This research revealed the RAMs' policy objectives (inferred from economic theories introduced in Chapter 1) at the multilateral trading system and how these motivations guided their policy performances before and after WTO accession. After a broad overview of all the RAMs on the basis of available cross-country data (in Chapter 2), the four case studies further analyzed the performance of selected RAMs (from Chapter 3 onwards) to observe how countries possessing specific characteristics (transition economies pursuing domestic reforms; export-oriented economies; large economies; and economies that suffered from costs as previous outsiders to the multilateral trading system) engaged in relevant liberalization schemes of the multilateral trading system (WTO accession, the Doha Round, and dispute settlement). While individual case studies mainly presented how the presence of these characteristics affected each country's policy behaviors based on the hypotheses inferred from the relevant theories of trade agreements and negotiations, observed correlations can be confirmed firmly only when compared with the results of other cases featuring the absence of the same characteristics. For instance, to verify importance of an economy's export orientation in pursuing reciprocal trade liberalization, there must be holistic comparison of policy behaviors between export-oriented economies and non-export-oriented ones. To verify hypotheses on this firm footing, the first section of this final chapter compares findings from the four case studies to draw grand conclusions of the entire research, after presenting their brief overviews. Two hypotheses (1 on commitment and 3 on

K. Takamiya, *Recently Acceded Members of the World Trade Organization*, https://doi.org/10.1007/978-981-13-9159-0_7

domino) out of four were found to be valid, while the others (those related to reciprocity, including Hypotheses 2-a on juggernaut and 2-b on terms of trade externality) were either rejected or confirmed only with nuanced or inconclusive findings on the relevance of their underlying theories.

The overall research has been formulated around the existing economic theories that served as the guide to investigate the RAMs' policy objectives for engagement in the multilateral trading system. However, it is possible to observe the same phenomenon also through other lenses that supplement these theories. Among them, what is probably worth looking into further would be the role of institutional processes built into different schemes of multilateral trade liberalization. This last chapter concludes with some introductory remarks on the latter as a preface for possible future research, as well as relevant policy recommendations.

1 Summary Findings from Case Studies

1.1 *Factual Overviews of Country Cases*

Georgia. As a country in transition to a market economy, Georgia utilized market access commitments for WTO accession with the aim to catalyze and consolidate its own unilateral trade liberalization. Like the case of other low-income economies in transition from the former Soviet Union, backed with the support by international financial institutions (IFIs), the country made very extensive market access commitments for WTO membership, with an average bound tariff rate at the single-digit level. However, the economy was neither export-oriented nor large, and there was no obvious reason to stay engaged in reciprocal trade liberalization of the Doha Round, such as mobilizing export interests and containing terms of trade externality. Georgia disengaged itself from the DDA market access negotiations initially with a defensive posture and, instead, proceeded with post-accession unilateral liberalization outside of the multilateral trading system. As the country's autonomous liberalization was accelerated after the Rose Revolution in 2003, the country departed even further from the WTO track of trade liberalization, and the feature of the disengagement changed from defensiveness to aloofness, particularly on NAMA for which the country nearly eliminated most of the remaining tariffs in 2006. Georgia had no major concern of targeted discrimination by the incumbent WTO members, and there was no apparent attempt to redress such costs of previous non-membership through accession, dispute settlement, and the Doha Round.

People's Republic of China. China was also a transition economy, and the government utilized the WTO accession commitment to push its domestic reform. The country made extensive market access commitments, albeit at the somewhat moderate level (compared with those of the low-income economies in transition, including Georgia) of the average bound tariff rate of about 10%. Also, the country has been suffering from targeted discrimination by its trading partners, and tried to remove the costs of previous non-member status through accession negotiations. However, most of them were kept imposed even after China's WTO accession, and the country resorted to the Doha Round and the dispute settlement mechanism to cope with the part of remaining discrimination, especially those that lasted long such as the non-market economy (NME) designation and transitional product-specific safeguard (TPS). At the backdrop of the rising current account surplus, the country exhibited some positive sign of engagement in the DDA market access negotiations and suspended autonomous liberalization. While the government pursued exports interests through reciprocal trade negotiations, the domestic private businesses were not substantially involved in the decision-making. As the world's second largest economy, China should be able to affect terms of trade through its trade policy, but there was no obvious sign of consciousness on this issue among policy-makers and negotiators. While having been more positive than other large developing countries and RAMs, China fell short of taking on a leadership role to move the entire round forward.

Viet Nam. The gradualist approach was even more strongly reflected in Viet Nam's reform path (than China's) for transition to a market economy. Accordingly, the market access commitments were made at a level slightly higher than those of many other RAMs (the average bound rate exceeding 10%), and Viet Nam did not exhibit keen interest in early accession at the initial phase of membership negotiations. However, the country intensified its efforts of accession after the Doha Ministerial Conference in 2001 that approved China's accession and launched the DDA. China's membership raised concerns on competitive disadvantage among other transition economies of the Greater Mekong Subregion (GMS), especially in relation to the full implementation of the Agreement on Textile and Clothing exclusively among WTO members, and triggered domino expansion of multilateralism in the region. While Viet Nam redressed this particular cost of previous non-membership through WTO accession, the country continuously suffered from the NME designation and resorted to dispute settlement to cope with anti-dumping actions in the fishery sector by the trading partner. Viet Nam's external balance deteriorated significantly after its WTO membership and the country was not proactively engaged in the DDA market access negotiations, while sustaining efforts of cautious autonomous liberalization. However, disengagement from the multilateral negotiations was probably a reflection of concerns over broader post-accession macroeconomic destabilization, rather than receding export business interests. As a medium-sized economy, Viet Nam is less likely to have been able to affect terms of trade, which were not part of the government's concern.

Ecuador: Unlike the other RAMs covered by preceding case studies, Ecuador is not a transition economy, and domestic reform has not been a priority of the government. Accordingly, the country did not use market access commitments for WTO accession to leverage unilateral trade liberalization and bound its tariffs at the highest level across the RAMs (at the average rate exceeding 20%, together with Panama). After the WTO membership, there were even occasional departures from the accession commitments, including the recourse to balance of payments (BOP) safeguard at the time of the global financial crisis in 2009, and the government took no substantial initiative of autonomous liberalization. Rather, Ecuador joined the multilateral trading system to recover the cost of previous non-membership in the form of discrimination against its banana exports by the EU (that accorded preferences to ACP countries and discriminated against Latin American countries). Thus, the country repeatedly challenged the EU's banana import regime through WTO's dispute settlement mechanism, and proactively participated in the agriculture negotiations of the Doha Round. While the country's external balance improved in the course of the Doha Round, broader domestic export businesses were not involved in the decision-making process for the DDA negotiations and played no substantive roles in policy formulation. For Ecuador, the Doha Round was an extension of the banana disputes to defend its agricultural interests of the specific product. For a small economy with no capacity to affect international prices through its trade policy, terms of trade externality was not an issue of its concern in proceeding with reciprocal tariff-cutting negotiations of the Doha Round.

1.2 Cross-Country Comparison by Hypothesis

Among the theoretical propositions adopted in this research, Hypothesis 1 (*Reforming economies [especially, those in transition to a market economy] would make extensive market access commitments for WTO accession, while others would make little use of them.)*, Hypothesis 2-a (*Only export-oriented economies would stay proactively engaged in the post-accession market access negotiations of the Doha Round, while others would pursue autonomous liberalization.), and Hypothesis 2-b (Only large economies would stay proactively engaged in the market access negotiations of the Doha Round, while others would pursue autonomous liberalization.)* relate to market access negotiations. An underlying assumption is that market access negotiations for WTO accession and those under the Doha Round serve different objectives, while both of them ultimately serve trade liberalization. Whereas the former enhances the credibility of domestic reforms for unilateral liberalization by tying the government's hands to binding international agreements (as per the commitment theory[1]), the latter is conducted on the premise of reciprocity, to advance interests of domestic export businesses to drive mutual market opening vis-à-vis trading partners (as per the juggernaut theory[2]) or to contain terms of trade externality among large economies (as per the terms of trade externality theory[3]). Whereas all reform-minded countries would be engaged in the accession process to enhance their unilateral liberalization before the WTO membership, only export-oriented or large economies would stay engaged in the Doha Round to take advantage of reciprocity in the post-accession phase. Hypothesis 3

[1] Staiger and Tabellini (1987), and Maggi and Rodriguez-Clare (1998, 2007).

[2] Baldwin (2006, 2012).

[3] Bagwell and Staiger (1999, 2002).

(*Countries that face the discriminatory cost of prior non-membership would stay engaged in the relevant multilateral liberalization schemes, while others would refrain from such activities.*) relates to the cost of the previous non-WTO member status in the form of targeted discrimination by their trading partners. It presumes that countries join the trade agreement, one after the other, to remove such costs (as per the domino theory,[4]) and RAMs suffering from lasting discrimination are expected to use the multilateral trading system to redress these remaining competitive disadvantages.

Table 1 summarizes findings from case studies on Georgia, China, Viet Nam, and Ecuador by each hypothesis. Triple tick marks (✓✓✓) in the table indicate that the hypothesis was strongly verified for the country concerned. Double tick marks (✓✓) mean that the hypothesis was verified by available macroeconomic and policy data, but the qualitative inquiry in the case studies of actual policy-making brought about a nuanced confirmation, and a single tick mark (✓) indicates that the hypothesis was confirmed only by the data but relevance of its underlying theory was not conclusively verified by qualitative observations. Thus, more tick marks are an indication of a higher level of hypothesis verification. The x mark (×) indicates that the hypothesis was completely rejected even by the data. The rest of this section provides a review of case study findings for each hypothesis.

Table 1 Summary of case study results

	Georgia	*China*	*Viet Nam*	*Ecuador*
Market access negotiations				
Hypothesis 1 (commitment)	✓✓✓	✓✓✓	✓✓✓	✓✓✓
Hypothesis 2-a (juggernaut)	✓✓	✓✓	✓	✓
Hypothesis 2-b (terms of trade)	✓	✓	✓	×
Recovering cost of non-membership				
Hypothesis 3 (domino)	✓✓✓	✓✓✓	✓✓✓	✓✓✓

Note ✓✓✓ = strongly verified; ✓✓ = verified by data, with nuanced qualitative confirmation; ✓ = verified only by data, without any conclusive qualitative confirmation; × = rejected by both data and qualitative observations

[4] Baldwin (1995).

Hypothesis 1: Reforming economies (especially, those in transition to a market economy) would make extensive market access commitments for WTO accession, while others would make little use of them. Georgia, China, and Viet Nam were transition economies undertaking domestic reforms. With a clear objective of consolidating or catalyzing their own unilateral trade liberalization, these three countries made extensive market access commitments through WTO accession, albeit at different degrees in accordance with their reform orientations. In contrast, Ecuador is not a transition economy and had no intent to utilize the WTO accession commitments for the domestic reform purpose. Thus, the country bound its tariffs at relatively high levels among the RAMs. Interestingly, the extensiveness of market access commitments made by individual RAMs to secure WTO accession seems to reflect the pace and level of their broader structural reforms. Among the four RAMs, Georgia was ranked as the world's best performer (out of 185 economies) in terms of narrowing gaps with international best practices in the period of 2005–2012 by the World Bank's Doing Business report (see Table 8, Chapter 2), and its ranking in terms of the absolute level of business friendliness moved up from 37th in 2005 to 9th in 2009. The country bound tariffs for WTO accession at the lowest level. China's raking of catching up with international best practice was 12th, with an absolute ranking hovering between 83rd and 93rd in the same period. In line with its gradualist approach, the country made slightly less extensive accession commitments, at the average bound tariff rate at a marginally higher level. Viet Nam's absolute ranking was similar, between 78th and 104th, but the country was not ranked among the top 50 countries that narrowed the gap with international best practices. Thus, Viet Nam had been a more cautious gradualist than China, and its bound tariff level was higher. Ecuador's absolute ranking had been between 123rd and 139th and was also not one of the top 50 reformers. As a non-reformer, its average rate of tariffs bound for accession was among the highest across the RAMs.

The behaviors of all four RAMs verify Hypothesis 1 based on the commitment theory. Reforming economies (Georgia, China, and Viet Nam) made extensive market access commitments, in line with their respective reform approaches, while the non-reformer (Ecuador) did not. Consistently with the commitment theory prescription, transition economies were engaged in the tariff-cutting negotiations for the WTO membership. In contrast, Ecuador's objective for WTO membership was completely different (banana disputes alone) and the country made only modest accession commitments. In addition to the data-based confirmation above, differentiated levels of reform orientations and corresponding tariff binding were also confirmed by qualitative observations of case studies. For instance, Georgia's policy-makers appreciated the merit of trade liberalization and made explicit statements to utilize tariff binding as the commitment device. This was true also for China albeit within its gradualist approach and, to a lesser extent, Viet Nam as a more cautious gradualist. On the other hand, Ecuador had no intention to leverage reforms with tariff bindings, and deliberately set the bound tariff rates at the level much higher than the applied ones, based on the benchmark of the existing regional trade agreement. Ecuador's departures from the membership commitments in the post-accession period, highlighted by recourse to the BOP safeguard in 2009, were further testimonies of the fact that tariff bindings were not utilized as a commitment device for the domestic reform.

Hypothesis 2-a: Only export-oriented economies would stay proactively engaged in the post-accession market access negotiations of the Doha Round, while others would pursue autonomous liberalization. Case studies on China and Ecuador showed that both of them recorded an increasing current account and trade surplus toward the high time of the DDA market access negotiations in July 2008. These two RAMs showed a relatively positive sign of engagement in the reciprocal liberalization process, compared with other RAMs (in particular, the low-income economies in transition and the very recently acceded members). China advocated the formula-based tariff cuts among WTO members at the NAMA negotiations and Ecuador called for ambitious results of the agriculture negotiations. While having been proactively engaged in reciprocal market access negotiations of the Doha Round, they both refrained from autonomous trade liberalization in the post-accession phase, regardless of the presence (or absence) of the domestic reform objective (whereas China continued non-trade reforms autonomously in the post-accession period, Ecuador even reversed the reform path). Thus, notwithstanding the clear difference in the reform orientation, they were both actively engaged in the DDA market access negotiations. The common factor for these two RAMs was the enhanced export orientation toward 2008, implying that what explains their proactive engagement in the Doha Round was export interests, rather than domestic reforms.

On the contrary, Georgia and Viet Nam experienced a rise of the external account deficit in the post-accession period. In the absence of a strong export orientation in the post-WTO accession period, they had no strong mercantilist reasons to stay engaged in the reciprocal negotiation process of the Doha Round. Thus, the two opted to proceed with non-discriminatory trade liberalization autonomously outside of the WTO, rather than reciprocal tariff cuts through the Doha Round. This departure from the WTO track was most explicitly observed in the case of Georgia, whose government forcefully proceeded with its autonomous market-oriented reform particularly after the 2003 Rose Revolution. While the country ultimately accepted the 2008 December NAMA modality, that was just to reflect part of the preceding unilateral liberalization. As a very recently acceded member, Viet Nam was still in the transition period for implementing its terms of accession, and the country did not accept any further cuts of bound tariff rates at the Doha Round. However, outside of the WTO, it gradually began to reduce MFN applied tariffs autonomously beyond the accession commitments.

These observations uphold Hypothesis 2-a on the crude statistical grounds, but the qualitative findings were nuanced. Export-oriented economies showed signs of more positive engagement in the reciprocal market access negotiations at the Doha Round (while less exported-oriented economies pursued autonomous liberalization). However, the case studies' observations revealed somewhat nuanced findings on the relevance of the juggernaut theory as an explanation of relationships between a country's export orientation and engagement in the reciprocal trade negotiations. While the theory predicts that the domestic exporters at large act as the driving force for reciprocal trade liberalization, the case studies on China and Ecuador found no strong indication that their nationwide business associations actively lobbied the government even when the economy's exporting sector was expanding.[5] Export interests have been indirectly reflected in the government's own mercantilist position at the WTO but domestic businesses were not directly affecting the

[5] However, in the face of the need to rebalance the growth model and a rise of the inward-looking policy, even the government priority on the pursuit of export market access began to fade away over time (especially after the global financial crisis in 2008–2009). The development focus was also part of China's foreign policy consideration at the Doha Round. See Chapter 4.

country's negotiating stance for reciprocal liberalization. Closer examinations revealed that a majority of the export sector in China were foreign invested enterprises (rather than state-owned or other domestic enterprises), which might not have strong leverage to influence public policy, and the source of the rise in Ecuador's surplus was its exports of oil, a commodity that was not negotiated at the WTO. While relatively proactive compared with other developing countries, China still fell short of meeting the expectation from others to take a leadership role in the Doha Round. Ecuador's positive engagement in the negotiations was mainly directed to addressing the cost of the previous non-member status specifically in the banana sector (as better explained by Hypothesis 3 below), rather than the broad-based expansion of the overall export sector. Another interesting finding was that non-export-oriented economies that departed from the WTO track and switched to autonomous liberalization would not necessarily retain a defensive posture permanently. Georgia's case illustrated that, after autonomous liberalization eliminated nearly all remaining industrial tariffs, the country turned to become more accommodating at the Doha Round. In fact, similar attitudes are observable also from a few other WTO members that achieved nearly free trade, such as Hong Kong and Singapore. They are not necessarily active players at the WTO negotiations, but not defensive at the same time. These free traders that have virtually nothing left to liberalize or protect seem to be disinterested and exhibiting somewhat aloof attitudes in the multilateral negotiations.

Hypothesis 2-b: Only large economies would stay proactively engaged in the market access negotiations of the Doha Round, while others would pursue autonomous liberalization. The terms of trade externality theory presumes that large countries have an incentive to raise import duties up to the optimal tariff level, but such actions would place themselves in the Prisoner's Dilemma position of risking trade wars with others. According to this theory, large countries use the multilateral trading system to avoid this fate through coordinated tariff cuts on a reciprocal basis, while small countries do not. In fact, the indirect macroeconomic data supports this proposition, as reviewed in Chapter 2. Among case study countries, China—the world's second largest economy—exhibited the most positive attitude toward reciprocal tariff-cutting negotiations of the Doha Round, in comparison with most of the other RAMs. At the same time, some of the small- and medium-sized economies disengaged themselves from the market access negotiations of the Doha Round. However, Ecuador's case shows that even a small country stays proactively engaged in the reciprocal trade negotiations if it has another reason to do so. Moreover, case studies revealed that trade negotiators were not even conscious about the terms of trade concept. No RAMs covered in the case studies, including China, ever mentioned containment of the adverse terms of trade externality as their reason for the reciprocal cuts of import duties at the WTO.

While the available data mostly upholds Hypothesis 2-b, except for one case, findings from the actual policy-making and negotiation scenes reject the relevance of the terms of trade externality theory as an explanation of large countries' engagement in reciprocal trade negotiations. As far as the RAMs are concerned, relatively large economies within the group (such as China and, to a much lesser extent, Chinese Taipei) tended to be export-orientated at the same time. Between the two relevant motivations, pursuit of export interests (albeit by the government, rather than domestic businesses as assumed by the juggernaut theory), as opposed to containment of terms of trade externality, would better explain their relatively more positive engagement in the reciprocal market access negotiations. If the size of the economy ever matters, it probably relates to the leverage that economies with large imports markets could have in the negotiations vis-à-vis major trading partners, but the underlying motivations in such bargaining are mercantilist export interests, rather than containment of the terms of trade externality.[6] In conclusion, despite plausible verification on the basis of available statistics, no conclusive evidence was found in support of practical relevance of the terms of trade externality theory in explaining the RAMs' engagement in the Doha Round. The multilateral trading system is envisaged to have a function of avoiding potential trade wars, but it relates to coping with protectionist actions (including targeted discrimination assumed in Hypothesis 3) that are best resolved by the dispute settlement mechanism (DSM), rather

[6] On the other hand, small countries tend to be taken less seriously by trading partners in reciprocal bargaining, and they can simply free-ride on market access offers by major players on the MFN basis. This combination of reciprocity and MFN leaves no pressing reason for small countries to be proactively engaged in the negotiations of the GATT/WTO trade rounds. This view has been expressed by former World Bank economists (Finger & Winters, 1998).

than manipulation of terms of trade that could be addressed by reciprocal tariff cuts.

Hypothesis 3: Countries that face the discriminatory cost of prior non-membership would stay engaged in the relevant multilateral liberalization schemes, while others would refrain from such activities. Unlike Hypothesis 1 and Hypothesis 2 on broad trade policy objectives for market access negotiations with economy-wide implications, Hypothesis 3 addresses more specific costs of the previous WTO non-membership in the form of targeted discrimination maintained by trading partners (notably, the United States and the EU), as assumed in the domino theory. China, Viet Nam, and Ecuador faced relatively higher trade barriers in the pre-accession period, and redressing such disadvantage was clearly part of their motivations to join the multilateral trading system. While WTO accession accorded the MFN treatment (in particular, through provision of the permanent normal trade relations [PNTR] status by the United States), some of the specific discriminatory measures remained for an extended period of time, preserving part of the pre-membership costs. As inscribed in the terms of WTO accession, China and Viet Nam had to suffer from the NME designation in anti-dumping actions. In addition, China's terms of accession imposed another discriminatory provision of TPS. Likewise, Ecuador had long been troubled by the EU's discriminatory banana import regime. After joining the WTO, these three countries commonly used the DSM to cope with abuses of the remaining discrimination by the major trading partners (EC—Fasteners [China], EC—Footwear [China], United States—Tyres [China], United States—Shrimp [Viet Nam], and EC—Bananas III [Ecuador]). At the same time, where relevant, they also addressed these issues at the Doha Round (e.g., China's position on NME at the rules negotiations, and Ecuador's focus on bananas tariffs in the agriculture negotiations). On the other hand, Georgia enjoyed a relatively easy access to its trading partners' markets, even before it joined the WTO. Targeted discrimination was none of Georgia's concern (except at the time of war with Russia), and the country did not have to resort to the multilateral trading system for this purpose, both before and after its WTO membership.

Behaviors of RAMs uphold Hypothesis 3. In particular, the DSM was commonly utilized by discriminated RAMs and proved to be an effective mechanism to cope with the competitive disadvantage (except for one case where China's challenge against the recourse to TPS by the United States turned out to be unsuccessful). In contrast, targeted discrimination was not a major concern for Georgia, as it had relatively smooth access to export markets of its trading partners even before the WTO accession, and the country had no issues to be resolved after gaining membership. Thus, the case studies showed that, while RAMs that still faced unresolved discriminatory measures utilized the WTO in the post-accession period, the one free from such troubles did not. Removal of the cost of the previous non-membership was one important motivation for the concerned RAMs to stay engaged in the relevant WTO activities.

1.3 Implications of Case Study Results

A very visible finding from the four case studies is that, while Hypotheses 1 on commitment and 3 on domino were strongly upheld for all RAMs, Hypothesis 2-a on juggernaut and 2-b on terms of trade externality were not strongly confirmed for any. The former primarily relates to WTO accession and dispute settlement (with some elements of the Doha Round), and the latter is intended to explain the role of reciprocity of the DDA market access negotiations. Even where these reciprocity-related hypotheses were found to hold on the basis of available data, at best, closer observations in the case studies revealed only nuanced validity of their underlying theories. Among them, the complete lack of practical relevance of terms of trade externality has been pointed out previously by economists and is somewhat well known,[7] but what is probably more surprising is that there was also a limit in the explanatory power of the juggernaut theory that presents the crucial role of domestic export industries to push reciprocal trade liberalization.

According to the theory, one potential advantage of reciprocal trade liberalization at the GATT/WTO trade round over unilateral market opening would be that the former should have allowed the government to mobilize exports business interests as a counterweight against protectionism of import-competing industries. This way WTO members should be able to achieve a higher degree of liberalization at the trade rounds compared with the case of autonomous reform. However, as shown by

[7] Krugman (1991).

this research on the RAMs, such support from export businesses does not appear to be robust enough to get a forceful juggernaut rolling in the Doha Round. No doubt, the export-oriented RAMs have been relatively more proactive in the reciprocal negotiations, but it was more a result of the government's own position and there was no apparent sign of direct support to multilateral liberalization by domestic business at large. In the past, export business interests were the driving force of the previous GATT rounds, and this was true also for more recent successful trade talks completed after establishment of the WTO. For instance, it was direct actions by the private sector in the United States, the EU, and Japan that pushed the launch of the plurilateral negotiations of the original Information Technology Agreement (ITA) signed at the Singapore Ministerial Conference in 1996 (WTO, 2012), but such a business-driven mechanism does not appear to be working any longer for the Doha Round.[8]

Consistently with findings in this research on the RAMs, the lack of business interests in the Doha Round is also pointed out by external observers (McGuire, 2012; Narlikar, 2009). Clearly, the mechanism that used to work for reciprocal trade negotiations among developed countries in the past is no longer working for the Doha Round that involves developing countries more substantively. One plausible explanation is that the policy-making dynamics of developing countries are different from those of developed countries. The juggernaut theory implicitly assumes that the export businesses are domestic constituencies (connected to those in power) and market access for their products are negotiated at the WTO, but such a presumption does not necessarily hold in developing countries. As the case studies for China and Ecuador (the two RAMs with the rising current account surplus) showed, a majority of exporting businesses of the former were foreign investors (that may not have a lobbying route to the communist government) and the source of export growth of the latter was oil (a commodity that is not covered by the multilateral trading system). As a result, while export interests were pursued by the government, there was no direct support to the Doha Round by domestic industries in these RAMs, even when the economies

[8]Discussions at the 2014 WTO Public Forum on "ICC World Trade Agenda post-Bali business priorities" organized by the International Chamber of Commerce on 1 October 2014 in Geneva. See the WTO Web site: http://www.wto.org/english/forums_e/public_forum14_e/programme_e.htm.

enhanced their export orientation. While this research did not examine the industrial structure of all developing countries, it showed that the domestic policy-making dynamics at least in these RAMs appear to be different from those of developed countries as assumed in the juggernaut theory.

This does not mean that domestic businesses have no stake in developing countries' involvement in the multilateral trading system. In fact, where their specific export interested were adversely affected by actions by foreign governments, they took initiatives in turning toward the WTO dispute settlement mechanism, as the case studies on China, Viet Nam, and Ecuador showed. For instance, the Vietnam Association of Seafood Exporters and Producers (VASEP) played a very proactive role in bringing in the shrimp disputes with the United States to the WTO. However, this type of proactive involvement of domestic businesses was observed only in defense of their specific interests through dispute settlement, but not at the Doha Round where broad-based market access for the broader export industries is negotiated. Ecuador's case showed that such specific business interests in bananas were extended to market access negotiations of the Doha Round, beyond DSM, but there was no sign of involvement by the broader export communities from domestic businesses.

As a big picture, overall, results of hypothesis examination showed that while the theories applicable primarily for WTO accession and dispute settlement (commitment and domino) were working as envisaged, those for reciprocal DDA market access negotiations (juggernaut and terms of trade eternality) were not. RAMs that made extensive market access commitments for the WTO membership literally utilized accession commitments as a commitment device to support domestic reforms. Also, RAMs that suffered from the targeted discrimination made repeated attempts to redress them through accession and subsequent engagement in the multilateral trading system. However, the same degree of theory relevance was not observed for juggernaut and terms of trade externality. This observation should provide at least a partial explanation on what works and what does not among different multilateral schemes of trade liberalization at the WTO—in particular, why the Doha Round faced deadlocks while accession and dispute settlement seem to have worked relatively well in the past. The potential motivations for engagement in the reciprocal trade negotiations are either pursuit of export business interests or containment of terms of trade externality, but neither of them were present nor sufficiently strong to move the entire round forward.[9]

2 Scope for Future Research and Policy Recommendations: Different Institutional Processes of Multilateral Liberalization

This book examined performance of the newly acceded members at the multilateral trading system primarily through the lens of its functions and policy objectives, as inferred from the existing economic theories on trade agreements. The research made intellectual contributions by assessing their practical relevance in the real world of trade negotiations and policy-making. At the same time, it is possible to look into the same subject further with other analytical lenses. One potential approach that could complement the book's theory-based observation is to investigate institutional aspects of various multilateral liberalization schemes, and such supplementary analysis may well be an interesting subject for future research.

To date, most existing literature on different modes of trade negotiations and agreements looked into multilateralism (GATT/WTO) on the one hand and regionalism (preferential trade agreements [PTAs]) on the other hand, or addressed comparison between the two. Unilateral liberalization is often treated as its own subject (usually interpreted as equivalent of autonomous liberalization without support by multilateral institutions), and bilateralism has been treated as a derivative of regionalism (typically, they both entail PTAs that cause discriminatory trade diversion and adverse spaghetti bowl effects). However, most of the research overlooks hybrid cases of these different institutional processes packaged into a single scheme of multilateral trade liberalization (perhaps with some limited important exception of attentions recently paid to the pursuit of plurilateralism in a multilateral framework[10]—most notably, ITA[11]).

[9]A more conventional explanation in the past was the notion of non-reciprocity built into the multilateral trading system (see Chapter 2) in effect deprived developing countries of the opportunity to resort to exchange of market access commitments (Laird, 1998), but this research revealed that what is also missing presently in the Doha Round is the strong domestically conceived motivations to resort to reciprocal liberalization on the part of developing countries.

[10]Woolcock (2013).

[11]Mann and Liu (2009).

Two different approaches of multilateral market access liberalization covered by this research, namely, WTO accession and the Doha Round, comprise unique sets of institutional processes. Both approaches are multilateral, in a sense that they are conducted under the WTO's multilateral auspices and the results are extended to all members on the MFN basis. However, the processes involved in these two schemes are different in terms of: (a) subject of the policy dialogue (as addressed in this research); (b) mode of negotiations; and (c) venue of final approval. Essentially, the focus of the WTO accession process is "unilateral" liberalization of a single applicant country and its market access commitments are negotiated "bilaterally" with interested parties (while compliance with the broader WTO rules are examined "plurilaterally" at the Working Group on accession), before the final approval is accorded "multilaterally" by consensus among all WTO members. Thus, by institutional design, the WTO accession entails unilateral, bilateral, and multilateral processes as its integral elements. This hybrid approach is quite different from the all-through multilateral approach of the Doha Round, whereby trade polices of all WTO members are negotiated simultaneously by multiple parties and then approved by them. Rather, the WTO accession process is similar to the business processes of IFIs' policy-based lending (PBL) (whereby one borrower country's unilateral reform is bilaterally discussed with the IFI mission, for an ultimate multilateral approval by the Executive Board), that are probably more familiar to many developing countries that undertook economic policy reforms in the past (see Table 2).

The hybrid approach of the WTO accession and IFIs' policy-based lending is much more streamlined in terms of the nature of procedural steps involved, in comparison with the all-through multilateral approach of the Doha Round. The unilateral reform focus of the former allows concentrating on the policy of one country alone, and bilateral negotiations avoid complication of simultaneous multi-party bargaining. In principle, the best results of these bilateral negotiations are automatically extended across the board on the MFN basis, without necessitating complicated multilateral negotiations. While the final approval under the hybrid approach is still accorded multilaterally by the entire membership (through consensus at the WTO General Council or voting by IFI's Executive Board), substantive decisions have already been made in the earlier bilateral process. Under the old GATT system, especially in its early history preceding the Kennedy Round, trade rounds were

Table 2 Different approaches of multilateral tariff liberalization

	WTO accession	*IFI's PBL*	*WTO DSM*	*WTO DDA*
Subject of liberalization	**Unilateral** (one applicant's own domestic reform)	**Unilateral** (one member's own domestic reform)	**Unilateral** (one respondent's ruling compliance)	**Multilateral** (reciprocal "concessions" among many members)
Mode of negotiations	**Bilateral** (focused market access negotiations)	**Bilateral** (between an IFI mission and a member)	**Bilateral** (complainant/s vs. respondent)	**Multilateral** (TNC and other WTO bodies)
Venue of final approval	**Multilateral** (by consensus, at the General Council)	**Multilateral** (voting by the Executive Board)	**Multilateral** (by negative/reverse consensus, at DSB)	**Multilateral** (by consensus, at the Ministerial Conference)

Note WTO accession requires approval by the Ministerial Conference. However, Article IV of the WTO Agreement stipulates that the General Council conducts the functions of the Ministerial Conference in intervals of the latter's meetings. DDA = Doha Development Agenda; DSB = Dispute Settlement Body; DSM = dispute settlement mechanism; IFI = international financial institution; TNC = Trade Negotiations Committee

conducted primarily on the basis of bilateral requests and offers among principal suppliers of particular industrial products (mainly developed countries).[12] However, this bilateral approach has been replaced partially or entirely by the formula approach in the later rounds, and the number of parties increased from one round to the other. The Doha Round placed particular emphasis on participation of all WTO members[13] and adopted the formula-based approach of market access liberalization by them.

In terms of delivering results, the unilateral-bilateral-multilateral hybrid approach appears to have been working better than the

[12] See Laird (1998) of the WTO secretariat. GATT Article XXVIII stipulates that modification of schedules is initially negotiated and agreed with the contracting parties that have a principal supplying interest.

[13] For instance, Director-General Roberto Azevêdo mentioned "*I will be doing everything I can to ensure that all Members are involved and that all voices are heard.*" in the lead to the Bali Ministerial Conference in 2013. See the WTO news release dated 9 September 2013 on "General Council: Azevêdo launches 'rolling set of meetings' aimed at delivering success in Bali" posted at the WTO Web site: http://www.wto.org/english/news_e/news13_e/gc_09sep13_e.htm.

all-through multilateral approach in support of trade liberalization involving developing countries. As shown in Chapter 2, the RAMs that went through the accession process generally managed to achieve a higher degree of non-discriminatory trade liberalization (in terms of the bound tariff rates) compared with other developing countries that participated in the Uruguay Round, and those that made extensive membership commitments brought about more visible trade expansion.[14] Likewise, in the past, developing countries liberalized their trade more extensively (in terms of the applied tariff rates) under the IMF-World Bank programs than through the GATT Uruguay Round. Available empirical research further showed that the IFI's program indeed led to increased openness of the borrowing countries.[15] Incidentally, the WTO dispute settlement process, which generally worked better, also takes this hybrid approach (while liberalization usually takes place on the side of the respondent, rather than the complainant filing the dispute), except where a third party is involved.

According to well-cited research by the World Bank economists, most of the MFN-based tariff cuts by developing countries were carried out as their own unilateral reforms (including both autonomous tariff cuts and those supported by WTO accession and IFIs' policy-based lending) since the 1980s, rather than through the Uruguay Round (World Bank, 2005).[16] Relatively speaking, the multilateral trade rounds did not

[14] Subramanian and Wei (2007).

[15] Mike Finger's internal work within the World Bank statistically showing the positive result of adjustment lending is cited by other World Bank economists (Hoekman & Winters, 2002). To the contrary, another cross-country empirical work by Rose (2005) concluded that the IMF membership and program did not lead to higher trade, but it does not appear to be focusing on the counties that were under the IMF programs with trade-related conditionality. A more recent study by Wei and Zhang (2010), which differentiated 77 countries that actually had trade reform conditions out of 99 that had IMF programs in 1993–2003, found that conditionality was associated with increases in trade openness and the positive results came from the programs with strong country ownership.

[16] This finding is presented in the World Bank's *2005 Global Economic Prospects: Trade, Regionalism, and Development*. Its background paper "A Note on Sources of Tariff Reductions in Developing Countries 1983-2003" by Will Martin and Francis Ng, dated 27 October 2004, analyzed trade liberalization of relatively large developing countries that accounted for 90% of developing country imports in 1990. Out of the weighted average tariff reductions of 18.6% percentage points (from 29.9% to 11.3%), a decline of only 5% points was caused by the Uruguay Round and the rest came from various forms of unilateral liberalization, such as autonomous market opening, World Bank/IMF adjustment

necessarily work effectively in support of trade liberalization by developing countries (while these did work extremely well, in the past, for a handful of rich countries including four largest economies under the old GATT system[17]) and, at least to date, the Doha Round does not seem to be an exception. However, there are other multilateral approaches that did work at the WTO and other international institutions, such as accession and policy-based lending.[18] These are essentially aimed at supporting each country's own unilateral reforms through relatively simple processes.

It may perhaps be a smart move for international communities to design a multilateral liberalization scheme for developing countries based on the model that actually worked in the past, rather than the approach that was tested but consistently failed. In principle, each country can utilize the WTO accession for non-discriminatory market opening only once at the time of its membership. Thus, a new multilateral approach of trade liberalization should ideally be established to support developing counters that have already joined the WTO and need further external support in the post-accession phase.

One such scheme that can be implemented without substantial changes to the WTO's current institutional setting would be more proactive use of the trade policy review mechanism (TPRM) as a venue for policy dialogues between each member and the WTO secretariat. The WTO's TPRM is similar to the IMF's Article IV consultations, in a sense that the staff of the multilateral institution bilaterally surveys mostly the

programs, and WTO accession. Regional trade agreements were estimated to have further reduced the tariff level by around 2% points. See Martin and Ng (2004).

[17]The United States, the EU, Japan, and Canada used to be called the "quad," and led the past multilateral trade rounds back then.

[18]This does not mean that all of past WTO accessions and IFI policy-based lending were successful. IFIs' experiences show that successful reform programs require strong country ownership (IMF, 2002; Johnson & Wasty, 1993; World Bank, 2001), as initially pointed out by Gustav Ranis (1995) in his "On Fast-Disbursing Policy-Based Loans" prepared for the US and Multilateral Development Bank Task force. The observation on primacy of country ownership may be valid also for the WTO accession process. For instance, among RAMs observed in this research, Ecuador was less willing to reform at the time of WTO membership negotiations and did not achieve a high degree of trade liberalization through accession (Chapter 6). Sally (2008) emphasized importance of the country ownership for trade policy reforms ("liberalism from below"), rather than external pressures by international organizations ("liberalism from above"), based on his observations of East Asian experiences.

unilateral economic policy of each country, before the results are discussed multilaterally by the entire membership. However, given the limited purpose of just enhancing transparency, the content of the TPRM staff report tends to be only descriptive, with few prescriptive elements (if any), and the findings do not appear to be used actively for follow-up reforms by the country under review through the WTO. In contrast, the IMF's Article IV consultation mission occasionally acts also as the review mission for the lending program, and the findings feed into the design of the reform package. A similar approach of effective utilization of the existing policy surveillance scheme could possibly be adopted in the WTO, within its unique constraints.

Another potential approach outside of the WTO but still within the multilateral system[19] of global economic governance would be to reactivate use of IFIs' policy-based lending to address trade policy reforms. Until the 1990s, trade liberalization was strongly featured in structural adjustment programs of the IMF and the World Bank, but use of trade-related conditionality by these institutions has been substantially reduced by now.[20] One of the reasons was launch of the DDA at the WTO in 2001, that was then expected to carry over the task of supporting developing countries' trade liberalization. Given the DDA's long stalemate, other multilateral institutions could bridge the gap at least temporarily and mainstream trade policy reform back into their operations again, ideally in close partnership with the WTO.

References

Bagwell, K., & Staiger, R. W. (1999). An economic theory of GATT. *American Economic Review, 89*(1), 215–248.

Bagwell, K., & Staiger, R. W. (2002). *The economics of the world trading system.* Cambridge: MIT Press.

[19]Outside of the multilateral systems, another possible approach to catalyze non-discriminatory trade liberalization would be for countries that already concluded preferential trade agreements to extend their preferential tariff rates unilaterally to non-members of the agreements on the MFN basis. See Menon (2014). In practice, this would mean that countries that formed preferential trade agreements would still observe GATT Article I on MFN without resorting to MFN exceptions under GATT Article XXIV on customs unions and free-trade areas.

[20]See Independent Evaluation Office of the IMF (2005a, 2005b, 2009), and World Bank Independent Evaluation Group (2006).

Baldwin, R. E. (1995). A domino theory of regionalism. In R. Baldwin, P. Haaparanta, & J. Kiander (Eds.), *Expanding membership of the European Union* (pp. 25–48). Cambridge: Cambridge University Press.

Baldwin, R. E. (2006). Multilateralising regionalism: Spaghetti bowls as building blocs on the path to global free trade. *The World Economy, 29*(11), 1451–1518.

Baldwin, R. E. (2012). Preferential trading arrangements. In A. Narlikar, M. Daunton, & R. M. Stern (Eds.), *The Oxford handbook on the World Trade Organization* (pp. 632–654). Oxford: Oxford University Press.

Finger, J. M., & Winters, L. A. (1998). What can the WTO do for developing countries? In A. O. Kruger (Ed.), *The WTO as an international organization* (pp. 365–392). Chicago: University of Chicago Press.

Hoekman, B., & Winters, L. A. (2002). A tribute to J. Michael Finger. In B. Hoekman, A. Mattoo, & P. English (Eds.), *Development, trade, and the WTO: A handbook* (pp. xiii–xvii). Washington, DC: World Bank.

International Monetary Fund. (2002). *Guidelines on conditionality.* Washington, DC: Author.

International Monetary Fund. (2005a). *Review of fund work on trade.* Washington, DC: Author.

International Monetary Fund. (2005b). *Trade conditionality under fund-supported programs, 1990–2004 (background paper to the review of fund work on trade).* Washington, DC: Author.

International Monetary Fund. (2009). *International financial statistics year book 2009.* Washington, DC: Author.

Johnson, J. H., & Wasty, S. S. (1993). *Borrower ownership of adjustment programs and the political economy of reform* (World Bank Discussion Papers No. 199). Washington, DC: World Bank.

Krugman, P. (1991, November/December). The move toward free trade zones. *Economic Review—Federal Reserve Bank of Kansas City, 76*(6), 5–25.

Laird, S. (1998). *Multilateral approaches to market access negotiations* (Trade Policy Review Division Staff Working Paper TPRD-98-02). Retrieved from World Trade Organization website: http://www.wto.org/english/res_e/reser_e/tp9802_e.htm.

Maggi, G., & Rodríguez-Clare, A. (1998). The value of trade agreements in the presence of political pressures. *Journal of Political Economy, 106*(3), 574–601.

Maggi, G., & Rodríguez-Clare, A. (2007). A political-economy theory of trade agreements. *American Economic Review, 97*(4), 1374–1406.

Mann, C., & Liu, X. (2009). The information technology agreement: sui generis or model stepping stone? In R. Baldwin & P. Low (Eds.), *Multilateralizing regionalism: Challenges for the global trading system* (pp. 182–216). Geneva: WTO.

Martin, W., & Ng, F. (2004). *A note on sources of tariff reductions in developing countries 1983-2003*. Unpublished manuscript.

McGuire, S. (2012). What happened to the influence of business? Corporations and organized labour in the WTO. In A. Narlikar, M. Daunton, & R. M. Stern (Eds.), *The Oxford handbook on the World Trade Organization* (pp. 320–339). Oxford: Oxford University Press.

Menon, J. (2014). Multilateralisation of preferences versus reciprocity when FTAs are underutilized. *The World Economy, 37*(10), 1348–1366.

Narlikar, A. (2009). Reforming the multilateral trading system—Lessons of the Doha negotiations. In F. Trentmann (Ed.), *Is free trade fair trade? New perspectives on the world trading system* (pp. 47–57). London: Smith Institute.

Ranis, G. (1995). *On fast-disbursing policy-based loans*. Unpublished manuscript.

Rose, A. K. (2005). Which international institutions promote international trade? *Review of International Economics, 13*(4), 682–698.

Sally, R. (2008). *Trade policy, new century: The WTO, FTAs and Asia rising*. London: Institute of Economic Affairs.

Staiger, R. W., & Tabellini, G. (1987). Discretionary trade policy and excessive protection. *American Economic Review, 77*(5), 823–837.

Subramanian, A., & Wei, S. (2007, May). The WTO promotes trade, strongly but unevenly. *Journal of International Economics*, 72(1), 151–175.

Wei, S., & Zhang, Z. (2010). Do external interventions work? The case of trade reform conditions in IMF supported programs. *Journal of Development Economics, 92*, 71–81.

Woolcock, S. (2013). *Getting past the WTO deadlock: The plurilateral option?* (RSCAS Policy Paper No. RSCAS PP 2013/08). San Domenico di Fiesole (FI): European University Institute.

World Bank. (2001). *Adjustment lending retrospective: Final report*. Washington, DC: Author.

World Bank. (2005). *Global economic prospects 2005: Trade, regionalism, and development*. Washington, DC: Author.

World Bank Independent Evaluation Group. (2006). *Assessing World Bank support for trade, 1987–2004: An IEG evaluation*. Washington, DC: World Bank.

World Trade Organization. (2012). *15 years of the information technology agreement: Trade, innovation and global production networks*. Geneva: Author.

Appendix

K. Takamiya, *Recently Acceded Members of the World Trade Organization*, https://doi.org/10.1007/978-981-13-9159-0

Procedures of Accession to the World Trade Organization

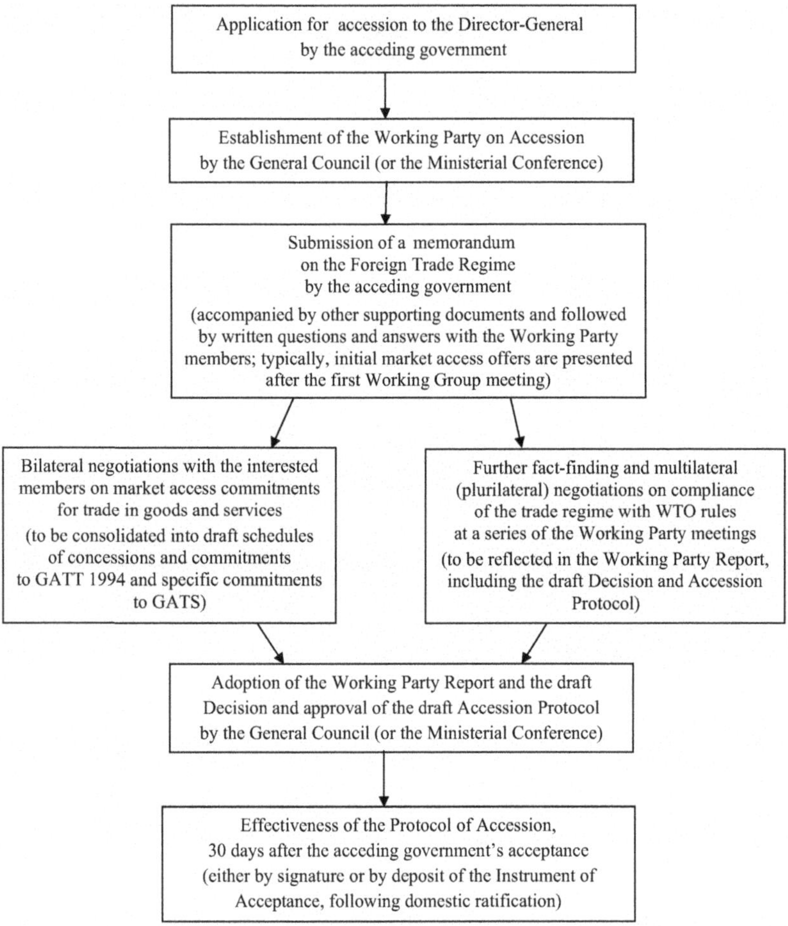

GATT = General Agreement on Tariffs and Trade; GATS = General Agreement on Trade in Services; WTO = World Trade Organization

Source WTO (1995c, 2010a, 2014c), P. J. Williams (2008)

Bibliography

Abass, A. (2004). The Cotonou trade regime and WTO law. *European Law Journal, 10*(4), 439–462.

Adlung, R., & Roy, M. (2005a). *Turning hills into mountains? Current commitments under the GATS and prospects for change* (Staff Working Paper ERSD-2005-01). Retrieved from WTO website: http://www.wto.org/english/res_e/reser_e/ersd200501_e.htm.

Adlung, R., & Roy, M. (2005b). Turning hills into mountains? Current commitments under the general agreement on trade in services and prospects for change. *Journal of World Trade, 39*(6), 1161–1194.

All Change: China's Economy and the WTO. (2011, December 10). *The Economist, 401*(8763), 45–46.

Allee, T. L., & Scalera, J. E. (2012). The divergent effects of joining international organizations: Trade gains and the rigors of WTO accession. *International Organization, 66*(2), 243–276.

Anderson, K. (1999). *Vietnam's transforming economy and WTO accession.* Singapore: Institute of Southeast Asian Studies.

Anderson, K. (2002). Peculiarities of retaliation in WTO dispute settlement. *World Trade Review, 1*(2), 123–134.

Anderson, K., Huang, J., & Ianchovichina, E. (2004a). Will China's WTO accession worsen farm household incomes? *China Economic Review, 15,* 443–456.

Anderson, K., Huang, J., & Ianchovichina, E. (2004b). The impact of WTO accession on Chinese agriculture and rural poverty. In D. Bhattasali, S. Li, & W. Martin (Eds.), *China and the WTO: Accession, policy reform, and poverty reduction strategies* (pp. 101–116). Washington, DC: World Bank.

K. Takamiya, *Recently Acceded Members of the World Trade Organization*, https://doi.org/10.1007/978-981-13-9159-0

Asian Development Bank. (2013). *Key indicators for Asia and the Pacific 2013* (44th ed.). Manila: Author.

Auffret, P. (2003). *Trade reform in Viet Nam: Opportunities with emerging challenges*. Washington, DC: World Bank.

Bacchetta, M., & Drabek, Z. (2002). *Effects of WTO accession on policy-making in sovereign states: preliminary lessons from the recent experience of transition countries* (Development and Economic Research Division Staff Working Paper DERD-2002-02). Retrieved from World Trade Organization website: http://www.wto.org/english/res_e/reser_e/derd200202_e.htm.

Bagwell, K., & Staiger, R. W. (1999). An economic theory of GATT. *American Economic Review, 89*(1), 215–248.

Bagwell, K., & Staiger, R. W. (2002). *The economics of the world trading system*. Cambridge: MIT Press.

Bagwell, K., & Staiger, R. W. (2011). What do trade negotiators negotiate about? Empirical evidence from the World Trade Organization. *American Economic Review, 101*(4), 1238–1273.

Baldwin, R. E. (1994). *Toward an integrated Europe*. London: Centre for Economic Policy Research.

Baldwin, R. E. (1995). A domino theory of regionalism. In R. Baldwin, P. Haaparanta, & J. Kiander (Eds.), *Expanding membership of the European Union* (pp. 25–48). Cambridge: Cambridge University Press.

Baldwin, R. E. (2006). Multilateralising regionalism: Spaghetti bowls as building blocs on the path to global free trade. *The World Economy, 29*(11), 1451–1518.

Baldwin, R. E. (2012a). Preferential trading arrangements. In A. Narlikar, M. Daunton, & R. M. Stern (Eds.), *The Oxford handbook on the World Trade Organization* (pp. 632–654). Oxford: Oxford University Press.

Baldwin, R. E. (2012b). The case for a multilateral trade organization. In A. Narlikar, M. Daunton, & R. M. Stern (Eds.), *The Oxford handbook on the World Trade Organization* (pp. 29–39). Oxford: Oxford University Press.

Baldwin, R. E. (2014). WTO 2.0: Governance of 21st century trade. *Review of International Organizations, 9*(2), 261–283.

Basra, H. (2012). Increased legalization or politicization? A comparison of accession under the GATT and WTO. *Journal of World Trade, 46*(4), 937–960.

Beruchashvili, T. (2001). *Accession to the World Trade Organization: The case of Georgia*. Retrieved from United Nations Economic and Social Commission for Asia and Pacific website: http://www.unescap.org/oes/speca/docs/Divisions/TID/Accession_to_WTO-Tashkent/Georgia finalpaper.pdf.

Beseler, H. F. (2002). The EU-China negotiations: Breaking the deadlock. In H. Holbig & R. Ash (Eds.), *China's accession to the World Trade Organization: National and international perspectives* (pp. 3–13). London: RoutledgeCurzon.

Bhagwati, J. (2002a). *Free trade today*. Princeton: Princeton University Press.

Bhagwati, J. (2002b). Introduction: The unilateral freeing of trade versus reciprocity. In J. Bhagwati (Ed.), *Going alone: The case for relaxed reciprocity in freeing trade* (pp. 1–30). Cambridge: MIT Press.

Bhagwati, J. (2008). *Termites in the trading system: How preferential arrangements undermine free trade*. Oxford: Oxford University Press.

Bhagwati, J., & Sutherland, P. (Co-chairs). (2011). *The Doha round: Setting a deadline, defining a final deal—Interim report*. Retrieved from the Graduate Institute Geneva website: http://graduateinstitute.ch/files/live/sites/iheid/files/sites/ctei/shared/CTEI/Baldwin/Publications/Chapters/Regionalism/The_Doha_round_Setting_a_deadline,defining_a_final_deal.pdf.

Bhattasali, D., Li, S., & Martin, W. (2004). Impacts and policy implications of WTO accession for China. In D. Bhattasali, S. Li, & W. Martin (Eds.), *China and the WTO: Accession, policy reform, and poverty reduction strategies* (pp. 1–17). Washington, DC: World Bank.

Braga, C. A. P., & Cattaneo, O. (2009a). Introduction. In C. A. P. Braga & O. Cattaneo (Eds.), *The WTO and accession countries* (Vol. 1, pp. xi–xlvii). Cheltenham: Edward Elgar.

Braga, C. A. P., & Cattaneo, O. (2009b). *Everything you always wanted to know about WTO accession (But were afraid to ask)* (Policy Research Working Paper, WPS5156). Retrieved from World Bank website: http://www-wds.worldbank.org/external/default/WDSContentServer/WDSP/IB/2009/11/05/000158349_20091105161912/Rendered/PDF/WPS5116.pdf.

Broda, C., Limão, N., & Weinstein, D. (2006). *Optimal tariffs: The evidence* (Working Paper No. 12033). Retrieved from National Bureau of Economic Research website: http://www.nber.org/papers/w12033.

Brookings Institution. (2011). *From popular revolution to effective reforms: The Georgia experience*. Retrieved from Brookings website: http://www.brookings.edu/~/media/events/2011/3/17%20saakashvili/20110317_saakashvili_transcript.pdf.

Business Association of Georgia. (2013). *Georgia's long-term economic development concept*. Tbilisi: Author.

Cañizares, C. P. (1995). el ingreso del ecuador a la organización mundial de comercio [Entry of Ecuador to the World Trade Organization]. *AFESE, 25*. Retrieved from the AFESE website: http://www.afese.com/img/revistas/revista40/artCristianEspinoza.pdf.

Central Institute for Economic Management. (2010). *Impacts of international economic integration on Vietnam's economy after three years of WTO membership*. Hanoi: Author.

Central Institute for Economic Management. (2013). *Đánh giá tổng thể tình hình kinh tế - xã hội Việt Nam sau 5 năm gia nhập tổ chức Thương mại Thế giới* [Assessing the overall economic situation—Vietnamese society after 5 years of joining WTO]. Hanoi: Financial Publisher.

Charnovitz, S. (2008). Mapping the law of WTO accession. In M. E. Janow, V. Donaldson, & A. Yanovich (Eds.), *The WTO: Governance, dispute settlement, and developing countries* (pp. 855–920). Huntington: Juris.

China and the WTO: Long March. (1999, April 1). *The Economist.* Retrieved from: http://www.economist.com/node/320544/print.

Chuanshui, Z., & Yang, Y. (2000). China's textile and clothing exports in the post Uruguay round. In P. Drysdale & L. Song (Eds.), *China's entry to the WTO: Strategic issues and quantitative assessments* (pp. 175–193). London: Routledge.

Cong, D. T. (2010). Catfish, shrimp, and the WTO: Vietnam loses its innocence. *Vanderbilt Journal of Transnational Law, 43*(5), 1235–1264.

Cooper, W. H. (2012). *The Jackson-Vanik amendment and candidate countries for WTO accession: Issues for congress.* Washington, DC: Congressional Research Service.

Davis, C. L. (2006). Do WTO rules create a level playing field? Lessons from the experience of Peru and Vietnam. In J. S. Odell (Ed.), *Negotiating trade: Developing countries in the WTO and NAFTA* (pp. 219–256). Cambridge: Cambridge University Press.

Dickson, I. (2003). China's interest in the World Trade Organization's deregulation in international textiles trade. In D. Z. Cass, B. G. Williams, & G. Barker (Eds.), *China and the world trading system: Entering the new millennium* (pp. 175–201). Cambridge: Cambridge University Press.

Drabek, Z., & Bacchetta, M. (2004). Tracing the effects of WTO accession on policy-making in sovereign states: Preliminary lessons from the recent experience of transition countries. *World Economy, 27*(7), 1083–1125.

Drabek, Z., & Woo, W. T. (2010). Who should join the WTO and why? A cost-benefit analysis of WTO membership. In Z. Drabek (Ed.), *Is the World Trade Organization attractive enough for emerging economies? Critical essays on the multilateral trading system* (pp. 249–294). Basingstoke: Palgrave Macmillan.

Egger, P., & Larch, M. (2008). Interdependent preferential trade agreement memberships: An empirical analysis. *Journal of International Economics, 76,* 384–399.

Elsig, M. (2010). The World Trade Organization at work: Performance in a member-driven milieu. *The Review of International Organizations, 5*(3), 345–363.

Elsig, M. (2011). Principal-agent theory and the World Trade Organization: Complex agency and 'missing delegation'. *European Journal of International Relations, 17*(3), 495–517.

Eschenbach, F., & Hoekman, B. (2006). Services policies in transition economies: On the EU and WTO as commitment mechanism. *World Trade Review, 5*(3), 415–443.

Ethier, W. J. (2004). Political externalities, nondiscrimination, and a multilateral world. *Review of International Economics, 12*(3), 303–320.

Ethier, W. J. (2007). The theory of trade policy and trade agreements: A critique. *European Journal of Political Economy, 23*, 605–623.

European Communities. (1991, October 12). Notice of initiation of anti-dumping proceeding concerning imports of bicycles originating in Taiwan and the People's Republic of China (91C 266/07). *The Official Journal of the European Communities* (No. C 266/6-No. C 266/7).

European Communities. (2000, July 14). Council regulation (EC) No. 1524/2000 of 10 July 2000 imposing a definitive anti-dumping duty on imports of bicycles originating in the People's Republic of China. *The Official Journal of the European Communities* (L175/39-L175/52).

European Union. (2005, July 14). Council regulation (EC) No. 1095/2005 of 12 July 2005, imposing a definitive anti-dumping duty on imports of bicycles originating in Vietnam, and amending regulation (EC) No. 1524/2000 imposing a definitive anti-dumping duty on imports of bicycles originating in the People's Republic of China. *The Official Journal of the European Union* (L183/1-L183/36).

European Union. (2006, October 6). Council regulation (EC) No. 1472/2006 of 5 October 2006, imposing a definitive anti-dumping duty and collecting the provisional duty imposed on imports of certain footwear with uppers of leather originating in the People's Republic of China and Vietnam. *The Official Journal of the European Union* (L275/1-L275/41).

Evenett, S. J., & Braga, C. A. P. (2005). WTO accession: Lessons from experience (Trade Note 22, June 6). Retrieved from World Bank website: http://www-wds.worldbank.org/external/default/WDSContentServer/WDSP/IB/2005/07/28/000160016_20050728140916/Rendered/PDF/331270TradeNote22.pdf.

Evenett, S. J., & Braga, C. A. P. (2006). WTO accession: Moving the goalposts? In R. Newfarmer (Ed.), *Trade, Doha, and development: A window into the issues* (pp. 231–243). Washington, DC: World Bank.

Evenett, S. J., & Gage, J. (2005). Evaluating WTO accessions: The effect of WTO accession on national trade flows. In M. Kennett, S. J. Evenett, & J. Gage (Eds.), *Evaluating WTO accessions: Legal and economic perspectives* (pp. 194–220). Retrieved from World Bank website: http://siteresources.worldbank.org/INTRANETTRADE/Resources/WBI-Training/EvaluatingWTOAccessions_partI.pdf.

Felbermayr, G., & Kohler, W. (2010). Does WTO membership make a difference at the extensive margin of world trade? In Z. Drabek (Ed.), *Is the World Trade Organization attractive enough for emerging economies? Critical essays on the multilateral trading system* (pp. 217–248). Basingstoke: Palgrave Macmillan.

Feng, H. (2006). *The politics of China's accession to the World Trade Organization: The dragon goes global.* London: Routledge.
Ferrantino, M. J. (2010). Policy anchors: Do free trade agreements and WTO accessions serve as vehicles for developing-country policy reform? In Z. Drabek (Ed.), *Is the World Trade Organization attractive enough for emerging economies? Critical essays on the multilateral trading system* (pp. 91–138). Basingstoke: Palgrave Macmillan.
Finger, J. M., & Winters, L. A. (1998). What can the WTO do for developing countries? In A. O. Kruger (Ed.), *The WTO as an international organization* (pp. 365–392). Chicago: University of Chicago Press.
Food and Agriculture Organization of the United Nations. (2011). *Banana Statistics 2011.* Rome: Author.
Francois, F. F., & Martin, W. (2002). Binding tariffs: Why do it? In B. Hoekman, A. Mattoo, & P. English (Eds.), *Development, trade, and the WTO: A handbook* (pp. 538–547). Washington, DC: World Bank.
Francois, J. F., & Spinanger, D. (2004). WTO accession and the structure of China's motor vehicle sector. In D. Bhattasali, S. Li, & W. Martin (Eds.), *China and the WTO: Accession, policy reform, and poverty reduction strategies* (pp. 191–210). Washington, DC: World Bank.
Fugazza, M., & Robert-Nicoud, F. (2010). *The 'emulator effect' of the Uruguay round on US regionalism* (CEP Discussion Paper No. 973). Retrieved from Centre for Economic Performance website: http://cep.lse.ac.uk/pubs/download/dp0973.pdf.
Gadbaw, M. (1998). WTO accession: A private sector view. In F. M. Abbott (Ed.), *China in the world trading system: Defining the principles of engagement* (pp. 81–86). Cambridge, MA: Kluwer Law International.
General Agreement on Tariffs and Trade. (1984). *China—Request for observer status* (L/5712). Geneva: Author.
General Agreement on Tariffs and Trade. (1986). *China's status as a contracting party: Communication from the People's Republic of China* (L/6017). Geneva: Author.
General Agreement on Tariffs and Trade. (1987). *China's status as a contracting party: Memorandum on China's foreign trade regime* (L/6125). Geneva: Author.
General Agreement on Tariffs and Trade. (1988a). *Contracting parties, forty-fourth session: China—Statement by Qian Jiadong, ambassador, permanent representative (speaking as an observer)* (SR.44/ST/28). Geneva: Author.
General Agreement on Tariffs and Trade. (1988b). *Working party on China's status as a contracting party: Communication from China* (Spec(88)37). Geneva: Author.
General Agreement on Tariffs and Trade. (1991). *Contracting parties, forty-seventh session: China—Statement by H.E. Mr. Fan Guoxiang, ambassador and*

permanent representative (speaking as an observer) (SR. 47/ST/6). Geneva: Author.

General Agreement on Tariffs and Trade. (1993a). *Accession of Ecuador: Memorandum of the foreign trade regime* (L/7202). Geneva: Author.

General Agreement on Tariffs and Trade. (1993b). *EEC—Member states' import regime for Bananas: Report of the panel* (DS/32/R). Geneva: Author.

General Agreement on Tariffs and Trade. (1994a). *EEC—Import regime for bananas: Report of the panel* (DS/38/R). Geneva: Author.

General Agreement on Tariffs and Trade. (1994b). *The fourth ACP-EEC convention of Lomé: Decision of 9 December 1994* (L/7604). Geneva: Author.

General Agreement on Tariffs and Trade. (1994c). *Contracting parties, forty-ninth session: China—Statement by Yufeng Tang, Minister-Counsellor, Deputy Permanent Representative (speaking as an observer)* (SR.49/ST/18). Geneva: Author.

General Agreement on Tariffs and Trade. (1994d). *Contracting parties, fiftieth session: China—Statement by Mr. Long Yongtu, Assistant Minister, Ministry of Foreign Trade and Economic Cooperation (speaking as an observer)* (SR.50/ST/19). Geneva: Author.

General Agreement on Tariffs and Trade. (1994e). *Multilateral trade negotiations, the Uruguay round, trade negotiations committee, Meeting at ministerial level, Marrakesh (Morocco), 12–15 April 1994: China—Statement by Gu Yongjiang, Vice-Minister for Foreign Trade and Economic Cooperation* (MTN.TNC/MIN(94)/ST/45). Geneva: Author.

Georgia's Election: The End of Saakashvili's Reign. (2013a, November 2). *The Economist, 409*(8860), 56.

Gerhart, P. M. (2003). The two constitutional visions of the world trade organization. *University of Pennsylvania Journal of International Economic Law, 24*(1), 1–75.

Gertler, J. L. (1998). The process of China's accession to the World Trade Organization. In F. M. Abbott (Ed.), *China in the world trading system: Defining the principles of engagement* (pp. 65–74). Cambridge, MA: Kluwer Law International.

Gertler, J. L. (2002). Negotiating China's protocol of accession. In S. Ostry, A. S. Alexandroff, & R. Gomez (Eds.), *China and the long march to global trade: The accession of China to the World Trade Organization* (pp. 22–29). London: Routledge.

Gertler, J. L. (2003). China's WTO accession—The final countdown. In D. Z. Cass, B. G. Williams, & G. Barker (Eds.), *China and the world trading system: Entering the new millennium* (pp. 55–67). Cambridge: Cambridge University Press.

Gertler, J. L. (2004). What China's WTO accession is all about. In D. Bhattasali, S. Li, & W. Martin (Eds.), *China and the WTO: Accession, policy reform, and poverty reduction strategies* (pp. 21–28). Washington, DC: World Bank.

Godoy, S., & Stiglitz, J. E. (2006). *Growth, initial conditions, law and speed of privatization in transition countries: 11 years later* (Working Paper No. 11992). Retrieved from National Bureau of Economic Research website: http://www.nber.org/papers/w11992.

Goldstein, J. (1998). International institutions and domestic politics: GATT, WTO, and the liberalization of international trade. In A. O. Kruger (Ed.), *The WTO as an international organization* (pp. 133–152). Chicago: University of Chicago Press.

Goldstein, J. (2012). Trade liberalization and domestic politics. In A. Narlikar, M. Daunton, & R. M. Stern (Eds.), *The Oxford handbook on the World Trade Organization* (pp. 64–82). Oxford: Oxford University Press.

Green, S. (2004). *China's quest for market economy status* (Chatham House Briefing Note). Retrieved from Royal Institute of International Affairs website: https://www.chathamhouse.org/sites/files/chathamhouse/public/Research/Asia/bnmay04.pdf.

Grossman, G. M., & Helpman, E. (1994). Protection for sale. *The American Economic Review, 84*(4), 833–850.

Gruber, L. (2001). Power politics and the free trade bandwagon. *Comparative Political Studies, 34*(7), 703–741.

Grynbeg, R., Dugal, M., & Razzaque, M. A. (2006). *An evaluation of the terms of accession to the World Trade Organization: A comparative assessment of services and goods sector commitments by WTO members and acceding countries.* London: Commonwealth Secretariat.

Guth, E. (2012). The end of the banana saga. *Journal of World Trade, 46*(1), 1–31.

Hanh, P. T. H. (2011). Does WTO accession matter for the dynamics of foreign direct investment and trade? Vietnam's experience. *Economics of Transition, 19*(2), 255–285.

Hawkins, D. G., Lake, D. A., Nielson, D. L., & Tierney, M. J. (2006). Delegation under anarchy: States, international organizations, and principal-agent theory. In D. G. Hawkins, D. A. Lake, D. L. Nielson, & M. J. Tierney (Eds.), *Delegation and agency in international organizations* (pp. 3–38). Cambridge: Cambridge University Press.

Hoekman, B., & Roy, J. (2000). Benefiting from WTO accession and membership. In B. Hoekman & J. Zarrouk (Eds.), *Catching up with the competition: Trade opportunities and challenges for Arab countries* (pp. 307–324). Ann Arbor: University of Michigan Press.

Hoekman, B., & Winters, L. A. (2002). A tribute to J. Michael Finger. In B. Hoekman, A. Mattoo, & P. English (Eds.), *Development, trade, and the WTO: A handbook* (pp. xiii–xvii). Washington, DC: World Bank.

Hoekman, B. M., & Kostecki, M. M. (2009). *The political economy of the world trading system: The WTO and beyond* (2nd ed.). Oxford: Oxford University Press.

Huang, C. (2009). Bilateralism and multilateralism: Taiwan's trade liberalization trajectory. *The Hague Journal of Diplomacy, 4*, 37–59.

Huerta, C. M. (2010). *Ecuador y el caso del banano* [Ecuador and the banana disputes]. *AFESE, 57*, 133–149.

Ianchovichina, E., & Martin, W. (2001, December). Trade liberalization in China's accession to WTO. *Journal of Economic Integration, 16*(4), 421–445.

Ianchovichina, E., & Martin, W. (2004). Economic impacts of China's accession to the WTO. In D. Bhattasali, S. Li, & W. Martin (Eds.), *China and the WTO: Accession, policy reform, and poverty reduction strategies* (pp. 211–236). Washington, DC: World Bank.

Independent Evaluation Office of the International Monetary Fund. (2009). *Evaluation report: IMF involvement in international trade policy issue.* Washington, DC: International Monetary Fund.

International Finance Corporation, Ministry of Planning and Investment, & World Bank. (2006, December 13). *Vietnam business forum: Vietnam consultative group meeting 2006.* Hanoi: Vietnam Business Forum Secretariat.

International Monetary Fund. (1997). *Georgia: Enhanced structural adjustment facility policy framework paper, 1997–1999.* Retrieved from IMF website: http://www.imf.org/external/np/pfp/georgia/geor-01.htm.

International Monetary Fund. (1998a). *Georgia: Recent economic developments and selected issues* (IMF Staff Country Report No. 98/99). Washington, DC: Author.

International Monetary Fund. (1998b). *Vietnam: Selected issues and statistical annex* (IMF Staff Country Report No. 98/30). Washington, DC: Author.

International Monetary Fund. (2000). *Ecuador: Selected issues and statistical annex* (IMF Staff Country Report No. 00/125). Washington, DC: Author.

International Monetary Fund. (2002). *Guidelines on conditionality.* Washington, DC: Author.

International Monetary Fund. (2003a). *Direction of trade statistics yearbook 2003.* Washington, DC: Author.

International Monetary Fund. (2003b). *Georgia: 2003 article IV consultation—Staff report; staff statement; and public information notice on the executive board discussion annex* (IMF Staff Country Report No. 03/346). Washington, DC: Author.

International Monetary Fund. (2003c). *Ecuador: Selected issues and statistical appendix annex* (IMF Staff Country Report No. 03/91). Washington, DC: Author.

International Monetary Fund. (2004a). *World economic outlook (September): The global demographic transition*. Washington, DC: Author.

International Monetary Fund. (2004b). *Georgia: Ex post assessment of Georgia's performance under fund-supported programs—Staff report; staff supplement; public information notice on the executive board discussion; and statement by the executive director for Georgia* (IMF Staff Country Report No. 04/26). Washington, DC: Author.

International Monetary Fund. (2004c). *Georgia: Request for three-year arrangement under poverty reduction and growth facility—Staff report; staff supplement; press release on the executive board discussion; and statement by the executive director for Georgia* (IMF Staff Country Report No. 04/165). Washington, DC: Author.

International Monetary Fund. (2005a). *Review of fund work on trade*. Washington, DC: Author.

International Monetary Fund. (2005b). *Trade conditionality under fund-supported programs, 1990–2004 (background paper to the review of fund work on trade)*. Washington, DC: Author.

International Monetary Fund. (2006a). *Georgia: Poverty reduction strategy paper progress report* (IMF Staff Country Report No. 06/360). Washington, DC: Author.

International Monetary Fund. (2006b). *People's Republic of China: 2006 article IV consultation—Staff report; staff statement; and public information notice on the executive board discussion* (IMF Staff Country Report No. 06/394). Washington, DC: Author.

International Monetary Fund. (2007a). *Vietnam: 2007 article IV consultation—Staff report; staff supplement and statement; and public information notice on the executive board discussion; and statement by the executive director for Vietnam* (IMF Staff Country Report No. 07/387). Washington, DC: Author.

International Monetary Fund. (2007b). *Staff report on the multilateral consultation on global imbalances with China, the Euro area, Japan, Saudi Arabia, and the United States*. Washington, DC: Author.

International Monetary Fund. (2008). *International financial statistics year book 2008*. Washington, DC: Author.

International Monetary Fund. (2009). *International financial statistics year book 2009*. Washington, DC: Author.

International Monetary Fund. (2010a). *Direction of trade statistics yearbook 2010*. Washington, DC: Author.

International Monetary Fund. (2010b). *Vietnam: 2010 article IV consultation—Staff report and public information notice* (IMF Staff Country Report No. 10/281). Washington, DC: Author.

International Monetary Fund. (2011a). *Articles of the agreement of the International Monetary Fund (1944)*. Washington, DC: Author.

International Monetary Fund. (2011b). *World economic outlook (September): Slowing growth, rising risks*. Washington, DC: Author.

International Monetary Fund. (2011c). *People's Republic of China: 2011 article IV consultation* (IMF Country Report No. 11/192). Washington, DC: Author.

International Monetary Fund. (2012a). *Direction of trade statistics yearbook 2012*. Washington, DC: Author.

International Monetary Fund. (2012b). *People's Republic of China: 2012 article IV consultation* (IMF Country Report No. 12/195). Washington, DC: Author.

International Monetary Fund. (2013). *People's Republic of China: 2013 article IV consultation* (IMF Country Report No. 13/211). Washington, DC: Author.

International Monetary Fund. (2018a). *Viet Nam: 2018 article IV consultation* (IMF Country Report No. 18/215). Washington, DC: Author.

International Monetary Fund. (2018b). *World economic outlook (October): Challenges to steady growth*. Washington, DC: Author.

Jiang, L. (2005). The WTO dispute settlement mechanism and China's participation. In H. Gao & D. Lewis (Eds.), *China's participation in the WTO* (pp. 303–314). London: Cameron May.

Johnson, J. H., & Wasty, S. S. (1993). *Borrower ownership of adjustment programs and the political economy of reform* (World Bank Discussion Papers No. 199). Washington, DC: World Bank.

Jones, K. (2009). The political economy of WTO accession: The unfinished business of universal membership. *World Trade Review, 8*(2), 279–314.

Josling, T. (2003). Bananas and the WTO: Testing the new dispute settlement process. In T. E. Josling & T. G. Taylor (Eds.), *Banana wars: The anatomy of a trade dispute* (pp. 169–194). Oxford: CABI.

Josling, T. E., & Taylor, T. G. (Eds.). (2003). *Banana wars: The anatomy of a trade dispute*. Oxford: CABI.

Kavadze, A., Ukleba, M., & Katamadze, V. (2003). *Georgia's path to the multilateral trading system*. Tbilisi: Forma.

Keck, A., & Low, P. (2004). *Special and differential treatment in the WTO: Why, when and how?* (Economic Research and Statistics Division Working Paper ERSD-2004-03). Retrieved from World Trade Organization website: http://www.wto.org/english/res_e/reser_e/ersd200403_e.htm.

King, C. (2004). A rose among thorns: Georgia makes good. *Foreign Affairs, 83*(2), 13–18.

Koremenos, B., Lipson, C., & Snidal, D. (2004). The rational design of international institutions. In B. Koremenos, C. Lipson, & D. Snidal (Eds.), *The rational design of international institutions* (pp. 1–39). Cambridge: Cambridge University Press.

Koukhartchouk, O., & Maurel, M. (2003). *Accession to the WTO and EU enlargement: What potential from trade increase?* London: Centre for Economic Policy Research.

Krugman, P. (1991, November/December). The move toward free trade zones. *Economic Review—Federal Reserve Bank of Kansas City, 76*(6), 5–25.

Krugman, P. (1997). What should trade negotiators negotiate about? *Journal of Economic Literature, 35*(1), 113–120.

Krugman, P. R., & Obstfeld, M. (1997). *International economics: Theory and policy* (4th ed.). Reading, MA: Addison-Wesley.

Laborde, D., Martin, W., & Mensbrugghe, D. V. D. (2012). Implications of the Doha market access proposals for developing countries. *World Trade Review, 11*(1), 1–25.

Lacey, S. (2007). The view from the other side of the table: WTO accession from the perspective of WTO members. In J. Streatfeild & S. Lacey (Eds.), *New Reflections on International Trade* (pp. 75–98). London: Cameron May.

Laird, S. (1998). *Multilateral approaches to market access negotiations* (Trade Policy Review Division Staff Working Paper TPRD-98-02). Retrieved from World Trade Organization website: http://www.wto.org/english/res_e/reser_e/tp9802_e.htm.

Langhammer, R. J., & Lücke, M. (1999). WTO accession issues. *World Economy, 22*(6), 837–873.

Lanoszka, A. (2001). The World Trade Organization accession process: Negotiating participation in a globalizing economy. *Journal of World Trade, 35*(4), 575–602.

Lawrence, R. Z. (2006). *China and the multilateral trading system* (Working Paper No. 12759). National Bureau of Economic Research website: http://www.nber.org/papers/w12759.

Lawrence, R. Z. (2008). China and the multilateral trading system. In B. Eichengreen, Y. C. Park, & C. Wyplosz (Eds.), *China, Asia, and the new world economy* (pp. 145–167). Oxford: Oxford University Press.

Lim, C. L., & Wang, J. Y. (2010). China and the Doha development agenda. *Journal of World Trade, 44*(6), 1309–1331.

Lissovolik, B., & Lissovolik, Y. (2004). *Russia and the WTO: The "gravity" of outsider status* (Working Paper No. WP/04/159). Retrieved from the International Monetary Fund website: http://www.imf.org/external/pubs/ft/wp/2004/wp04159.pdf.

MacFarlane, S. N. (2004). Georgia's revolution and the region: Is it catching? *The World Today, 60*(2), 14–15.

Maggi, G., & Rodríguez-Clare, A. (1998). The value of trade agreements in the presence of political pressures. *Journal of Political Economy, 106*(3), 574–601.
Maggi, G., & Rodríguez-Clare, A. (2007). A political-economy theory of trade agreements. *American Economic Review, 97*(4), 1374–1406.
Mallon, G., & Whalley, J. (2004). *China's post accession WTO stance* (Working Paper No. 10649). Retrieved from National Bureau of Economic Research website: http://www.nber.org/papers/w10649.
Manger, M. S. (2009). *Investing in protection: The politics and proliferation of preferential trade agreements between north and south.* Cambridge: Cambridge University Press.
Mann, C., & Liu, X. (2009). The information technology agreement: sui generis or model stepping stone? In R. Baldwin & P. Low (Eds.), *Multilateralizing regionalism: Challenges for the global trading system* (pp. 182–216). Geneva: WTO.
Martin, M. F. (2012). *U.S.-Vietnam economic and trade relations: Issues for the 112th congress.* Washington, DC: Congressional Research Service.
Martin, W. (2003). Implication of reform and WTO accession for China's agricultural policies. In S. D. Rozelle & D. A. Summer (Eds.), *Agriculture trade and policy in China: Issues, analysis and implications* (pp. 1–27). Aldershot: Ashgate.
Martin, W. (2010). Development implications of WTO accession procedures. In Z. Drabek (Ed.), *Is the World Trade Organization attractive enough for emerging economies? Critical essays on the multilateral trading system* (pp. 13–36). Basingstoke: Palgrave Macmillan.
Martin, W., & Ng, F. (2004). *A note on sources of tariff reductions in developing countries 1983-2003.* Unpublished manuscript.
Mattoo, A. (2003). China's accession to the WTO: The services dimension. *Journal of International Economic Law, 6*(2), 299–339.
Mattoo, A. (2004). The services dimension of China's accession to the WTO. In D. Bhattasali, S. Li, & W. Martin (Eds.), *China and the WTO: Accession, policy reform, and poverty reduction strategies* (pp. 117–139). Washington, DC: World Bank.
McGinnis, J. O., & Movsesian, M. L. (2000). The world trade constitution. *Harvard Law Review, 114*(2), 511–605.
McGuire, S. (2012). What happened to the influence of business? Corporations and organized labour in the WTO. In A. Narlikar, M. Daunton, & R. M. Stern (Eds.), *The Oxford handbook on the World Trade Organization* (pp. 320–339). Oxford: Oxford University Press.
Menon, J. (2009). Managing success in Viet Nam: Macroeconomic consequences of large capital inflows with limited instruments. *ASEAN Economic Bulletin, 26*(1), 77–95.

Menon, J. (2014). Multilateralisation of preferences versus reciprocity when FTAs are underutilized. *The World Economy, 37*(10), 1348–1366.

Messerlin, P. A. (2004). China in the WTO: Antidumping and safeguards. In D. Bhattasali, S. Li, & W. Martin (Eds.), *China and the WTO: Accession, policy reform, and poverty reduction strategies* (pp. 29–47). Washington, DC: World Bank.

Michalopoulos, C. (1998). *WTO accession for countries in transition* (Policy Research Working Paper No. 1934). Retrieved from World Bank website: http://www-wds.worldbank.org/external/default/WDSContentServer/WDSP/IB/1998/06/01/000009265_3980702115733/Rendered/PDF/multi0page.pdf.

Michalopoulos, C. (2002). WTO accession. In B. M. Hoekman, A. Mattoo, & P. English (Eds.), *Development, trade, and the WTO: A handbook* (pp. 61–70). Washington, DC: World Bank.

Milner, H. V. (1988). *Resisting protectionism: Global industries and the politics of international trade*. Princeton: Princeton University Press.

Milner, H. V. (1997). *Interests, institutions and information: Domestic politics and international relations.* Princeton: Princeton University Press.

Milthorp, P. (2009). WTO accessions: The story so far. *The Hague Journal of Diplomacy, 4*, 103–112.

Ministry of Planning and Investment. (2003). *Foreign investment policy of Vietnam in the process of international economic integration.* Retrieved from World Bank website: http://siteresources.worldbank.org/INTRANETTRADE/Resources/WBI-Training/vietFIP_dat.pdf.

Narlikar, A. (2003). *International trade and developing countries: Bargaining coalitions in the GATT & WTO.* London: Routledge.

Narlikar, A. (2009). Reforming the multilateral trading system—Lessons of the Doha negotiations. In F. Trentmann (Ed.), *Is free trade fair trade? New perspectives on the world trading system* (pp. 47–57). London: Smith Institute.

Narlikar, A. (2011). Editorial: Small states in multilateral economic negotiations. *The Roundtable, 100*(413), 135–139.

Narlikar, A. (2012). Collective agency, systemic consequences: Bargaining coalitions in the WTO. In A. Narlikar, M. Daunton, & R. M. Stern (Eds.), *The Oxford handbook on the World Trade Organization* (pp. 184–209). Oxford: Oxford University Press.

National Secretariat of Planning and Development. (2013). *Good living national plan 2013–2017: A better world for everyone—Summarized version.* Quito: Author.

Ninh. (2013). Foreword. In D. M. Pham, D. Mishra, K. Cheong, J. Arnold, A. M. Trinh, H. T. N. Ngo, & H. T. P. Nguyen, *Trade facilitation, value creation, and competitiveness: Policy implications for Vietnam's economic growth—Summary report* (p. vii). Washington, DC: World Bank.

Odell, J. S. (2001). Case study methods in international political economy. *International Studies Perspectives, 2*(2), 161–176.

Odell, J. S. (2010). Negotiating from weakness in international trade relations. *Journal of World Trade, 44*(3), 545–566.

Office of the United States Trade Representative. (2006). *Trade facts—May 2006: U.S.-Viet Nam bilateral WTO accession agreement—Ensuring a level-playing field for U.S. textile and apparel industries.* Retrieved from U.S.-Vietnam Trade Council website: http://www.usvtc.org/trade/wto/coalition/URTR-VietnamTextileBenefits05Sep06.pdf.

Osakwe, C. (2011). Developing countries and GATT/WTO rules. *Minnesota Journal of International Law, 20*(2), 365–436.

Papava, V. (2006). The political economy of Georgia's Rose Revolution. *Orbis, 50*(4), 657–667.

Papava, V. (2009). The "rosy" mistakes of the IMF and the World Bank in Georgia. *Problems of Economic Transition, 52*(7), 44–55.

Papava, V., & Beridze, T. (1997). Industrial policy and trade regime in Georgia. *Eurasian Studies, 3*(4), 65–78.

Pelc, K. J. (2011). Why do some countries get better WTO accession terms than others? *International Organization, 65*(4), 639–672.

Petersmann, E.-U. (1986). Trade policy as a constitutional problem: On the 'domestic policy functions' of international trade rules. *Aussenwirtschaft, 41*, 405–439.

Pietras, J. (1998). The role of the WTO for economies in transition. In A. O. Kruger (Ed.), *The WTO as an international organization* (pp. 353–362). Chicago: University of Chicago Press.

Polouektov, A. (2002). Non-market economy issues in the WTO anti-dumping law and accession negotiations: Revival of a two-tier membership? *Journal of World Trade, 36*(1), 1–37.

Pomfret, R. (2010). Regional trading arrangements and WTO membership: Substitutes or complements? In Z. Drabek (Ed.), *Is the World Trade Organization attractive enough for emerging economies? Critical essays on the multilateral trading system* (pp. 176–195). Basingstoke: Palgrave Macmillan.

Pregelj, V. N. (2005a). *Normal-trade-relations (most-favored-nation) policy of the United States.* Washington, DC: Congressional Research Service.

Pregelj, V. N. (2005b). *The Jackson-Vanik amendment: A Survey.* Washington, DC: Congressional Research Service.

Putnam, R. D. (1988). Diplomacy and domestic politics: The logic of two-level games. *International Organization, 42*(3), 427–460.

Qin, J. Y. (2003). "WTO-plus" obligations and their implications for the World Trade Organization legal system: An appraisal of China accession protocol. *Journal of World Trade, 37*(3), 483–552.

Ranis, G. (1995). *On fast-disbursing policy-based loans.* Unpublished manuscript.

Regan, D. H. (2006). What are trade agreements for? Two conflicting stories told by economists, with a lesson for lawyers. *Journal of International Economic Law, 9*(4), 951–988.

Rhodes, S. A., & Jackson, J. H. (1999). United States law and China's WTO accession process. *Journal of International Economic Law, 2*(3), 497–510.

Rodríguez, F., & Rodrik, D. (2000). Trade policy and economic growth: A skeptic's guide to the cross-national evidence. *NBER Macroeconomics Annual, 15*, 261–325.

Rogowski, R. (2004). Commerce and coalitions: How trade affects domestic political alignments. In J. A. Frieden & D. A. Lake (Eds.), *International political economy: Perspectives on global power and wealth* (4th ed., pp. 318–326). London: Routledge. (Original work published 2000).

Rose, A. K. (2004a, March). Do we really know that the WTO increase trade? *American Economic Review, 94*(1), 98–114.

Rose, A. K. (2004b). Do WTO members have more liberal trade policy? *Journal of International Economics, 63*, 209–235.

Rose, A. K. (2005). Which international institutions promote international trade? *Review of International Economics, 13*(4), 682–698.

Rose, A. K. (2007). Do we really know that the WTO increases trade? Reply. *American Economic Review, 97*(5), 2019–2025.

Rose, A. K. (2010). The effect of membership in the GATT/WTO on trade: Where do we stand? In Z. Drabek (Ed.), *Is the World Trade Organization attractive enough for emerging economies? Critical essays on the multilateral trading system* (pp. 195–216). Basingstoke: Palgrave Macmillan.

Saakashvili, M. (2004, November 30). Fulfilling the promise of the rose revolution Georgia's progress. *The New York Times*. Retrieved from: http://www.nytimes.com/2004/11/30/opinion/30iht-edsaakash_ed3_.html.

Sales, M., & Jackson, J. H. (2000). Procedural overview of the WTO EC—Banana dispute. *Journal of International Economic Law, 3*(1), 145–166.

Sally, R. (2008). *Trade policy, new century: The WTO, FTAs and Asia rising*. London: Institute of Economic Affairs.

Sally, R. (2011). *Chinese trade policy after (almost) ten years in the WTO: A post-crisis stocktake* (ECIPE Occasional Paper No. 2/2011). Brussels: European Centre for International Political Economy.

Sam, P. V., & Thu, V. T. (2005). Preparation by Viet Nam's banking sector for WTO accession. In P. Gallagher, P. Low, & A. Stoler (Eds.), *Managing the challenges of WTO participation: 45 case studies* (pp. 621–633). Cambridge: Cambridge University Press.

Sapir, A. (2001). Domino effects in Western European regional trade, 1960–1992. *European Journal of Political Economy, 17*, 377–388.

Siphana, S. (2005). *Cambodia enters the WTO: Lessons learned for least-developed countries*. Retrieved from Asian Development Bank Institute website: http://

www.adbi.org/research-policy-brief/2005/10/11/1430.cambodia.wto.lessons/.

Smith, J. M. (2006). Compliance bargaining in the WTO: Ecuador and the banana dispute. In J. S. Odell (Ed.), *Negotiating trade: Developing countries in the WTO and NAFTA* (pp. 257–288). Cambridge: Cambridge University Press.

Smith, M. G. (1996). Accession to the WTO: Key strategic issues. In J. J. Scott (Ed.), *The world trading system: Challenges ahead* (pp. 167–181). Washington, DC: Institute for International Economics.

Snyder, F. (2001). The origins of the 'nonmarket economy': Ideas, pluralism and power in EC anti-dumping law about China. *European Law Journal, 7*(4), 369–424.

Special Report—World Economy: In My Backyard—Trade. (2013b, October 12). *The Economist, 409*(8857), 16.

Staiger, R. W., & Tabellini, G. (1987). Discretionary trade policy and excessive protection. *American Economic Review, 77*(5), 823–837.

Staiger, R. W., & Tabellini, G. (1999). Do GATT rules help governments make domestic commitments? *Economics and Politics, 11*(2), 109–144.

Startup, J. (2005). From catfish to shrimp: How Vietnam learned to navigate the waters of "free trade" as a non-market economy. *Iowa Law Review, 90*(5), 1963–1990.

Stolper, W., & Samuelson, P. (1941). Protection and real wages. *Review of Economic Studies, 9*(1), 58–73.

Stovall, J. G., & Hathaway, D. E. (2003). US interests and the banana trade controversy. In T. E. Josling & T. G. Taylor (Eds.), *Banana wars: The anatomy of a trade dispute* (pp. 151–167). Oxford: CABI.

Subramanian, A., & Watal, J. (2000). Can TRIPS serve as an enforcement device for developing countries in the WTO? *Journal of International Economic Law, 3*(3), 403–416.

Subramanian, A., & Wei, S. (2007, May). The WTO promotes trade, strongly but unevenly. *Journal of International Economics*, 72(1), 151–175.

Tang, M., & Wei, S. (2009). The value of making commitments externally: Evidence from WTO accessions. *Journal of International Economics, 78*, 216–229.

Tarr, D. (2007). *Russian WTO accession: What has been accomplished, what can be expected* (Policy Research Working Paper No. 4428). Retrieved from World Bank website: http://www-wds.worldbank.org/external/default/WDSContentServer/WDSP/IB/2007/12/04/000158349_20071204105142/Rendered/PDF/wps4428.pdf.

Thephavong, B., Iemsouthi, K., & Vilavong, B. (2005). Laos: The textile and garment industry in the post-ATC era. In P. Gallagher, P. Low, & A. L. Stoler

(Eds.), *Managing the challenges of WTO participation: 45 case studies* (pp. 316–325). Cambridge: Cambridge University Press.

Thinh, D. V. (2003). *Tariff reduction and NTB removal roadmap during WTO accession: A state-owned company.* Retrieved from World Bank website: http://siteresources.worldbank.org/INTRANETTRADE/Resources/WBI-Training/viet-tariffreduc_thinh.pdf.

Tomz, M., Goldstein, J. L., & Rivers, D. (2007). Do we really know that WTO increases trade? Comment. *American Economic Review, 97*(5), 2005–2018.

Tsogtbaatar, D. (2005). Mongolia's WTO accession: Expectations and realities of WTO membership. In P. Gallagher, P. Low, & A. L. Stoler (Eds.), *Managing the challenges of WTO participation: 45 case studies* (pp. 409–419). Cambridge: Cambridge University Press.

Tumbarello, P. (2005). *Regional trade integration and WTO accession: Which is the right sequencing? An application to the CIS* (Working Paper No. WP/05/94). Retrieved from International Monetary Fund website: http://www.imf.org/external/pubs/ft/wp/2005/wp0594.pdf.

Tumbarello, P. (2007a). *Are regional trade agreements in Asia stumbling or building blocks? Implications for the Mekong-3 countries* (Working Paper No. WP/07/53). Retrieved from International Monetary Fund website: http://www.imf.org/external/pubs/ft/wp/2007/wp0753.pdf.

Tumbarello, P. (2007b). Vietnam's WTO accession: Opportunities and challenges. In International Monetary Fund, *Viet Nam: Selected issues* (IMF Country Report No. 07/385). Washington, DC: International Monetary Fund.

Tyagi, M. (2012). Flesh on a legal fiction: Early practice in the WTO accession protocols. *Journal of International Economic Law, 15*(2), 391–441.

United Nations. (2001, July 25–27). Accession to the World Trade Organization: Issues and recommendations for Central Asian and Caucasian economies in transition. In *Proceedings and papers presented at the subregional workshop on accession to the World Trade Organization, economies in transition, Tashkent.* New York: United Nations.

United States Department of Commerce. (2003a). *Fact sheet: Final determination in the antidumping duty investigation of certain frozen fish fillets from Vietnam.* Retrieved from International Trade Administration website: http://www.ita.doc.gov/media/FactSheet/0603/catfish_final_061703.html.

United States Department of Commerce. (2003b). Notice of final antidumping duty determination of sales at less than fair value and affirmative critical circumstances: Certain frozen fish fillets from the Socialist Republic of Viet Nam. *Federal Register, 68*(120), 37116–37121. Retrieved from United States International Trade Commission website: http://www.usitc.gov/trade_remedy/731_ad_701_cvd/investigations/2002/frozen_fish_fillets_from_vietnam/final/PDF/fr_commerce_determination.pdf.

United States Department of Commerce. (2004). Final determination of sales at less than fair value: Certain frozen and canned warmwater shrimp from the Socialist Republic of Vietnam. *Federal Register, 69*(235), 71005–71010. Retrieved from International Trade Commission website: http://www.usitc.gov/trade_remedy/731_ad_701_cvd/investigations/2004/shrimp/final/PDF/fr_commerce_determination_vietnam.pdf.

United States General Accounting Office. (2002). *World Trade Organization: Selected U.S. company views about China's membership*. Washington, DC: Author.

United States International Trade Commission. (2003). *Certain frozen fish fillets from Vietnam* (Investigation No. 731-TA-1012 [Final]). Washington, DC: Author.

United States International Trade Commission. (2005). *Certain frozen or canned warmwater shrimp and pawns from Brazil, China, Equador, India, Thailand, and Vietnam* (Investigation Nos. 731-TA-1063-1068 [Final]). Washington, DC: Author.

U.S.-Vietnam Trade Council. (2006). *Vietnam WTO accession issues in brief: Textile safeguards*. Retrieved from the U.S.-Vietnam Trade Council website: http://www.usvtc.org/trade/other/textiles/TextileMemo04may06.pdf.

Van, D. N., Thanh, P. C., & Sa, L. K. (2005). Vietnam. In S. J. Evenett (Ed.), *Preparing for WTO accessions: Insights from developing countries*. Retrieved from World Bank website: http://siteresources.worldbank.org/INTRANETTRADE/Resources/WBI-Training/PreparingforWTOAccessions.pdf.

VanGrasstek, C. (2001). Why demands on acceding countries increase over time: A three-dimensional analysis of multilateral trade diplomacy. In United Nations Conference on Trade and Development, *WTO Accession and Development Policies* (UNCTAD/DITC/TNCD/11) (pp. 78–95). Retrieved from United Nations Conference on Trade and Development website: http://unctad.org/en/Docs/ditctncd11_en.pdf.

Vermulst, E., & Graafsma, F. (2006). Recent EC anti-dumping practice towards China and Vietnam: The great leap backward? *International Trade Law and Regulation, 12*(5), 124–129.

Vietnam and the United States: Case of the Ghostly Catfish. (2002, December 14). *The Economist, 365*(8303), 35.

Viet Nam and the WTO: Market Maker. (2006, 2 November). *The Economist, 381*(8502), 100.

Vietnam Association of Seafood Exporters and Producers. (2010). Viet Nam brings shrimp case against U.S. to WTO. *Vietfish International, 7*(2). Retrieved from: http://www.vietfish.org/20100420110657640p49c64t52/viet-nam-brings-shrimp-case-against-us-to-wto.htm.

Vietnam Association of Seafood Exporters and Producers. (2011). Despite shrimp dumping 'zeroing" victories at WTO, Vietnam sees continuing trade challenges. *VASEP News, 1*(28), 7. Retrieved from: http://www.vasep.com.vn/pic/VasepNew/swfEbook/VASEP_News_No-28_2011.swf.

Wei, S., & Zhang, Z. (2010). Do external interventions work? The case of trade reform conditions in IMF supported programs. *Journal of Development Economics, 92*, 71–81.

Whalley, J. (2006). China in the world trading system. *CESifo Economic Studies, 52*(2/206), 215–245.

Williamson, J. (1990). What Washington means by policy reform. In J. Williamson (Ed.), *Latin American adjustment: How much has happened?* (pp. 7–20). Washington, DC: Institute for International Economics.

Williams, P. J. (2008). *A handbook on accession to the WTO*. Cambridge: Cambridge University Press.

Woolcock, S. (2013). *Getting past the WTO deadlock: The plurilateral option?* (RSCAS Policy Paper No. RSCAS PP 2013/08). San Domenico di Fiesole (FI): European University Institute.

World Bank. (1987). *Ecuador: Country economic memorandum* (Report No. 6592-EC). Washington, DC: Author.

World Bank. (1999). *Russian trade policy reform for WTO accession* (World Bank Discussion Paper No. 401). Washington, DC: Author.

World Bank. (2001). *Adjustment lending retrospective: Final report*. Washington, DC: Author.

World Bank. (2003). *Georgia: An integrated trade development strategy* (Report No. 27264-GE). Washington, DC: Author.

World Bank. (2005). *Global economic prospects 2005: Trade, regionalism, and development*. Washington, DC: Author.

World Bank. (2009). *Georgia: Poverty assessment* (Report No. 44400-GE). Washington, DC: Author.

World Bank. (2011). *Leveraging trade for development and inclusive growth: The World Bank Group trade strategy, 2011–2021*. Washington, DC: Author.

World Bank. (2012a). *Fighting corruption in public services: Chronicling Georgia's reforms*. Washington, DC: Author.

World Bank. (2012b). *Taking stock: An update on Vietnam's recent economic development*. Hanoi: Author.

World Bank. (2013). *Georgia: Sustaining rapid economic growth—Country economic memorandum* (Report No. 79532-GE). Washington, DC: Author.

World Bank Group. (2009). *Enterprise surveys country note series: Georgia—Running a business in Georgia*. Retrieved from World Bank website: http://documents.worldbank.org/curated/en/2009/01/11143000/running-business-georgia.

World Bank Independent Evaluation Group. (2006). *Assessing World Bank support for trade, 1987–2004: An IEG evaluation*. Washington, DC: World Bank.
World Bank & International Finance Corporation. (2006). *Doing business 2007: How to reform*. Washington, DC: Authors.
World Bank & International Finance Corporation. (2007). *Doing business 2008*. Washington, DC: Authors.
World Bank & International Finance Corporation. (2008). *Doing business 2009*. Washington, DC: Authors.
World Bank & International Finance Corporation. (2009). *Doing business 2010: Reforming through difficult times*. Washington, DC: Authors.
World Bank & International Finance Corporation. (2010). *Doing business 2011: Making a difference for entrepreneurs*. Washington, DC: Authors.
World Bank & International Finance Corporation. (2012). *Doing business 2012: Doing business in a more transparent world*. Washington, DC: Authors.
World Bank & International Finance Corporation. (2013). *Doing business 2013: Smarter regulations for small and medium-size enterprises*. Washington, DC: Authors.
World Trade Organization. (1995a). *The results of the Uruguay round of multilateral trade negotiations: Legal texts*. Geneva: Author. (Original work published by the GATT Secretariat 1994).
World Trade Organization. (1995b). *Communication from China* (WT/ACC/CHN/1). Geneva: Author.
World Trade Organization. (1995c). *Report of the working party on the accession of Ecuador* (WT/L/77). Geneva: Author.
World Trade Organization. (1995d). *Accession to the World Trade Organization: Procedures for negotiations under article XII—Note by the secretariat* (WT/ACC/1). Geneva: Author.
World Trade Organization. (1996a). *Accession of Vietnam: Memorandum on the foreign trade regime* (WT/ACC/VNM/2). Geneva: Author.
World Trade Organization. (1996b). *European Communities—Regime for the importation, sale and distribution of bananas: Request for consultation by Ecuador, Guatemala, Honduras, Mexico and the United States* (WT/DS27/1). Geneva: Author.
World Trade Organization. (1996c). *European Communities—Regime for the importation, sale and distribution of bananas: Request for establishment of the panel* (WT/DS27/6). Geneva: Author.
World Trade Organization. (1997a). *Accession of Georgia: Memorandum of the foreign trade regime* (WT/ACC/DEO/3). Geneva: Author.
World Trade Organization. (1997b). *European Communities—Regime for the importation, sale and distribution of bananas: Complaint by Ecuador—Report of the panel* (WT/DS27/R/ECU). Geneva: Author.

World Trade Organization. (1997c). *Appellate body: European Communities—Regime for the importation, sale and distribution of bananas: Report of the appellate body* (WT/DS27/AB/R). Geneva: Author.

World Trade Organization. (1998a). *European Communities—Regime for the importation, sale and distribution of bananas: Arbitration under Article 21.3(c) of the understanding on rules and procedures governing the settlement of disputes—Award of the arbitrator Said El-Naggar* (WT/DS27/15). Geneva: Author.

World Trade Organization. (1998b). *European Communities—Regime for the importation, sale and distribution of bananas: Request for the establishment of a panel by the European Communities* (WT/DS27/40). Geneva: Author.

World Trade Organization. (1998c). *European Communities—Regime for the importation, sale and distribution of bananas: Recourse to article 21.5 of the DSU* (WT/DS27/41). Geneva: Author.

World Trade Organization. (1999a). *Working party on the accession of Georgia: Report of the working party on the accession of Georgia to the World Trade Organization* (WT/ACC/GEO31). Geneva: Author.

World Trade Organization. (1999b). *Ministerial conference, third session, Seattle, 30 November–3 December—Viet Nam: Statement by H.E. Mr. Truong Dinh Tuyen, Minister of Trade* (WT/MIN(99)ST/81). Geneva: Author.

World Trade Organization. (1999c). *Dispute settlement body: 19 November 1999* (WT/DSB/M/71). Geneva: Author.

World Trade Organization. (1999d). *European Communities—Regime for the importation, sale and distribution of bananas: Recourse by the United States to article 22.2 of the DSU* (WT/DS27/43). Geneva: Author.

World Trade Organization. (1999e). *European Communities—Regime for the importation, sale and distribution of bananas: Recourse by the United States to article 22.7 of the DSU* (WT/DS27/47). Geneva: Author.

World Trade Organization. (1999f). *European Communities—Regime for the importation, sale and distribution of bananas: Request by the European Communities for arbitration under article 22.6 of the DSU* (WT/DS27/46). Geneva: Author.

World Trade Organization. (1999g). *European Communities—Regime for the importation of sale and distribution of bananas: Recourse to article 21.5 of the DSU by Ecuador—Report of the panel* (WT/DS27/RW/ECU). Geneva: Author.

World Trade Organization. (1999h). *European Communities—Regime for the importation, sale and distribution of bananas: Request by the European Communities for arbitration under article 22.6 of the DSU* (WT/DS27/53). Geneva: Author.

World Trade Organization. (1999i). *European Communities—Regime for the importation, sale and distribution of bananas: Recourse by Ecuador to article 22.2 of the DSU* (WT/DS27/52). Geneva: Author.

World Trade Organization. (1999j). *Ministerial conference, third session, Seattle, 30 November–3 December—Ecuador: Statement by H.E. Mr. José Luis Ycaza Pazmiño, Minister of Foreign Trade, Fisheries, and Tourism* (WT/MIN(99) ST/35). Geneva: Author.

World Trade Organization. (2000a). *European Communities—Regime for the importation, sale and distribution of bananas: Request by the European Communities for arbitration under article 22.6 of the DSU—Decision by the arbitrators* (WT/DS27/ARB/ECU). Geneva: Author.

World Trade Organization. (2000b). *European Communities—Regime for the importation, sale and distribution of bananas: Recourse to article 22.7 of the DSU by Ecuador* (WT/DS27/54). Geneva: Author.

World Trade Organization. (2000c). *Dispute settlement body: 30 November 2000* (WT/DSB/M/91). Geneva: Author.

World Trade Organization. (2001a). *Ministerial conference, fourth session, Doha, 9–14 November 2001: Ministerial declaration—Adopted on 14 November 2001* (WT/MIN(01)/DEC/1). Geneva: Author.

World Trade Organization. (2001b). *Committee on agriculture, special session: WTO agriculture negotiations—Proposal by Jordan* (G/AG/NG/W/140). Geneva: Author.

World Trade Organization. (2001c). *Committee on agriculture, special session: Sixth special session of the committee on agriculture, 22–23 March 2001—Statement by Jordan* (G/AG/NG/W/147). Geneva: Author.

World Trade Organization. (2001d). *Committee on agriculture, special session: WTO negotiations on agriculture—Submission by Croatia* (G/AG/NG/W/141). Geneva: Author.

World Trade Organization. (2001e). *Ministerial conference, fourth session, Doha, 9–13 November 2001—Georgia: Statement by H.E. Mrs. Tamar Beruchashvili, Deputy Minister of Foreign Affairs* (WT/MIN(01)/ST/106). Geneva: Author.

World Trade Organization. (2001f). *Ministerial conference, fourth session, Doha, 9–13 November 2001—Viet Nam: Statement by H.E. Mr. Luong van Tu, Vice-Minister of Trade* (WT/MIN(01)/ST/149). Geneva: Author.

World Trade Organization, (2001g). *European Communities—Regime for the importation, sale and distribution of bananas: Notification of mutually agreed solution* (WT/DS27/58). Geneva: Author.

World Trade Organization. (2001h). *Dispute settlement body: 5 November 2001* (WT/DSB/M/112). Geneva: Author.

World Trade Organization. (2001i). *Ministerial conference, fourth session, Doha, 9–14 November 2001: European Communities—The ACP-EC partnership agreement: Decision of 14 November 2001* (WT/MIN(01)/15). Geneva: Author.

World Trade Organization. (2001j). *Ministerial conference, fourth session, Doha, 9–14 November 2001: European Communities—Transitional regime for the EC autonomous tariff rate quotas on imports of bananas: Decision of 14 November 2001* (WT/MIN(01)/16). Geneva: Author.

World Trade Organization. (2001k). *Working party on the accession of China: Report of the working party on the accession of China* (WT/ACC/CHN/49). WTO: Author.

World Trade Organization. (2001l). *Ministerial conference, fourth session, Doha, 9–13 November 2001: Report of the working party on accession of China* (WT/MIN/01/3). Geneva: Author.

World Trade Organization. (2001m). *Accession of the People's Republic of China: Decision of 10 November 2001* (WT/L/432). Geneva: Author.

World Trade Organization. (2002a). *Negotiation group on market access: Market access for non-agricultural products—Contribution from Oman* (TN/MA/W/14). Geneva: Author.

World Trade Organization. (2002b). *Negotiation group on market access: Market access for non-agricultural products—Proposal by the People's Republic of China* (TN/MA/W/20). Geneva: Author.

World Trade Organization. (2002c). *Committee on agriculture, special session: Summary report on the thirteen meeting of the committee on agriculture special session held on 6 September 2002—Note by the secretariat* (TN/AG/R3). Geneva: Author.

World Trade Organization. (2002d). *Negotiating group on market access: Minutes of the meeting held in Centre William Rappard on 2 August 2002* (TM/MA/M2). Geneva: Author.

World Trade Organization. (2002e). *Negotiating group on market access: Minutes of the meeting held in Centre William Rappard on 30 October 2002* (TN/MA/M/3). Geneva: Author.

World Trade Organization. (2003a). *Negotiation group on market access: Market access for non-agricultural products—Communication form Albania, Croatia, Georgia, and Moldova* (TN/MA/W/29). Geneva: Author.

World Trade Organization. (2003b). *Ministerial conference, fifth session, Cancún, 10–14 September 2003: Proposal on flexibility provisions for recently acceded members—Communication from China* (WT/MIN(03)/W/8). Geneva: Author.

World Trade Organization. (2003c). *Negotiation group on market access: Market access for non-agricultural products—Proposal by the People's Republic of China, corrigendum* (TN/MA/W/20/Corr.1). Geneva: Author.

World Trade Organization. (2003d). *Negotiating group on rules: Proposal of the People's Republic of China on the negotiation on anti-dumping* (TN/RL/W/66). Geneva: Author.

World Trade Organization. (2003e). *Ministerial conference, fifth session, Cancún, 10–14 September 2003—Georgia: Statement by H.E. Mrs. Tamar Beruchashvili, Deputy Minister of Foreign Affairs* (WT/MIN(03)/ST/106). Geneva: Author.

World Trade Organization. (2003f). *Committee on agriculture, special session: Summary report on the nineteenth meeting of the committee on agriculture special session held on 1 July 2003—Note by the secretariat* (TN/AG/R9). Geneva: Author.

World Trade Organization. (2003g). *Negotiating group on market access: Minutes of the meeting, held in the Centre William Rappard on 26–28 May 2003—Chairman: ambassador P-L. Girard (Switzerland)* (TN/MA/M/8). Geneva: Author.

World Trade Organization. (2003h). *Committee on agriculture, Special session: Summary report on the seventeenth meeting of the committee on agriculture special session held on 28 February 2003—Note by the secretariat* (TN/AG/R7). Geneva: Author.

World Trade Organization. (2003i). *Ministerial conference, fifth session, Cancún, 10–14 September 2003—China: Statement by H.E. Lu Fuyuan, Minister of Commence* (WT/MIN(03)/ST/12). Geneva: Author.

World Trade Organization. (2003j). *Negotiating group on Market access: Minutes of the meeting held in the Centre William Rappard on 14–16 April 2003* (TN/MA/M7). Geneva: Author.

World Trade Organization. (2004a). *Doha work programme: Decision adopted by the general council on 1 August 2004* (WT/L/579). Geneva: Author.

World Trade Organization. (2004b). *Ministerial conference, sixth session, Hong Kong, 13–18 December 2005: Doha work programme—Ministerial declaration adopted on 18 December 2005* (WT/MIN(05)/DEC). Geneva: Author.

World Trade Organization. (2004c). *Negotiating group on market access: Minutes of the meeting, held in the Centre William Rappard on 9–11 June 2004—Chairman: Ambassador S.H. Jóhannesson (Iceland)* (TN/MA/M/13). Geneva: Author.

World Trade Organization. (2005a). *Negotiation group on market access: Market access for non-agricultural products—Communication form Armenia, Georgia, Kyrgyz Republic and Republic of Moldova* (TN/MA/W/56). Geneva: Author.

World Trade Organization. (2005b). *Negotiation group on market access: Market access for non-agricultural products—Communication form Armenia, Georgia, Kyrgyz Republic and Republic of Moldova—Revision* (TN/MA/W/56/Rev.1). Geneva: Author.

World Trade Organization. (2005c). *Committee on agriculture, special session: Communication form Armenia, Georgia, the Kyrgyz Republic and the Republic of Moldova* (TN/AG/GEN/10). Geneva: Author.

World Trade Organization. (2005d). *Committee on agriculture, special session: Communication form Armenia, Georgia, the Kyrgyz Republic and the Republic of Moldova—Corrigendum* (TN/AG/GEN/10/Corr.1). Geneva: Author.

World Trade Organization. (2005e). *Ministerial conference, 6th session, Hong Kong, 13–18 December 2005: Georgia—Statement by H.E. Mr. Irakli*

Chogovadze, Minister of Economic Development (WT/MIN(05)/ST/156). Geneva: Author.

World Trade Organization. (2005f). *Trade policy review body: Trade policy review, Ecuador—Draft minutes of meeting* (WT/TPR/M/148). Geneva: Author.

World Trade Organization. (2005g). *Trade policy review body: Trade policy review report by the secretariat, Ecuador—Revision* (WT/TPR/S/148/Rev.1). Geneva: Author.

World Trade Organization. (2005h). *Committee on agriculture, special session: Summary report on the thirty-first and thirty-second formal special sessions of the committee on agriculture, held on 19 April and 3 June 2005* (TN/AG/R/20). Geneva: Author.

World Trade Organization. (2005i). *Ministerial conference, sixth session, Hong Kong, 13–18 December 2005: Ecuador—Statement by H.E. Mr. Jorge Illingworth, Minister of Foreign Trade, Industrialization, Fisheries and Competitiveness* (WT/MIN(05)/ST/148). Geneva: Author.

World Trade Organization. (2005j). *Ministerial conference, sixth session, Hong Kong, 13–18 December 2005: China—Statement by H.E. Bo Xilai, Minister of Commerce* (WT/MIN(05)/ST/59). Geneva: Author.

World Trade Organization. (2006a). *Committee on agriculture, special session: Communication form small low-income economies in transition, recently acceded to the WTO—Proposal by Armenia, the Kyrgyz Republic and the Republic of Moldova* (TN/AG/GEN/16). Geneva: Author.

World Trade Organization. (2006b). *Committee on agriculture, special session: Communication form Armenia, the Kyrgyz Republic and the Republic of Moldova* (TN/AG/GEN/21). Geneva: Author.

World Trade Organization. (2006c). *Trade negotiations committee, negotiating group on market access: Market access for non-agricultural products—Position of the Kingdom of Saudi Arabia as a newly acceded member, communication from Saudi Arabia* (TN/C/W/45, TN/MA/W/81). Geneva: Author.

World Trade Organization. (2006d). *General council, committee on agriculture (special session), negotiating group on market access: Recently acceded members—Communication from Ecuador and Panama* (WT/GC/W/565, TN/AG/W/2, TN/MA/W/73). Geneva: Author.

World Trade Organization. (2006e). *Working party on the accession of Viet Nam: Accession of Viet Nam—Report of the working party on the accession of Viet Nam to the World Trade Organization* (WT/ACC/VNM/48). Geneva: Author.

World Trade Organization. (2006f). *Trade policy review body, 19 and 21 April 2006: Trade policy review—People's Republic of China: Minutes of meeting* (WT/TPR/M/161). Geneva: Author.

World Trade Organization. (2006g). *Trade policy review body: Trade policy review report by the secretariat—People's Republic of China, revision* (WT/TPR/S/161/Rev.1). Geneva: Author.

World Trade Organization. (2006h). *Trade policy review body: Trade policy review report by the People's Republic of China* (WT/TPR/G/161). Geneva: Author.

World Trade Organization. (2007a). *Negotiating group on market access: Market access for non-agricultural products—Negotiating proposals by recently acceded members (RAMs)* (TN/MA/W/83). Geneva: Author.

World Trade Organization. (2007b). *Committee on agriculture special session: Negotiating proposals by recently acceded members (RAMs)* (TN/AG/GEN/24). Geneva: Author.

World Trade Organization. (2007c). *World trade report 2007—Six decades of multilateral trade cooperation: What have we learned?* Geneva: Author.

World Trade Organization. (2007d). *Committee on agriculture, special session: Negotiations on agriculture—Communication from Albania* (TN/AG/GEN/28). Geneva: Author.

World Trade Organization. (2007e). *International trade statistics 2007.* Geneva: Author.

World Trade Organization. (2008a). *Negotiating group on market access: Fourth revision of draft modalities for non-agricultural market access* (TN/MA/W/103/Rev.3). Geneva: Author.

World Trade Organization. (2008b). *Committee on agriculture, special session: Revised draft modalities for agriculture* (TN/AG/W/4/Rev.4). Geneva: Author.

World Trade Organization. (2008c). *Negotiating group on market access: Market access for non-agricultural products, non-agricultural market access (NAMA) negotiations—Communication from Albania* (TN/MA/W/99). Geneva: Author.

World Trade Organization. (2008d). *Negotiating group on rules: Statement on anti-dumping negotiations—Communication from Brazil; Chile; China; Columbia; Costa Rica; Hong Kong, China; Indonesia; Israel; Japan; Korea, Rep. of; Malaysia; Mexico; Norway; Pakistan; Singapore; Switzerland; the Separate Customs Territory of Taiwan, Penghu, Kinmen and Matsu; Thailand; and Viet Nam* (TN/RL/W/233). Geneva: Author.

World Trade Organization. (2008e). *European Communities—Regime for the importation, sale and distribution of bananas: Second recourse to article 21.5 of the DSU by Ecuador—Report of the panel* (WT/DS27/RW2/ECU). Geneva: Author.

World Trade Organization. (2008f). *European Communities—Regime for the importation, sale and distribution of bananas: Recourse to article 21.5 of the DSU by the United States—Report of the panel* (WT/DS27/RW/USA). Geneva: WTO.

World Trade Organization. (2008g). *European Communities—Regime for the importation, sale and distribution of bananas: Second recourse to article 21.5 of the DSU by Ecuador; European Communities—Regime for the importation, sale and distribution of bananas: Recourse to article 21.5 of the DSU by the United States—Reports of the appellate body* (WT/DS27/AB/RW2/ECU, WT/DS27/AB/RW/USA). Geneva: Author.

World Trade Organization. (2008h). *Trade policy review body: Trade policy review—Report by China* (WT/TPR/G/199). Geneva: Author.
World Trade Organization. (2008i). *Trade policy review: Report by the secretariat—China, revision* (WT/TPR/S/199/Rev.1). Geneva: Author.
World Trade Organization. (2008j). *United States—Definitive anti-dumping and countervailing duties on certain products from China: Request for consultations by China* (WT/DS379/1). Geneva: Author.
World Trade Organization. (2009a). *Ministerial conference, seventh session, Geneva, 30 November–2 December 2009: Communication from the group of recently acceded members (RAMs)* (WT/MIN(09)/6). Geneva: Author.
World Trade Organization. (2009b). *Trade policy review body, 8 and 10 December 2009: Trade policy review, Georgia—Record of the meeting* (WT/TPR/M/224). Geneva: Author.
World Trade Organization. (2009c). *Committee on balance-of-payments restrictions: Notification under paragraph 9 of the understanding on the balance-of-payments provisions of the general agreement on tariffs and trade 1994—Communication from Ecuador* (WT/BOP/N/65). Geneva: Author.
World Trade Organization. (2009d). *Committee on balance-of-payments restrictions: Consultations with Ecuador—Background document by the secretariat, revision* (WT/BOP/S/15/Rev.1). Geneva: Author.
World Trade Organization. (2009e). *Committee on balance-of-payments restrictions: Consultations with Ecuador—Basic document supplied by Ecuador: Overview of the situation and outlook for the balance-of-payments taking into account internal and external factors that affect the situation* (WT/BOP/G/15). Geneva: Author.
World Trade Organization. (2009f). *Committee on balance-of-payments restrictions: Report (2009) of the committee on balance-of-payments restrictions* (WT/BOP/R/96). Geneva: Author.
World Trade Organization. (2009g). *Dispute settlement body: 11 December 2008* (WT/DSB/M/260). Geneva: Author.
World Trade Organization. (2009h). *Geneva agreement on trade in bananas: Communication from Brazil, Columbia, Costa Rica, Ecuador, European Union, Guatemala, Honduras, Mexico, Nicaragua, Panama, Peru and the Bolivarian Republic of Venezuela* (WT/L/784). Geneva: Author.
World Trade Organization. (2009i). *International trade statistics 2009*. Geneva: Author.
World Trade Organization. (2009j). *European Communities—Definitive anti-dumping measures on certain iron or steel fasteners from China. Request for consultations by China* (WT/DS397/1). Geneva: WTO.
World Trade Organization. (2009k). *United States—Measures affecting imports of certain passenger vehicle and light truck tyres from China: Request for consultations by China* (WT/DS399/1). Geneva: Author.

World Trade Organization. (2009l). *China—Measures related to the exportation of various raw materials: Request for consultations by the United States* (WT/DS394/1). Geneva: Author.
World Trade Organization. (2009m). *China—Measures related to the exportation of various raw materials: Request for consultations by the European Communities* (WT/DS395/1). Geneva: Author.
World Trade Organization. (2009n). *China—Measures related to the exportation of various raw materials: Request for consultations by Mexico* (WT/DS398/1). Geneva: Author.
World Trade Organization. (2009o). *10 benefits of the WTO trading system.* Geneva: Author.
World Trade Organization. (2010a). *Technical note on the accession process: Note by the secretariat—Revision* (WT/ACC/10/Rev/4). Geneva: Author.
World Trade Organization. (2010b). *Technical note on the accession process: State of play and information on current accessions, note by the secretariat—Revision* (WT/ACC/11/Rev.9). Geneva: Author.
World Trade Organization. (2010c). *Trade policy review body: Trade policy review report by the secretariat, Georgia—Revision* (WT/TPR/S/224/Rev.1). Geneva: Author.
World Trade Organization. (2010d). *Trade policy review body, 8 and 10 December 2009: Trade policy review, Georgia—Record of the meeting, addendum* (WT/TPR/M/224/Add.1). Geneva: Author.
World Trade Organization. (2010e). *United States—Anti-dumping measures on certain shrimp from Viet Nam: Request for consultations by Viet Nam* (WT/DS404/1). Geneva: Author.
World Trade Organization. (2010f). *United States—Anti-dumping measures on certain shrimp from Viet Nam: Request for the establishment of a panel by Viet Nam* (WT/DS404/5). Geneva: Author.
World Trade Organization. (2010g). *Trade policy review: Report by the secretariat—China, revision* (WT/TPR/S/230/Rev.1). Geneva: Author.
World Trade Organization. (2010h). *Trade policy review body, 31 May and 2 June 2010: Trade policy review—People's Republic of China: Minutes of meeting* (WT/TPR/M/230). Geneva: Author.
World Trade Organization. (2010i). *European Union—Anti-dumping measures on certain footwear from China: Request for consultations by China* (WT/DS405/1). Geneva: Author.
World Trade Organization. (2010j). *European Communities—Definitive anti-dumping measures on certain iron or steel fasteners from China: Report of the panel* (WT/DS397/R). Geneva: Author.
World Trade Organization. (2010k). *United States—Definitive anti-dumping and countervailing duties on certain products from China: Report of the panel* (WT/DS379/R). Geneva: Author.

World Trade Organization. (2010l). *United States—Measures affecting imports of certain passenger vehicle and light truck tyres from China: Report of the panel* (WT/DS399/R). Geneva: Author.

World Trade Organization. (2011a). *Ministerial conference, eighth session, Geneva, 15–17 December 2011: Ministers/heads of delegations meeting of the group of recently acceded members (RAMs)* (WT/MIN(11)/22). Geneva: Author.

World Trade Organization. (2011b). *United States—Anti-dumping measures on certain shrimp from Viet Nam: Report of the panel* (WT/DS404/R). Geneva: Author.

World Trade Organization. (2011c). *Trade policy review body: Trade policy review—Report by Ecuador* (WT/TPR/G/254). Geneva: Author.

World Trade Organization (2011d). *European Union—Anti-dumping measures on certain footwear from China: Report of the panel* (WT/DS4065/R). Geneva: Author.

World Trade Organization. (2011e). *European Communities—Definitive anti-dumping measures on certain iron or steel fasteners from China: Report of the appellate body* (WT/DS397/AB/R). Geneva: Author.

World Trade Organization. (2011f). *United States—Definitive anti-dumping and countervailing duties on certain products from China: Report of the appellate body* (WT/DS379/AB/R). Geneva: Author.

World Trade Organization. (2011g). *United States—Measures affecting imports of certain passenger vehicle and light truck tyres from China: Report of the appellate body* (WT/DS399/AB/R). Geneva: Author.

World Trade Organization. (2011h). *Dispute settlement body, 5 October 2011: Minutes of the meeting* (WT/DSB/M/304). Geneva: Author.

World Trade Organization. (2011i). *China—Measures related to the exportation of rare earth, tungsten and molybdenum: Request for consultations by the United States* (WT/DS431/1). Geneva: Author.

World Trade Organization. (2011j). *China—Measures related to the exportation of various raw materials: Report of the panel* (WT/DS394/R, WT/DS395/R, WT/DS398/R). Geneva: Author.

World Trade Organization. (2012a). *United States—Anti-dumping measures on certain shrimp from Viet Nam: Request for consultations by Viet Nam* (WT/DS429/1). Geneva: Author.

World Trade Organization. (2012b). *Trade policy review body: Trade policy review report by the secretariat, Ecuador—Revision* (WT/TPR/S/254/Rev.1). Geneva: Author.

World Trade Organization. (2012c). *European Communities—Regime for the importation, sale and distribution of bananas (Guatemala; Honduras; Mexico; United States) (DS16); European Communities—Regime for the importation, sale and distribution of bananas (Ecuador; Guatemala; Honduras; Mexico; United States) (DS27); European Communities—Regime for the importation, sale and distribution of bananas (Panama)(DS105); European*

Communities—Regime for the importation, sale and distribution of bananas (Guatemala; Honduras; Mexico, Panama; United States) (DS158); European Communities—Regime for the importation of bananas (Colombia) (DS361); European Communities—Regime for the importation of bananas (Panama) (DS364); European Communities—The ACP-EC partnership agreement—Recourse to arbitration pursuant to the decision of 14 November 2001 (Brazil; Colombia; Costa Rica; Ecuador; Guatemala; Honduras; Nicaragua; Panama and Venezuela) (WT/L/616); European Communities—The ACP-EC partnership agreement—Second recourse to arbitration pursuant to the decision of 14 November 2001 (Brazil; Colombia; Costa Rica; Ecuador; Guatemala; Honduras; Nicaragua and Panama) (WT/L/625): Notification of a mutually agreed solution (WT/DS27/98). Geneva: Author.

World Trade Organization. (2012d). *Trade policy review: Report by the secretariat—China, revision* (WT/TPR/S/264/Rev.1). Geneva: Author.

World Trade Organization. (2012e). *Trade policy review body, 12 and 14 June 2012: Trade policy review, China—Record of the meeting* (WT/TPR/M/264). Geneva: Author.

World Trade Organization. (2012f). *Dispute settlement body, 23 July 2012: Minutes of the meeting* (WT/DSB/M/320). Geneva: Author.

World Trade Organization. (2012g). *China—Measures related to exportation of various raw materials: Reports of the appellate Body* (WT/DS394/AB/R, WT/DS395/AB/R, WT/DS398/AB/R). Geneva: Author.

World Trade Organization. (2012h). *15 years of the information technology agreement: Trade, innovation and global production networks*. Geneva: Author.

World Trade Organization. (2012i). *WTO accessions: 2012 annual report by the Director-General* (WT/ACC/19). Geneva: Author.

World Trade Organization. (2012j). *United States—Countervailing and anti-dumping measures on certain products from China: Request for consultations by China* (WT/DS449/1, G/L/1001, G/SCM/D92/1, G/ADP/D95/1). Geneva: Author.

World Trade Organization. (2013a). *Trade policy review body: Trade policy review report by the secretariat, Viet Nam—Revision* (WT/TPR/S/287/Rev.1). Geneva: Author.

World Trade Organization. (2013b). *Trade policy review body: Trade policy review—Report by Viet Nam* (WT/TPR/G/287). Geneva: Author.

World Trade Organization. (2013c). *United States—Anti-dumping measures on certain shrimp from Viet Nam: Request for the establishment of a panel by Viet Nam* (WT/DS429/2/Rev.1). Geneva: Author.

World Trade Organization. (2013d). *United States—Certain methodologies and their application to anti-dumping proceedings involving China: Request for consultations by China* (WT/DS471/1, G/L/1060, G/ADP/D100/1). Geneva: Author.

World Trade Organization. (2014a). *Trade policy review body: Trade policy review report by the secretariat, China* (WT/TPR/S/300). Geneva: Author.

World Trade Organization. (2014b). *China—Measures related to the exportation of rare earth, tungsten, and molybdenum: Reports of the panel* (WT/DS431/R, WT/DS432/R, WT/DS433/R). Geneva: Author.

World Trade Organization. (2014c). *Accession to the World Trade Organization: Procedures for negotiations under article XII—Note by the secretariat* (WT/ACC/22). Geneva: Author.

World Trade Organization. (2014d). *China—Measures related to the exportation of rare earth, tungsten, and molybdenum: Reports of the appellate body* (WT/DS431/AB/R, WT/DS432/AB/R, WT/DS433/AB/R). Geneva: Author.

World Trade Organization. (2014e). *United States—Anti-dumping measures on certain shrimp from Viet Nam: Report of the panel* (WT/DS429/R). Geneva: Author.

World Trade Organization. (2014f). *United States—Countervailing and anti-dumping measures on certain products from China: Report of the panel* (WT/DS499/R). Geneva: Author.

World Trade Organization. (2014g). *United States—Countervailing and anti-dumping measures on certain products from China: Report of the panel—Addendum* (WT/DS499/R/Add.1). Geneva: Author.

World Trade Organization. (2014h). *United States—Countervailing and anti-dumping measures on certain products from China: Report of the appellate body* (WT/DS499/AB/R). Geneva: Author.

World Trade Organization. (2014i). *United States—Countervailing and anti-dumping measures on certain products from China: Report of the appellate body—Corrigendum* (WT/DS499/AB/R/Corr.1). Geneva: Author.

World Trade Organization. (2015a). *European Communities—Definitive anti-dumping measures on certain iron or steel fasteners from China—Recourse to article 21.5 of the DSU by China: Report of the panel* (WT/DS397/RW). Geneva: Author.

World Trade Organization. (2015b). *European Communities—Definitive anti-dumping measures on certain iron or steel fasteners from China—Recourse to article 21.5 of the DSU by China: Report of the panel*—Addendum (WT/DS397/RW/Add.1). Geneva: Author.

World Trade Organization. (2015c). *United States—Anti-dumping measures on certain shrimp from Viet Nam: Report of the appellate body* (WT/DS429/AB/R). Geneva: Author.

World Trade Organization. (2015d). *United States—Anti-dumping measures on certain shrimp from Viet Nam: Report of the appellate body*—Corrigendum (WT/DS429/AB/R/Corr.1). Geneva: Author.

World Trade Organization. (2016a). *European Communities—Definitive anti-dumping measures on certain iron or steel fasteners from China—Recourse to article 21.5 of the DSU by China: Report of the appellate body* (WT/DS397/AB/RW). Geneva: Author.

World Trade Organization. (2016b). *European Communities—Definitive anti-dumping measures on certain iron or steel fasteners from China—Recourse to article 21.5 of the DSU by China: Report of the appellate body*—Addendum (WT/DS397/AB/RW/Add.1). Geneva: Author.

World Trade Organization. (2016c). *Trade policy review body: Trade policy review report by the secretariat, Georgia—Revision* (WT/TPR/S/328/Rev.1). Geneva: Author.

World Trade Organization. (2016d). *United States—Measures Related to Price Comparison Methodologies: Request for consultations by China* (WT/DS515/1, G/L/1169, G/ADP/D115/1). Geneva: Author.

World Trade Organization. (2016e). *European Union—Measures Related to Price Comparison Methodologies: Request for consultations by China* (WT/DS516/1, G/L/1170, G/ADP/D116/1). Geneva: Author.

World Trade Organization. (2017a). *United States—Measures Related to Price Comparison Methodologies: Request for consultations by China—Addendum* (WT/DS515/1/Add.1, G/L/1169/Add.1, G/ADP/D115/1/Add.1). Geneva: Author.

World Trade Organization. (2017b). *Committee on regional trade agreements, Council for trade in services: Notification of regional trade agreement—Protocol of Accession of Ecuador to the trade agreement between the European Union and its member states, of the one part, and Columbia and Peru, of the other part* (WT/REG380/N/1, S/C/N/876). Geneva: Author.

World Trade Organization. (2018a). *Committee on regional trade agreements: Treaty on the Eurasian Economic Union (EREA), EAEU—Accession of Armenia, EAEU—Accession of the Kyrgyz Republic—General incident calculation: Notes by the secretariat* (WT/REG358/2, WT/REG363/2, WT/REG/366/2). Geneva: Author.

World Trade Organization. (2018b). *United States—Anti-dumping measures on fish fillets from Viet Nam—Request for consultations by Viet Nam* (WT/DS536/1 G/L/1208 G/ADP/D122/1). Geneva: Author.

WTO Department, Ministry of Commerce (Ed.). (2013). *Basic Instruments and selected documents on the negotiations for China's accession to the World Trade Organization*. Beijing: China Commerce and Trade Press.

Yongtu, L. (2002). Negotiating entry: Key lessons learned. In C. A. Magariños, L. Yongtu, & F. C. Sercovich (Eds.), *China in the WTO: The birth of a new catching-up strategy* (pp. 25–35). New York: Palgrave Macmillan.

Zhang, Y., & Yang, G. (2004). China as a WTO member in the first two years. In M. Matsushita & D. Ahn (Eds.), *WTO and East Asia: New perspectives* (pp. 313–325). London: Cameron May.

Zheng, Z. (2003). Economic globalization and development of China's foreign economic cooperation and trade. In D. Lu, G. J. Wen, & H. Zhou (Eds.), *China's economic globalization through the WTO* (pp. 5–12). Aldershot: Ashgate.

Index

K. Takamiya, *Recently Acceded Members of the World Trade Organization*, https://doi.org/10.1007/978-981-13-9159-0

D

G

H

The manufacturer's authorised representative in the EU is Springer Nature Customer Service Centre GmbH, Europaplatz 3, 69115 Heidelberg, Germany. If you have any concerns regarding our products, please contact ProductSafety@springernature.com

Printed and bound by CPI Group (UK) Ltd, Croydon, CR0 4YY
25/09/2026
02222902-0013